African Families and the Crisis of Social Change

African Families and the Crisis of Social Change

Edited by
Thomas S. Weisner,
Candice Bradley,
and Philip L. Kilbride

In collaboration with A.B.C. Ocholla-Ayayo,
Joshua Akong'a, and Simiyu Wandibba

BERGIN & GARVEY
Westport, Connecticut • London

Library of Congress Cataloging-in-Publication Data

African families and the crisis of social change / edited by Thomas S.
Weisner . . . [et al.].
p. cm.
Includes bibliographical references and index.
ISBN 0–89789–473–1 (alk. paper).—ISBN 0–89789–519–3 (pbk.)
1. Family—Africa—Congresses. 2. Social change—Africa—
Congresses. 3. Intergenerational relations—Africa—Congresses.
I. Weisner, Thomas S., 1943–
HQ691.A697 1997
306.85′096—dc21 96–45346

British Library Cataloguing in Publication Data is available.

Library of Congress Catalog Card Number: 96–45346
ISBN: 0–89789–473–1
0–89789–519–3 (pbk.)

First published in 1997

Bergin & Garvey, 88 Post Road West, Westport, CT 06881
An imprint of Greenwood Publishing Group, Inc.

Printed in the United States of America

The paper used in this book complies with the
Permanent Paper Standard issued by the National
Information Standards Organization (Z39.48–1984).

10 9 8 7 6 5 4 3 2 1

To the people of Kenya
and to Susan, Jeffrey, and Michael Weisner
and Daniel, John, Mark, and Camille Byrne
and Nancy, Buz, Rusty, and Rachel

Contents

Illustrations

TABLES

TABLES (CONTINUED)

FIGURES

FIGURES (CONTINUED)

MAPS

Foreword

Beatrice Whiting and John Whiting

This volume is a landmark in the development of collaboration between social scientists of different nationalities. It includes papers stimulated by a conference held in Kakamega, Kenya, in August of 1992, including contributors from East Africa, Europe, and the United States. It exemplifies the type of communication between international scholars that promises to advance our knowledge of human development and the process of family change. The authors, most of whom have worked in western Kenya, agreed to focus on a transcultural process, social change, in an institution, the family, that appears in some form in every society, each approaching the theme from a different point of view. Western Kenya provides a setting that shares many common cultural elements. As a result of this type of collaboration the reader acquires a kaleidoscopic view of the many facets of the process of social change as it impinges on family life.

This type of coequal collaboration requires communication in an international language and the acceptance of shared basic concepts and methodologies. Up until recently this type of communication between scholars from different nations has been difficult. In previous decades most social science research has been conducted by western scholars assisted by members of the community being studied, who serve as informants, interpreters, or apprentices, but not as full collaborators in research, since western-trained social scientists were very few. Although these collaborations were productive and valuable, the few university-trained social scientists at that time made research collaboration, as we have defined it, rare. Ideally, full research collaborators should participate in the planning of the research, the goals, and the methodology. They should share a language such that the concepts and methodology are mutually understood. Such an international language is taught in institutes of higher learning.

University-trained individuals were seldom available as collaborators of this kind to early ethnographers and students of non-western cultures, and this was certainly true in many parts of sub-Saharan Africa. Although Leakey, when he collected his data on the Southern Kikuyu of the Central Province of Kenya (Leakey, 1977), claimed that the elders he worked with were collaborators and not just informants, none of them was university trained or able to read the manuscript. The collaboration of Malinowski and Kenyatta that appeared in *Facing Mt. Kenya* (1938) is closer to our ideal. This treatise on "the tribal life of the Gikuyu" was written by Kenyatta when he was a member of a seminar directed by Malinowski at the London School of Economics. Kenyatta wrote the book for a British audience and with Malinowski's advice used concepts familiar to this Western audience, translating the elements of Kikuyu social structure into language that could be understood by an educated British public. The book became widely known in Kenya during the independence struggle and afterwards, as an example and stimulus for many other works that came later, as Kenyans increasingly began writing about their own cultures.

By now there are universities in most nonwestern countries where social science concepts are taught in an international language. Kenya has been a leader in promoting formal education in English, and now, as this volume illustrates, collaboration as well as independent research by Kenyans is widespread. Collaboration is bidirectional: Western researchers come to learn Kenyan research goals, questions, and methods, and Kenyans learn those of the West. The increase in collaboration between Western and nonWestern communities was anticipated by a group of social scientists who met in Chicago in 1964 to discuss cross-national research in human development. Robert LeVine and both of us attended this conference. At one of the discussions it was suggested that the widespread presence of people with university education throughout the world provided a pool of scholars who could be invited to collaborate in, and hopefully eventually to initiate, cross-national research. This idea was implemented by the establishment of the Child Development Research Unit (CDRU) attached to the University of Nairobi and financed by the Carnegie Corporation of New York.

When we asked Arthur Porter, who was the principal of the university at the time, if we could attach our research unit to the university, he asked us what good it would do for Kenya. We replied that we doubted whether our research results would be of any immediate use to Kenya, but that we intended to train some of the university students. They then would be available as collaborators with social scientists from other parts of the world, able to communicate in international projects in the study of social issues. They would also benefit from social science research training by developing their own research goals and agenda and beginning to train cadres of students for succeeding generations. In addition to assisting students of the universities of East Africa by apprenticing them to research projects designed by professors and advanced graduate students from the United States at that time, we arranged for Carnegie fellowships for individuals selected from the CDRU apprentices to receive further overseas training. Twelve such fellowships were granted.

Several of the authors of the present chapters are former members of CDRU. Weisner, one of the editors of this volume and one of the initiators of the conference that spawned it, collected the data for his doctoral thesis as a CDRU research fellow. Susan Abbott, Carolyn Edwards, Sara Harkness, Robert LeVine, Ruth and Robert Munroe, and Charles Super have all been members of the CDRU staff. All of the Americans affiliated with the CDRU collected their data with the assistance of university students who were then studying in Kenya. Prof. Priscilla Kariuki, who coauthored the chapter with Whyte, was such a student, and conducted research as a member of CDRU, as did Prof. Ezra Maritim, now the dean of Kenyatta University College. Prof. George Eshiwani, who assisted in sponsoring the conference and is now the vice-chancellor of Kenyatta University College, was also director of the Child Development Research Unit after it moved to that university.

Other Kenyan conference organizers and contributors to this volume have had a similar pattern of international collaboration through other sponsors. Prof. Joshua Akong'a, chair of the anthropology department at Moi University, worked with Prof. Marc Swartz at the University of California at San Diego after obtaining his B.A. in sociology at the University of Nairobi. He then returned to Kenya to the Center for African Studies, where he trained a number of Kenyan anthropologists. Dr. Joseph Ssennyonga received his training at the University of Sussex with T. Scarlett Epstein, an anthropologist with long-standing interests in comparative studies of culture and demography. Prof. A. B. C. Ocholla-Ayayo, former acting director of the Population Studies and Research Institute (PSRI), received his Ph.D. at the University of Uppsala in Sweden, an international center for social anthropological research.

Some of the collaborative links formed over the past three decades of research in Kenya have come about in unexpected ways. T. Scarlett Epstein encouraged Bradley to do a restudy of Ssennyonga's Maragoli fieldsite. Bradley in turn sponsored two University of Nairobi students, including James Onyango Ndege, whose master's research took place in the same fieldsite. Bradley had studied with us while we were at the University of California, Irvine, and later linked up with Weisner in the organization of the books and conference.

Although the international collaboration represented in this volume is to be highly commended, it is but the first step toward meeting the challenge of the postmodern critics who claim that all ethnographies and social science studies written by western scholars, even if they occurred in the context of collaborative relationships of various kinds, are inherently "biased," even impossible. They should consider a type of true collaboration that is developing as a consequence of conferences and books such as these, which facilitated communication between social scientists from different countries. This collaboration starts at the planning stage, with concepts and method agreed upon, and the data analyzed, by the team. For example, Maritim, who received a doctorate from the Harvard School of Education, and Edwards plan a collaborative project. Super and Harkness have also proposed collaborative work with Maritim. Bradley is already actively working with several Kenyan collaborators, through her association as a faculty member at the Population Studies and Research Institute, University of Nairobi. Prof. Kilbride, of Bryn Mawr College, who has been a research associate at the Institute of

African Studies since 1976, and Prof.Wandibba have worked together in the past and have shared a number of Ph.D. students as well. Kilbride, Wandibba, Kariuki, and others are currently undertaking a joint collaborative study of the growing problem of street children in Kenya. Others previously or presently associated with the institute who have collaborated in the current volume include Drs. Cattell and Nasimiyu, while others participated in the conference. Various other teams are forming between members of the conference and authors of the chapters of this book.

As a further sign of progress in this kind of collaboration, a related volume, entitled *Social Dynamics, Family Change and Human Development in Kenya*, is planned for publication in Kenya, edited by Profs. Ocholla-Ayayo, Akong'a, and Wandibba with the collaborative assistance of Weisner, Bradley, and Kilbride. This volume will be made available at a relatively modest cost accessible to Kenyans—seldom possible for work published in the West. Many students who attended the conference in Kenya and wrote papers will have their work appear in this volume, for many their first research publication.

The Kenyan social scientists attending the conference were somewhat bewildered by the anxieties of the more extreme, relativistically inclined post-modern anthropologists in the United States. Most voiced the opinion, reflected in their papers, that it was possible to build an empirical discipline that could study topics such as those covered in this volume all over the world, using concepts that could be validly defined in any culture, as well as models and constructs of particular relevance to Kenya, generated by Kenyans. The next steps are cross-cultural studies designed by collaborating international teams. Is the process of social change and its effect on family similar in other parts of the world? Communication among peers can lead to true international collaboration and the development of our comparative knowledge of universal aspects of human development. This volume is a landmark in progress toward this goal.

REFERENCES

Kenyatta, Jomo. (1961 (1938)). *Facing Mt. Kenya. The tribal life of the Gikuyu. With an introduction by B. Malinowski.* London: Secker & Warburg.

Leakey, L. S. B. (1977). *The southern Kikuyu before 1903.* London: Academic Press.

Acknowledgments

Our book grew out of a conference held in Kakamega, Western Province Kenya in August of 1992: "Intergenerational relations and ecology in Western Kenya." The conference was successful and exciting, bringing together some forty researchers who had worked in this region. Thirty-seven papers were presented at the meetings, which extended over three days. Presenters included thirteen scholars from Europe and North America, along with twenty-four from Kenya and Uganda. A number of the African presentations were by senior scholars, with others by graduate and postgraduate students, some of whom had the opportunity to present their first major research work to an international audience.

Funding for the conference in Kakamega that led to our book came from the Rockefeller Foundation, the World Bank EXTIE Program, the Institute for Intercultural Studies, and from the Division of Social Psychiatry, Department of Psychiatry, UCLA. We are very grateful to these organizations and their officers for their support. In addition, the conference was sponsored in Kenya by the Population and Social Research Institute, University of Nairobi, Prof. A.B.C. Ocholla-Ayayo; by the Institute for African Studies, Prof. Simiyu Wandibba, Director; and by the Department of Anthropology, Moi University, Eldoret, Kenya, Prof. Joshua Akong'a. These institutes and scholars are our collaborators as well as hosts in Kenya and it was a pleasure to work with them. In addition to the papers and authors in our book, another twenty papers and presentations were made at the conference by other scholars and by Kenyan graduate and postdoctoral students. We are hoping that this larger collection, including the many other excellent presentations from the conference in Kakamega, will be published in Kenya in a relatively inexpensive edition, accessible to Kenyan students and general readers.

Dr. Sharon Sabsay at UCLA and Ray Shoemaker did fantastic jobs as our editors; this book could not have happened without their dedication and commitment. Paula Block-Levor did a terrific job working with us on the index. Rhodora Maliksi-Farmer assisted Weisner in countless ways to send out proposals to raise the funds, get out letters and reports, and keep track of everything. Thanks to Christina von Mayrhauser for help with references and last-minute proofreading.We also had excellent editorial support at Greenwood from Lynn Flint, Lynn Taylor, and Lynn Zelem. Our thanks to Donna Crandall of the UCLA Media Laboratory, MR-RC, and Deanna Knickerbocker of the Center for Advanced Study in the Behavioral Sciences for assistance with maps and A. B. C. Ocholla-Ayayo and Population Studies and Research Institute for supplying the current map of administrative units in western Kenya. Most of all, we thank the Kenyan participants in all the research work reported in these chapters; they are at the heart of the story each author in our book is telling.

The editors acknowledge the participation of Professor Gideon Were in our conference and note here with sadness the untimely death of this pioneering scholar whose contributions to social science and history are so significant. We are also saddened at the recent death of one of our contributors, Prof. Ruth Munroe, who was a leader in comparative research in human development.

Weisner would like to thank the wonderful people and communities in Kisa Location, Kakamega District, who participated off and on in some twenty years of fieldwork, the University of Nairobi, and the Child Development Research Unit, initially supported by the Carnegie Corporation and founded and first directed by John and Beatrice Whiting, and now part of Kenyatta College, for sponsorship and support. This volume was completed while Weisner was a fellow at the Center for Advanced Study in the Behavioral Sciences. He is grateful for financial support at the Center provided by the National Science Foundation Grant #SBR-9022192 and the William T. Grant Foundation Grant #95167795.

Bradley would like to acknowledge her debt to the Population Studies and Research Institute of the University of Nairobi, especially Prof. H. W. O. Okoth-Ogendo, Prof. A. B. C. Ocholla-Ayayo, and Prof. John Oucho. She also thanks Dr. Joseph Ssennyonga and the people of Igunga Sublocation, Maragoli, especially the extended families of Jothamu Mudiri and Joseph Makindu. This book and the conference from which it grew would not have been possible without the support and friendship of Tom Weisner, along with the several thousand email messages that went into this book's creation. Thanks, Tom!

Kilbride is grateful to all of the many Kenyans who, during numerous visits to Kenya since 1967, have helped him in countless ways to better understand the significance of community in the human experience. He is especially indebted to the Nangina hospital community in Funyula, Samia Location, for all their support and kindness.

Introduction: Crisis in the African Family

Candice Bradley and Thomas S. Weisner

We are accustomed to hearing that Africa is in crisis. Images of Africa in crisis appear in literature, art, academic writing, and the media. From the Yeats-inspired title of Achebe's *Things Fall Apart* to articles in the *New York Times*, Africa is described as a "continent in crisis," an "imperiled continent," an "entire continent . . . near the brink of collapse," and perhaps even a "rough beast, its hour come round at last" that "[s]louches towards Bethlehem to be born." Images of African crisis, personified as starving children in deserts and filthy villages, bombard us from the television set accompanied by pleas for donations and the voices of rock stars singing arm in arm. We hear of famine and overpopulation, warfare, ecological degradation, and dreaded diseases. Yet beyond the din of transient media events and academic fashions is a set of very real problems, some enduring, some recurring, and some worsening with time. These problems include public health and food scarcity concerns, high fertility, political instability and civil disorder, lagging economic growth, and loss of infrastructure.

Our focus is the African *family* in crisis. This too is a common media theme. For example, television news segments have covered such topics as overpopulation in Kenya and Zimbabwe, Ugandan AIDS orphans, female circumcision in north Africa, and the explosion of urban street children in Africa's major cities. A recent *New York Times* article described elite Kenyan women who choose to have children but not to marry. Writings on the crisis in the African family, both academic and popular, focus on the disintegration of the multigenerational family, the breakdown of morals, the loss of economic viability, the dispersion of family members, and the loss of values, language, and cultural traditions in the wake of colonialism, modernization, and marginalization.

But the perception of crisis in the African family is not merely one of western imagining. It reflects the concerns and values expressed by Africans themselves in scholarship, film, literature and poetry, the popular media, and political dis-

Africa and East Africa

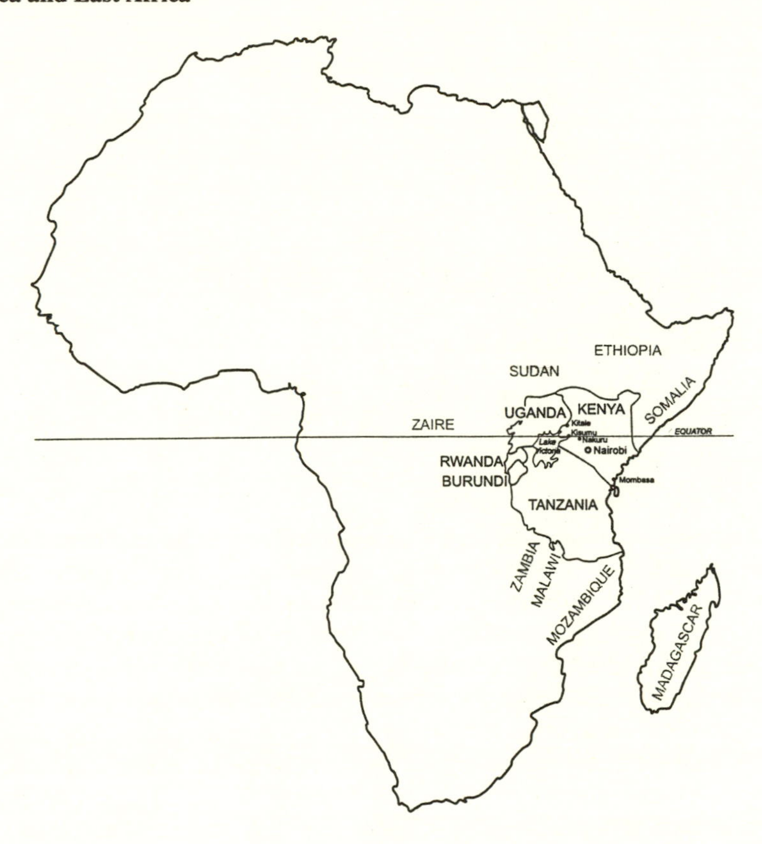

Kenya

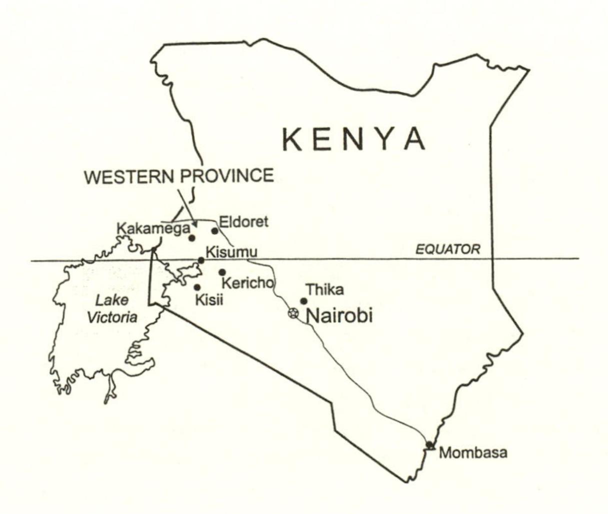

Administrative Units in Western Kenya Described in *African Families*

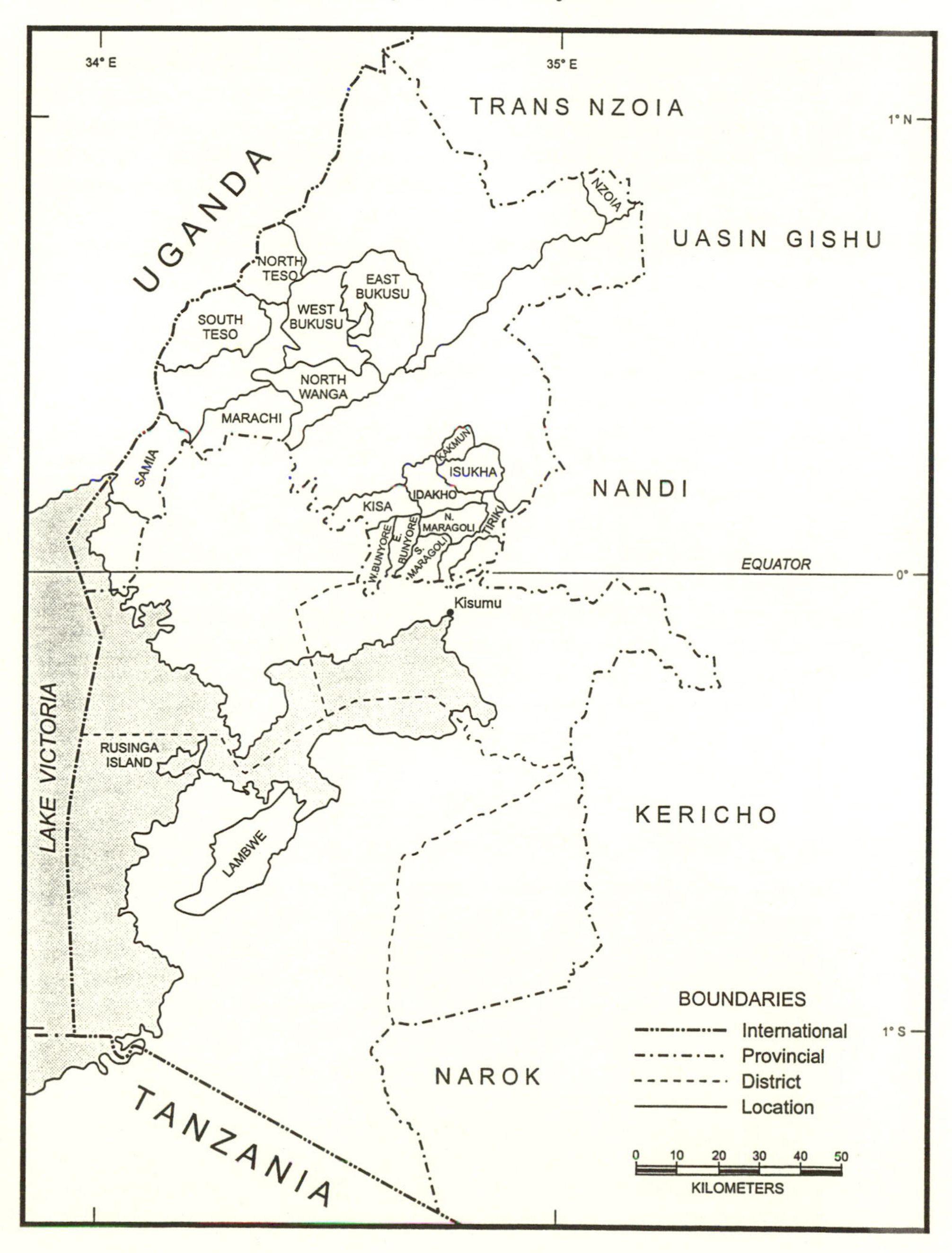

course at every level of government. There is a broad-based and realistic perception that the African family has changed dramatically, and not necessarily for the better.

A crisis is an acute change, a turning point most often associated with serious personal concerns and insecurity, illness, ecological damage, and economic or political instability. The perception that Africa is in a crisis may have roots in earlier centuries, perhaps originating partly in what some have described as the pathologizing of African society. However, the consensus both within and outside Africa is that a crisis of development is very real. "Africa in crisis" may be a sensational Euro-American media phenomenon, but it is also a realistic rubric for a broad range of contemporary problems effecting African economy, ecology, politics, and development. It is especially pertinent to discussions of health, gender, children, the elderly, and population—the topics of our book.

We examine changing family life in Africa primarily through focus on western Kenya and eastern Uganda. The issues affecting the family in western Kenya echo throughout the African continent. The various ethnic groups found in western Kenya and discussed in this book include Abaluyia, Kalenjin, Luo, and Gusii; also included are neighboring ethnic groups in central Kenya and eastern Uganda (see maps). The larger region includes the arid Rift Valley to the shores of Lake Victoria and the slopes of Mt. Elgon and is bisected by the Kenya-Uganda border. Although ecologically diverse, it is an area of extremely high population density, with several expanding urban centers. The people living here are primarily farmers, herders, traders, laborers, and urban dwellers, speaking many languages, practicing different religions, and living in a variety of ecological settings with different degrees of industrialization. Western Kenya has much in common with other densely populated regions throughout Africa (although regional and national differences across regions are great) and is a microcosm of the myriad changes affecting the family throughout Africa.

AFRICAN FAMILY IN DECLINE?

Popenoe (1988) outlines one kind of change or family crisis: the idea that families are in "decline" in the industrial West. He argues that family groups are becoming internally deinstitutionalized, carrying out fewer traditional functions, losing power relative to the state, and becoming smaller and more unstable and that the cultural value of familism is weakening in favor of self-fulfillment and egalitarianism (pp. 8–9).

The evidence from our African data are important with regard to family decline. The families and communities studied in our volume are changing, often gaining or losing resources and sharing power with delocalized forces that are part of a wider world system. But the family is not declining in all the senses Popenoe identifies. The African family circumstances described in our study suggest that the institutional structures of Kenyan families are becoming more diverse but are still highly salient; that some functions (support and care for children, care of the elderly, control of property, health care, nutritional status) are as strong as ever, although changing in form and perhaps not as homogeneous or as reliable; that the state affects the economy and polity differently than it directly impinges on the domestic world; and that family life has become more unstable more because of migration and fertility change than a change in the values of familism per se.

Our book focuses on what family change means to Kenyans themselves, what the different manifestations of change are, and what the shape of future resilience and continuity is in the Kenyan family. Our authors have not focused on blame or moral judgments regarding who and what caused or is responsible for family crises, although this topic certainly matters. The consequences and adaptive responses of families are our main focus.

Concerns in Africa about the family have some parallels in the contemporary United States and Europe. In the United States, where a third of the births now occur outside marriage, the issue of family change has been articulated at every level of the social and political structure. For example, during the early 1990s Vice President Dan Quayle called for a return to "family values." Quayle's call underscored a widely held desire to recapture an aspect of United States culture that has changed radically since the 1950s. The imagined tranquillity and quality of life of that era, a remembrance or yearning that is itself contested, is a part of the feeling that contemporary family life is in crisis in comparison.

A desire to return to traditional values is a theme also found in Africa and reflects a perception that life was better before the present—before colonialism, incorporation into the capitalist world-economy, and development. This nostalgia for the past is a centerpiece of many African novels (e.g., *Things Fall Apart*) and a component of several papers in this volume. For example, Nasimiyu (this volume) argues that women's usufruct rights to land were better protected and food sources were more secure in precolonial Bungoma (also see Håkansson and LeVine, Kilbride and Kilbride, and Cattell, this volume). Ocholla-Ayayo (this volume) shows that Kenyans believe sexual mores have deteriorated over time. Whyte and Whyte and Kariuki (this volume) argue that prior nutritional regimes were better than present ones, due to more resilience and a wider range of naturally occurring foods.

However, we urge caution when evaluating informants' memories of a better past, for example, a time when women were better treated, adolescent sexuality was better guarded within the cultural context (Ocholla-Ayayo, this volume, Kilbride and Kilbride, this volume) or in-laws and elders were properly honored (Bradley, this volume, Cattell, this volume). Although we have empirical evidence that Kenyans believe things have gotten worse, we must look elsewhere for confirmation, if it is available at all. In other words, the perception of "breakdown"—the loss of traditions, values, and culture—and also the changes that have actually occurred, are valuable data. But memories and reminiscences occur in the present and should not be mistaken for the realities of the past.

Such reminiscences may not be quite veridical about the past, but they can help defend the predictability of life (Marris, 1975, p. 3). Defending the predictability of life involves comparing current circumstances to an idealized and internalized model inherited from past family experiences. They are defended to the extent that they are primordial, emotionally-salient experiences from childhood and earlier adult life and reinforced by contemporary cultural practice. Family ideals may not be attainable and ideals and practices are changing, but they remain culturally and psychologically important to the imagined cultural careers of contemporary Kenyans. There are prototypical cultural models for creating and sustaining family life which continue to have a force in contemporary Kenyan communities.

Hence our data suggest that a unidimensional image of the African family as "breaking down" is unsupported. Many studies in this volume (e.g., Weisner, Akong'a, Håkansson and LeVine, Munroe and Munroe, Wandibba, Edwards) suggest significant continuity and adaptive resilience in the face of contemporary changes. These include continuity in psychological themes around family (Akong'a; Weisner), gender (Munroe and Munroe, Håkansson and LeVine, and Nasimiyu), and the elderly. Our evidence suggests that Kenyan family adaptation is an ongoing struggle, a historically continuous cultural project to create a meaningful, sustainable, and coherent pattern of everyday life. Our authors often report that similar adaptive struggles took place in the past. Thus, rather than breakdown, we see selective crises that arise when, for a variety of reasons, family members can no longer effectively engage in the shared adaptive project, tied to primordial, defended cultural models of family life experienced in the past and partially reinforced in the present, that is the heart of family life.

CULTURE, FAMILIES, HOUSEHOLDS

Our authors speak of cultures, tribes, and different local communities in Kenya. But were there in the past, and are there today, cultures, or tribes, or communities in Kenya, or were there only colonial and/or locally-defined groups in shifting, historically variable configurations? We and our authors accept the importance and relevance of cultural communities without overly reifying them. We believe that cultures and tribes are useful as analytical categories and real in the world of Kenyan families and communities. It has long been recognized in anthropology, including work in Africa (Southall, 1970), that the extent of homogeneity in a cultural community, or human population, is an empirical question, not inherent in the use of culture or tribe as category. Brightman's (1995, p. 541) review of the criticisms of the culture concept in anthropology makes this point:

> Neither in earlier disciplinary history nor as deployed in recent anthropological writing does the culture concept consistently exhibit the attributes of ahistoricism, totalization, holism, legalism, and coherence with which its critics selectively reconstitute it. These [critics' conceptions of culture] are invented images of culture, both arbitrary and partial with respect to a much more diverse and versatile field of definition and use.

Our evidence suggests that there is substantial local homogeneity within the various cultural communities studied in our volume, as well as many common features shared among them. Sub-Saharan Africa and Kenya include meaningfully different human populations, or "interactional networks within which mating and other communicative processes tend to be concentrated" (LeVine et al., 1994, p. 12). Populations share a local ecology, symbol systems for encoding that ecology, and social organizations and cultural rules for adapting to it.

We have organized our family studies of adaptation and change around five topics: economy, human development, gender and fertility, the elderly, and health. Although all the papers focus on one or more of these topics, there is no single unifying theoretical perspective. The authors have diverse views on theory and method. Theoretical perspectives articulated in the papers include ecological, psychoanalytic, ecocultural, historical materialist, symbolic, feminist, and modernization or delocalization. Most papers use a multimethod approach, combining quantitative and qualitative methods. Ethnography combines with comparative and cross-cultural, demographic, psychological, historiographic, and public heath survey methodologies. With authors coming from Africa, Europe, and North America, these perspectives and methods represent different traditions through which social scientists come to understand the same or similar problems.

Likewise, units of analysis vary. Some authors, for example, measure data for individuals, while others also collect data from units they call "households" or "families." Clearly, households and families are constituted differently and would call for different methods. In western Kenya, for example, a household is easily defined as "those who share a cooking pot." This definition can accommodate two women living with children, a Logoli grandmother living with three grandchildren and an unmarried pregnant daughter, or a multigenerational household consisting of parents, their sons and cowives, their biological children, and any number of foster children, all of whom eat from the same pot. To collect data on *families* related by blood and marriage in contemporary Kenya requires a research design including travel to other regions and cities, locating kin who remain part of the family estate but live elsewhere in the country. "Household" and "family" would then overlap but remain analytically distinct as units for analysis and conceptualization.

Most recent publications about the problems at issue in this book focus on households. This is because "family" has ceased to be a viable unit for *economic* research. This shift to studying households is primarily due to the very perception that there is a crisis of the family throughout the contemporary world. The concept of "household" has taken root, replacing the notion of family that was used over the previous 150 years (Wallerstein, 1974). In the United States up to the 1950s, households and families were still synonymous for the majority of domestic units census takers encountered. These were spoken of by demographers as "true families." But for the last forty years the proportion of households containing "true families" has declined. Eventually, the concept of "family" was no longer identifiable as a group of people living in a house.

In addition, the notion of family became tainted with evolutionist or developmentalist assumptions, namely, that the nuclear family was the most modern or advanced family form (Smith & Wallerstein, 1992). But families are often not constituted in this nuclear way—not in the United States or in Africa. This encouraged feminists, anthropologists, and political scientists to use the term "household" instead (see, for example, Netting, Wilk, & Arnould, 1984).

But something is lost in the transition from studying families to households. As a unit of analysis, "household" nearly always implies economic and political variables and relations. For example, a household is commonly defined as an institution with fluid boundaries, where people pool income, allocate tasks, make decisions, and reproduce class and ethnic relations (Smith & Wallerstein, 1992). Household, in this economic sense, is also used as a unit of analysis in several papers in this volume.

However, our deeper concern with "family" emphasizes not only the "household" as a coresidential, economic unit but also the family as a complex institution that binds together individual households. The family in Africa in this wider view is connected by blood, marriage, adoption, and *shared cultural, economic, and psychosocial tools for adaptation.* The role of families in social support, moral judgments, and economic exchanges and as the unit carrying important values and practices being used by communities today is clear in many of the studies in our volume. Furthermore, our African colleagues talk of families in these ways. The notion of a crisis in the African *family*, where African values and traditions are reproduced and transmitted, is one that is very real to them and to the communities we studied.

The African family can be seen from a variety of perspectives and levels of analysis, but always as an intergenerational, multilocal, psychosocial community linked to local, national, and global economies and polities. Although many chapters in this book make such linkages to different levels, we do not lose sight of the family as the center of our interest. European interests, the Kenyan state, the world economic order—these matter to the contemporary, partially delocalized African family, but they do not in any sense replace the importance of the family in the actions and thoughts and feelings of Kenyans themselves.

CULTURE, FAMILY, AND ECONOMY

Hence, our focus on the family and regional communities of Western Kenya does not suggest lack of acknowledgment of the world system in which it exists. As Moore comments regarding how community studies in Africa relate to a global perspective in anthropology itself: "The global political-economy is in sight, even from the food gardens of the most peripheral settlements. Intense local study is a method of investigation, not a definition of the anthropological problem" (1993, p. 4).

In this respect the evidence from the studies in this book supports the notion that colonization had many of its effects "from the bottom up, through the remaking of the inhabited environment" (Comaroff & Comaroff, 1992, p. 67), as well as through the state and the economy and formal ideologies, and that domestic life was central in the remaking of the local environment.

Western Kenya and eastern Uganda share with other African countries a history punctuated by the colonial experience. In essence, the economic history of Africa over the last several hundred years was dominated by the process of incorporation into the capitalist world economy. The colonial and postcolonial periods may be viewed as two phases of incorporation and capitalist intrusion. Thus, when scholars write about economic change in Africa they almost invariably make these factors central in the analysis.

The authors writing about the economics of family change in this volume have both the global and the local system in sight. For example, Kilbride and Kilbride explore changing family life in East Africa using the concept "delocalization" as a centerpiece. Delocalization is similar to Appadurai's (1991) term "deterritorialization," and perhaps also to the world-systems theory concept of "peripheralization." Western Kenya may be thought of as a delocalized, or peripheralized, landscape. This is a place in which some men and women, perhaps identifying as Abaluyia or Luo or Kalenjin, travel back and forth from their city homes to the rural homes where they hope to be buried someday. Western Kenya is delocalized in the sense that it has become for many a kind of bedroom community for Kenya's major cities. It is a labor market and food-producing region, with inextricable links to the wider world. These links are made by people who travel back and forth and through radio, television, newspapers, commodities, sexually transmitted diseases, and family planning information. Yet it is also a place that is economically, politically, and culturally often very distant in experience, in family practices and customs, and in locally meaningful systems of social participation.

Of course, western Kenya was never isolated and unconnected to other ethnic groups and places, before or after colonial influence. The region was settled during the Bantu diaspora of preceding centuries, and some men and women can remember, as young children, the first settlement of their current lineage lands. Trade and intermarriage was extensive with groups in Uganda and all the way to the coast. But the sheer scale of the colonial and postcolonial eras, the asymmetry of the impact, the comprehensiveness of it in every domain of life, makes this delocalization of a different order of magnitude and force in the life of the region.

Our authors find that local variations in access to resources affect how resources are allocated within the household (de Wolf, M. Whyte). Resource allocation decision making is also affected by changing access to education, women's status, and polygyny (Ssennyonga). Wandibba compares the economic and domestic roles of children across two generations, providing new ethnographic data on children's local knowledge of their ecology. Super and Harkness provide some of the most detailed cross-sectional data currently available on two different patterns of community response to modernization in Kokwet and provide evidence for these at both the family and individual child and mother levels. Younger, better educated, and Christian-affiliated families have more access to cash and school fees for their children, and their children are less likely to be found away from their homes doing subsistence tasks. However, infant and child health measures were unaffected by modernity. Younger and more educated women bear children earlier and with smaller birth intervals and these greater risks to health offset any gains from better education or access to health care.

Several authors in this volume evaluate change in Africa during the colonial and postcolonial period using a modernization, or westernization, perspective. By the term "modernization," these authors do not refer to a simplistic modernization theory. Modernization theory, in which states are thought of as either modern or modernizing, has been critiqued by most disciplines. World-system theorists, for example, argue that societies do not necessarily proceed teleologically toward modernization, but rather argue that, in a single world-system, peripheral areas may be marginalized. As such, they fail to develop in the ways expected by modernization theory, instead becoming labor and raw material supplying regions for core areas and states. This follows from Frank's (1966) notion of the "development of underdevelopment." However, when the authors in this book use the term "modernization," they mean the intrusion of capital and its infrastructure, as well as the ways in which the relations of capitalism are reproduced (e.g., media, national education), and recognize that many parts of Kenya are underdeveloped or marginalized relative to core cities such as Nairobi and countries such as England or the United States.

HUMAN DEVELOPMENT, AGING, AND CHANGING FAMILY VALUES

There are universal problems facing all families and cultural communities in raising children. LeVine et al. (1994, p. 12) for instance, argue that four adaptive needs—subsistence, reproduction, communication, and social regulation—shape human child care and that these are always socially and culturally organized. Each of these adaptive problems are represented in our chapters, in sections covering economics, fertility, health, aging, or cultural values and development. Our authors write about changing systems of social support for children and the elderly and women (Abbott, Bradley, Cattell, Sangree, Kilbride, Håkansson and LeVine, Ssenyonga, Nasimiyu, Munroe and Munroe, Weisner), moral judgments (Edwards), health and survival for children (Ocholla-Ayayo, Whyte, Whyte and Kariuki), and parental strategies for responding to modernity (Super and Harkness, Wandibba, de Wolf).

The adaptive challenge facing families and communities everywhere is to provide a daily routine of life for children that is relatively stable and sustainable in a local ecology, provides for subsistence needs, is meaningful and appropriate within the communities' moral worlds, and is congruent with the resources parents and children have available to them. "Sustaining" a daily routine means adapting it to a local ecology and the family resource base. That is, it refers to survival, work, wealth, and resources. To sustain a routine means dealing with the resources and constraints available and perceived in the world. It requires an assessment of class, gender, and power and the ecology surrounding the family and community. A "meaningful" routine is one that has moral and cultural significance and value for family members—a routine of cultural activities that meets at least some valued cultural goals. It is also a routine of life that is interpretable within some shared cultural developmental model in a community.

Many of our studies argue for a continuing, coherent set of moral ideals and cultural models—albeit, of course, changing constantly because of delocalization—guiding African families in this adaptive project of organizing their parenting practices and daily routines of life. There are many examples of an interesting mix of cultural coherence, continuity, and change with regard to cultural models of family life in our volume. The continuity in our studies of family life derives in part from the importance of locally situated family practices that still encode (in symbols, practices, beliefs, and institutions) useful ways to deal with some of the universal adaptive problems facing families.

Edwards finds that there are changes in moral reasoning and judgments across the generations—but not a different moral world. Munroe and Munroe present evidence for a culture complex of gender socialization that continues to reproduce gender-determined child rearing patterns and parenting roles. Abbott compares parenting beliefs between Kikuyu and Appalachian communities and clearly finds central tendencies and continuities in each group. Weisner finds continuity in shared caretaking of children and in notions of social support, including sibling caretaking within a culture complex encouraging its continued modified practice. Akong'a argues that core cultural values are crucial to psychosocial adaptation in Kenya and outlines some of these core institutionalized values concerns. Håkansson and LeVine show continuity in men's and women's life course strategies and life goals among the Gusii, as well as contemporary changes in Gusii women's and men's strategies as men and women age. Both women and men jockey for power and resources, with women relying on their children if they can and with men increasingly isolated if they cannot take additional wives. S. LeVine has summarized how change has accentuated this *prior* cultural and psychological pattern among Gusii:

> [I]t would appear that these women, like most others of their age group in Gusii society, are bound to live psychologically and physically isolated lives—alone, for the most part, with their children.... [W]omen seemed to be condemned to rather solitary lives in which they pursued their daily activities alone for the most part, with little opportunity to meet with others in neutral circumstances. If a lack of trust was always a feature of Gusii culture, the contemporary social and economic situation has further emphasized this characteristic. (1979, pp. 369–370)

Whereas change can produce an exaggeration of previous cultural practices, more often it produced syncretism, active strategic manipulation of the old and the new, and community heterogeneity. Whiting (1996, pp. 29–30), for example, has shown how contemporary Kikuyu mothers still valued the social behaviors of obedience, respect for elders, generosity, and good-heartedness. At the same time, more modern Kikuyu mothers valued cleverness, confidence, inquisitiveness, and bravery or boldness in their children, social behaviors they perceived might help them in school and the new state and economy. They expressed ambivalence about such values as cleverness or boldness, recognizing the difficulty of combining these behaviors with obedience.

Our studies of aging and generational differences, like the work on parenting and social support for children, show considerable ambivalence among elderly, as well as their children and siblings, about their circumstances. Elderly are dependent on children's earnings from cash in ways never anticipated. The elderly are being put to work caring for children and continuing to manage family farms and herds, at a time in life when their cultural ideals were to sit quietly and receive respect and recognition. This is hard logistically and physically for elders. It is also difficult and unexpected socially, since elders' roles and interpersonal expectations are changed. It is also a struggle emotionally—there is a sense among elders in Western Kenya that they have been "betrayed" or denied something they thought would be theirs by their children and siblings, since they are not receiving the honor and respect they deserve.

Men's and women's circumstances are often very different, as is clear from the chapters by Ssennyonga, Håkansson and Levine, and Cattell. Elders' experiences of delocalization is profound, but often they are actually collaborating in family persistence and continuity for their children and grandchildren! The theme of remembrance is also especially relevant for the elderly: Have the elderly not always experienced loss and recalled the past and its promises in idealized ways?

Taken together, these studies vividly capture many of the concerns driving the ecocultural adaptations of Kenyan families. In the face of sometimes overwhelming difficulties, parents are struggling to achieve such a sustainable and meaningful routine of everyday life for their children, their elders, and themselves. It is this human adaptive project in family life that is a focus of our volume.

CONCLUSION

The moral and cultural concerns of families in the current crisis of delocalization in western Kenya are hardly local in the sense of being limited to that part of the world. That is, these are not "East African problems." These problems are recognizable in varying forms everywhere. Kilbride and Kilbride compare concerns with child abuse, infanticide, and elder neglect and abuse in Kenya with North America, for instance. The impossible demands placed on some women in Kenya, especially those with no husband or an absent one, to provide for their children with inadequate resources is a problem found throughout the world, and evidence for this comes from a number of the studies.

The intergenerational study of family change at the local community level is, in our view, a key to understanding family adaptation and is a theme of the fieldwork and design of many of the studies in this volume. It is not the only important way, but it is an essential complement to surveys, historical and political economic studies, or other approaches. These chapters suggest new hypotheses and longitudinal studies at every turn: What will be the cultural model and expectations for social support in the current generation of Western Kenyans? How will local behavioral adaptations for HIV and sexual conduct finally emerge in these communities? How will the parents now viewing their own elderly generation view aging and its rights and obligations? How will the fertility decline now under way in the region be reflected in changing gender roles and economic obligations? How will the different strategies for economic adaptation across families within cultural groups discovered by the authors in our volume affect their children's life course into the next generation?

The family adaptive project vividly seen in these studies is shared by families everywhere: to sustain a way of life for kin that has cultural and emotional meaning. The Kenyan communities our authors have studied are trying to achieve this in the face of often desperate economic, sociohistorical, demographic, and political circumstances. The diversity and complexity of how families have adapted shows continuity, delocalization, fragmentation, and loss. The extent to which families are succeeding offers some hope and should be counted as a real achievement of contemporary Kenyan communities.

NOTE

A note on terminology and maps: We used standard Kenya spelling of basic terms (such as Luyia and Abaluyia). However, Abaluyia communities vary in spelling and usage of some terms. Authors' usage was followed in those circumstances, and so some terms and phrases will differ slightly in spelling across chapters. All the western Kenya communities described in the volume are shown on the detailed map of administrative units. These include communities where extensive fieldwork was done (such as Samia and Maragoli) or communities where comparative data are presented (such as Nzoia and Teso). Communities outside western Kenya are near other centers shown on the Kenya map (such as Gusii near Kisii Town, Kikuyu near Thika, Gisu near the Kenya–Uganda border, Kokwet south of Kericho, and so on).

REFERENCES

Appadurai, Arjun. (1991). Global ethnoscapes: Notes and queries for a transnational anthropology. In Richard G. Fox (Ed.), *Recapturing anthropology*. Santa Fe, NM: School of American Research.

Brightman, Robert. (1995). Forget culture: Replacement, transcendence, relexification. *Cultural Anthropology, 10*, 509–546.

Comaroff, Jean, & Comaroff, John L. (1992). Home-made hegemony: Modernity, domesticity, and colonialism in South Africa. In Karen Tranberg Hansen (Ed.), *African encounters with domesticity* (pp. 37–74). New Brunswick, NJ: Rutgers University Press.

Frank, André Gunder. (1966). The development of underdevelopment. *Monthly Review, 28*, 17–35.

Gray, R. F., & Gulliver, P. H. (Eds.) (1964). *The family estate in Africa. Studies in the role of property in family structure and lineage continuity*. Boston: Boston University Press.

LeVine, Robert A., Dixon, Suzanne, LeVine, Sarah, Richman, Amy, Leiderman, P. Herbert, Keefer, Constance H., and Brazelton, T. Berry (1994). *Child care and culture. Lessons from Africa*. Cambridge: Cambridge University Press.

LeVine, Sarah. (1979). *Mothers and wives. Gusii women of East Africa*. Chicago: University of Chicago Press.

Marris, P. (1975). *Loss and change*. New York: Doubleday/Anchor Books.

Moore, Sally F. (1993). Changing perspectives on a changing Africa: The work of anthropology. In Robert H. Bates, V.Y. Mudimbe, & Jean O'Barr (Eds.), *Africa and the disciplines: The contributions of research in Africa to the social sciences and humanities* (pp. 3–57). Chicago: University of Chicago Press.

Netting, Robert, Wilk, Richard R., & Arnould, Eric J. (1984). *Households: Comparative and historical studies of the domestic group*. Berkeley, CA: University of California Press.

Popenoe, David. (1988). *Disturbing the nest: Family change and decline in modern societies*. New York: Aldine de Gruyter.

Smith, J., & Wallerstein, I. (1992). *Creating and transforming households: The constraints of the world-economy*. Cambridge: Cambridge University Press.

Southall, Aidan. (1970). The illusion of tribe. *Journal of Asian and African Studies, 5*, 28–50.

Whiting, B. B. (1996). The effect of social change on concepts of the good child and good mothering: A study of families in Kenya. *Ethos, 24*, 3–35.

HUMAN DEVELOPMENT, VALUES, AND FAMILY CHANGE

1

Psychological and Institutional Defense Mechanisms in Times of Change

Joshua Akong'a

INTRODUCTION

In psychology and psychiatry, the processes through which individuals attempt to maintain a satisfactory balance between instinctual desires and their gratifications are known as psychological defense mechanisms. These mechanisms are triggered by an influx of stimuli that are either more or less intense than expected, and they are deployed to combat the onslaught of anxiety and frustration that may ensue. Psychological defense mechanisms constitute an early warning system that enables individuals to adjust, consciously or unconsciously, to prevailing environmental conditions as part of their socio-psychological adaptation.

Some psychologists and psychiatrists who have written on this subject have failed to recognize that there is a relationship between psychological defense mechanisms, which are cognitive and universal, and the social institutions that support them. The ethnographic literature, especially of African societies, is replete with descriptions of institutions, some of whose functions may not be readily apparent unless they are viewed as symbolic institutional defenses that protect individuals and society from disruption. Many of these institutional or social defense mechanisms may support the development and deployment of the psychological defense mechanisms responsible for the development and protection of the mind and superego. By discussing the symbolic function of certain social institutions from a cross-cultural perspective, this chapter will demonstrate, first, that there is a direct correspondence between effective psychological defense mechanisms and the existence of institutional defense mechanisms and, second, that the disintegration of traditional institutions in the rapid social and cultural change taking place in African societies has destroyed institutional defense mechanisms. The consequence has been social and cultural disruption in the name of modernization. But change need not bring about psychological upheavals in individuals nor the social disruption that has been experienced by African societies.

A brief description of some psychological defense mechanisms is provided to illustrate their functions in stabilizing the psychological and social bearing of the individual. Then examples of institutional defense mechanisms that have assisted individuals in various societies to readapt to situations that would otherwise have been disruptive are presented as a preamble to an understanding of the fundamental issue of what happens to the institutional and psychological bases of societies in times of rapid sociocultural change.

This discussion is not necessarily exhaustive, as there are other defense mechanisms, such as biological ones, that are not considered here. This is a conceptual exposition intended to demonstrate the direct relationship between social institutions, the workings of the mind, and what underlies human behavior. It is a psychological interpretation of psychic and social phenomena and derives its strength from the power of interpretation rather than from description per se. However, it certainly has its own biases and subjective underpinnings.

My goal in this chapter, in addition to defining and giving examples of defenses at psychological and social levels in Kenya and elsewhere, is to argue that social science in the past may have overemphasized the sharing of culture and its role in smoothly and easily maintaining law and order. We need to explore the contrary, dangerous aspects of our common human nature that defense mechanisms both reveal and help defend against. Further, I think that the current overwhelming changes and dislocations confronted by Kenyan families, many of which are reviewed in this volume, have seriously threatened, and indeed sometimes overwhelmed, both psychological and traditional social and institutional defense mechanisms. A certain kind of desperation and dehumanization is in the process of occurring unless these defenses can be restored and strengthened (among many other economic, social, and other changes needed). Individuals in Kenya today sometimes are exercising a kind of false individualism and free will, made "false" to the extent that change and breakdown in familial and societal institutions has occurred without sufficiently supportive and culturally meaningful alternatives arising to replace them. This breakdown has led to increases in overindulgent, deviant or immature behavior to some extent, since the institutions that would normally provide local cultural rationality, control, and defenses are unavailable.

PSYCHOLOGICAL DEFENSE MECHANISMS

Under normal circumstances, individuals are socialized to be able to control, postpone, or delay instinctual desires until conditions prevail that are favorable or suitable for their gratification. When there is an imbalance between instinctual desires and their gratification, individuals experience anxiety, a signal of danger. In order to protect the psyche from experiencing pain, a pleasure principle is triggered the purpose of which is to deflect psychological, physical, or social pain or discomfort. The process by which this pleasure principle modifies or rechannels the libidinal energy is what is referred to here as a psychological defense mechanism. The following descriptions of some of these mechanisms should reveal how they function to protect individuals and to facilitate re-adaptation to different situations. The classical, neo-Freudian defense mechanisms include repression, denial, displacement, rationalization, sublimation, isolation, projection, scapegoating, turning against self, identification, and regression, among others. After briefly defining and giving examples of each, I will turn to the institutional defenses that accompany them.

Repression

According to Conger and Peterson, "in repression, anxiety-producing impulses [and] memories . . . are kept from conscious awareness" (1984, p. 65). Repression is a process by which individuals attempt to bar unwanted thoughts, such as the wishful fantasies that occur in daydreaming, from consciousness. It is a type of forgetting that protects individuals from feeling the pain or guilt they would experience if such thoughts were made conscious. To some extent, repression is achieved by conscious or deliberate effort.

Denial

Denial is refusal to admit the existence of an anxiety-provoking reality. For example, in a patrilineal, patrilocal, and patriarchal society—as most of the Kenyan societies are—a man believed to be dominated by his wife or thought to have feminine characteristics would be held in contempt by his peers. Such a man might be among the first to decry such characteristics in others as being unworthy of a man, in a conscious or unconscious effort to deny them in himself.

Denial can manifest itself as ambivalence—a criminal who becomes a convert and an active street preacher and a victim of cruelty who becomes a social worker or counselor are examples. In these instances, individuals express in behavior the obverse of what they consciously or unconsciously feel. Denial is a compensation, in which a real or perceived weakness is disguised by the exaggeration of a behavior that distracts from the one deemed undesirable. The student weak in academics who excels in sports is a common example.

Displacement

In displacement, a destructive response or emotion engendered by one person or object is transferred to another. For example, a man who does not get a promotion or is belittled by his boss may turn his anger and frustration against his family, becoming touchy and violent. Displacement may also manifest itself through withdrawal, which "involves the direct avoidance of or flight from threatening situations or people" (Conger and Petersen, 1984, p. 68). Instead of passing time together in a room and risking temptation, friends of the opposite sex may decide to go and watch a football match.

Rationalization

Rationalization "involves providing . . . socially acceptable reasons for . . . behavior or attitudes, when the real reason would not be acceptable to one's conscience, and hence, would, if permitted into awareness, lead to painful anxiety and guilt" (Conger & Petersen, 1984, p. 68). This implies that an impulse appears in consciousness but devoid of the corresponding significance. This results in defensive intellectualization, that is, an attempt to substitute a good reason for the real one. It is, in fact, deceptive reasoning. A chain-smoker who realized that those around him may get concerned about his habit might in the past have preemptively informed them that they should not become concerned about his smoking habit because it has been scientifically proven that sufficient doses of nicotine are good for the body.

Sublimation

Sublimation is a process by which a desire is forgotten in the process of participating in other unrelated activities, thus using up the psychic energy that would have been expended on the original desire. This protects the psyche from the original desire, which would otherwise be frustrating or anxiety provoking. Sublimation of social or private life is usually characteristic of successful career men and women such as doctors, lawyers, professors, and politicians, who spend long hours at their places of work in order to succeed. In fact, Sigmund Freud, the father of psychoanalytic psychology, believed that sublimation in the long run contributes positively to the growth of civilization. This is not to imply, however, that all sublimation contributes positively to the well-being of individuals and societies.

Isolation

Isolation is the process by which a thought or act that would create anxiety is barred from memory. A person who fears an injection, for example, must pretend that it will not be painful until he has been injected—and may do this by forgetting he or she has the appointment until the last minute. A woman who faints in the process of rape would be succumbing to the psychological process of isolation, the means by which an experience that would be too painful to bear psychologically in a conscious state is made devoid of the accompanying emotion and can be literally forgotten in conscious memory.

Projection

In projection, individuals attribute their own wishes and impulses to others. Politicians who cry foul by claiming "money has been spent by others to finish me" may themselves be involved in scheming against their own political adversaries. In this case, the emotional state is the same, but the object to which the wishes and impulses are attributed is reversed.

Scapegoating

In the process of scapegoating, the explanation given for a failure is not the actual reason for the failure. A weak student who blames his or her failure wholly on victimization by a teacher is scapegoating.

Turning against Self

Some people, usually those who possess weak superegos, blame themselves for mistakes they have not committed or for mistakes committed by others. Because they cannot easily and eloquently explain or justify something that has happened, they end up taking responsibility for it to avoid further embarrassment, even when they are conscious that they are lying. Sometimes they accept blame to cover up the mistakes of those they respect or love. Such people are easily taken advantage of. The overuse of this technique of adaptation is a symptom of severe psychological malfunction.

Identification

Identification involves imagining, feeling, and desiring to behave as though one were another person. Identification arises in situations in which there is a discrepancy between the perceived and the true self. Therefore individuals aspire to become what they are not, as reflected in another person. They form a mental representation of an observed act, relate it to themselves, and attempt to imitate it. Identification is, therefore, the process of performing a role in fantasy so that when the time comes for performing it in reality, the mind is ready. Identification becomes a problem when individuals identify with inappropriate or incorrect persons or objects, that is, incorrect from the point of view of being adaptive to what is socially acceptable.

Regression

Regression involves "the re-adaptation of a response that was characteristic of an earlier phase of development . . . [which was] successful and rewarding in an earlier, simpler period" (Conger & Petersen, 1984, p. 68). Temper tantrums may be regressive behavior, as may certain psychosomatic illnesses such as headaches, stomachache, and fatigue, which are consciously or unconsciously aimed at avoiding activities that would be frustrating. A child who hates a particular teacher may become sickly because it is acceptable to be sick and to stay at home, rather than stay healthy and have to face the hated teacher.

The list of psychological defense mechanisms is long and can by no means be exhausted in a brief chapter such as this one. What should be made clear is that these mechanisms develop as part of one's experience in the course of maturation and should not necessarily be considered pathological. In fact, their effective deployment takes place in people Carl Rogers would refer to as "fully functioning" (Morris, 1988, p. 472). These are the people who are self-directed and independent, even though their choices may not always be correct ones. They are people who are not easily swayed by others, who are principled, open to new experience, and willing and able to take risks.

The more experiences one has, the more psychological mechanisms one is likely to develop in response to frustrating experiences. The development of psychological defense mechanisms is analogous to the process by which the body develops antibodies against new diseases in order to survive.

Several defense mechanisms may be deployed, simultaneously or in succession, during any one psychological or social event. The *overdeployment* of any one defense mechanism could be a symptom of severe psychological and, consequently, social malfunction.

People are also provided with culturally constituted social institutions as means of obtaining honest and socially approved livelihoods. These are the institutions I have referred to as *social* or *institutional* defense mechanisms. For these contexts, the appropriate deployment of psychological defense mechanisms at the proper time in balanced proportions is a manifestation of normal adaptation to the psychological, social, and physical environments. A person so adapted can be said to possess a normal and effective superego, since the deployment of any one defense mechanism is done after (largely unconscious) planning, evaluation, and decision making, in order to assist in adaptation to the local culture and economy.

INSTITUTIONAL DEFENSE MECHANISMS

Societies attempt consciously or unconsciously to deal with insufficient psychological defense mechanisms through mechanisms built into the social structure—hence social or institutional defense mechanisms. An institution is a fixed mode of thought or pattern of behavior held by a group of individuals. Institutions are normally culturally constituted, as they differ from one society to another in structure and function.

According to Kardiner and others, there are primary and secondary institutions. Primary institutions include a people's mode of livelihood, social organization, child-training practices, and so on. Secondary or derived institutions, on the other hand, are created by society to satisfy or reconcile the needs and conflicts of individuals, which constitute basic personality and which are, therefore, the products of primary institutions. Secondary institutions include religion, dreams, myths, songs, initiation ceremonies, and similar social structures (Kardiner, 1967; Ember & Ember, 1985).

Social or institutional defense mechanisms are secondary institutionalized behaviors that either impede or facilitate the fulfillment of certain basic needs or desires that are either prescribed or proscribed, but which either way would be difficult to satisfy, either because of the structure of the society or because of the inadequate development of the superego and, therefore, the existence of weak psychological defense mechanisms in individuals. There exist in all societies institutionalized patterns of behaviors designed to provide individuals with social and psychological satisfaction that would not otherwise have been possible. Thus, there is an association between social institutions and psychological processes, as the human mind is used to stability and is thrown into chaos in unstable social and physical conditions.

Using a structural analytical framework, Melford Spiro (1961) identified three types of institutional defense mechanisms. The first type is mechanisms that are both culturally proscribed and socially and psychologically disruptive. From Spiro's explanation one is tempted to conclude that this behavior, even though it may be habitual or even institutionalized, is neither adaptive for the individual nor integrative for society. He points out that "[t]he resolution of inner conflict is achieved at the price of mental illness and/or social punishment for the individual, or of the breakdown of social control for society" (Spiro, 1961, p. 483). Little attention has been focused on this type of human behavior and, as a result, little is known about it. For example, engaging in incest, which is against both social convention and the law, may bring about the consequences cited by Spiro. We need to know more about what motivates people to act against social convention. In the past, anthropologists may have overemphasized the sharing of culture and the need for maintenance of law and order. We have been afraid to ask questions that would point to contrary aspects of human nature and social well-being.

The second type of institutional defense mechanisms is those that are culturally approved and socially and psychologically integrative. These may apply to normal, expected behavior or to behavior that may not be against social convention but may not necessarily be mainstream. For example, many street preachers in Kenyan towns, judging on the basis of their own confessions, are former criminals who would probably be participating in criminal activities if they were not preaching. From this viewpoint, street preaching is a type of displacement or reaction formation. The institution of street preaching, which is both individually and socially acceptable, therefore protects the individual from inner conflicts as it "utilizes materials which form the social or cultural system for the distortion of a forbidden motive and hence, its disguised gratification" (Spiro, 1961, p. 484).

According to Spiro, the above-mentioned institutional defense mechanisms are idiosyncratic or personally constituted, in the sense that they are individual improvisations that are non-adaptive from the point of view of the first kind of institutional defense mechanism and adaptive from the point of view of the second.

The third type is institutional defense mechanisms that are not only culturally constituted but also socially and psychologically integrative. Spiro presents three examples to demonstrate this type of institutional defense mechanisms: in-law avoidance, through which incest was avoided and friendly relations maintained; political ritual protest in traditional African societies, in which role reversal was occasionally permitted to provide opportunity for the oppressed to vent repressed desires; and ritual food distribution by chiefs among the Ifaluk. Culturally constituted institutional defense mechanisms are pervasive. Additional cross-cultural examples should demonstrate their significance to the stability and integration of individuals and societies, at least in traditional societies. The description and interpretation of well known institutional defense mechanisms from outside Africa should make it possible to understand better those that have existed in Africa in general, and in Kenya in particular, and the impact rapid sociocultural changes have had on them.

ETHNOGRAPHIC CASE STUDIES

Among the Plains Indians of the United States of America, boys were socialized to the violent lifestyle of warriors and buffalo hunters. Society expected men to become brave, cunning, and strong (Thayer, 1980). Some boys, however, failed to approximate the expected ideal military, aggressive, and independent character traits. Such men became either *shamans* or *berdache* as full-time occupations from which they earned their living and sociopsychological well-being. A *berdache* was a transvestite—a man who dressed like a woman, used makeup, and easily mixed with women. The *berdache* can be said to have assumed the female role on the basis of psychological considerations as a result of lack of masculinity. In such situations, the very society that looked down upon women as inferior human beings permitted some of its men to become *berdache*, providing them with culturally acceptable means of gratifying a proscribed drive for dependence and enabling them to find meaning in life. Some of those who could not face up to this reality of leading a feminine lifestyle after dreaming about the moon or a hermaphrodite buffalo, which in American Indian cosmology was feminine in character, committed suicide. Others became *shamans*. Becoming a *berdache* was an institutional defense mechanism that gave meaning to the life of someone who otherwise would have been dismissed as a nonperson. Such men were good at matchmaking since they could mix freely with both men and women.

In South America among the Black Carib (Broude, 1988, p. 908) existed the *couvade*, in which on the birth of a child, as well as during the mother's pregnancy, the father performs acts or simulates states natural or proper to the mother, or abstains for a time from certain foods or activities as if he were physically affected by the birth. Many reasons have been put forward to explain the existence of this institution, including the fact that it constitutes a network of magical practices associated with important but unpredictable events, of which pregnancy, childbirth, and early infancy are examples (Broude, 1988, p. 909). Psychoanalysts explain the prevalence of this institution in this particular society as resulting from cross-sex identification (the Oedipus complex) that was not resolved in childhood and at the secondary level in adolescence because of the absence of initiation rituals. It definitely cannot be a manifestation of the desire by men to imitate the process of giving birth by women because of status envy. If this assumption is correct, then the motivational factors underlying *couvade* must be similar if not the same as those involved in *machismo*. *Machismo* is the belief in male dominance and is manifested in exaggerated expression of virility through such behaviors as intransigence in male–female relations, boasting about masculinity, expression of aggression in sexual relations, and acting out on the street.

In societies in which *machismo* is institutionalized, such as Southern Italy, Spain, Catholic South America, and, to some extent, the black community in the United States, a wide dichotomy is drawn between the good, hardworking, faithful wife and the wayward, wretched husband, a drunkard who spends much of his money on beer, women, and friends since these are the things which identify a real man. The pursuit of military glory, which rejoices in seeing others suffer; narcissism, which is egoistic behavior that leads to an over-evaluation of one's own attributes or achievements; and pugnacity, the manifestation of quarrelsome or aggressive tendencies as part of one's personality, are some of the aspects of *machismo*. *Machismo* can, therefore, correctly be viewed as hyper or protest masculinity—the conscious or unconscious denial by men who manifest feminine characteristics that they are feminine and, therefore, an attempt by such men to reassert their masculinity.

Thus, the behavior of men who preoccupy themselves with womanizing, boasting to others of being super men, or raping and murdering their victims—phenomena that are already very common in Kenya—is highly suggestive. Their obsession with dominating women and sometimes other men finds its unconscious base in their questionable masculinity.

The more logical explanation of *couvade*, in contradistinction to *machismo*, is that in *couvade* the male has been overwhelmed by the dominance of feminine characteristics, while in machismo these are fervently denied through reaction formation. It would not be stretching the point too far to point out here that bullfighting, which is an age old institution in Spain and Mexico, and the Mafia in Italy are elaborations of the same cultural complex based on *machismo*.

Taking an example from closer to home, among the Muslim Swahili of the Kenyan Coast there is strict segregation of members of the household on the basis of age and sex. Except for husband and wife, no two members of the opposite sex are expected to pass time together in one room in the absence of a third party, while boys and girls are not expected to be present in the same room as their mothers or fathers, when the parents are entertaining their peers from other households. The mutual exclusiveness of these dyadic relations are based on the honor of the men in the household, which can easily be tainted by free movement in the household and between the members of one household and others (Akong'a, 1979). The non-Muslim Nyakyusa of Southern Tanzania evolved an even more effective way of segregating members of the household by creating villages based on the age of men. This ensured that mature sons and their wives, when they got married, did not share the same village as their fathers and mothers (Wilson, 1963).

Socially, the Swahili may have feared the potential of incest among primary relatives in a society where cousin marriages are preferred. Among the Nyakyusa, on the other hand, the institution of age villages acted against potential incest between sons and stepmothers and between fathers-in-law and daughters-in-law. Since there was potential for sons seducing their young stepmothers and fathers seducing their sons' wives, the two sets of members of the family were expected to live in exclusive villages. One can go further to observe that among the Swahili, more especially, the potential for boys identifying with their mothers is very high, and in the two communities segregation on the basis of age and sex was a defense mechanism against unresolved Oedipal conflicts. This may account for the premium placed on same age, same sex, "good company" through which vital personal or cultural information could be transmitted (Wilson, 1963; Akong'a, 1979; Swartz, 1982).

Still in the family arena, it could be stated that most of the traditional types of marriage, especially in Africa, are institutional defense mechanisms. In levirate marriage, for example, a man is expected to inherit the wife and children of his deceased brother, paternal cousin, or clansman so classified. Many reasons have been cited to justify this institution. The widow and her children gain a husband

and father respectively, someone already familiar to them, providing them with both material and psychological support. Probably more important is the fact that the widow retains some of the property of the deceased for use by herself and her children, which is eventually inherited by her male children when they are grown up and married.

Sororate marriage involved the acquisition by the widower of his deceased wife's unmarried sister or paternal cousin. The marriage was based on the belief that the sister to the deceased woman would be a better surrogate mother for her children than some other woman or cowife.

On the other hand, woman to woman marriage, which is still common among the Kamba, Kikuyu, Kipsigis, and Gusii, involves an elderly woman bringing into her household a younger woman after fulfilling all the expectations pertaining to marriage negotiations. The main purpose of this "marriage" is for the younger woman to give to the older one children sired in secret by a man selected either by the older woman or by the younger woman herself.

In the past, a variant of such marriages took place among the Luyia. A barren woman who was subject to contempt from her co-wives or her husband asked her brother or paternal male cousin for a daughter who would bear children for her. Unlike other communities, where the husband of the "marrying" woman cannot touch the bride, who is the wife of an assumed son, among the Luyia the bride was given to the "marrying" woman's husband to have children with her in the same way Sarah gave her Egyptian slave girl to Abraham (Genesis 15:2–3). In addition to seeking children, women "marrying" others were motivated by jealousy, realizing that the property entrusted to them by their husbands for themselves and their children would be inherited by other women's children if they did not have their own. Therefore society permitted a woman in a patrilineal, patrilocal, and patriarchal society, in which the normal order of things is for men to marry women and have children, to "marry" other women to satisfy their quest for children for social and psychological satisfaction.

In ghost marriage, which is still practiced among the Kamba and the Gusii, a couple negotiates for the marriage of a deceased son, and a stepbrother or paternal cousin is chosen to sire children with the bride on behalf of the deceased.

In Kenya there existed the institution of the "senior bachelor," referred to variously as *omusumba* among the Luyia, *musumba* among the Luo, *omosomba* among the Gusii, and *chiriya* among the Rendille. *Omusumba* was a man who had already passed the time when he was expected to marry, either because he had not tried to do so or for lack of motivation. In a society in which all men were expected to marry and have children, this was considered unusual and unfortunate. Doubts were cast as to whether the man was impotent, bewitched, or just foolish.

Apart from the misfortune of being a senior bachelor, *omusumba* was usually a destitute with no independent means of livelihood, even though his parentage and relatives were known. He was usually slow in thinking and lacking in personal initiative. Although such men were considered reliable and could be trusted with assisting women in collecting and splitting firewood, fetching water, and babysitting, they were not necessarily hardworking enough to be offered full time employment. They were therefore offered odd jobs in order allow them to earn food and, sometimes, shelter.

In terms of psychological development, such men had not developed a strong superego, yet they were neither criminals nor mad. They were simply dismissed as childish or foolish—people who had matured only in body. As a result, children were cautioned not to abuse them or laugh at them, because this was considered a state of mind which the victim did not choose and which could be acquired by any person, especially those who treated such people with contempt. It was also believed that making such persons conscious that they were not normal might force them into committing suicide, leading to a curse.

Similarly, *jakowiny,* among the Luo, and *nduwa*, among the Kamba, were men of no fixed abode who provided free labor in a widow's home in exchange for food, shelter, and sometimes sexual favors. They could also be called upon to perform ritual functions considered polluting or beneath the dignity of the male members of the next lineage or clan. For example, after all the burial rites had been performed, there was still ritual coitus that was supposed to remove the death spell from the home. In the case of the death of a premarital baby, ritual coitus had to be performed with the child's mother. An outsider of no fixed abode was therefore appropriate, for he would not lay claim on the girl as his wife.

Among the Rendille, the senior bachelor had other very important functions in society. He was used as a spy in enemy villages to warn his own village when it would be appropriate to stage a livestock raid; he was able to do this because he could freely mix with women and children without suspicion because of his psychological and social conditions. It was believed that since he did not participate in sexual relations as a matter of course, his saliva had the potency to heal snake bites. He was sent with the *gumo* stick to the home of the bride-to-be to exchange it for her as part of the process of marriage. He was also knowledgeable regarding the herbs to be used for treating women. In many respects, then, except for his sex identity, the *chiriya* of the Rendille was similar in function to the *berdache* among Native Americans (Thayer, 1980, p. 290).

In Kenyan societies, other institutional defense mechanisms would include polygyny, rituals and ceremonies, and myths and songs. The list is inexhaustible.

In analyzing briefly selected social institutions, I hope I have demonstrated that there is a relationship between those institutions and certain states of mind. This implies the existence of close relationships not only between goals and the means of their attainment but also between institutional and psychological defense mechanisms as a consequence. Thus, in some cases, proscribed goals such as dependency may be attained by individuals through culturally acceptable means (as in the institutions of *berdache*, *couvade*, or *omusumba*), which provide the individual with psychological satisfaction and in the process protect society from disruption. In other cases, however, well-intentioned goals may lack culturally acceptable means of attainment, leading to the deployment of personally constituted means that may not always be in conformity with societal expectations. The girl who becomes pregnant premaritally because of inner conflicts or social pressure and who, as a result, cannot get married may be a case in point.

In general, institutional defense mechanisms are pervasive in any one society, since they relate to each of the stages of one's life cycle. That is to say, changes in status and roles, changes in situations and contexts, and so on expose individuals to different institutional and psychological defense mechanisms. In each one, individuals are guided by the culture of their society to be able to deploy appropriate psychological defenses to their own and society's advantage within the institutional frameworks available to them.

This is in part why rapid social and cultural change may take place to the disadvantage of individuals and society if it is not well managed. In situations of rapid social, cultural, structural, technological, or ecological change, a disjunction develops between the various previously integrated elements that held society together. A social condition identified by Emile Durkheim as *anomie* may arise, in which the prevailing norms are no longer operating effectively, while the new ones have not yet been fully perceived or even conceptualized. At such a point, the society and its norms provide no effective goals nor means for their attainment. The people who try to follow the old norms find themselves looked upon as old fashioned, since the old ways of doing things have been relegated to the status of historical anachronisms, while those who adopt new ways, though they may be considered modern or progressive, are guided not by what is generally accepted in society but by personally constituted improvisations.

There are certain types of people who stand in more danger of being taken advantage of and being exposed to suffering than others in such situations. These are the likes of *omusumba*, the physically and mentally handicapped, and the young, who may not differentiate the normal from the unique and who may not know what to do next even if they do. A society that is changing quickly and in which personally constituted mechanisms of goal attainment are prevalent creates its own momentum for further change. This is the point at which a society should be held accountable for providing its members with practical and moral guidance. Given time, some societies develop psychological and institutional mechanisms for cushioning the effects of change on some of the individuals affected, as happened in Uganda during Amin's traumatic rule (Ngabo-Lutaaya, 1982), or achieve a new equilibrium in which the unusual becomes normal (Du Bois, 1967, p. 101).

In some cases, societies become overwhelmed by change, as happened among the Native Americans in the Prairies during the colonization of the plains and west. As a consequence of war, missionary activities, and the introduction of farming, those Native Americans who did not die physically died socially and psychologically (Erikson, 1963). For this reason the disintegration of the traditional culture, social structure, and belief systems is cause for great concern. Many African societies, overwhelmed by change, economic stress (brought about partly by high population growth rate), and adverse climatic and political conditions, are growing desperate.

Even processes of "delocalization," which "involves persistence of tradition and even creating of new cultural forms" (Kilbride & Kilbride, 1990, p. 60; see also Kilbride & Kilbride, this volume), have not all been positive, although they hold the best chance for continuity in the face of change. The processes of delocalization, popularly referred to as syncretization, have been more acceptable, and therefore very successful, in the area of religion. With the introduction of Christianity that came with colonialism, some traditional African beliefs and institutions came to be viewed, especially in Kenya, as "primitive and repugnant to civilization and morality" by Christians. In Africa, Christianity developed variant expressions that borrowed from both systems, creating a Christianity as experienced in the African context. Since the ideal moralities of the two systems were not incompatible, as missionaries had at first believed, syncretic religions in Africa can be considered modern institutional defense mechanisms, designed to accommodate both new and old beliefs and to protect Africans psychologically from the feeling that their religious belief and practice are inferior to those of the Western world. The high rate of premarital pregnancies in Kenya demonstrates that in some areas of life such new mechanisms have not emerged soon enough (see Ocholla-Ayayo, this volume). The example of African Christianity should demonstrate that institutional defense mechanisms are instruments of adaptation. Even though they may be a reflection of previous maladjustment, they manifest successful re-adaptation.

HIGH ADOLESCENT FERTILITY IN KENYA

In Kenya, up to 31.9% of the children born are born to women between the ages of fifteen and twenty-four. What is surprising is that 93% of the women in this age bracket have never been married (Government of Kenya, 1979, p. 2). The contribution of premarital pregnancies to overall fertility is therefore quite large. Various reasons have been cited for the prevalence of premarital pregnancies, but I wish to focus on the breakdown of the traditional kinship and belief systems as one of the main factors underlying this phenomenon. In addition to the problems these changes can create for children and single mothers (see Kilbride & Kilbride, this volume), the transformation and loss of the previous culturally constituted norms and institutions regarding marriage leads, in my view, to the loss of social and psychological defenses that such institutions in part represent, and that provide assistance in maturation and in avoiding damaging and destructive behaviors that otherwise can and do occur.

In traditional African society, children belonged to an extended family, which gave them very wide and varied experiences on how to relate with others. In initiation ceremonies that marked an abrupt change from childhood to adult status, the youth were taught their society's lore, moral codes, beliefs, and taboos. This abrupt exposure to vital facts of life pertaining to adult status at the onset of puberty enabled them to enter adolescence with clear vision, knowledge, and status, and, therefore, without some of the major psychological conflicts experienced by adolescents in the western world. The breakdown of traditional family and kinship systems and the prevalence in African society of marital problems, broken marriages, rural to urban migration, single parent households, conflicts in religious teaching, and conflicts and contradictions between African and western cultures have adversely affected the process of socialization, leaving the youth unprepared to face the world.

With the breakdown of the system of avoidance behavior, for example, premarital and extramarital sexual relations have become common even among relatives, further complicating an already complicated issue. Because the institutions that had the capacity to restrain them from individualistic and deviant tendencies have broken down, individuals are exercising free will that derives more from immaturity than from mature, rational decision making, and premarital pregnancies have become more common. At a time when age of menarche and age of first sexual experience are dropping, adolescent fertility is inevitably high.

Thomas (1965) has identified four motivational preconditions for social action:

1. The wish for experience. People crave excitement and adventure, sometimes as an end in itself rather than as a means to a goal. There is a cathartic element which expresses itself through acts of courage, advance, attack, pursuit, and so on. The desire for experience is exploratory and may be indulged in disregard of other's views. The fact that it is provocative need not necessarily evoke hostile response.
2. The wish or desire for security. This desire is in opposition to the desire for experience; it is expressed through avoidance of experience or through timidity.
3. The wish or desire for response. This desire is related to the tendency to seek signs of appreciation from and to give signs of appreciation to other individuals. It is supposed to be the most social of the four wishes.
4. The wish or desire for recognition. This desire is expressed through the struggle for position, that is, through the effort to secure recognized social status.

These wishes are important, because human beings have the power to make decisions and to exercise free will. Their wishes, therefore, define the situation or context of social action before or during interaction. Every group or society has norms, or laws, values, and the like, that prescribe or should prescribe behavior in given situations. This is why one's knowledge of one's status, role, and situation is important in projecting appropriate behavior. Under normal circumstances, individuals, having internalized social expectation, need not define a situation every time they want to exhibit certain behavior. It is taken for granted and done as if by reflex. However, because individuals are not the same in status and role, and because situations differ from moment to moment, confusion, misunderstanding, and conflict often result as people have varying definitions of the situation in which they are operating. The point is that situations are redefined when there is a challenge, strain, or crisis that calls for new action or a new point of view. Such redefinitions depend on prevailing psychological, biological, physical, social, and cultural factors.

Because traditional mechanisms of moderation of behavior are breaking down, there may no longer be a balance among Thomas's four wishes as ideally there should be. The result has been overindulgence in the realization of one person's wish at the expense of all the others. For example, because there are no institutional mechanisms that define their status as children and clearly demark their transition into adulthood, youths may engage in sexual activities with as many partners as possible in an attempt to prove to themselves and their partners that they are grown-ups, when in fact they are not.

Taking a Freudian approach to interpreting motivational factors underlying the behavior of premarital mothers, Simpson says that such pregnancy is not accidental, as metaphorically expressed in most African societies. He states:

> We know the pervasive force of the unconscious in human motivation and the cumulative effect of motives stemming from the early life history.... The girl, not understanding her own motives and the driving forces in her environmental situation, tends to deny responsibility for what happened. She thinks of herself as a victim of circumstance without being able to realize that circumstances can be made. (Simpson, 1966, p. 471)

Thus pregnancy may be not consciously planned but a consequence of whatever happens.

Girls in many societies of technologically less developed countries become premaritally pregnant because of cultural stereotypes of women as irrational, gullible, easily confused, and unable to make rational independent judgments about what is good for them. In Africa, women were traditionally considered to be almost infantile in their expectations and behavior. This is why it was almost taboo for women to initiate sexually oriented responses. In rural Bangladesh, girls are reported to become premaritally pregnant because "men speak only with their lips and not with their hearts when they tell women they love them and want to marry them, as is shown by the fact that when the woman becomes pregnant, the man just leaves her. The other side of this situation is the expectation that women believe men much too readily when courting, that women are too trusting" (Howes, 1983, p. 48). The situation is no different in the Caribbean. According to Freilich and Coser, "The men spend considerable time and energy discussing their own sexual exploits and such conversations always include statements concerning 'fooling.' A great man is able to fool many women into believing all his promises" (Freilich & Coser, 1974, p. 87).

Increasing numbers of girls become pregnant outside marriage in this manner, and this is certainly well understood in Kenya as it is elsewhere. This attitude and practice is often opposed and contested. It is not merely accepted as an inherent part of "Kenyan (male) culture." It is often viewed, both in public and private debate, as a cover-up for promiscuity and exploitation and has been described as such in national newspapers.

CONCLUSION

One of the things that created stability in the social fabric of society and in the minds of individuals in it was the mystification of certain facts of life. Max Gluckman once wrote, "To say that African rituals (the locus of much mystification) have this high degree of particularism is not to deny that they deal with some of the general problems of social existence which have faced men everywhere" (Gluckman, 1956, p. 121).

The importance of mystification of reality can also be found in what the philosopher Walter Stace once wrote, "There is plenty of evidence that human happiness is almost wholly based upon illusions of one kind or another. But the scientific spirit, or the spirit of truth, is the enemy of illusions and therefore the enemy of human happiness" (Stace, 1989, cited in Nyangweso, 1992).

The implications are that the rapid process of secularization taking place in our society (see Hill, 1973) as a result of rapid social, cultural, political, economic, and environmental changes is not for the good of society unless at the same time new institutions are being brought into existence to take care of the old and new needs, which in the past were either satisfied or denied satisfaction through mystification of reality. The rapid changes taking place in our society which have denied children the rights and privileges historically associated with childhood, should be curbed so that children are permitted the full cycle of social and psychological growth before they are called upon to play the roles associated only with adult status in the past. Because of their pervasive impact, rapid changes should always be managed in order to minimize their deleterious consequences. Many such destructive changes, whether or not they are of human origin, can be influenced by human intention and will. Building these new familial and other institutions in Kenya surely will require economic, spiritual, political, and other kinds of investments. But to fully rebuild them will also require us to take into account the importance of psychological processes and their sometimes dangerous and threatening character, since psychological processes and social institutions are so closely interconnected, in my view.

REFERENCES

Akong'a, J. J. (1979). *Social training: Perspectives on obedience and autonomy in boys among the Swahili of Mombasa, Kenya and the upper middle class of La Jolla, California, USA*. Unpublished doctoral dissertation, University of California, San Diego.

Broude, G. J. (1988). Rethinking the *couvade*: Cross cultural evidence. *American Anthropologist, 90*, 902–911.

Conger, J. J., & Petersen, A. C. (1984). *Adolescence and youth: Psychological development in a changing world*. New York: Harper and Row.

Du Bois, C. (1967). The people of Alor. In Abraham Kardiner (Ed.), *The psychological frontiers of society* (pp. 101–258). New York: Columbia University Press.

Ember, C. R., & Ember, M. (1985). *Anthropology* (4th ed.). New Jersey: Prentice Hall.

Erikson, E. H. (1963). *Childhood and society*. New York: W.W. Norton and Company.

Freilich, M., & Coser, L. (1974). Structural imbalances of gratification: The case of the Caribbean mating system. In R. Laub Coser (Ed.), *The family: Its structures and functions* (pp. 78–93). New York: St. Martins Press.

Gluckman, M. (1956). *Custom and conflict in Africa*. London: Basil Blackwell.

Government of Kenya (December 1979). *Major highlights of the Kenya fertility survey* (Vol. 4, No. 2). Nairobi: Ministry of Economic Planning and National Development.

Hill, M. (1973). *Sociology of religion*. London: Heinemann Educational Books.

Howes, H. (1983). Representations of rural women in Bangladesh. *Sussex Anthropology, 5*, 21–26.

Kardiner, A. (1967). *The psychological frontiers of society*. New York: Columbia University Press.

Kilbride, P. L., & Kilbride, J. C. (1990). *Changing family life in East Africa: Women and children at risk*. University Park: Pennsylvania State University Press.

Morris, C. G. (1988). *Psychology: An introduction* (6th ed.). New Jersey: Prentice Hall.

Ngabo-Lutaaya, L. (1982). Buyaaye *as an adaptive response to social, economic and political disorganization in Uganda during the rule of Idi Amin*. Unpublished master's thesis, University of Nairobi.

Nyangweso, Mary. (1992). *The influence of Christianity on Abanyole beliefs and practices about death and afterlife*. Unpublished master's thesis, Department of Religions, Moi University.

Simpson, G. (1966). *People in families: Sociology, psychoanalysis and the American family*. Cleveland: World Publishing.

Spiro, M. E. (1961). An overview and suggested reorientation. In F. L. K. Hsu (Ed.), *Psychological anthropology approaches to culture and personality* (pp. 459–497). Homewood, IL.: Dorsey Press.

Swartz, M. J. (1982). *The way the world is: Cultural processes and social relations among the Mombasa Swahili*. Berkeley: University of California Press.

Thayer, J. S. (1980). The Aberdache of the Northern Plains: A socio-religious perspective. *Journal of Anthropological Research, 36*, 287–293.

Thomas, W. I. (1965). The four wishes and the definition of the situation. In Talcott Parsons, Edward Shils, Kaspar D. Naegele, & Jess R. Pitts (Eds.), *Theories of society* (pp. 741–744). New York: Free Press.

Wilson, M. (1963). *Good company: A study of Nyakyusa age villages*. Boston: Beacon Press.

2

Support for Children and the African Family Crisis

Thomas S. Weisner

INTRODUCTION

There is a growing crisis in many parts of Africa, fueled by population pressure, land and food scarcity, and public health concerns regarding mortality and HIV. Sub-Saharan Africa has the highest under-five child mortality rate of any world region, about two hundred per one thousand live births in 1990. The per capita rate of increase of gross national product between 1970 and 1980 was .2 percent, the lowest in the world—by comparison, the rate for India was 1.4 percent and for the rest of Asia 2.7 percent. The number of calories consumed per day per capita is the lowest in the world. Public investment in social welfare on a per capita basis is declining in Africa, while military expenditures increase. African nations have been experiencing a net transfer of assets to the developed world since around 1983 (Barnett & Bleikie, 1992; Coquery-Vidrovitch, 1988; Ocholla-Ayayo, this volume; UNICEF, 1992; Weisner, 1994). Although elites and some middle class families are improving, African families overall are getting poorer compared to the rest of the world and relative to their own previous experiences over the past two generations.

In previous generations, the poor and exploited in Africa were primarily the socially isolated and abandoned. Family membership, and the access to labor and security that family membership provided, were at least a partial guarantee of social support, although certainly not the guarantee of an easy or safe life or a life free from the possibility of famine, war, family exploitation, and suffering. Participation in large family and homestead groups in the past provided security from predators, both human and nonhuman, and sufficient labor to obtain food, raise livestock, and perhaps even expand one's territory. Not to have access to labor and sociality in the family group was to risk poverty. Lack of social participation in one's community and family was considered morally inappropriate and socially threatening. Since labor came from family and kin, loss of kin led to poverty. In a land-rich African ecology, loss of labor and the social ties necessary to obtain labor was both economically hazardous and morally inappropriate (Frank & McNicoll, 1987; Iliffe, 1987).

The world around many African families is expanding from the one in which poverty and threats to individual survival usually came to the socially isolated. Today there are increasing threats to those who are participating in family and community life. Participation in rapidly changing family situations and in communities that are overpopulated or lacking land for the first time has meant that even those in families are now at greater risk.

This crisis is one of survival and resource control in times of scarcity, rooted in national and international politics, economics, and public health. But there is also a crisis in how the cultures of the region are redefining intergenerational relationships and social support. Some elderly worry that they no longer can expect to receive assistance and security from their children, and indeed they are having to care for grandchildren and the lands of their own children while parents are gone, for instance (Cattell, this volume; Sangree, this volume). Women are having more children outside of the patrilineal descent system and without formal marriages (Håkansson & LeVine, this volume, Kilbride & Kilbride, this volume, Ssennyonga, this volume). Women are struggling to better control their own fertility decisions in the midst of conflicting pressures from their mates and families (Bradley, this volume; Frank & McNicoll, 1987). Brothers are said to be less likely to assist each other in marriage arrangements than they have been in the past. They may also not be monitoring as carefully the circumstances of their sisters who have married into other lineage groups. Abuse and neglect of children and the elderly is apparently growing in Kenya, at least in some kinds of family situations (Bradley, 1995; Kilbride & Kilbride, 1990, this volume). Malnutrition among children is a continuing problem facing mothers expected to provide for children without adequate resources or family supports (Whyte & Kariuki, this volume). A certain cultural control and conservatism regarding sexuality and childbirth that characterized East African communities in prior generations is being transformed today into increased promiscuity (Ocholla-Ayayo, this volume; Kilbride & Kilbride, this volume; Whyte & Kariuki, this volume). In the midst of rapid changes like these and a growing concern regarding the future of families and children in Africa, the role of the African family system in providing support, nurturance, and care for family and community members is as essential as it has ever been.

The loss of family and community support systems is a matter of powerful concern in Africa, because sociality and "socially distributed nurturance" within the family unit are at the heart of important cultural values throughout the continent (Serpell, 1992). Family solidarity may be crucial in helping African communities to survive the current crises. If the "true secret" of any society lies in part in how it manages to survive (Goubert, quoted in Coquery-Vidrovitch, 1988, p. 44), understanding the nature of shared social support in African families and communities is critical to the future of Kenya and Africa. African communities flourished and survived in the past in considerable part because of their successful elaboration of shared social allegiance and support in corporate groups. This long tradition of African "communal solidarity" and shared social support indeed can assist in meeting some of the problems facing the continent today (Lesthaeghe, 1989, p. 11–12; Serpell, n.d.).

Shared support and the hierarchical, communal family authority and resource control that go with it are learned early in childhood and in emotionally salient contexts. Their significance lasts, therefore, throughout life and becomes a part of the *cultural careers* and life plans of adults (Goldschmidt, 1990). In this way, life goals regarding family support and obligations enter the public national debates concerning what is wrong and what is of value in Kenyan society, including debates about how to correct these wrongs, and how to sustain the strengths of Kenyan families and communities. The sharing of caretaking and support therefore has a significance in addition to its social organizational and functional importance. It helps in the psychological task of defending the predictability of life, as Peter Marris has put it (Marris, 1975, p. 3). It provides a prototypical cultural and psychological model for creating and sustaining personal meaning and for defining the life goals central to Kenyans' cultural careers.

The men and women I talked with, in Kisa Location and Nairobi alike, wanted to achieve as part of their life goals what families everywhere hope for: *a sustainable, congruent, and meaningful routine of everyday life.* A sustainable routine is one that can be maintained in the cultural and ecological circumstances of the world around that family. Sustainability has to do with subsistence, mortality, migration, and survival in local ecologies. A congruent routine is one that takes appropriate account of the people available in the family—their talents, temperaments, gender, and numbers. It takes account of who is available for assistance, for example. A meaningful routine is one that provides cultural coherence and intrapsychic satisfaction, peace of mind, and a sense of moral and emotional appropriateness. A meaningful routine is one that is seen as morally and emotionally appropriate for the family and community.

Families are proactive agents in their adaptive struggles to achieve such a meaningful routine and cultural career, not just hapless victims of economic and political circumstances, powerful as these circumstances surely are. The culture complex of shared social support, held in the mind as a part of life goals and cultural careers, is a tool Kenyan families use to sustain a routine, to make it congruent with available people in their worlds, and to make this routine culturally and personally meaningful (Weisner, 1993a). It also becomes a part of what parents and children alike psychologically defend as a valued life goal.

The contemporary circumstances of many families in Kisa (and others described in this volume) do *not* meet an important test: Many families in Kenya are unable to sustain the kind of family routines they desire. In the contemporary era, efforts to construct such a daily routine leads to nonsurvival and nonsustainability, a lack of congruence, and nonmeaningfulness. Millions of Kenyan families and children today neither have their basic needs met nor possess a sense of basic predictability in life. Shared social support is not possible for them, but they hope for it. They continue to defend its possibility, if not predictability, in their lives. This is how the African family crisis is experienced.

Any support system for children, whether based on shared caretaking or not, has certain features recognizable around the world. These universal features include affection, physical comfort, assistance, shared solving of problems, provision of food and other resources, protection against harm and aggression, and a coherent moral and cultural understanding of who can provide support and the appropriate ways to do so (Weisner, 1993b). The African cultural complex of socially distributed social support attempts to meet these needs for children and families while responding to other cultural, economic and institutional constraints and opportunities in the region.

This chapter summarizes and reviews the antecedents, correlates, and consequences of this system of shared family management and support, particularly during childhood. Its antecedents and correlates lie in African demography, ecology, and sociohistorical traditions. Its consequences are, I will argue, important for childhood attachment, emotional expression, social behaviors such as aggression, nurturance, and responsibility, school achievement, gender roles, the domestic economy, and cognitive style. It is still widespread in its practice and of profound meaning and importance in Kenya and elsewhere in Africa. This system of shared family caretaking of children and socially distributed nurturance of children is not without its social and psychological costs for families and children, and these costs are also considered in the contemporary context. Although declining in importance in some ways, it remains a pattern of support that is still culturally, morally, and economically powerful. Even as current public culture and the world economy seem to conspire against its practice, shared family support for children remains a deep influence in Kenyan society.

SHARED MANAGEMENT, CARETAKING, AND SOCIALLY DISTRIBUTED SUPPORT

Among the varied forms of shared domestic management and family social support is sibling caretaking—older children doing child care, usually in the context of other domestic chores and tasks, under the overall management of adults in the home. In this kind of system children are expected to turn to parents, siblings, cousins, aunts, grandparents, and socially recognized others for help. In turn, they are often expected to assist others in their family. Parents may manage and direct their family caretaking system without directly providing care themselves. Children may spend time living with other kin and participating in the care of others away from their natal home (Bledsoe, 1980).

A number of features of socially distributed support in shared management family systems often co-occur and can be found in many places around the world (Weisner, 1987, 1989a; Weisner & Gallimore, 1977). The following list of features is based on studies of shared caretaking and social support from Kisa Location in western Kenya, as well as reviews of other studies done throughout the region and elsewhere in Africa and the world.

1. Child caretaking often occurs as a part of indirect *chains* of support in which one child (under a mother's or other adult's management) assists another, who assists a third, who in turn assists another child.
2. Children look to other children for assistance and support as much or more than to adults;
3. Girls are much more likely to do caretaking and domestic tasks than boys. Boys clearly provide support, caretaking, and nurturance to other children as well, although more infrequently as they reach late middle childhood.
4. Mothers provide support and nurturance for children as much by ensuring that *others* will consistently participate in doing so as by doing so directly themselves.
5. Care often occurs in the context of other domestic work done by children.
6. Aggression, teasing, and dominance accompany nurturance and support and come from the same people; dominance of these kinds increases with age.
7. Support is often indirect and delayed, not necessarily organized around exclusive dyadic relationships between child and caregiver.
8. Food is a powerful cultural concern, used to threaten, control, soothe, and nurture.
9. Verbal exchange and elaborated question-framed discourse rarely accompanies support and nurturance for children; negotiations regarding rights and privileges between children and dominant caretakers are infrequent.
10. Social and intellectual competence in children is judged in part by a child's competence in doing domestic tasks, acting socially appropriately, doing childcare, and nurturing and supporting others.
11. Children are socialized within this system both through apprenticeship learning of their family roles and responsibilities and through self-ascribed cultural standards and beliefs about their appropriate role behavior according to age and gender. Girls, for instance, tend to over-report to others that they are responsible for caring for others, while boys tend to under-report.

THE ECOLOGICAL AND CULTURAL COMPLEX SUSTAINING SHARED MANAGEMENT AND SUPPORT

Socially distributed support for children within a shared-management family caretaking system occurs in Kisa Location and elsewhere as part of a culture complex. This culture complex includes demographic, familial, subsistence, and psychological/emotional elements.

Demographic

High fertility and declining mortality are characteristic, although a population can be at any stage of the demographic transition and still practice shared caretaking (Bradley, this volume; Caldwell, 1982; Hewlett, 1991; LeVine and White, 1986). This is because child caretakers can be drawn from other families; each domestic group and family unit is not solely responsible for providing all its own caretakers for itself. Indeed, the culture complex serves to redistribute children and adults across households and families to assist in support.

Family and Household

Large households and joint families characteristically practice shared caretaking; polygyny, particularly where it accompanies large homesteads and many coresident children, might encourage shared care where cowives are on good terms and encourage it. Polygyny rates vary widely in Western Kenya and are generally declining rapidly among most communities in Kenya (see Håkansson & LeVine, this volume, for such declines and reasons for it among the Gusii), but can be very high, as in Ssennyonga's 1987 report (this volume) that 56 percent of women on Rusinga Island are in polygynous unions. Families with members living in more than one household often utilize shared caretaking in the current wage migration economic system in many areas. Rural–urban and other kinds of migration in which there is a pattern of commuting and sharing of family personnel and resources also often accompanies shared support systems (Weisner, 1976a). Shared support bolsters chain and commuting migration patterns. High *variability* in family composition, size, and fertility within communities is characteristic (Hewlett, 1991); since kin-related households are at all stages in their developmental cycles, children are often moving among families. High fertility and high migration often are accompanied by such variability.

Child lending, fosterage, and adoption practices are common. These practices often include the use of child nurses "loaned" from one family to another; in stratified communities, higher-status households are more likely to receive such child nurses from lower status households (Bledsoe, 1980; Bledsoe & Isiugo-Abanihe, 1989; E. Goody, 1982; J. Goody, 1969; Schildkrout, 1973; Weisner, 1982). *Sibling* caretaking is a common cultural practice as well, along with the use of cousins, hired nurses, and other relatives also available for caretaking, depending on the kinship system and residence norms in the community (Leiderman & Leiderman, 1974b; 1977; Munroe & Munroe, this volume; Whiting & Whiting, 1975; Weisner & Gallimore, 1977).

Clear gender-role differences are present in domestic and caretaking tasks during this juvenile period, with girls more involved in these tasks (Bradley, 1993; Munroe & Munroe, this volume; Shibadu, 1978). Whiting and Edwards (1988:125) report that mothers direct task commands to girls far more than to boys and that girls do far more chores and child care; "to state the situation in the baldest terms, girls work while boys play."[1] Munroe and Munroe (1971) found that siblings in Vihiga cared for infants about half the time, with girls caring for infants of either sex and boys caring almost exclusively for male babies. (However, by 1978, no sex differentiation in preference for male or female babies was observed, and sibling care of infants declined for girls as their school attendance rose from 69% to 96%.)

There is no presumption of equality between parents and children within the household and family. As age generally confers authority, children are expected to invest in the family estate with their labor and social attention and emotional ties (Bradley, this volume; Caldwell, 1982). Hierarchy and deference in family authority and management patterns often are culturally elaborated; expectations of obedience are high, punishment is often swift for mistakes, and overt verbal praise or positive recognition from adults is very infrequent. Recognition and support for children comes from inclusion in family activities and recognition in schools, sports, churches, and peer situations (S. LeVine, 1979; Weisner, 1989a).

Subsistence and Work

The use of children as joint managers and caretakers is related to heavy maternal domestic workloads that require women to work away from their homes (Minturn & Lambert, 1964; Whiting & Whiting, 1975) or require heavy work in the domestic domain. Caretaking is only one among many tasks assigned a child caretaker/domestic manager (Burton, Brudner, & White, 1977; Whiting & Edwards, 1988). Children apprentice for and assume tasks including caretaking and domestic tasks during and following the five year to seven year age-period transition. This juvenile period in child development is one in which children are ready cognitively and socially for assuming such tasks (Rogoff, Sellers, Pirrotta, Fox, & White, 1975; Rogoff, Newcombe, Fox, & Ellis, 1980; Weisner, 1996).

Psychological and Emotional

Children become closely attached to their child caretakers as well as to their mothers. Children and caregivers retain close bonds with mothers but also show a pattern of diffused attachment and ties to particular siblings or other caretakers (Reed & Leiderman, 1981; Leiderman & Leiderman, 1974a). Social competence and "intellectual" intelligence in children are inextricably tied together, with judgments regarding both made in part on the basis of children's social and task-sharing skills in providing caretaking and support for others. Being "smart" includes being competent in social support (Nerlove, Roberts, Klein, Yarbrough, & Habicht, 1974; Nerlove, Roberts, & Klein, 1975; Serpell, n.d.; Super, 1983). Also, there is high moral value placed on family social support. That is, shared caretaking and support is not seen only as a convenient, available way to keep one's household going (although it does assist in that goal); shared support is also viewed as a morally valuable, appropriate way to respond to meeting this goal (Edwards, this volume; Nsamenang, 1992).

These features are very likely to be associated with shared caretaking and support among children in much of Africa. Their tendency to co-occur makes them part of a culture complex. At the same time, these features all have varied in African history and are changing dramatically today. They do not inevitably co-occur, nor is shared care precluded even when only some of these circumstances are present. Thus this pattern for support and caretaking by children is an ideal–typical culture complex, not a template followed in every family in just one way. It is a recognizable, available option for parents in a cultural community, perhaps among other options, rather than a monolithic practice. Since this pattern of support assists in family adaptation to varying, changeable conditions, shared support will vary in profile in each particular cultural community. It is also predictable that families within any community will vary in their practice of shared caretaking; in fact, such expectable variation is a part of the complex itself.

Any culture complex looks somewhat different in each of its local adaptations, in each cultural community and, for that matter, in each family within a community. The developmental cycle of the family ensures that there will be such diversity within a community. Several papers in this volume are devoted to the analysis of important local cultural variations in Western Kenyan communities that affect the local practice of sibling caretaking and socially distributed care of children (de Wolf, M. Whyte, Edwards, and Super & Harkness). Furthermore, children within a family will vary in the extent to which they were involved in these practices; birth order, gender, temperament, school experiences, and a host of other factors will predictably produce variation. I emphasize this because no community or family or individual will see their own experience somehow exactly mirrored in the ideal–typical portrait of shared support. What should be seen, however, are practices and beliefs that many will have experienced in part or have seen clearly in other families.

RURAL–URBAN PATTERNS OF SHARED MANAGEMENT AND SOCIAL SUPPORT IN KISA LOCATION

I studied the practice of shared caretaking and support in Kisa Location and Kariobangi Estate, Nairobi, between 1968 and 1983 (Weisner, 1976b). The unit for analysis is shown in Figure 2.1 (Weisner, 1973a). This is a characteristic social

Figure 2.1
Design of Network and Census Samples

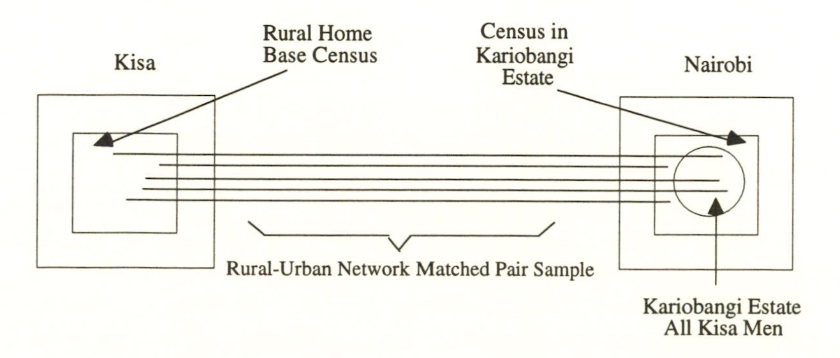

unit in systems of chain and commuting migration. Family members commute between residences during the year, and related families try to find inexpensive urban housing near one another. For this reason, many families from certain subclans and lineages in Kisa Location lived near one another in Kariobangi Estate, sharing knowledge of housing and services and jobs. I located twenty-four men from a few sublocations in Kisa who were living in Kariobangi. I then matched each man with a brother or close patrilineal kinsman resident in Kisa location. These twenty-four matched pairs of men, along with their families and coresident kin, constituted the rural–urban comparative sample.

Most Kisa families then (and now) had duolocal or multilocal residence, with frequent commuting and high income remittance from urban wage earners to rural homes. Household surveys were done in both communities (Kisa and Kariobangi), and intensive research was done in the forty-eight matched-pair households, twenty-four in each place. Sixty-eight children between the ages of two and eight were observed between 1969 and 1972. Data from ethnographic fieldwork, school grades and exam scores, and child cognitive tests were collected during four field studies: 1968–1970, 1972, 1978, and 1983 (Weisner, 1976d).

Figure 2.2
Percentage of Individuals Connected for Different Numbers of Steps, Men and Women, Knowing and Visiting Relationships

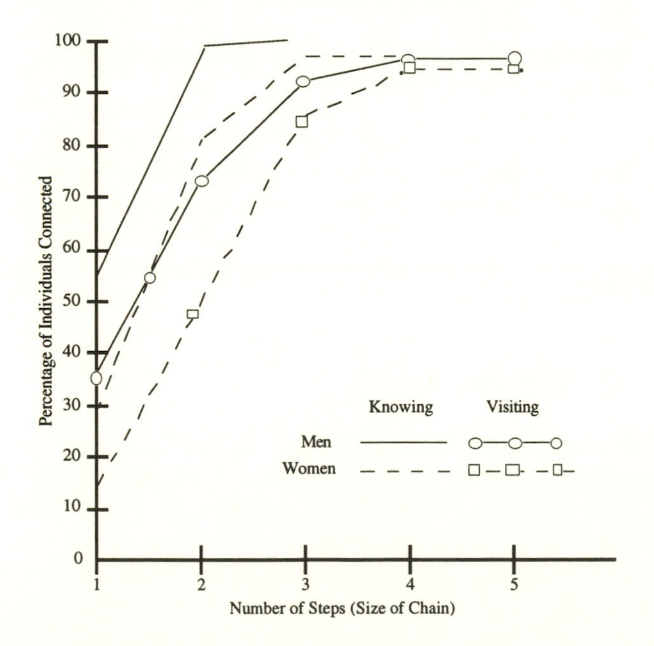

The rural–urban social unit used for these studies has sociometric relational closeness as well as cultural significance. Figure 2.2 presents a network connectedness measure for men and women in forty-eight households, showing how closely men are in fact in contact. "Contact" is measured by asking whether the men and women in the rural–urban network sample know one another directly or indirectly or visit each other's homes. For example, 55 percent of the men in the total rural–urban network knew each other directly, and 99 percent knew each other through only one intermediary. By one intermediary I mean that they knew another man in the network who in turn knew the person they did not know directly. Similarly, 37 percent of the men visited one another directly, 75 percent visited another man who in turn visited another person in the network, and 90 percent were within two links of one another in terms of family visiting connections. Women in the forty-eight households were somewhat less directly connected to one another by patterns of visiting or knowing one another. All the women, of course, had married into these subclans from outside their husband's natal communities because of norms of clan exogamy and viri-patrilocal residence. Thus their overall connectedness measures would expectedly be lower than their husbands' (Weisner, 1976a). Nonetheless, the wives of the men matched in the rural–urban sample were highly likely to know and visit one another.

This rural–urban sample reflects a social unit that contemporary Kisa families recognize, that they used for social support, and that has sociometric significance. It exists because of the economic and sociocultural integration of Kisa into the national and international world, and it shows the proactive, creative adaptations Kisa families have made in response to that dislocation.

CORRELATES AND CONSEQUENCES OF SHARED MANAGEMENT FOR CHILDREN IN RURAL–URBAN NETWORKS

Studies using this rural–urban network matched sample showed a shared management system of social support in active use and its influence on children's social behavior, cognitive development, and school performance.

The observational studies, for instance, showed how frequent multiple caretaking was and how common it was for family members other than parents to provide direct assistance and nurturance under the overall supervision of parents. For example, siblings provided as much nurturance for children as did mothers, with girls over twice as likely as boys to do so (Figure 2.3). Multiple caretaking is not

Figure 2.3
Nurturant Interactions (Direct Care and Emotional Support), by Dyad and Residence

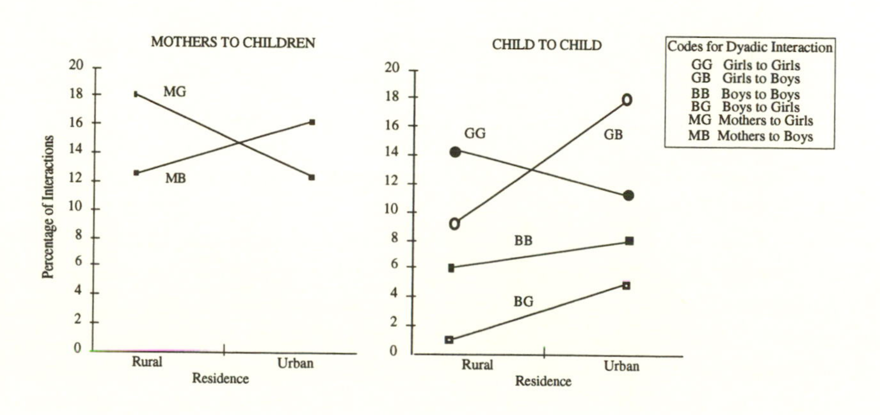

a rural practice alone; such caretaking and support was about as common in Nairobi as it was in Kisa in the 1970s and 1980s.[2]

Children were sociably interacting with other children (both boys and girls) nearly half the time (48%) and with mothers about 10 percent to 15 percent of the time they were observed (Figure 2.4). Sociability declined somewhat in family situations in Nairobi (urban) compared to those in Kisa (rural). The general pattern, in which children experienced the benefits of support as well as the costs and pain of hierarchy and control by others in the extended family, held for both urban and rural settings. Sibling care seems to be an experience in which children simulta-

Figure 2.4
Sociable Interaction (Affection, Physical Contact, Seeks Proximity, Sitting Together) by Dyad and Residence

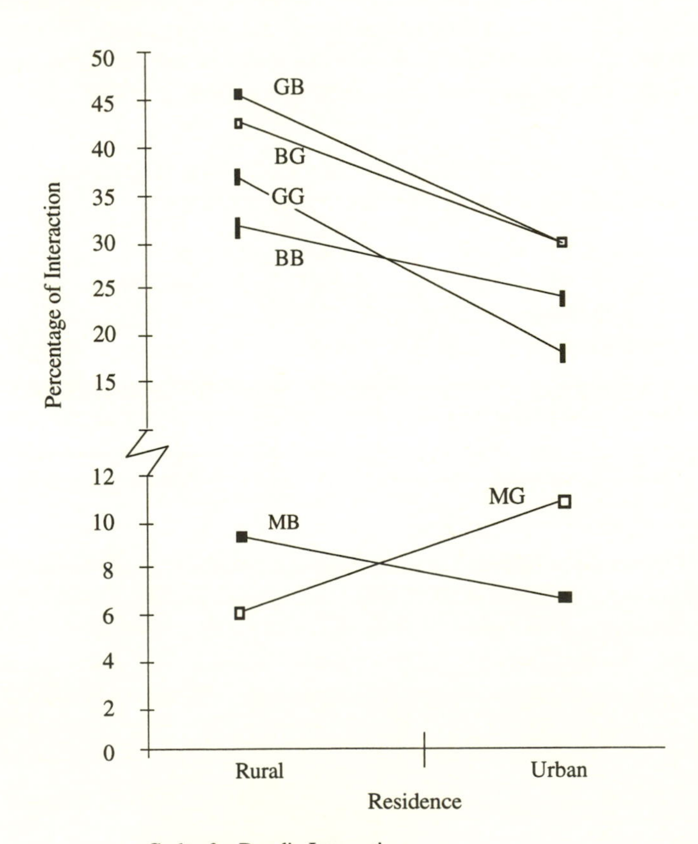

Codes for Dyadic Interaction

GG Girls to Girls
GB Girls to Boys
BB Boys to Boys
BG Boys to Girls
MG Mothers to Girls
MB Mothers to Boys

neously experience both protection and nurturance on the one hand, and dominance, teasing, and even exploitation by their caretakers on the other.

Thus caretaking relationships are far from all positive, nurturant, and sociable. Figure 2.5 shows the percentage of interactions in which children were observed to be assaulting, insulting, annoying, or in various ways dominating and teasing other, mostly younger children. There is considerably more such dominance between children than between mothers and children. In addition, boys appear to be somewhat more dominant and aggressive in the rural areas, where they are less supervised and monitored by adults. Gender differences present in rural data disappear in urban situations among these children ages three to eleven.

Figure 2.5
Dominance (Physical Assaults, Insulting, Annoying Others, Seeking Submission) by Dyad and Residence

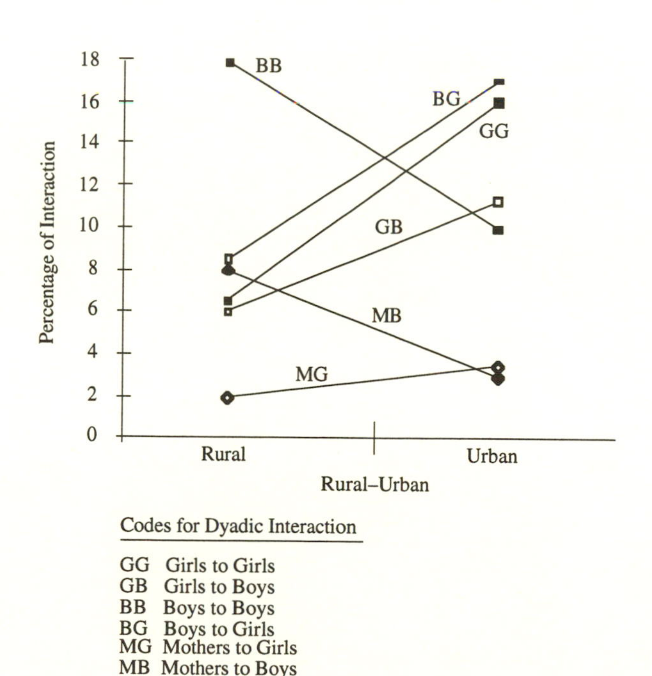

Families living in Nairobi usually left some of their children in Kisa, and the nature of tasks and shared management changed dramatically as the result of this breakup of the sibling group. Older children were more likely to be needed for farm work, and so they often remained behind in the rural areas. There were a number of other reasons for this. Parents believed that older children were more likely to succumb to the dangers of city influence they perceived—violence, "roaming about," drinking, wasting money. Older children customarily sleep in separate houses from their parents, and urban housing is far too costly to provide easily. Many parents also preferred that children use Luluyia as well as Kiswahili and English in school, and only local Kisa schools would ensure this. Older children could more easily and safely be left in Kisa.

The absence of older children from Nairobi households was a contributing factor in some of the differences between urban and rural children in their social behavior. Urban resident children showed more disruptive and aggressive behaviors, less sociability, and less shared task performance than did rural resident children, and sought out their mothers for interaction (and disturbed them) more (Figures 2.3–2.6). Normally older children (and perhaps other adults) would be caretaking younger children and assisting in the management of the family domestic routine (Weisner, 1979b). Older children normally, in rural areas, buffer such negative interactions between parents and children and engage in more sociable and shared task interactions.

Figure 2.6
Dominance in Children's Interactions by Age, Gender, and Residence

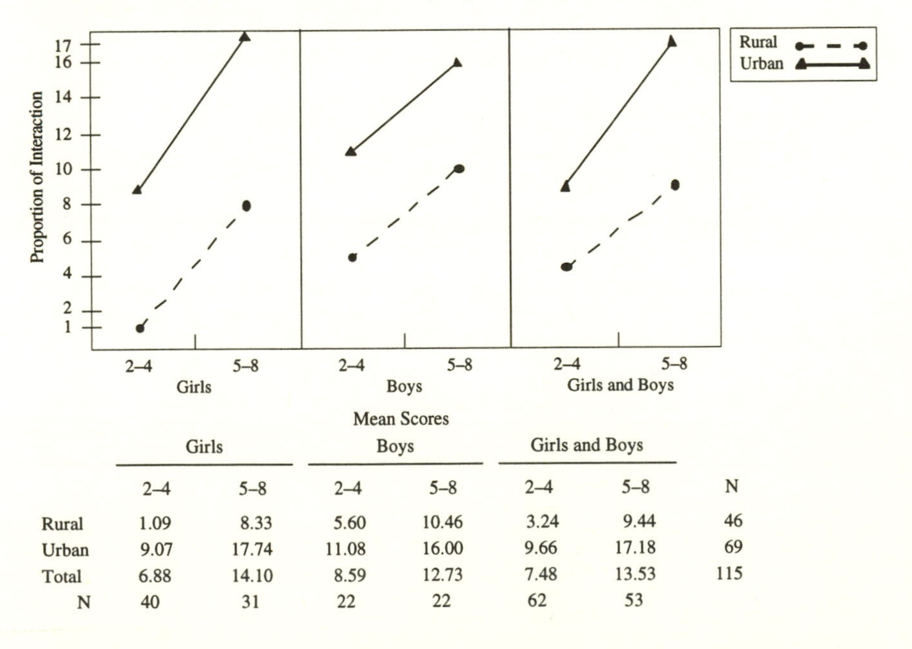

Mean Scores

	Girls		Boys		Girls and Boys		
	2–4	5–8	2–4	5–8	2–4	5–8	N
Rural	1.09	8.33	5.60	10.46	3.24	9.44	46
Urban	9.07	17.74	11.08	16.00	9.66	17.18	69
Total	6.88	14.10	8.59	12.73	7.48	13.53	115
N	40	31	22	22	62	53	

Other factors that might plausibly have influenced differences in social behavior were unrelated in our study. For example, education levels of parents (in a range from none to Form II, with a median of four years in the Kisa–Nairobi sample) were unrelated to the decision by parents to use shared caretaking, their beliefs about the practices, or their committment to it as a cultural pattern in their community. Levels of modernity or reported maternal stress also were unrelated to the overall educational levels of parents. Indeed, our studies showed that mothers in families with a resource base in the city (from husbands' wages or trade) and a functioning rural farm or shop reported feeling somewhat *less* psychophysiological stress than women exclusively dependent on the city (e.g., living full time in the city without a rural homestead residence available to them) or the rural farm economy (with no source of urban wage income and remittances, or rural wage income such as from teaching) (Weisner & Abbott, 1977; Abbott & Weisner, 1979). Such women seemed to have more alternative sources of wealth, influence, and social capital, although some complained of their husbands taking urban wives or girlfriends and not supporting their rural families.

Cognitive assessments of children ages five to eleven in both Kisa and Nairobi showed only small or no differences in the children's overall tested ability due to urban or rural residence. There were large differences, though, in the style with which children approached the kinds of cognitive tasks we presented to them. Urban resident children were bolder with the testers and tried out more solutions to the problems presented to them. However, the proportion of correct responses did not differ between city resident and country resident children. Urban resident and predominantly urban-schooled children did give more partially correct answers to most of the cognitive tasks administered, however, and had better facility in English and Kiswahili because of their greater exposure to both languages in Nairobi (Weisner, 1976c). Their greater number of attempts at answering questions gave them more partially correct answers.

Children who participated more often in shared caretaking did not suffer in their school performance because of their tasks as caretakers. Those children observed to participate more actively in sibling caretaking and "distributed nurturance" of other children in fact did slightly better in primary school (as assessed by final exams administered at the school or the national Kenya Primary Examination), as I established when I returned to Kisa in 1983 and assembled data on the school achievements of the children. Children often "played school" with their siblings and cousins while caretaking and managing the domestic work, and literacy and numeracy skills seemed to be woven into everyday routines. Classroom activities often depended on group recitation and sharing of scarce books and other materials. It is possible (although I did not specifically test this) that children with the social and managerial skills garnered through shared support and caretaking systems at home might (other influences being equal) do better in the kinds of classroom circumstances common in Kisa location (Weisner, 1996).

NURTURANCE, SUPPORT, AND LIFE PLANS: DEFENDING THE PREDICTABILITY OF LIFE

These studies in Kisa and among Nairobi commuting migrants from Kisa clearly show the importance of child caretaking during the 1960s and 1970s and its strong influence on the following aspects of child development: gender roles, attachment, and trust; nurturance and dominance; school achievement; cognitive styles; and task competence, among others. Nonetheless, is a culture complex like child caretaking, with its shared social support and nurturance, merely a slowly declining victim of modernization and delocalization, soon to disappear? It is certainly changing in many ways, but nonetheless child caretaking is not disappearing and continues to be a strong and continuing influence on families and on all age groups. This continuing influence also appears in regard to gender roles (Munroe & Munroe, this volume), moral judgments (Edwards), attitudes towards modernization (Super & Harkness), support for the elderly (Sangree, Cattell) and other domains as well.

But whatever its significance for children, what does shared support represent for adults struggling to survive in the contemporary world? If shared caretaking is a practice more salient in childhood and under pressure in the contemporary world, how or why would it matter later in life—that is, what would make it an important influence in Kenya's contemporary cultural and personal circumstances?

The culture complex of shared support remains salient perhaps because it was (and continues to be) learned and reinforced in emotionally powerful situations within the family. Akong'a (this volume) describes the defenses established by or brought to the forefront during change. The processes of defense, denial, sublimation, and projection, in some cultural form, may all be visible in processes of change and adaptation. However, there is also another quite powerful representation of the way in which social change is experienced and internalized by individuals. This psychological process is what Peter Marris has called "the impulse to defend the predictability of life . . . a fundamental and universal principle of human psychology" (1975, p. 3).

This psychological process involves the human experience of matching a prior schema of the world of relationships or resources with the experience of the moment and accommodating the new experience to the prior schema. Defending the predictability of life in this sense is a cultural process as well as a psychological one. Men and women carry with them cultural models of support, and these models are what we defend in the face of change. Their expectations regarding nurturance, shared support, and hierarchy are embedded in such prior schemas and so influence behavior throughout life. My argument here is that Kenyans' life goals and their cultural careers—that is, the cultural models that help organize their lives and give them meaning—include the goals of continually recreating shared support and nurturance for themselves and their families. Kenyans are defending the predictability of life today by using their formative experiences with shared support when they were children.

The cultural models that we defend drive our *life goals*. Organized within a cultural community, these goals are a part of "life plans," defined by Robert LeVine as "a people's collective representation of the life course viewed as an organized system of shared ideals about how life should be lived and shared expectancies about how lives are lived" (R. LeVine, 1980, p. 82).

Goldschmidt (1990) has developed a related concept of the "cultural career," one that includes the culturally motivating representations regarding the life course and adds the satisfaction of physical needs and what he calls the universal "hunger for affect," worth, and self-esteem. "By career, I mean that trajectory through life which each person undergoes, the activities he or she engages in to satisfy physical needs and wants and the even more important social needs and wants. The career, then, is activated in the service of both the physical being and the symbolic self (Goldschmidt, 1990, p. 107)."

R. LeVine described the life plan for Gusii men as being divided into reproductive, economic, and spiritual careers. He described the Gusii homestead as a social and moral "prototype" of the constraints and opportunities and moral imperatives of these life careers. Similarly, children's and parents' experiences with socially shared support within the homestead is a "prototype experience" in this sense. Gusii men, for example, strive for "ever-expanding cycles of exchange," and compete for roles as both investor and supervisor of resources and kin. LeVine also describes a sense of "potency" as a goal, where potency is judged by the size of one's family and the extent of one's economic holdings and networks (1980, p. 97). This notion of the homestead and its support network as a moral and psychological prototype suggests immediately how formative experiences in shared caretaking in childhood would be used by Kenyans as prototypes that would be defended long after childhood.

Sarah LeVine (1979) has done a parallel study of Gusii women at various stages of married life prior to reaching elderhood. Although their circumstances and individual lives varied, she describes women as having heavy domestic and childcare obligations, with few relationships of trust, living in a community in which fears are constant in the midst of a hostile environment, in which men dominate and control women. As her children grow to maturity, however, a Gusii woman can look forward to increasing ritual involvement and responsibility, increasing assistance, respect, and authority in her homestead, and, ideally, support from her sons and grandchildren. Håkansson and R. LeVine (this volume) in fact show the effects of such economic and marital changes on Gusii life careers.

The culture complex of socially distributed support, with the kin dominance and hierarchical relationships that go with it, drives the life plans and goals of Kenyans. Its prototypical forms are used to defend the predictability of life. Sibling caretaking, nested within this culture complex, is one such prototypical form and experience for children. The rural–urban network sample described in this chapter for Kisa certainly reflects changing life circumstances, but shared caretaking remains as an important cultural practice. Hence men and women, and boys and girls, are not merely defending the predictability of some (now utterly long past) cultural image of shared support. As children become parents and then elders, they see and feel the worth of participating in the system. Although the culture complex of shared support itself may be changing, it is far from being replaced, since it influences the cultural careers that motivate millions of Kenyans.

Of course, this process of defending prototypical forms of cultural life might be understood in other ways as well. For instance, it might be viewed as the psychodynamic principle of sustaining the belief that there is continuity and consistency in close relationships, or "object relations." Seen another way, "defending predictability" could describe a "stubborn" individual, clinging to false beliefs, that is, someone who would be called "in denial." Defending the predictability of life also can appear as a justification for oppression of one person or group over another or for the intrusion of a state-imposed "predictability" into the lives of those opposing that other group, or the state. Whatever the usefulness of these other conceptions, defending the predictability of life, seen as a *cultural matching process*, is free from clinical or invidious implications and is a very common process in everyday life experience.

The Ideal Life Career in Kisa

Experiences in the system of socially shared support clearly influenced the ideal life careers of men in Kisa and Kariobangi. I asked many men and a smaller group of women in their forties to sixties, what they wanted out of life—that is, what did they see as their imagined good or ideal life career? I asked them to imagine their lives as a whole. When they "retired" as elders, for instance, what would their goals for life look like in practice? What activities would be going on? What life goals are they striving for now that would be represented successfully in the final periods of life?

These men all had had urban wage-labor migration experience, were living either in Kisa or Nairobi, were in midlife, and had between no education and Form II (about ninth or tenth grade). None were among the educated or financial elite, but they represented the range of variation in life experience of most Kisa men of their era. There was considerable variation in what different individuals said. Each conversation, each person's image of his or her life goals, was in some ways unique, in some ways characteristic of most Luyia, and in some ways what men and women everywhere might want. Each man's cultural career was still in process. But here is a summary script, a synthesis, a prototypic snapshot:

> I am sitting comfortably outside my house within my homestead. Children and grandchildren, many of them, live here or come to visit, particularly my sons. Smoke curls out of the cooking huts, chickens and animals are abundant, and the many people who come to visit pay their respects and defer to my opinions. My wife and daughters-in-law are cooking for me, take me to the clinic when I have needed to go, and make sure I have money to travel to markets, to funerals of our kin, and occasionally to town for visits. My lands are sufficient, and my wife (or wives) has ample to feed everyone and to entertain. I have sons and daughters employed by the government or major industries like the breweries or railroads, with good salaries, who send me and my wife money. My wife and daughters-in-law are able to provide for the children and grandchildren, and I see the children out doing well in school and working here as well. My daughters are married to successful men, have had many children, and can send them to school. They often are here visiting me. I can assist my brothers and their children at times, and I have done well compared to my siblings and age mates in our clan. I frequently walk to and from the market or church or chief's compound or local court—and everyone knows my name. I have helped to build our church or the nursery school addition or to add roofing to the primary school, and my work was praised at the gatherings to organize and fund-raise.

Five Themes in Kisa Men's Life Stories: Hierarchy, Alliances, Sociality, Property, and Potency

Socially distributed support and affiliation appear as central issues in these life stories. Five themes appeared over and over as goals in these men's pasts, presents, and futures: enjoying the *deference and respect* of others; being a part of a rich network of all kinds of *alliances*; *sociality* within the clan and lineage; *accumulation* of wealth and property, including entrepreneurship; and a feeling of *potency*. Each of these themes is echoed in the culture complex and practice of socially distributed support. The concerns over hierarchy, alliances, sociality, and potency are clearly a part of shared social support.

Hierarchy. These are men who imagined themselves in the ideal Abaluyia role of hierarchy and respect: They delegate a great deal, are delegated to very little. The absence of this kind of deference is a major source of the "complaint discourse" described by Cattell (this volume). Sangree's Tiriki elders (this volume) wanted this too, but complain bitterly that along with their status as elders, they have to work caring for their grandchildren and doing farm work. The Samia grandparents of Kilbride and Kilbride (this volume) report feeling stigmatized to some extent because their responsibilities for childcare do not permit them this status.

These men's cohorts—especially their full and classificatory siblings—are now their only age peers who can influence them, and ideally men want to be first among these peers. Kisa men would mention this comparative frame of reference with their age mates, siblings, and cousins. These discussions of close kin and affines were cautious, clouded, sometimes filled with jealousy and anger from life-long enmities over things done and not done, given and not given. LeVine mentions in his discussion of the Gusii that "The most common motive one can be certain of for Gusii men and women is wanting to move with one's age-mates; the most common anxiety one can attribute to them is that of being left behind. . . . The reference group of age peers sets the standards by which individuals evaluate themselves and react with a sense of satisfaction or jealousy (R. LeVine, 1980, pp. 93–94)."

A social network of alliances. Family support and survival depend on implicit and explicit alliances with other families. Men described their cultural careers as culminating in successful alliances—for marriage, trade, wealth, protection from threats, and honor—and their life's end as a time when such alliances were recognized in the forms of visits from many others, with one's name and lineage known far and wide. Funerals at the end of such a cultural career, with hundreds in attendance, represent the fulfillment and projection of such a life into the community's future social alliances.

Sociality. These men imagined themselves to be at the top of a system of socially distributed support for others. Their name and home would be known widely, and they were surrounded by their lineage kin, wife or wives, children, grandchildren, and visiting affines. Kisa men hoped that they had made a lasting, to-be-remembered impression on their lineage. They make this impression physically on the land, in their name and memory of themselves, and economically and materially through wealth, trade networks, and social networks.

Accumulation and property. Sons often complain about the delays fathers make in allocating their lands and other property to them and their wives. The Kisa men I talked with retained their entrepreneurial ideals, including their goal to control property even as the wider economy militated against these efforts. Entrepreneurship means more than having a shop or trading with others, although those are certainly widespread occupational roles and ideals. Rather, the men meant owning an expanding network of resources. The ideal of traveling widely and, through contacts and strategic trading, earning money, is a long-standing feature of the Kisa economy and of East African economies generally. This type of trade economy long antedates British or Arab colonial penetration.

Kisa men and women take remarkable risks just in trying to find employment through wage labor migration, raising subsistence and cash crops, finding enough cash to send their children to schools, and enduring the harsh conditions of travel and living circumstances in cities in accomplishing these goals. There is no insurance to repay them if their wealth is stolen and no ready police assistance if their lives or their family's lives are in danger. But there is little overt commentary about the memory or excitement of risk taking. There is an implicit understanding that *all* transactions and subsistence activities entail substantial risk. To have survived these risks is to have led a successful life career, and a network of kin is essential to having survived. Outlasting the envy, jealousy, and witchcraft that go with such success represents a risk overcome.

Potency. LeVine defines potency as numbers of children and power and invulnerability in one's economic, reproductive, and spiritual cultural careers (1980, p. 97). Having many children, perhaps having several wives, having control over others, receiving deference from others, overcoming social and physical risks, and moving in a wide social field are all signs of social potency, and Kisa men hope and strive for all these. Ancestors who had this kind of social potency are better remembered and continue to have an impact on the living. Shared support systems are involved in all these kinds of cultural signs of potency and could not have been achieved at all without participation in shared support.

In this regard, Kisa men appear to think of their life goals in terms of *both* "lineal" and "lateral" life course strategies (cf. Håkansson & LeVine, this volume). Lineal ties can provide services and resources from one's own children and from one's brothers' children; lateral ties through a man's marriage(s) can provide resources from spouses and married daughters.

CONCLUSION

There are many local variations on these common themes in life goals. De Wolf, Super and Harkness, and many of the other papers in this volume richly illustrate these in different communities throughout Western Kenya. Bradley, Nasimiyu, and many others show women's life courses and their cultural careers. Younger men, those more educated, and Protestants are more likely to favor independence among sons and in one's own life (Edwards, this volume). Variations in marriage patterns, residence rules, incidence of polygyny, allocation of domestic resources, land, cattle, cash crops, and remittances, the control of corporate lineages as opposed to cooperatives or domestic groups or individual entrepreneurs—all these local variations matter as to how parents and children strategize in seeking their life goals and the social support for a valorized, culturally meaningful life.

Men and women complained bitterly at times that they were not going to be able to achieve many of these life goals. In spite of all the dislocations and disappointments in their lives, these men hoped to be able to maintain a daily routine of life that is predictable enough and that they could defend. Although often not successfully achieved as a goal, shared family management and socially distributed care and nurturance are likely to continue in Kenya both as a powerful cultural model and as a practical means to provide support for children and other kin. Edwards' findings on moral judgments among Abaluyia and Kipsigis showed, for instance, that "all the men—young and old, married and unmarried—shared a common vocabulary for talking about the underlying issues and moral conflicts raised. . . . The core values of respect, harmony, interdependence, and unity were not only alive and well, they were stressed over and over as the central virtues of family living" (p. 82). The Luyia were particularly likely to invoke the ideal of "reasonableness" in deciding difficult dilemmas, compared to the Kipsigis emphasis on more "respectful" relationships and loyalty.

Although the application of moral rules may differ, there appeared to continue to be an overlapping set of moral terms, arguments, and conceptions shared by most informants through the 1970s. What would a restudy in the 1990s of the moral discourse around socially shared support show? One clue comes from Cattell's survey of the elderly in Samia (this volume), which shows the persistence of a family morality based on principles of intergenerational contracts of reciprocity and change. Yet Kilbride and Kilbride, Ocholla-Ayayo, Nasimiyu, and others show a darker side of serious troubles in families, including neglect.

Shared support and many of its specific practices seem to be compatible with rising levels of education, rural–urban migration, and different patterns of residence, as the data from Kisa and many of the other communities studied in our volume indicate. The practice of shared caretaking and support is also compatible, in my view, with a steadily lowering total fertility rate (say, a rate in Kenya that came down to about 4 percent or so—if not as low as the current European/North American level of 2 percent). Many features of the culture complex remain in place: the high variability in fertility across families, variability in residence patterns, age and sex-specific fosterage, continued high maternal and family workloads, and others.

Since shared, socially distributed caretaking is a part of a culture complex with deep (if, therefore, no doubt also ambivalent and conflicted) emotional and moral significance, held as a cultural model, containing goals that are part of the cultural career, it is unlikely that changes in some parts of that complex (such as declining fertility, or increasing parental participation in care, or increasing family investment in education) would eliminate it. The propensity to defend the predictability and meaningfulness of life would be at stake. Indeed, changes in one part of such a culture complex will call for changes in other parts of it that assist in ongoing adaptation.

Given the ubiquitousness of the rural–urban familial group as a part of this complex, it is perplexing to see study after study in which the unit of analysis for social research continues to be a geographically localized place such as a village, an urban housing estate, or a location or district-defined sample. Although such geographically localized sampling frames may have their uses for particular purposes, it is quite apparent that these geographically based units no longer represent the social fields of action for families in Kenya today. They do not reflect the core cultural model of the social and economic "landscape" held by Kenyans (Cohen & Atieno Odhiambo, 1989). Given the obvious social significance in Kenya today of dispersed family groups occupying several different subsistence niches, it is surprising that individualistic, survey sample based sampling strategies are used so often, rather than sampling units that have greater social and cultural meaning (Ross & Weisner, 1977; Super & Harkness, this volume; Weisner, 1973b, 1981). We can miss seeing the family and social community as a support if only such individualistic units are used.

It would be extremely valuable for the next waves of social research studies in East Africa to be designed in the future to consider the value of sampling frames and definitions of "communities" and "families" that will reflect today's meaningful social worlds. This is not to criticize the many outstanding studies in this volume and elsewhere that use other kinds of samples. The valuable findings and insights of these studies show how useful they still can be. Yet these studies often reflect the local community consequences of actions taken by others (husbands, lovers, natal kin, children, wage earners, traders, Nairobi investors and politicians, and so forth) who live and work elsewhere and so are not themselves in the sample.

Under current conditions of rapid change, resource scarcity, and high but declining total fertility rates, it would be a cause of concern if adaptive strategies in addition to shared management and socially distributed nurturance were *not* being actively explored. However, it would be of even greater concern if the tradition of socially distributed family nurturance were to be lost as an important cultural model and set of social practices available to Kenyans and others for the social support and nurturance of future generations of children. It would be a loss for this tradition to be replaced by alternatives such as the socially isolated conjugal family, mother-headed single-parent household, or state-provided caretaking in schools, to mention only three. Shared support is increasingly *complementary* to these alternatives, but it is unlikely to be replaced. The persistence of the traditions of shared social support as seen in the cultural careers and life plans of Kenyans and their continued defense of the predictability of these traditions is a sign of resilience. Shared family support will be important for confronting the formidable adaptive tasks facing Kenyan families in the next generations.

NOTES

Portions of this paper are adapted from Weisner (1996). Professor Anna Simons made helpful comments, as did Christina von Mayrhauser, who also assisted with references. Research funds or conference support have been provided by the Rockefeller Foundation, the Institute for Intercultural Studies, the World Bank, the United States National Institute of Mental Health, the Carnegie Corporation of New York, the Child Development Research Unit of Kenyatta University College, Nairobi, the Academic Senate research grant program of UCLA, and the Department of Psychiatry and Biobehavioral Sciences of UCLA. This chapter was completed while Weisner was a Fellow at the Center for Advanced Study in the Behavioral Sciences. I am grateful for financial support at the Center provided by the National Science Foundation Grant #SBR-9022192 and the William T. Grant Foundation Grant #95167795.

1. Although girls have far more specifically household and domestic chores than boys, boys do have chores—herding, ploughing, or transport, for instance—that keep them occupied and often away from home.

2. However, the sheer amount of such care is greater in the rural areas, particularly in the absence of the mother or other kin and in the context of many other household chores.

REFERENCES

Abbott, S., & Weisner, T. S. (1979). Modernization, urbanization, and stress: A controlled comparison from East Africa. In A. McElroy & C. Mathiasson (Eds.), *Sex roles in changing cultures* (Occasional Papers in Anthropology, No. 1, pp. 155–165). Buffalo: State University of New York–Buffalo.

Barnett, T., & Bleikie, P. (1992). *AIDS in Africa: Its present and future impact.* New York: Guilford Press.

Bledsoe, C. H. (1980). *Women and marriage in Kpelle society.* Stanford: Stanford University Press.

Bledsoe, C. H., & Isiugo-Abanihe, U. (1989). Strategies of child-fosterage among Mende grannies in Sierra Leone. In R. J. Lesthaeghe (Ed.), *Reproduction and social organization in sub-Saharan Africa* (pp. 442-474). Berkeley: University of California Press.

Bradley, C. (1993). Women's power, children's labor. *Behavior Science Research, 2,* 70–96.

Bradley, Candice. (1995). Women's empowerment and fertility decline in western Kenya. In Susan Greenhalgh (Ed.), *Situating fertility: Anthropology and demographic inquiry* (pp. 157–178). Cambridge: Cambridge University Press.

Burton, M. L., Brudner, L. A., & White, D. R. (1977). A model of the sexual division of labor. *American Ethnologist, 4,* 227–251.

Caldwell, J. (1982). *Theory of fertility decline.* London: Academic Press.

Cohen, D. W., & Atieno Odhiambo, E. S. (1989). *Siaya: The historical anthropology of an African landscape.* Athens, Ohio: Ohio University Press.

Coquery-Vidrovitch, C. (1988). *Africa: Endurance and change south of the Sahara.* Berkeley: University of California Press.

Frank, O., & McNicoll, G. (1987). An interpretation of fertility and population policy in Kenya. *Population and Development Review, 16,* 85–106.

Goldschmidt, W. (1990). *The human career: The self in the symbolic world.* Cambridge, MA: Blackwells.

Goody, E. (1982). *Parenthood and social reproduction: Fostering and occupational roles in West Africa.* Cambridge: Cambridge University Press.

Goody, J. (1969). Adoption in cross-cultural perspective. *Comparative Studies in Society and History, 11,* 55–78.

Hewlett, B. (1991). Demography and childcare in preindustrial societies. *Journal of Anthropological Research, 47,* 1–37.

Iliffe, J. (1987). *The African poor: A history.* New York: Cambridge University Press.

Kilbride, P. L., & Kilbride, J. C. (1990). *Changing family life in East Africa. Women and children at risk.* University Park, PA: Pennsylvania State University Press.

Leiderman, P. H., & Leiderman, G. F. (1974a). Affective and cognitive consequences of polymatric infant care in the East African highlands. *Minnesota Symposium on Child Psychology, 8,* 81–109.

Leiderman, P. H., & Leiderman, G. F. (1974b). Familial influences on infant development in an East African agricultural community. In E. J. Anthony & C. Koupernek (Eds.), *The child in his family: Children at psychiatric risk (Vol. 3).* New York: Wiley.

Leiderman, P. H., and Leiderman, G. F. (1977). Economic change and infant care in an East African agricultural community. In P. Herbert Leiderman, S. R. Tulkin, & Anne Rosenfeld (Eds.), *Culture and infancy* (pp. 405–438). New York: Academic Press.

Lesthaeghe, R. (1989). Introduction. In R. Lesthaeghe (Ed.), *Reproduction and social organization in sub-Saharan Africa* (pp. 1–12). Berkeley: University of California Press.

LeVine, R. (1980). Adulthood among the Gusii of Kenya. In N. Smelser & E. Erikson (Eds.), *Themes of work and love in adulthood* (pp. 77–104). Cambridge: Harvard University Press.

LeVine, R., & White, M. I. (1986). *Human conditions: The cultural basis of educational development.* London: Routledge & Kegan Paul.

LeVine, R., Dixon, S., LeVine, S., Richman, A., Leiderman, P. H., Keefer, C. H., & Brazelton, T. B. (1994). *Child care and culture: Lessons from Africa.* Cambridge: Cambridge University Press.

LeVine, S. (1979). *Mothers and wives: Gusii women of East Africa.* Chicago: University of Chicago Press.

Marris, P. (1975) *Loss and change.* New York: Doubleday/Anchor Books.

Minturn, L., & Lambert, W. (1964). *Mothers of six cultures.* New York: Wiley.

Munroe, R. H. & Munroe, R. L. (1971). Effects of environmental experience on spatial judgments in an East African society. *Journal of Social Psychology, 83,* 15–22.

Nerlove, S. B., Roberts, J. M., and Klein, R. E. (April 1975). Dimensions of *listura* ("smartness"): Community judgments of rural Guatemalan children. In P. Draper (Chair), *Experimental Correlates of Cognitive Abilities.* Symposium conducted at the biennial meeting of the Society for Research in Child Development, Denver.

Nerlove, S. B., Roberts, J. M., Klein, R. E., Yarbrough, C., & Habicht, J. P. (1974). Natural indicators of cognitive development: An observational study of rural Guatemalan children. *Ethos, 2,* 265–295.

Nsamenang, B. A. (1992). Early childhood care and education in Cameroon. In M. E. Lamb, K. J. Sternberg, C-P. Hwang, & A. G. Broberg (Eds.), *Child care in context: Cross-cultural perspectives* (pp. 419–439). Hillsdale, NJ: LEA Press.

Reed, G., & Leiderman, P. H. (1981). Age-related changes in attachment behavior in polymatrically reared infants: The Kenyan Gusii. In T. H. Field, A. M. Sostek, P. Vietze, & P. H. Leiderman (Eds.), *Culture and early interactions* (pp. 215–234). Hillsdale, NJ: LEA Press.

Rogoff, B., Newcombe, N., Fox, N., & Ellis, S. (1980). Transitions in children's roles and capabilities. *International Journal of Psychology, 15*, 181–200.

Rogoff, B., Sellers, M. J., Pirrotta, S., Fox, N., & White, S. H. (1975). Age of assignment of roles and responsibilities to children: A cross-cultural survey. *Human Development, 18*, 353–369.

Ross, M. H., & Weisner, T. S. (1977). The rural–urban migrant network in Kenya: Some general implications. *American Ethnologist, 4*, 359–375.

Schildkrout, E. (1973). The fostering of children in urban Ghana: Problems of ethnographic analysis in a multi-cultural context. *Urban Anthropology, 2*, 48–73.

Serpell, R. (1992). African dimensions of child care and nurturance. In M. E. Lamb, K. J. Sternberg, C-P. Hwang, and A. G. Broberg (Eds.), *Child care in context: Cross-cultural perspectives* (pp. 463–476). Hillsdale, NJ: LEA Press.

Serpell, R. (n.d.). *Afrocentrism: What contribution to the science of developmental psychology?* Manuscript in author's possession.

Shibadu, G. C. (1978). *Children's labour contributions in Hamisi Division (Kakamega).* Unpublished Bachelor of Arts dissertation, University of Nairobi.

Super, C. (1983). Cultural variations in the meaning and use of children's "intelligence." In J. B. Deregowski, S. Dziurawiec, & R. C. Annis (Eds.), *Expiscations in cross-cultural psychology* (pp. 199–212). Lisse, The Netherlands: Swets & Zeitlinger.

UNICEF . (1992). *The state of the world's children 1992.* New York: Oxford University Press.

Weisner, T. S. (1973a). The primary sampling unit: A nongeographically based rural–urban example. *Ethos, 1*, 546–559.

Weisner, T. S. (1973b). Studying rural–urban ties: A matched network sample from Kenya. In W. O'Barr, D. Spain, & M. Tessler (Eds.), *Solving problems of survey research in Africa* (pp. 122–134). Evanston: Northwestern University Press.

Weisner, T. S. (1976a). The structure of sociability: Urban migration and urban–rural ties in Kenya. *Urban Anthropology, 5*, 199–223.

Weisner, T. S. (1976b). Kariobangi: The case history of a squatter resettlement scheme in Kenya. In W. Arens (Ed.), *A century of change in eastern Africa* (pp. 77-99). The Hague: Mouton.

Weisner, T. S. (1976c). Urban–rural differences in African children's performance on cognitive and memory tasks. *Ethos, 4*, 223–250.

Weisner, T. S. (1976d). Consequences of rural–urban migration for families and children in Kenya: Some results and suggested research orientations. *Kenya Education Review, 3*, 108–115.

Weisner, T.S. (1979a). Some cross-cultural perspectives on becoming female. In C. B. Kopp (Ed.), *Becoming female: Perspectives on development* (pp. 313–331). New York: Plenum Press.

Weisner, T.S. (1979b). Urban–rural differences in sociable and disruptive behavior of Kenya children. *Ethnology, 18*, 153–172.

Weisner, T.S. (1981). Cities, stress, and children: A review of some cross-cultural questions. In R. H. Munroe, R. L. Munroe, and B. B. Whiting (Eds.), *Handbook of Cross-Cultural Human Development* (pp. 783–808). New York: Garland STPM Press.

Weisner, T.S. (1982). Sibling interdependence and child caretaking: A cross-cultural view. In M. Lamb & B. Sutton-Smith (Eds.), *Sibling relationships: Their nature and significance across the lifespan* (pp. 305–327). Hillsdale, NJ: Lawrence Erlbaum Associates.

Weisner, T. S. (1987). Socialization for parenthood in sibling caretaking societies. In J. Lancaster, A. Rossi, J. Altmann, & L. Sherrod (Eds.), *Printing across the life span* (pp. 237–270). New York: Aldine Press.

Weisner, T. S. (1989a). Social support for children among the Abaluyia of Kenya. In D. Belle (Ed.), *Children's social networks and social supports* (pp. 70–90). New York: Wiley.

Weisner, T. S. (1989b). Comparing sibling relationships across cultures. In P. Zukow (Ed.), *Sibling interactions across cultures: Theoretical and methodological issues* (pp. 11–25). New York: Springer-Verlag.

Weisner, T. S. (1993a). Siblings in cultural place: Ethnographic and ecocultural perspectives on siblings of developmentally delayed children. In Z. Stoneman & P. Berman (Eds.), *Siblings of individuals with mental retardation, physical disabilities, and chronic illness* (pp. 51–83). Baltimore: Brooks.

Weisner, T. S. (1993b). Overview: Sibling similarity and difference in different cultures. In C. Nuckolls (Ed.), *Siblings in South Asia: Brothers and sisters in cultural context* (pp. 1–17). New York: Guilford Press.

Weisner, T. S. (1994). The crisis for families and children in Africa: Change in shared social support for children. *Health Matrix: The Journal of Law and Medicine, 4*, 1–29.

Weisner, T. S. (1996). Cultural adaptations and the 5–7 transition: Caretaking and socially distributed support. In Sameroff, A., & Haith, M. (Eds.), *Reason and responsibility: The passage through childhood* (pp. 295–326). Chicago: University of Chicago Press.

Weisner, T. S., & Abbott, S. (1977). Women, modernity and stress: Three contrasting contexts for change in East Africa. *Journal of Anthropological Research, 33*, 421–451.

Weisner, T. S., and Gallimore, R. (1977). My brother's keeper: Child and sibling caretaking. *Current Anthropology, 18*, 169–190.

Weisner, T. S., Gallimore, R., & Tharp, R. (1982). Concordance between ethnographer and folk perspectives: Observed performance and self-ascription of sibling caretaking roles. *Human Organization, 41*, 237–244.

Whiting, B. B. (1996). The effect of social change on concepts of the good child and good mothering: A study of families in Kenya. *Ethos, 24*, 3–35.

Whiting, B. B., & Edwards, C. (1988). *Children of different worlds: The formation of social behavior*. Cambridge, MA: Harvard University Press.

Whiting, B. B, and Whiting, J. W. M. (1975). *Children of six cultures. A psychocultural analysis*. Cambridge: Harvard University Press.

3

Morality and Change: Family Unity and Paternal Authority among Kipsigis and Abaluyia Elders and Students

Carolyn Pope Edwards

Periods of rapid social and economic change entail dramatic transformations of value systems and priorities. In Kenya, as elsewhere, urbanization, industrialization, formal education, and rapid population growth have stressed traditional systems of shared family management and support that were historically integral to the social fabric (Kilbride & Kilbride, this volume; Bradley, this volume). It is equally apparent, however, that the core cultural values—the system that Weisner (this volume) calls "socially distributed family nurturance"—have not gone away. As this volume amply documents, for example, norms of respect for elders still prevail in Tiriki (Sangree this volume), norms of helping the aged in Samia (Cattell, this volume), and norms supporting high fertility and large family size in Kericho (Suda, 1992).

How best, then, to look and listen for inevitable changes in values controlling kinship relations? How can we hear whether the central themes of family morality, such as "respect," "harmony," and "unity" in Kenya, have been eroded or replaced by economic, educational, and demographic change? And then how to determine the implications of the findings for social policy? The questions may be more complicated than they seem. For example, many in Kenya today are worried about the seemingly increasing numbers of socially isolated, poverty-stricken old people in rural communities (e.g., Cox with Mberia, 1977). But are the traditional obligations of caring for elder parents actually changing? Instead, it could be that the appearance of increased numbers of aged poor is simply a by-product of population increase and longevity, without either the values or the underlying patterns of help-giving having changed at all. Or, alternatively, it could be that the numbers of elderly poor do reflect changes in patterns of help-giving behavior, but that these changes may be the result, not of weakening values regarding care for the old, but rather of changing residential patterns and competing financial obligations facing adults who have both elderly parents and children in school. The answers have practical significance. With regard to obligations to care for elderly parents, for example, if the underlying values regarding care for aged parents are actually weakening or changing, then the solution would be to provide new systems of societal assistance to fill that gap; on the other hand, if the values are still intact but merely losing out to higher priorities, then the solution would be to find ways to assist the younger generation to continue to fulfill obligations that they still recognize as valid. To tackle contemporary social problems best, then, it is critical to know how people today understand and cope with their multiple and sometimes conflicting role obligations.

Yet studies of value change rarely permit a close look at how individuals use and understand key moral concepts involving role relations and obligations. Instead, studies more often involve comparisons of behavioral indicators such as owning or using modern consumer goods, obtaining a certain level of education, or holding a certain kind of job. Household studies allow close examination of the actual help and resources exchanged between target individuals, such as elderly parents and their children. Or, if the focus is on espoused values, then value priorities and shared perspectives may become the issue. Parents may be asked to list what values they wish to promote in their children, or case-study informants may be asked to reflect on the changes they have seen in their lifetimes (e.g., Davison, 1989). Alternatively, survey techniques may be employed to assess people's value priorities, with possibilities of larger sample size and more complex statistical treatment of the data. For instance, subjects may be asked to identify or describe themselves by completing sentence stems such as "I am ________," or to rate or rank order statements chosen to represent different value positions or goals (e.g., Rokeach & Ball-Rockeach, 1989; Triandis, 1989; Triandis, McCusker, & Hui 1990).

Yet all of these techniques have in common that they assume we know what informants mean when they use moral words. The survey methods, for instance, assume that all respondents understand more or less the same thing when they rate statements such as "A wife should respect and obey her husband" or "The young owe obedience and care to the old," as if there were a universally agreed upon meaning within a society or community for moral terms such as "respect," "obedience," and "care." Instead, as this chapter will show, individuals' understandings of key moral terms may be overlapping enough for them to communicate and dispute with one another but still show important distinctions that deeply affect what they mean to say. It is in the way that informants weave different concepts together into a fabric of an argument—rather than the way they respond to isolated statements taken out of context—that best reveals their underlying explanatory system.

This chapter will examine the underlying concepts of paternal authority and family unity and understanding put forward by Kipsigis and Abaluyia men engaging in discussion of moral dilemmas focused on family roles. It presents thematic and statistical analyses of the values of paternal authority, as put forward by representatives of two generations of rural Kipsigis and Abaluyia men. The work rests on a reanalysis of interview data originally collected in 1972–1973 to test the cross-cultural validity of a cognitive-structuralist stage theory of moral development (cf. Edwards, 1974, 1975, 1978, 1979, 1982, 1985, 1986; Harkness, Edwards, & Super 1981; Snarey, 1985). For this study, Kenyan informants of several different language groups and age and education levels were individually interviewed using a series of hypothetical moral dilemmas, requiring them not only to make decisions but also to justify why they thought one or another decision to be right. All of the moral dilemmas contained story characters related by kinship; in answering the probing questions, the informants provided insight not only into the complexity of their moral judging processes but also into their core moral values regarding parent–child and husband–wife roles and obligations. Reviewing this material now in the light of issues concerning the changing family in contemporary Western Kenya, it is striking to see how active the informants were in interpreting the changing nature of Kenyan society and values, as well as how individualized and personalized their responses were. The data, though readily scorable in terms of Lawrence Kohlberg's six stages of moral judgment, nevertheless also contain rich information about the informants' moral understanding that was never captured by the moral-stage system that rated informants on a scale from one to six.

In the first section of the chapter, the men's values are described. Within each subgroup of informants, orientation toward paternal authority is summarized—starting from those men most strongly oriented to hierarchical authority and going to those least so. It is seen that within subgroups there is a substantial range and variation of moral orientations toward authority. In addition, across subgroups there are certain general, though subtle, differences between the Kipsisis and Abaluyia informants in their typical way of talking about paternal authority, and these will be described. Quotations are used to convey precisely the meanings put forward by the men.

Underlying this thematic analysis is a cognitivist perspective on values as elements of cultural meaning systems. According to this theoretical framework, culture is conceived to consist of *learned and shared systems of understanding, communicated primarily through natural language* (D'Andrade 1992). Put another way, culture is "chunked" into meaningful packages of knowledge, "schemas," that allow a person to accomplish four critical tasks: construct an individualized mental reality, respond affectively to events and experiences, make behavioral choices, and communicate and interact with others. In constructing a moral meaning system, individuals creatively draw elements from the culture around them, actively make selections among the alternative ideas available, and may even introduce revisions. Therefore, theories are needed to explain why different individuals make the choices they do and how cultural meaning systems evolve over time through repackagings of old elements and introductions of new ones. In order to construct such theories, social scientists must make use of texts from formal interviews or naturalistic conversations and then link that content to information about the backgrounds and experiences of informants and the general social context. The moral judgment interviews analyzed in this paper offer an example of such a body of texts.

Following the thematic analysis, a correlational analysis is presented to address the individual differences in informants' orientations to authority. Given the obvious variation that is seen in the texts, the question arises, Are the individual differences at all related to such general factors as ethnic group, social position, age, education, and religion—factors that may be associated with degree of modernization and hence be expected to relate to attitudes toward traditional values? It was hypothesized that (1) older and (2) less schooled subjects would be found to be more likely to advocate traditional strong paternal authority than those informants who were younger and more educated. Similarly, (3) religious traditionalists (non-Christians) were expected to be more authority-oriented than Christians; and among Christians, Roman Catholics were expected to advocate more strongly traditional authority than the members of Protestant denominations (in accordance with Munroe and Munroe's [1986] finding that Protestant Logoli schoolchildren were more individualistic than Roman Catholics). Between Kipsigis and Abaluyia, no differences were predicted a priori other than those that might co-occur with differences in education and religion, since in both groups traditional family patterns have involved public emphasis on status hierarchies based on age and sex (LeVine, 1973), including such beliefs as that old men and women may curse their adult children when grossly neglected by them (Saltman, 1977; Wagner, 1949). (For maternal–child relations, see Super & Harkness, this volume; Weisner, this volume; Whiting & Edwards, 1988). To undertake this correlational analysis, informants' overall orientation to paternal authority was indexed using the dichotomous choice ("yes/no" type) questions from the moral dilemma interviews.

SAMPLE AND METHODOLOGY

In 1972–1973, forty-seven males and fourteen females living in seven communities in the Central and Western provinces of Kenya were interviewed (Edwards, 1975). These subjects belonged to five different ethnic groups (Kikuyu, Meru, Kipsigis, Abaluyia, and Ismaili). The Kipsigis and Abaluyia will be the focus of this paper.

Seven University of Nairobi students served as the staff of interviewers. The students, upper level majors in the social sciences, participated in a training seminar where they mastered the technique of Piagetian clinical interviewing, whose goal is to find out not only what the interviewer believes to be right but also the structure of the reasons behind that deliberative choice. During the December school holidays, the student interviewers headed home and conducted interviews with subjects of their own ethnic group. The interviewers selected as informants both adults residing in their local area and secondary students also home for vacation. The Kipsigis interviewer went to Sigor Location, fifty miles from Kericho. The two Abaluyia interviewers went to North Wanga Location, fifty miles from Kisumu, and Idakho Location, twelve miles from Kakamega.

The adult informants they selected were all community leaders, that is, persons considered "moral leaders" in their locales. They had reputations as responsible and honest citizens noted for giving sound and wise advice and counsel. Most of them were officers or members of local civic organizations or church groups; some were also holders of local political office. About half were nonschooled, the others had some primary education. Most were peasant farmers, though other occupations represented were schoolteacher, trader, shopkeeper, and mason. They identified themselves as traditionalists (non-Christians), Roman Catholics, and members of various Protestant denominations (Anglican, Church of God, Salvation Army, African Inland Church, African Gospel Church). The secondary school informants, in contrast, were intended to provide a comparison group to the community leaders. They were on the whole younger and more educated than the community leaders; their interviews offer a sampling of the moral thought and values of the "new generation" in the communities. They ranged from Form 1 to Form 5; most were attending school in Western Province. The majority of the students identified themselves as Roman Catholics. Although the university interviewers were instructed to collect data on both male and female subjects equally, they had much more success recruiting male subjects. Accordingly, the qualitative analysis to follow will consider the data from males only, since there were too few female interviews to permit balanced comparison. (However, the women's data are included in the quantitative analysis.) This male sample includes a total of twenty-five individuals: six Kipsigis community adults (aged thirty-two to seventy-five); five Kipsigis secondary students (aged twenty to twenty-seven); eight Abaluyia community adults (aged thirty-six to seventy-two); and six Abaluyia secondary students (aged seventeen to twenty).

All of the interviewers were equipped with tape recorders to record their interviews, which lasted from one to two hours each. The interviewers had previously translated the moral dilemmas and probing questions into their own home language, and they conducted the community adult interviews in that language. They interviewed the secondary school students either in that same language or in English, whichever the informant preferred. The interviews were later transcribed in full and translated into English by the students at the University of Nairobi.

The interviewers told informants the purpose of the research was to understand their ideas of right and wrong by having them discuss some hypothetical moral dilemmas with no right or wrong answers. Four hypothetical dilemmas were used, three of which had been drawn directly from the work of Kohlberg (Kohlberg, 1981, 1984; Kohlberg, Levine, & Hewer, 1983) but adapted in minor details to suit the Kenyan setting (cf. reviews in Edwards, 1979, 1982, 1985, 1986; Snarey, 1985). The fourth dilemma, similar in format but entirely new and especially tailored to Kenyan core values, grew out of the intensive discussions conducted in the training seminar.

Of the four dilemmas, two proved best in eliciting familial values and will be the subject of this paper: "Daniel and the School Fees" (developed in the training seminar) and "James and the Nairobi Show" (adapted from Kohlberg). These dilemmas are presented in Table 3.1. Note that both dilemmas involve authority and obedience issues between a father and a son: "Daniel and the School Fees" focus-

Table 3.1
Two Moral Dilemmas

Moral Dilemma 1: Daniel and the School Fees

A man, Daniel, managed to complete his secondary school education (Form 4) on the basis of school fees given him by his brother. Afterwards he married and took his wife to live with his parents in the rural area, while he got a job in the city. Eight years later, when his first son was ready to go to primary school, his mother and father came to him and said, "Your brother who educated you has been in an accident and cannot work, so you must begin to pay for the education of your brother's child." This child was the same age as his own son. The man, Daniel, did not have enough money to pay school fees for both his own son and his brother's child. His wife said he must put his own son first.

Questions

1. What should Daniel do in this situation? Should he put his son or his brother's child first? Why?
2. What obligation does he have to his brother who educated him?
3. What does he owe his son?
4. Should he obey his parents in this case? Do you think a grown son has to obey all of his parents' wishes? Why, or why not?
5. What should a grown son do for his parents?
6. Is it more important to maintain harmonious relations with his wife or his brother and parents? Why?
7. Would you condemn Daniel if he just moved his wife and children to the city and did not pay for the education of his nephew? Why or why not?
8. Would you yourself expect your eldest children to help their younger brothers and sisters with school fees? Why, or why not?

Moral Dilemma 2: James and the Nairobi Show

James is a 14-year-old boy who wanted to go to the Nairobi Show very much. His father promised him that he could go if he saved up the money himself. So James worked hard and saved up the shillings it cost to go to the Show, and a little more besides in case he saw something at the Show he wanted to eat or drink or buy to take home. But just before the Show was going to start, his father changed his mind. Some of his father's friends decided to go to town to drink beer, and James' father was short of money. So he told James to give him the money he had saved. James did not want to give up going to the Nairobi Show, so he thought of refusing to give his father the money.

Questions

1. Should James refuse to give his father the money? Why or why not?
2. What is the best reason you can think of to justify James' refusing to give his father the money?
3. What is the best reason you can think of to justify James' giving his father the money?
4. Who actually has the right to the money, the son or the father? Why?

Table 3.1 (continued)

5. Does the father have the authority to tell the son what to do in a case like this? Why? What should be the authority of a father over a son, in general? At what age does this authority grow less? Why at that age? Why is it good for a father to have this authority over a young son?
6. What does a son owe his father in a case like this? Why is it good for a son to obey his father most of the time? Can you think of specific examples where a son does not have to do what his father says?
7. Whose conduct in the story was unfair? Why was it unfair?
8. Why should a promise be kept, by anyone? Why is it important for people to keep their promises? What would the community be like if people did not keep their word?
9. What effect does it have on a son if his father breaks promises to him? In the case of this story, what effect will it have on James?10.Would a good father, a respected man in the community, do to his son what James' father did in this story; that is, promise him he could go to the Show if he earned the money, and then change his mind? What effect does it have on a father if his son breaks a promise to his father?
10. Would a good father, a respected man in the community, do to his son what James' father did in this story; that is, promise him he could go to the Show if he earned the money, and then change his mind? What effect does it have on a father if his son breaks a promise to his father?
11. If a son breaks a promise to his father, is that better or worse or just the same than if a father breaks a promise to a son? Why?

---

es on a grown son and his conflicting role obligations to his various close relatives, while "James and the Nairobi Show" involves an adolescent son's relationship to his father.

Table 3.2 presents a capsule summary of the background information of the twenty-five men, in the order in which they are mentioned in the following discussion. Table 3.3 presents the sides they took on five key questions: (1) Should Daniel pay school fees for his son or his nephew? (2) Should Daniel prefer harmony with his wife or with his parents? (3) Should a grown son obey his parents? (4) Should James give his father the money he earned himself or refuse? (5) Does James's father have the authority to ask for that money in this situation?

ANALYSIS AND FINDINGS

Thematic Analysis of the Texts

Concepts of the Kipsigis community leaders. As a group the Kipsigis community leaders were strongly concerned with intergenerational family unity and interdependence and with upholding the authority of the male head of household. The core value of "respect" was variously used by men to include such meanings as to fulfill one's role obligations; to reciprocate; to obey parental commands, advice, or requests; to treat aged parents generously; to receive discipline from el-

Table 3.2
Description of Informants (in Order of Mention)

Case No.	Age	Highest Year of Schooling	Occupation	Religion	Marriage Type
Kipsigis Elders					
K1	45	Standard 3	manual worker (school)	traditional	polygynous
K2	54	0	farmer	traditional	monogamous
K3	48	0	farmer & shopkeeper	African Gospel Church	polygynous
K4	55	Standard 3	agricultural assistant	African Inland Church	monogamous
K5	32	Standard 4	mason	African Gospel Church	monogamous
K6	75	0	farmer & subchief	African Inland Church	polygynous
Kipsigis Students					
K7	20	Form 2	secondary student	Roman Catholic	not married
K8	20	Form 1	secondary student	Roman Catholic	not married
K9	22	Form 5	secondary student	Roman Catholic	not married
K10	22	Form 5	secondary student	African Gospel Church	not married
K11	27	Form 2	secondary student	Roman Catholic	not married

Case No.	Age	Highest Year of Schooling	Occupation	Religion	Marriage Type
Abaluyia Elders					
A1	50	Standard 2	farmer	Roman Catholic	monogamous
A2	43	Standard 6	farmer	Roman Catholic	polygynous
A3	52	Standard 4	trader	Roman Catholic	monogamous
A4	36	Standard 7	primary teacher	Anglican	monogamous
A5	53	0	farmer	Church of God	monogamous
A6	36	Standard 7	primary teacher	Roman Catholic	monogamous
A7	72	0	farmer	Church of God	monogamous
A8	51	Standard 4	farmer	Salvation Army	polygynous
Abaluyia Students					
A9	18	Form 4	secondary student	Roman Catholic	not married
A10	19	Form 3	secondary student	Roman Catholic	not married
A11	19	Form 3	secondary student	Roman Catholic	not married
A12	17	Form 2	secondary student	Roman Catholic	not married
A13	20	Form 3	secondary student	Church of God	not married
A14	20	Form 4	secondary student	Roman Catholic	not married

ders; and to treat subordinates well, listening to their advice and ruling them by peaceful means. They evidenced a strong sense of moral reciprocity. They were much more likely than the other groups in the sample to refer to community elders, or old men, as a moral reference group. They were also most likely to name as a moral motivating force the paternal sanctions of blessing, cursing, and repudiating. Four of the six said it would be more important for a man to maintain harmony with his parents and brother than with his wife; two even spoke of the wife as a potentially divisive force in the father–son relationship. While they strongly believed that economic progress and the means to a "good life" come through members of the family helping one another over time, they also believed a man should become "self-reliant." One man even suggested that a father wants his son to leave the father's land at adulthood and clear the way for younger siblings.

Case K1, a farmer with three years of education and one of the two non-Christians, said that Daniel should educate his nephew first, in order to maintain "love and peace" with his brother and out of reciprocity: He would not have "become economically strong" if his brother had not helped him. When asked what Daniel owes his son, this man was unique in saying, "Nothing in particular, in terms of school fees." He clearly stood for the authority of the elder generation and the solidarity of the patrilineal line, achieved through harmonious feelings and cooperative exchanges. He spoke of both paternal sanctions: the sanction of cursing his son, thereby ruining his material prosperity, and the sanction of repudiating the son and "leaving him aside." He saw the wife as introducing a divisive element into the father–son relationship.

A grown son should obey [all his parents' wishes] because parents are the elderly people who have had a long time experience and knowledge about the world. When the son is faced with a problem, his parents will help him, and this therefore calls for obedience.

[What should a grown son do for his parents?] A grown son should help his parents in any activities that are being done at home, such as farming.

[Is it more important for Daniel to have harmonious relations with his brother and parents or with his wife?] It is more important to maintain harmonious relations with his brother and parents because they can be able to work hand in hand. They can do *Harambee* ['pull together' in a self-help group]. If we leave our parents alone, they can spoil and curse us, because we have developed rudeness. One has a different relationship with a wife than with parents: In a family a man must do everything through force or against the wife's resistance, indicating he is not on such good terms with his wife; but when a man visits his parents, there is always peace.

Similarly, for the James dilemma, Case K1 argued that James cannot refuse his father and risk losing his blessings. The father has authority in James' situation because "If you don't have any authority over your son, then things will never work out well. Your son may not even help you if you don't have authority over him.

...There is no occasion when the son should disobey his father. When you can't do anything about the rudeness of your son, then you have to just leave him aside."

The son should love and obey his father because of what the father has done for him. This obedience continues up until the son is about eighteen, "when the son can work for himself and become self-reliant." But note: the father–son respect relationship is not one-way, it is reciprocal: "The son should obey his father, and the father should obey his son. If my son shows me respect, then I have to show him respect also. I don't want my son to respect me, while I can't reciprocate."

The other religious traditionalist, Case K2, was an unschooled man of fifty-four years. Like Case K1, this man argued that Daniel should educate his nephew before his own son out of a feeling of reciprocity, "because his brother educated him. And then his brother's children will also in future take care of his children. They will educate his children." But Daniel should under no circumstances abandon his son in terms of his monetary obligation, paying the son's brideprice, lest his son become proud and ungenerous towards his father. "[What does he owe his son?] Daniel should pay the brideprice of his son. . . . Even if the son could pay his own brideprice, the father should still contribute; otherwise the son will say, 'Why did you not help me?' If you let your son pay his own brideprice, he will be proud and say, 'I paid the brideprice by myself, without your help.'"

Case K2 said that a grown son should obey all of his parents' wishes, again for the sake of reciprocity: so that his own children will obey him to the same degree. The son should buy clothes and build a house for his parents, which will secure their blessings. When asked whether it is more important to maintain harmony with wife or parents, he placed parents first: "After developing a good relation with my parents, I will go and teach my wife that we should develop harmonious relations to the same degree. I give priority to my parents, because they are my parents. My wife takes the second priority."

Yet, in answering the James dilemma, this man said James should refuse his father because "his father made a mistake" by instructing his son to work, then seeking his money. "The father should tell his friends he has no money." But Case K2 also believed that James's father does have the authority to ask for the money: "If you are my son, I can tell you what I want you to do," and furthermore, "The son wants to respect his parents." The father's authority does not become less until the son has married, at about twenty years of age, and is considered an adult with his own family responsibilities. At this point the son's formal status in society changes: "He develops his own family authority and begins to issue instructions to his children. He also comes into the category of older people."

The community leader with strongest ideas about how a father must encourage his sons to strike out on their own was Case K3, a forty-eight-year-old, non-schooled farmer and shopkeeper, member of the African Gospel Church. He considered Daniel's repaying his debt to his brother a matter of "respect."

Daniel should show great respect to his brother, because he was the one who brought him into a good position where he can see what is good for himself. The education he has received is the key to his success. . . . Daniel should not think of himself only.

[Does a grown son have to obey his parents?] Yes, a grown son should obey all of his parents' wishes. If your parents have done something good for you, then you must show them respect and obedience. You should build them a house and provide them with food and clothing.

When asked whether it is more important to maintain harmonious relations with wife or parents, he placed the wife first. This was not, however, because he favored separation or autonomy of the husband–wife unit but because he saw the husband–wife relationship as the source of harmonious extended family relations.

When the husband and wife have harmonious relations, then a harmonious chain of good relations can develop among the siblings and parents too. The good relationship between husband and wife is a stepping stone. Marriage ties make a husband and wife united as one. . . . The two of them develop good relationships toward their parents. You understand your parents when both of you understand each other.

This man's concern with proper respect for parents was also seen in his answers to the James dilemma, where he took the position that the father had the right to the money because in instructing James to work and earn, the father was actually teaching him self-reliance. He had a great deal to say about the father–son relationship:

[Does the father have the authority to tell the son what to do in a case like James's?] Yes, more fathers at present tell their son to do so. Even in the past, a father would tell his son, "I will no longer buy any cloth for you. You are now able to buy it for yourself. You can be employed in a farm to drive the oxen, or go to the White Highlands to pick pyrethrum, or you can go to the tea estates to pluck tea, to get the money for your cloth. You are a grown-up person; give me a chance to look after the younger ones. . . ." Your father tells you these words so that you can know that you are a grown up person and you should look for your own property. This is another way of teaching. Your father loves you when you have a job, but if you are not employed and are with him most of the time and causing some disturbance, then he can't have any love for you. . . . Your father will think that you are not able to think ahead.

[At what age does this authority grow less?] Things have changed in the present days. In the old days, a child of fifteen years was able to look for employment. He would stay away until he comes for initiation to grant him the status of manhood. After initiation, he would begin to realize he has to look for his own brideprice money so that the father would only give him additional brideprice. At the age of fifteen, a child had nothing in particular to do for his father. At this age, children began to loiter. [What does a father owe his son in a case like this?] The son should know that whatever the father tells him is nothing but advice on how to lead a proper life. . . . The son might think that the father is against him; he might forget that his father is planning to get him into a proper way. It is like when your father is chasing you to go to school. You can't say that he doesn't love you, but he doesn't want you to stay at home with nothing to do. He wants you to use the school fees and buy the knowledge through those school fees he has paid.

This man had not only a keen sense for the father's proper guiding authority but also a belief that the mother may undermine a harmonious father-son relationship.

A father and mother may be on bad terms, and sometimes the mother does not like the way the father instructs his son. If she has nurtured a grudge against the father [common in cases where the father has misused the bridewealth], she will instruct the son to disobey the father. A clever son should . . . not follow the mother's instructions. Some mothers can even tell their son to kill the father! Other sons see how much the mothers love them, therefore they accept the mothers' instructions. A woman's ways are never adequate. . . . The mother can spoil the son to the extent that the son will never again be on good terms with his father. The son and mother can be the enemies of the father. . . . The father will never trust a son who breaks a promise to him. The father can't call him his son, and there is nothing valuable that he will see in him.

A man with many views similar to Case K2 was Case K4, a fifty-five-year-old agricultural assistant, member of the African Inland Church, who had attended three or four years of school in the early 1930s. He argued that Daniel should educate his nephew first "to repay the debt" and show his "great friendship with his brother who educated him." He believed that a grown son should continue to obey all of his parents' wishes, although this obedience has limits and must be reciprocal: "The parents should not, for example, take all the child's property by force. If the parents take things by force, there is no reason the son should obey. [What should a grown son do for his parents?] A grown son should obey his parents, and the parents should also listen to him."

When asked whether it is more important to maintain harmonious relations with wife or parents, Case K4 chose the parents. Like Case K3, he had a great deal to say about the selfishness and divisiveness of wives.

The wife may not bring unity among the brothers and parents. Wives usually say a lot of things against the husband's brothers and parents, and this may cause hatred. The husband turns around and shows more love to his wife alone, and leaves the others out. This is not good. He should only maintain harmonious relations with his wife on certain desirable issues, their own family matters. A husband is supposed to be more clever than the wife. The usual aim of a wife is to cause a split. She is not pleased to see that some things are given to the parents.

This man, however, also said that James should refuse to give his father the money, and he was the only Kipsigis leader to repudiate the father's reason for asking: "The father was going to misuse the money on beer. A beer party is wasteful."

While he agreed that James' father has the authority to ask for the money, he went on to say that the father's authority is limited and reciprocal:

There are certain things in which the father has to exercise more authority. . . . The son should be instructed not to be wasteful and he should also obey advice. [Yet] there are also certain things that the child has to tell the parents, and the parents also must obey and do as the child says. There is a knowledge that the father has, and he should pass it on to his children. The son also has a portion of knowledge which the father lacks, and therefore the father must listen to his son. There should be equal understanding between the son and the father. When understanding exists, there is no word that is small: the son's advice is as big as the father's. Except that the greater authority remains with the father—but only for what is seen as necessary.

This authority should diminish at about age eighteen, or whenever the son is able to leave his father's land and earn his own money. In fact, it is good if he leaves home and clears the way for younger brothers and sisters: "If I allow one son to dominate my land or the other children, that is not good; he must go out and become economically independent somewhere else. . . . 'Strength' means to get wealth. You are not strong when you don't have wealth."

An interesting aspect of this man's thinking is that he sees the importance of the respectful father–son relationship in larger systems perspective: both over time and within the broader community.

What the son does is actually preparing for the future. If you obey your father, your children will also obey you in future. . . . A person will never be respected in a community if he never shows respect to his children. A respected man in the community cannot change his mind on whatever he has told his children. The children of a respected person tend even to receive discipline from the community members. The community members usually tell them, "We like your father, and we can't see the reason why you are misbehaving." The father will not be happy in his own heart. [What would the community be like if people did not keep their word?] The opinions of the people cannot coincide or converge. The people will be like animals, because they have no power to think over what they have done. There will be no progress in that community, no cooperation of any kind.

The first of the Kipsigis community leaders to favor the son over the nephew in the Daniel dilemma was Case K5, a thirty-two-year-old mason, member of the African Gospel Church, with four years of schooling: "In doing so he is helping his family . . . [but] Daniel should help his brother whenever he is able. Daniel shouldn't listen to his wife, but should know that his brother gave him great help."

This subject also had somewhat different ideas regarding obedience. He said a grown son should not obey his parents' wishes if they are based on tradition as opposed to a Christian way of life. His definition of "respecting" parents appears based on maintaining outward respectful behavior, however, and on the traditional consideration of avoiding being cursed. "[What should a grown son do for his parents?] He should respect his parents, that is, he should behave well before them. He should avoid drunkenness because this might cause his parents to curse him."

The weight Case K5 placed on maintaining close relations with parents is seen in the following answer. In spite of his stated preference for Christian over traditional values, note how he self-consciously describes his viewpoint as based on the Kipsigis way of life:

What is actually very important in Kipsigis is for a person to maintain harmonious relations with his siblings and parents, so that the wife will automatically follow. Parents are elderly persons, and you should maintain harmonious relations with them; they teach you about your future life. ...[Daniel shouldn't separate his family from them and go live in the city] ... By going to the town, they are becoming the enemies of the others and they are actually lost.

This man's concern with gaining blessings from the parent was also evident in his answer to why James should give his father the money he had earned to go to the Nairobi Show:

James should give his father the money because this is the only way one can show respect to his parent, and the parent will bless him for doing so. His parent will bless him to get more money in future. [Does the father have the authority to tell him what to do in a case like this?] Yes, the father knew that he was going to bless him to get more money and get a better life. A Kipsigis father can bless his son to stay [i. e., live] longer.

According to Case K5, the father's authority grows less when the son at age 18 is able to work for his own survival and is old enough to understand what is to be done. What is the basis of the authority system? According to this man, it derives both from Kipsigis tradition and from an expedient concern for one's future well-being: "It is something that has existed for a very long time that a son should obey his father most of the time. It is our traditional behavior. If you don't obey your parents, you will not get a satisfactory life."

The eldest of the Kipsigis community leaders, Case K6, was seventy-five years old, nonliterate, a member of the African Inland Church, and a subchief as well as a member of the school committee. He expressed his arguments clearly and forcefully, drawing upon proverbs and traditional concepts of cursing and blessing to justify his choices. Yet, unlike the others, he did not strongly side with the father's authority in either one of the dilemmas. He had little to say about respect: When asked to describe a respected man in the community, he said simply, "To be respected is to have wealth." Concerning the Daniel dilemma, this man favored educating the son before the nephew because a man rightfully solves his own problem before another's: "You know it is said, 'When sparks jump from the fire onto you as you are holding the baby, you have to knock them off yourself first—even though the baby is yours.'"

When asked whether a grown son must obey his parents, he replied that yes, a grown man should obey, but not necessarily in all things, because he must help himself also and because they had "great hardship" in bringing him up. He needs to help his aged parents when they are really lacking in the necessities, but otherwise he should be left to help himself.

Indeed, this man believed that it is more important for a man to maintain harmony with his wife than with his parents, "so that they can be self-reliant and have good understandings between themselves." Yet, while he thus argued for some autonomy of the grown man from his parents, he nevertheless did not want complete separation. He urged Daniel to maintain a close connection between grandparents and grandchildren and drew a multi-generational vision of family unity. "Yes, I would condemn Daniel [if he just took his wife and children away to live in the city]. If he had taken his children to town, his children would have less acquaintance with Daniel's parents. It would be better for him to leave his children at home, so that his children can be able to know his parents well."

Likewise, in addressing the James dilemma, Case K6 took a moderate position. He argued that James should refuse to give his father the money because it was "not good" and "not right" for the father to go ask the child to give him that money when the child "had saved the money for an intended purpose" and "in his heart this boy actually wanted to go to the Show." On the other hand, Case K6 felt the father has the authority to ask for the money, if he and his son have a good, respectful relationship: "Yes . . . if the son is the type who listens to what the father says. If the son does not listen to what his father says, that son is bad. Such a son is not even good in the eyes of the old men. The father has this much authority because that is his child. The father and son should be helping each other always; the father and the son are one."

It would be right for the father to ask for the money only if he faces genuine troubles:

> The father has the right to have it when he needs it. Before this boy can support himself, he has been using his father's money. . . . If this boy had refused to give his father the money, and if his father had left him alone and told him, "Let that money be enough [i.e., I will never give you anything more]," then the money would have troubled the son. . . . [Nevertheless] the father should use peaceful means to get the money. . . . But the son is still young and highly dependent on his father. . . . It is good for a son to obey his father most of the time, because in this way the son is trying to be good and is developing respectable behavior. . . . The father will bless him . . . but if he disobeys, the father will not be happy. The father's heart will dislike that son . . . and he will leave him alone . . . and that child will never succeed in what he wants to accomplish.
>
> [When does the father's authority grow less?] Generally when the son is between 25 and 30, the father's authority grows less. Because he now becomes an independent person who can lead himself and become self-reliant. By that time he also has a burden of his own to carry—his own children. . . . At that age you now consider him not as your child, but rather as a person of your clan.

What was striking was the judicious and balanced, multigenerational moral vision, laying out how both community and family are held together by mutual trust and appropriate obedience. In such a community or family, the old are listened to respectfully by the young, but they do not rule them arbitrarily or by force. Instead, they listen to the young in such a way as to convey their respect and understanding and desire to protect the integrity of a fragile system. Trust and respect can easily break down, and then the cooperation and continued progress of the group comes to a halt. Wealth, the basis of respect, can no longer grow.

When the people in a community don't keep their word, there will be misunderstandings. Nothing can be done in that community. People will not cooperate and there will be conflicts and quarrels. There will be no leaders in that community. [Instead] we need a community where when an old man sits and talks, the people will listen and obey his words. ...There will be communal work done in good spirit—work done in love.

[Likewise] fathers usually don't break promises to a son . . . because the father is the lawmaker, therefore he can't fail to say the truth. ... James's father is probably an alcoholic. ...Drinks have finished him and spoiled his brain so he no longer says the truth. ... The son comes to despise his father's words, and then the father leaves him alone. ...The mistrust between son and father will continue on. To cure this system is hard. Probably the grandfather originally showed this behavior to the father and now the father passes the same chain of breaking promises to his own son.

Concepts of the Kipsigis secondary students. The five Kipsigis secondary students, as can be seen in Table 3.3, made choices that closely paralleled those of the Kipsigis leaders, except that they were much more ready to say that a grown son need not obey his parents' wishes (Dilemma 1) and that James' father does not have the authority to demand his son's money (Dilemma 2). In the substance of their interviews, they were also more likely than the Kipsigis community leaders to speak of the educational benefits of the Nairobi Show; and they did not talk about the paternal sanction of blessing and cursing. However, the language of "respect," reciprocity, and family interdependency figured prominently in their discourse; as one said, "We need to be dependent." Three of the six spoke of Daniel's paying school fees a matter of "respecting" his brother and/or nephew. They also supported the traditional value of masculine authority: two warned that a wife can "mislead" a husband or interfere with his "communication" with his parents.

Case K7 was a twenty-year-old Roman Catholic attending Form 2 at Kabianga School in Kericho. Echoing the argument of Case K3, he stated that Daniel should educate his nephew first in order to "respect his brother," who educated him. He believed, however, that a son need not always obey his parents if they are leading him the wrong way, though he owes them respect and help: "In some cases a son would just obey his parents, but in some other ways he cannot. If a father told him to do something, he should do it, but if the father is leading me another way round, it is not good. I think a son would not follow that way. [What should a grown son do for his parents?] I think a grown son should just have respect to his parents. I think if there is any work to do, he just helps."

But he was oriented to closeness of the parent–child relationship. He argued that a man should not follow his wife when she is leading him away from his family of origin: "Daniel should stay in good terms with his brothers and parents, and later on with his wife, because if you just follow what your wife is saying, it is not good, because she leads you into a position where you can't communicate with your brothers and others."

The James dilemma was difficult for this young man because he felt strongly that James had the right to the money and yet, at the same time, that the father,

Table 3.3
Informants' Responses to Questions about Moral Dilemmas

	Dilemma 1 (Daniel)			Dilemma 2 (James)	
Case No.	Pay for son or nephew?	Harmony with wife or parents?	Must a grown son obey?	Give to father or refuse?	Does father have authority or not?
Kipsigis Elders					
K1	nephew	parents	yes	give	yes
K2	nephew	parents	yes	refuse	yes
K3	nephew	wife	yes	give	yes
K4	nephew	parents	sometimes	refuse	yes
K5	son	parents	sometimes	give	yes
K6	son	wife	sometimes	refuse	yes
Kipsigis Students					
K7	nephew	parents	sometimes	refuse	yes
K8	son	parents	no	give	yes
K9	son	wife	sometimes	give	yes/no
K10	nephew	parents	no	refuse	no
K11	nephew	wife	no	refuse	no
Abaluyia Elders					
A1	nephew	parents	yes	give	yes
A2	both	both	yes	give	yes
A3	both	both	sometimes	give	yes
A4	son	wife	sometimes	give	yes
A5	son	parents	yes	refuse	no
A6	son/both	no answer	no	refuse	no
A7	son	wife	sometimes	refuse	no
A8	son	wife	sometimes	refuse	no
Abaluyia Students					
A9	nephew	parents	yes	give	yes
A10	nephew	both	sometimes	give	yes
A11	nephew	both	yes	refuse	no
A12	both	wife	sometimes	refuse	no
A13	son	parents	no	refuse	no
A14	son	wife	no	refuse	no

although he was being unfair, had the authority to claim the money, simply because "he is the head," giving his son all the necessities. The father's authority, he said, diminishes whenever you leave school, around the age of eighteen, and are a "bit mature" and able to understand problems. When does a son not need to obey his father? "I myself am in school now, and if my father tells me to marry—when I have not yet decided to—that is the way I can refuse to obey."

At the end he concluded that the father–son relationship may deteriorate to fighting if either one breaks his promise to the other, but overall it is worse if the son disrespects the father: "The son will be against the father and not even help him. The father will never feel good and he will be against the son. . . . The father can't break the promise of the boy because he will break the good terms they have had."

Case K8, a twenty-year-old Roman Catholic attending Form 1 at Sigor Secondary School in Kericho District, argued that Daniel should help his brother and brother's family in other ways, but still pay the school fees for his own son first. He was another Kipsigis informant who felt respect must be reciprocal: "Daniel owes his son respect. His son should try to respect his father, because the son is under him." When asked about a grown son, he said he should not obey wrongful commands. He defined "respect" as showing obedience:

> A grown son should not obey all of his parents' wishes because the parents sometimes may tell you something which is not good in the eyes of the community. Perhaps you are told to steal; you should not try to steal. . . . [If I do] I will suffer, maybe be arrested by the government, and I will suffer without the aid of my father. Another example is that if I am told to go and elope with somebody's child without the knowledge of that child, I will be arrested also. . . . [What should a grown son do for his parents?] A grown son should try to respect his parents, obey his parents, and try to help his parents in the way he was helped. To obey is to have respect.

His sense of the importance of the parent–child relationship was made clear in his answer that Daniel should try to maintain harmonious relations with his parents first: "Before he married he was with his parents. And [now] after that he should try to copy what he was seeing in his family."

Furthermore, he stated James should give his father his money. The father has the authority to ask for it because "James is under his father" and as "a respect," even though the father was "wasting" the money on beer and the Nairobi Show would benefit James. The father's authority becomes less, Case K8 said, when the son becomes mature and independent, "when he is married," whatever the age, twenty to forty, at which he is actually living independently away from his father's supervision. "You are not going to be followed by your father when you are going to a faraway country—when you are far from your father's home—and you will not have troubles from your father at any time. . . . You have your property, your real property, not your father's property. So when you are not married, you are still depending on your father's property."

He concluded by speaking of the importance of promises in the context of maintaining interdependent community relations, based on communication. "A promise is a means of communication. . . . A community where people don't keep their word will be corrupted because everyone will be solitary. He will have to depend upon himself, not helping each other. . . . It is wrong to be independent. Maybe you are going to have some troubles which need the community to help you. We need to be dependent."

Case K9, a twenty-two-year-old Roman Catholic attending Form 5 at Kagumo Secondary School in Nyeri, felt Daniel should put his son first, "because he has the obligation to respect him" and so that "in future the son will not turn against him." In general, he felt a man should put the interests of himself and his family, in the sense of his wife and children, before obligations to other family members.

[Should a grown son obey all of his parents' wishes?] He should obey in some cases, but in others he should not. [What should a grown son do for his parents?] If he is well-educated and earning quite a big amount, he should be giving some to his parents if they come and ask him. But if the money is not enough to share with his parents, he should first of all see that his family are well served, and his parents later on.

[Is it more important to maintain harmonious relations with his wife or with his brothers and parents?] I think I should maintain harmonious relations first of all with my wife and later with my parents.

On the other hand, he strongly opposed severing relations with the parents: "I condemn [Daniel] for moving his family to the city. . . . He should leave his family to live in the reserve. . . . In that case, he will be breaking relations between his family and parents completely. . . . Just because you are not on good terms with your parents, that doesn't mean your family should not be in good terms with your parents."

Addressing the James dilemma, Case K9 underscored his concept of obedience by stating that James should give his father the money, because otherwise he would be "disobeying the father and yet he is still too young to support himself." He expressed contradictory ideas on the father's authority, first saying that father "has no authority in a case like this" because of "the hard working [that] James had just done" and then saying, "in our society there is no limit [to the father's authority] so long as you are still in school." The authority continues as long as you are "still young or still unable to support [your]self," or "after having got married you are left alone." But during the period the son is young, he should "owe respect" to his father even when his father seems to be saying something that seems wrong to him. The father may indeed have better judgment than the son about the best interests of the son, for example, if the son seems to want to use his father's limited funds for brideprice rather than for school fees, when actually it would be foolish to get married without the means of supporting himself and his family.

Case K10 was a twenty-two-year-old member of the African Gospel Church attending Form 5 at Alliance High School in Kikuyu. He echoed Case K9 in saying that Daniel should educate his nephew first to "respect his brother," who educated him. His concept of "respect" seemed very broad—encompassing notions of following the wishes of someone, as seen in these answers:

[What does he owe his son?] He ought to respect him. He ought to be respected also, but when the two sons are there—his brother's son and his very [own] son—he should respect his brother's son more than this very son of his. He should help his son. I think it should be only respect, nothing more.

[What should a grown son do for his parents?] In the first place, he should respect them if the parents are also very respectful. If the parents are not respectful, I think there should be a bit of understanding between them, rather than deep respect. It would be something like the respect [that is seen] not in the family circle but like you respect your villagers and the rest. He should help them if the parents are very old and can't help themselves, just doing something which is necessary, just building a house or digging the *shamba* ['garden'], looking after the cows.

Besides being the only Kipsigis informant to speak in these terms, he was also the only one who spoke of moral behavior as being related to "self-respect." "[Would you expect your older children to help your younger ones with school fees?] Yes, I think it is necessary for them to help themselves [each other], because they will be respecting themselves much better if they help [each other] than if I just try to help them all. I think that is the only way that better relationships will be established."

When asked about the James dilemma, this student argued that James should refuse the money because he had "the right" to it. "I doubt whether [the father] has authority [in a case like this] because the father had promised." He commented, "I think the boy was trying to respect his parents as far as possible," and then said something else about respect that no other informant did: "I think a son owes his father disrespect—no respect at all—because his father did not respect him."

When asked whether a son needs to obey all of his parents' wishes, Case K10 agreed with the other students in saying, no, he has only to obey those which are good, "those which are reasonable, for example, if someone is sick." He ought not to obey if his father advises him to go and steal something from someone. The authority of the father, which continues until the son is "mature," at age twenty-one or so and self-supporting, extends to "what is reasonable, and there shouldn't be any exploitation by the parents."

Yet he still said harmony with parents comes before that with a wife, who can lead a man into selfish ways: "The wife, I doubt whether she really knows the life history of the person. She doesn't know even how the person was educated and the rest. . . . As a married man, as the head of your family, you have to give at all times the directives, and if you try to follow your wife's, the wife can really mislead you at times, and you will end up being just considering yourself."

This student strongly opposed ungrateful, selfish behavior within the family: "[James' father] is very right to have authority over his son, because the son can be moved by the world until he is lost. Training means being disciplined in a family life."

Similarly, he shared with the others a vision of a cooperative community. "[What would a community be like if people did not keep their promises?] There is a disorganization in the community, and there is no work at all to be done in the community. Many hands could not do big work: for example, if there is a forest to be cleared, it ought to be cleared first by very many people because it is a very heavy work, and if there is a dangerous fire to be put out, many people are needed."

He condemned selfish behavior—not as being against Kipsigis custom, but as being universally wrong. He was the only Kipsigis informant in the sample who used such universalistic terms as these in defending familialistic values: "If [Daniel] doesn't want to help his brother who helped him that will be very bad indeed, very immoral. Moral behavior is something which is spiritually good, which is faultless. [What do you mean, spiritually good?] Something spiritually good is universal—universally good. There is nothing individual which is moral."

Case K11, at twenty-seven the oldest secondary student and the least oriented to paternal authority, was a Roman Catholic attending Form 2 in Kitale. He also said Daniel should educate the nephew first because "he has an obligation" and a "close relationship" with his brother. On the other hand, he did not consider this a matter of obedience to parents.

> It was not something in force. It was something suggested by the parents, to inform the man about the accident so that the man may think himself whether he could manage to help his brother or not. He should not obey; he is a big man, like his parents. [Should a grown son obey all of his parents' wishes?] No . . . if the parents ask you now that you should go and kill somebody, would you go and kill? So you must agree to what you think is right. . . . So the son should consider what the parents are saying. Some parents are saying things correctly, others might say things which are not correct in the real sense. [Examples?] Parents may tell you that you should not go and drink, when you are grown up. What about if you go out; are they following you just telling you not to drink?

He felt a grown son does owe his parents a sense that they are well cared for: "Suppose they become very old, what you should see is that they get enough clothes, and other than that, you should have to build nice houses for them so that they can see for the rest of their lives that, 'Our son has just built for us this and this.'"

This man also viewed harmony with the parents as following from harmony with the wife: "The relation starts first of all from the house, from inside the house where the people stay, [and then] it spreads out until the parents have to come to the same category. . . . They inherit from how you are staying. If we copy from the parents, maybe my wife can say, 'Now I am on the other side.'"

Addressing the James dilemma, Case K11 was the only Kipsigis informant to say James should refuse his father because attending the Nairobi Show was such "a very important thing to young people." He went on to discuss the educational benefits of attending the Nairobi Show and learning different things from all over the nation: "James should have to tell his father reasons why he is attending the Show. ...The father might think that the Show was like going to town. I justify it by saying that James was attending an educational film, maybe James was in school and he can learn more about education and different things. The show ground is where [you] learn different things from different parts of the country."

He was the first of the Kipsigis informants to feel James' father does not have any authority in a case like this, because James had been instructed by his father to go earn his own money and, now that he has got it, he must be treated as a grown-up who can control its use. He had definite ideas about the source and limitations of the father's authority.

The father has authority over a young son because the father is the person who develops a child's mind to have harmonious relations with the country or within the country. The father trains the child for good behavior in the community.

[What should be the authority of a father over a grown son?] In general, it is to ask him about home affairs: what they should do, what they should plant this year, what they should actually do to get extension of farming in the family; but not the matter of just coming to me saying, "How much are you getting? Let me have this and this."

The father's authority, this man argued, diminishes after marriage or after leaving school, at twenty, twenty-five, even thirty years of age. In speaking of this, he again makes clear his sense of identification with the whole country of Kenya: "Because you are now counted as a citizen of the country. When you are schooling, you are not a citizen, you are just taken as a child."

Concepts of the Abaluyia community leaders. The Abaluyia community leaders that I interviewed, as can be seen in Table 3.3, were much less likely than the Kipsigis leaders to say James' father has the authority to ask for his money and to say Daniel should favor his nephew. Instead, they either favored Daniel's son or else insisted he must treat both boys equally. However, they were quite similar to the Kipsigis leaders in the degree to which they chose harmony with wife versus parents, said that a grown son must obey, and recommended that Daniel give his father the money.

In the substance of their interviews, they expressed subtly different values from the Kipsigis informants. "Respect" seemed less of a touchstone value. Instead, many spoke about a kind of moral "reasonableness," or depth of moral knowledge, acquired through age, experience, and education. This concept included the following various meanings: not quarreling "thoughtlessly" or creating disharmony "stupidly"; learning how to seek out knowledge and make up one's own mind as a mature adult; making judicious, impartial decisions; as head of household, becoming "answerable" on all problems; listening to the advice and wisdom of elders and parents and "praising any good advice"; not mindlessly "complying with the old things"; wanting one's children to "advance in knowledge."

In addition, family unity was valued: They focused on the need for kinfolk to live together harmoniously, maintain communication, avoid quarrels and escalating tensions, and pull together to achieve economic progress and success. None spoke of the divisive influence of women; indeed, one man spoke of the wife as a "real friend." In speaking of what a grown son should do for his parents, they differed from the Kipsigis informants in adding "love" to the list of "respect" and "help." The father's authority, they seemed to say, consisted mainly of the limited responsibility to control the son's waywardness until such time as he can behave responsibly and authoritatively to build his "own family." While they were strongly interested in education and recognized the importance of progress and increasing "civilization," two men spoke explicitly of the need to continue to "follow traditional custom."

Case A1, a fifty-year-old Roman Catholic farmer with two years of schooling, served as a village Chairman. He was the only Abaluyia community leader to clearly favor Daniel's nephew. He felt Daniel must obey his parents in this case because he was educated by his brother and must reciprocate. Even a grown son should obey his parents, "because at such a stage you know what is right and wrong according to the rules." His obligation to his parents is to assume the mantle of responsibility: "[What should a grown son do for his parents?] A grown up son is like a father to others in the home. If his father dies, he becomes answerable to all issues in the home, and if anything goes wrong, he has to be responsible for it, and he takes care of all things in the home."

He felt the wife should fit into this system and also obey the parents: "You should all live together harmoniously. He who quarrels with his parents due to his wife is thoughtless. Your parents have cared for you for quite long, and when your wife comes, she is also to care for you, and so both of you should obey parents and live harmoniously with them."

He likewise felt that James should give his father the money, because "that which belongs to the son also belongs to the father, while that which belongs to the father also belongs to the son. All have a right to it." The father has the authority to ask for it, but the respect relationship should be reciprocal: "The son ought to obey his father, and if the son also tells his father something that is reasonable, the father should listen too. . . . If the father was not giving [James] anything, he too can refuse to give his father."

The father's authority grows less when the son gets married and comes to have authority in his own homestead.

Case A2, a forty-three-year old Roman Catholic farmer with six years of schooling, insisted that Daniel must help both boys. According to this man, it is an issue, not of reciprocity or respect, but rather of fairness: "It is not fair to educate only one of them and leave the other. In this case his parents would see that he is impartial and does not favor either of them."

Likewise, he had a strong sense of balance and maintaining closeness with both wife and parents.

> He should maintain good relations with both his wife on the one hand and with parents on the other. The reason is that his parents also maintained such loyalty and obedience to their parents, according to custom. . . . If he goes to town and forgets about his parents it would be bad because he will have deserted them. The mere fact that he has less money should not make him break away from those who cared for him and brought him up. He should do all he can to be in touch with them even if he has nothing.

> [What should a grown son do for his parents?] A grown son who has his own wife and children could assist his parents financially or materially if he can. But since he also has family members to assist, the help which he may give may also be limited.

Concerning the James dilemma, this man felt that James could give his father some and "remain with a little sum for entry to the Show." It was "not a must" for James to give the money; but on the other hand, "the father traditionally has authority over his son" to "show him what is right and wrong or how to conduct his general affairs in an acceptable way." Furthermore, perhaps his father was just trying to test James to "see the reaction" of this boy: "Despite the fact that James' father had promised him to go to the Show, he had a right to change his mind because of visitors who arrived and had to be entertained. This [giving by James] would show that he was a good, respectful son."

The father's authority continues until the son is about twenty years of age: "Even then, advice from parents may still be valuable. At an early age he [the son] is taught to be social to others and cooperate with them; he should visit relatives and friends and help them in times of difficulties. He is taught how to face life situations."

Finally, this man referred to the traditional council of elders as a moral reference group: "[Why should a promise be kept?] Traditionally, a promise was a sort of contract represented by an object, a cow. It must not be broken or the one who breaks it will lose. The promise was made in front of elders. If it was broken, traditionally elders often convened a meeting to reconcile the parties who have not kept their promises and there is hostility. The same elders will decide the proper action."

Case A3, a fifty-two-year-old Roman Catholic trader who had worked twenty years for the East African Railways, was one of two Abaluyia community leaders who insisted Daniel must find a way to school both son and nephew in the Daniel dilemma. "He should educate his brother's child. In this way he is directly helping his brother who helped him. . . . This is in accordance with customs. . . . At the same time, he should not throw away his son or fail to do all that is necessary for him. He should do all he can, even getting into debts, to support his own child and his brother's child.

This man had a keen sense of the importance of harmonious family relations and at the same time specific strategies a man must follow to maintain them. A man should give economic help to his parents and listen to their advice, then decide for himself what is reasonable to do.

When you disagree with a parent, you should not criticize what he tells you. You should rather praise any good advice that he may give on occasion. . . . [What should a grown son do for his parents?] If he is working, he should support them financially and materially. It is only when his parents are uneconomical, that is, when they spend money brought to them recklessly, that the son can think of refusing to help them. By refusing to help them he creates tensions: the social relations between them will be restrained, which is not good. Within a household, members should live harmoniously and cooperatively.

All adults—man, wife, and parents—must exercise restraint and a kind of balance if household tensions are to be contained.

The wife should try to maintain good relations with her husband's parents. Where they disagree, attempts should be made to reconcile them. A man should not disagree with his wife because of his parents; he should not side with his parents and send away his wife, because should he be unable to raise brideprice to find another wife, he could blame his parents. [Likewise] the parents should not interfere with their son's wife, because if she gets annoyed and deserts, the son would blame his parents. On the other hand, should he ignore his parents because of his wife, the parents will be disappointed and may not carry out traditional obligations when the son falls into difficulty. All these misunderstandings could be minimized when a son starts his own household.

Regarding the James dilemma, this man suggested James should give his father his money because "his father has a right to stop him from going to the Show. By going without permission, he violates acceptable rules." The father has authority to claim James' money because "he might have good reasons why he does not want his son to go to the Nairobi Show," for example, he might get lost there or see things not approved. A father has authority until a child is about sixteen years of age, when he becomes able to choose for himself what is right and wrong. Proper obedience in a son is important because it leads him into the right relation with the community elders: "The son has to obey and follow whatever he is told by his father. By so doing he learns to obey those who are older than himself and learns proper, acceptable behavior. A good child is welcomed by elders. He follows their advice and does as he is told to do. . . . A child who does not sit with elders will never know what is required. He will never know what is good and what is wrong."

The remaining Abaluyia community leaders argued that Daniel should put his son before his nephew. For example, Case A4, a thirty-six-year-old Anglican primary school teacher with a Standard 7 level of education, argued that it is only "human" for Daniel to put his own son first: "As a human being—although he has been helped—I am sure he has to look at his son first before he looks to anyone else's son."

A grown son, in general, should do some of the important things to help his parents if possible, for example, give them food and pay their taxes. He should obey some, but not all, of his parents' wishes; and harmony with his own wife comes first before harmony with parents: "She's the one who cares for your life more than your mother will do, because when you are grown up, you have not much dealings with the parents."

On the other hand, he also felt James should give his father the money, because he "has to respect his father" and because "James's money is, in fact, very little in comparison with what the father does for him." The father has the authority to claim the money "because he's a big man; he knows what should be done to the son and the whole thing remains to him to decide." The authority of the father continues until about the age of eighteen years, when the son becomes mature and can make his own decisions and "see some other different things on his own." The basis of this authority, as described by this school teacher, comes not from Abaluyia custom but from God: "Even in the Bible, we read that a child should obey his parent; and as he obeys his parent, he grows up to be a good citizen."

Still, he returns to sounding much like the other community leaders in speaking of the importance of a good relationship between father and son: "[What is the effect on a son if a father breaks a promise to him?] The effect is a son loses respect for his father, and then he becomes rude to him, and their life together is not cooperative. . . . The father loses friendship for the son, and therefore, there is almost no help between them in the family."

Case A5, a fifty-three-year-old Church of God farmer with no formal education, was a member of the Land Consolidation Committee. He echoed the others in saying a grown son owes his parents "love, obedience, and help in things like money," if he is working. If he is not working, he should help them with farm work.

Like many of the remaining Abaluyia leaders, he felt Daniel must put his own son first to preserve his future relationship with him: "If he starts with his nephew, his own son might, when he grows up, feel bad for having been left behind. This will lead to conflicts with the father, and such a thing is not good for the family."

Likewise, he argued that James should refuse his father the money because going to the Show is important for his development: "If he gives the father the money, the father is just going to waste it buying beer; then James will miss very important knowledge he would have gotten by going to the Show, and this might be a setback in his studies."

He did not believe the father has the authority to claim James's money, "because the son worked hard for it himself." On the other hand, he argued that harmony with parents has priority over harmony with wife because they are the source of all his assets and identity. "Because they have borne him, brought him up, and educated him. They gave him cattle to marry with and gave him a farm. If it were not for them, he would not have gotten that wife he has or those children. It is because of his parents that he is referred to as 'so-and-so's son.'"

The authority of a father should continue until the son is about age twenty and is old enough to look after himself and his own family. The father should control the son to see "that he does not indulge in drinking and going around with girls, moving about, and so on." Even when the son becomes independent, he is at first "not very grown up and you might find you still have authority over him to see that he takes proper care of his family."

When asked to think of specific cases in which a son does not have to obey his father, this man presented ideas never voiced by the Kipsigis informants, namely, that the father might cruelly try to create disharmony between son and mother: "You might have a cruel man who drinks, comes home, and beats the wife, and even tells the son to help him. Or he hates her and tells the son to do the same. The son should not follow him. This is a stupid thing to do and a wrong thing for a son to do to his mother."

Or he might try to interfere with the son's education: "Let's say, there is a father who wastes his money in drink and can't afford to pay school fees for his son. If the son goes, for example, to his uncle and gets school fees, and then the father asks him to give him the money, the son should not obey . . . because he will miss his education which is important for his life."

Case A6, a thirty-six-year-old Roman Catholic primary school teacher with a Standard 7 level of education, strongly felt Daniel must educate both boys, though educating the nephew was not "a must" but "a willingness." Unlike all the others, however, his reasons had much more to do with increasing the level of literacy in Kenya than with Daniel's relationship with family members:

In case we are talking about a country like Kenya, a country which is developing ... "*Harambee*," we are told, by the head of state, I mean, we should try to rectify things. . . . Daniel is not doing this [educating his nephew] to obey the brother, he's doing this to make the country develop, to make the country have less illiteracy. . . . He would also be very proud if his nephew is educated. . . . We cannot accept to comply with the old things.

His educational orientation was also seen in his argument for why James should refuse his father the money, since he had earned it himself, and besides:

[Does the father have the authority to tell his son what to do in a case like this?] If he's a right father, who knows and understands the Show—because the Show is where all peoples, farmers, can learn about agricultural machines—where in general people who are doing all kinds of things in the country can go to see any changes. . . . The father has got a right to advise his son on things that will make him learn the purpose of the country. James' father wanted the money to go to the bar; he is not going to learn anything from the drinks, and after drinking he becomes hopeless. . . . [Indeed] James could not be wrong to take this money and ask his father to go to the Show with him. ...

When asked what a grown son should do for his parents, this man said, "A grown son should obey his parents in actions and deeds." The authority of the father "these days" ends after the son has finished his schooling and has got a job, around age twenty-five.

This teacher's strong orientation to Kenya the nation rather than the Luyia people was evident throughout his interview: "[What would the community be like if people didn't keep their promises?] It is always important for people to keep the promises. If you get people who cannot keep promises in the community, or anyplace, or in a country—well, in this country there [would be] no purpose at all, no civilization can take place in such places."

Case A7, a seventy-two-year-old Church of God farmer with no formal education, was chairman of a primary school committee, a church committee, and the coffee board. He felt Daniel must help his own son first because "Daniel has now become a family man and is to look after it. If he now concentrates on his brother's family, his own won't grow up properly and his name won't be known." On the other hand, "I would expect him after some time to have saved some money to educate his nephew. If he doesn't, it would mean that he doesn't care about the help his brother gave him, and this is unfair."

According to this man, a grown son owes his parents "respect, love, and help" in the form of money, blankets, clothing, help in farming, and so on. He has to obey only those of his parents' wishes "which he thinks are right and beneficial to him," and harmony with his wife is more important than with parents because "it is his wife he is going to live with and bring up a family."

Likewise, he believed James should refuse his father the money, simply because it was he who "worked very hard to save the money." Moreover, "a good man would not prevent his son from going to a beneficial thing like the Show just because he wants the money to go and drink." A father has authority over his son until about the age of twenty, when the son is grown-up and has acquired enough knowledge about the world to look after himself. James' father does not have authority to claim his money in this case; his authority, in general, consists mainly of controlling waywardness:

> A father should see that his son does not become destructive. For instance, if I find my son destroying vegetables, or if I find that he has just taken my clothes to put on, I have a right to rebuke him. I have a right to beat him or rebuke him if he steals my chickens to go and sell, or if he steals my money. Also, I should see that he does not grow into a ruffian, waiting for people on the roads and beating them up.

The father has this authority so that the son "follows his father's good example: to do good things in order to be respected in the community when he grows up."

Case A8, the final Abaluyia community leader, was a fifty-one-year-old Salvation Army farmer with four years of primary schooling. He echoed Case A7, above, when he said Daniel should put his own son first: "Because he has now to start building up his own family, and if he devotes his money to the brother's family, then his family will lag behind."

Echoing others of the Abaluyia leaders, he felt a grown son owes his parents "help" in the form of food, clothing, and money and also "respect and love." In general, he did not think a grown son has to obey all of his parents' wishes because he "can think for himself" and "obey those wishes or advices he sees as right and beneficial to him." He went even beyond Case A7 in arguing for the importance of maintaining harmony with his wife: "Because the wife is the real friend. They live together, rear a family together, and therefore, they must agree with each other."

He was the most extreme informant in upholding Daniel's right to autonomy from his other relatives: "He has the right to do what he thinks is right, and if to him moving to the city is okay, I don't see why I should blame him. Moreover, his nephew is not a member of his own family; in this case the nephew's ties to him are weaker than those of his wife and his son."

Similarly, he argued that James should refuse his father the money because he worked hard for it and the Show will be beneficial to him. The father does not have the authority to claim the money in this case because "it is the son's money and he has the right to do what he wants." A father's authority, which continues until the son is about twenty-two and old enough to look after himself, consists mainly of controlling him from drinking, stealing, fighting, roaming, moving around with girls, and so on. In a more positive sense, "A good person knows what his son needs, and he is ready to provide him with everything and also satisfy his son's wants. A good man would also like his son's knowledge to advance by going to things like the Show."

Concepts of the Abaluyia secondary students. The Abaluyia secondary students that we interviewed generally agreed with the Kipsigis students in their choices on all five questions. In the substance of their interviews, however, they sounded much like the Abaluyia community leaders. They did not introduce new moral themes; instead, they emphasized how education is vital to the success of the individual, family, even the whole country of Kenya. They stressed the importance of good relations with wife and with parents in order to "live a good life." Like the Abaluyia community leaders, they appealed to the value of moral "reasonableness," including the need for a son to obey his father "to know the ways to respect people," to learn to think for oneself and not be led around by others, and to avoid waywardness (drunkenness, stealing, and other wrong and dangerous things). They recognized the obligation of a grown son to listen carefully and with understanding to his parents' advice but then make his own decisions about what is reasonable to follow. As one said, it has been "from the beginning of the world, actually, that you should respect your parents. . . I don't see why this should not be carried on."

Case A9, an eighteen year old Roman Catholic attending Form 4 at Namulungu Secondary School in North Wanga Location, was unusual among the Abaluyia students in believing that Daniel should educate his nephew out of gratitude and reciprocity to his brother. He believed a grown up son should be obedient to his parents because "however old he is, he has to obey the parents." A grown son owes his parents "respect," as well as "financial help," if they need it. Furthermore, harmony with parents is paramount, for the son's best interests lie with them: "If he has to live a good life, he has to live in very good relations with his parents and brothers. Better than his wife, I think. This is because even if you divorce your wife, or you do without your wife, your father—your parents, I mean—and your brothers remain your parents and brothers, even if you have a different wife."

Similarly, James should give his father the money "because he must obey his father; he is supposed to obey." The father does have the authority to tell his son what to do in a case like this: "Yes, he has . . . because his father can help him later. The son should obey because it is his father who brought him up. . . . So he has to do much to respect his father and to obey him."

When does the father's authority grow less? Surprisingly, this student said the authority does not grow less at any age. "He has to obey his father in order to know the ways to respect people and in order to have his father helping him all the time."

Case A10, a nineteen-year-old Roman Catholic attending Form 3 at Namulungu School, also said Daniel must help his nephew first, since his brother had helped him; however, "in this case, it is not a must, but it is according to the willingness of Daniel." His reasoning focused on the value of education, not just to the boys themselves, but to the world around them: "The present world doesn't need the one who is not educated, but it needs everyone to be educated."

He felt Daniel does have authority in a case like this, but in general, he should obey only when what they tell him is right and he can manage it. A grown son, he argued, owes his parents obedience only in cases where they aren't forcing him. However, he strongly advocated family unity and maintaining harmony with both wife and parents. He empathized with the needs of parents' and brother's households as well as James's:

"If a house is divided against itself it just falls," and here if Daniel separates himself from the wife, then obviously the house will fall, or the family will fall. . . . Not only should he make up a good relationship with the wife but also with the brothers and parents. The parents are the ones who gave him his wife, and here the brother is the one who educated him and made him to be employed. And also if Daniel can separate from his father's family, then obviously they will have no support; they will remain poor and die in a poor way, since the brother is unable to support himself.

Similarly, out of empathy with the father's needs for companionship, he argued that James should give his father the money. "If his father's friends are asking him to go with them to drink, and he doesn't have money, he is to ask James because James has got money. But if he does not ask for the money, so that the friends do not get anything, then at least the friendship will die."

The father has the authority to tell James what to do because "he is the one who brought him up." However, the authority grows less as the boy becomes a teenager, between thirteen and eighteen years of age, and "becomes somehow mature" and knows what is right and wrong and whether to obey the father or not.

This student concluded by affirming his sense of the whole world as his moral reference group:

[What would the community be like if people didn't keep their promises?] The world would be very much disorganized. And everyone will be termed a liar, which is wrong, to be a liar. Even God, when He created the world, said to keep His commandments. In case you disobey, then you may leave society. . . . People should have respect for each other, because in case there is no respect at all in the world, there will be calamity everywhere.

Case A11, a nineteen-year-old Roman Catholic attending Form 3 at Pehil Secondary School in Homa Bay, South Nyanza, echoed the others' arguments in saying Daniel must educate his nephew out of reciprocity to his brother. He also felt a grown up son has to continue to obey his parents and maintain harmony with both wife and parents because "they are all important. Without [either] one, I think your life should not be in a good mood." When asked what a grown son should do for his parents, he said he should "be ready to help them in everything they like or want" for the house or "in the family as a whole."

On the other hand, he felt James should refuse his father because the father was just going to use the money for drink, whereas James's aim was for education, "to learn very many new things that he had been hearing of." In fact, the father has no authority to prevent James from having access to information about the whole world: "As you know, the Show is where many things are brought from various countries, various places, various districts, and probably this son has never traveled to these countries." The father's authority should only be applied when the son is trying to misbehave. This authority continues until the son is married and has his own home and family.

Case A12, a seventeen-year-old Roman Catholic, in Form 2, the third of the students attending Namulungu School in North Wanga, felt Daniel should not choose between his son and nephew but instead divide the money between them. He did not feel a grown up son needs to obey his parents in everything, because the parents may be selfish—"the parents want money"—so he should neglect them a bit. Still, a grown son owes his parents help "until they die." Even if they educated the other children but not him, he can still help "to a little extent." He should maintain harmony most with his wife because she is the one with whom he lives: "He must at least just live with the wife, because he won't leave the wife and go live with the parents again. He has already established with the wife."

At the same time, he should not abandon his other relatives: "[Would you condemn Daniel if he just took his wife and children and went to live in the city?] Yes, he must stay there and persevere with that whole situation—the situation of the parents plus the family of the brother, rather than moving to the town, leaving them behind suffering. For they helped him very much."

Concerning the James dilemma, he felt James should refuse his father because he had earned the money himself and his father was breaking his word. His father does not have the authority to tell James what to do in a case like this because "it is too late." The father's authority, which continues until the son is settled into his own married life, should have some limits. The father may control the son regarding drinking and going out at night, but not regarding whether he gets women and girls. When asked why a son should obey his father, he told an anecdote about his own brother:

> I have a brother who, when the parents were trying to advise him, he was refusing. Sometimes when he was taken to school and changed to another, he said, "I am not a policeman to be taken from station to station." Therefore, when the parents refused to take him to school, he practiced stealing. And even now he is a thief. And though he is a thief, he is not living a happy life. He is worried all the time. He doesn't know when he will die, for a thief does not know if he shall die sometime.

Case A13, a twenty-year-old member of the Church of God, attending Form 3 at Musingu Secondary School on the boundary of Isukha and Idakho Locations, was one of the two Abaluyia students who argued Daniel should put his own son first, otherwise "his family won't progress quickly enough." A grown son, he said, does not need to obey his parents in everything, but rather only when they speak sensible and useful things. He owes them help in food, farming, and clothing, and "he has to love them and respect them."

He gave a singular answer to the question about whether Daniel should maintain harmony with wife or parents. He cautioned Daniel not to become womanlike by agreeing too much with his wife and, moreover, losing his inheritance by antagonizing his father.

If a son, for example, maintains strong harmonious relations with the wife, the latter might control him so much that he might adopt character[istic]s of a woman. He might even ignore his parents, and yet he is living in his father's home. The father might be annoyed, and he has the right of sending away this son. Probably this son may have no money to buy any other piece of land somewhere, and he may hang himself, causing great loss to the community.

Concerning the James dilemma, however, this student argued James should refuse his father because it is his money and "therefore he must fulfill his needs as he wants." The father does not have the authority to tell James what to do because he only wants the money for beer, which "isn't necessary as far as James is concerned." The father is supposed to teach his son not to steal and to be serious with his studies in order to gain the means to live in future. This authority diminishes when the son is around twenty-one and is no longer "called a boy but a man" and is able to marry and live his own life. When asked for specific examples of when a son need not obey his father, he again showed originality in his answer: "Again, his father may be a wizard; if he goes out to jump, and advises his son to follow him, the son should refuse, because this is not a good thing to do."

The final student, Case A14, another Roman Catholic, was a twenty-year-old attending Saint Peter's Secondary School in Mumias. He said Daniel must educate his own son first to avoid that son's blame when the son gets older. He owes his son education, especially in these modern times: "Especially on the side of education, it is very important these days." A grown son need not obey all of his parents' wishes because "some of them can mislead." Looking toward his own interests in the future, he should maintain harmony first of all with his wife: "The reason is that if the husband does not maintain a good relation with the wife because of the parents' advice, or other people's advice, then it's obvious they might end up in a divorce, and this would not help him in his family. Especially if the parents die, you should have your family, and if the family is not good, or there is no good relationship, you will end up in divorce and will not have a good life."

His relative detachment toward parents was also evident in his answer to what a grown son should do for his parents: "It depends on whether the parents can afford to live life by themselves . . . then there should be nothing he should do for them. In fact, it is the parents who should keep on helping him! But if at all the parents cannot afford to live by themselves, I think you can give small help which is necessary."

Unlike most of the others—Abaluyia and Kipsigis—he did not believe in reciprocity of helping obligations: "Well, what I know, if someone helps you, it is not necessary that you have also to help him, but you can help him also." Still, it would be wrong for Daniel to just move to the city and spend money on expensive living that he could be using to help his nephew.

This student, like those previous, felt James should refuse to give his father the money because he had taken the trouble to save this money himself, after his father told him to do so. The only reason to give the money would be "just to keep the relationship between his father and his friends good." The father has no authority in a case like this because by breaking his promise he is "contradicting himself" and being unfair. In general, his authority should concern preventing his son from doing wrong or dangerous things. This authority declines when the son reaches his early twenties and becomes mature. Why should a son obey his father most of the time? "[I]t has been like that from the beginning of the world, actually, that you should respect your parents. As a son you should respect your parents and the father especially. I don't see why this should not be carried on."

Yet, the respect should be reciprocal, in order that people in the family continue to listen to one another and trust each other: "The father should not break a promise to the son, and the son should not break a promise to the father. Both of them should keep their promises because they are people staying together in the family. Once somebody loses faith or hope in another, then it will have the same effect on both of them, so both of them should keep faith in the other."

Correlational Analysis of the Moral Choices

The thematic analysis has suggested that the sample individuals varied substantially in the moral choices they made and in their reasons justifying those choices. The four subsamples differed in their respective moral choices (for example, in whether they favored Daniel's nephew or son), but it appeared that they overlapped heavily in how they talked about family harmony, unity, and paternal authority. These moral values were clearly salient and important to all of the informants. Kipsigis and Abaluyia men differed stylistically in their emphasis on the touchstone values of "respect" versus "reasonableness," respectively. To the Kipsigis, attitudes of respect seemed most essential to finding ways for family members to get along, whereas, with the Luyia, attitudes of reasonableness seemed predominant. Even within each subsample, individual differences seemed to appear in the precise meanings the men applied to such key terms as "respect" and "paternal authority." Case K1, for example, argued that a son should always obey his father and may be cast aside if he cannot be controlled. Case K4, another Kipsigis elder, described a more equal relationship where both father and son listen to each other and the father has greater authority "only for what is seen as necessary." Case K5 defined respect as simply behaving well before parents and avoiding drunkenness.

But did the men's actual choices on the dilemmas, such as whether they thought Daniel should pay school fees for his son or nephew, tend to relate to the informants' objective situations, experiences, or position in life? It appeared, for example, that community elders were more likely than secondary students to answer that, "Yes, grown sons should obey their parents," rather than, "No, grown sons need not obey their parents." To systematically examine whether the background variables of ethnic group (Kipsigis versus Abaluyia), social position (community adult versus student), formal education (years of schooling), age (in years), and religion (non-Christian versus Roman Catholic versus Protestant) were associated with informants' moral choices, a correlational analysis was performed. To do this, the informants' answers on the five key questions in Table 3.3 were assigned numerical values. This could be done because the questions had dichotomous answers, such as "yes/no" or "give/refuse." In all cases, the choices indicating *higher* endorsement of paternal authority (e.g., "Yes, James's father does have the authority to ask for his money," or "Daniel should [obey his parents and] pay school fees for his nephew") were assigned a score of 0,whereas the choices indicating *lower* endorsement of parental authority (e.g., "No, James's father does not have the authority to ask for the money," or "Daniel should pay school fees for his son") were assigned the score of 1. (The few cases of undecided or halfway responses, such as "Sometimes the father does have authority, sometimes he doesn't," were assigned the compromise score of .5). In addition, TOTAL JAMES and TOTAL DANIEL indices were constructed by adding up the scores on all of the objective questions in each dilemma (see Table 3.4, footnotes a and b). Then, the background variables of Ethnic Group, Religion, and Social Position were also assigned nominal values, while those of Age and Education were quantified in years, and all five were correlated with the moral choice scores. The results are displayed in Table 3.4.

Two sets of correlations can be seen in this table: one set for what is referred to as the original sample (composed of the twenty-five men whose interviews have been described so far in this paper); and another for an augmented sample. This augmented sample was created to add power to the statistical analysis by adding subjects to increase the sample size. To the data on the twenty-five men were added parallel data on ten women (four Kipsigis community leaders, two Kipsigis secondary students, two Abaluyia community leaders, two Abaluyia secondary students), who had also been interviewed by the university students as part of the original study. In addition, data on twelve more Kipsigis community adults were available from a study by Harkness, Edwards, and Super (1981), conducted in the community referred to as Kokwet, using the same approach to moral judgment interviewing as Edwards (1974).

The findings for the Augmented Sample were clearly stronger than for the Original Sample, but the directions and magnitudes of the correlations were very similar; accordingly, the Augmented Sample results will be emphasized in this discussion. Of the three background variables—Education, Age, and Religion—by far the strongest predictor was Religion, followed by Education. Religion correlated significantly ($p < .05$) with five variables: DANIEL Q1 (School fees for son or nephew?), JAMES Q1 (Give the money or refuse?), JAMES Q5 (Does father have authority?), TOTAL DANIEL, and TOTAL JAMES. Examination of the means within subsamples showed that for all four groups, Protestants scored higher (i.e., were less authority-oriented) than Roman Catholics; while among Kipsigis elders (the only subsample with religious traditionalists), Christians scored higher than non-Christians. Similarly, more years of education correlated positively with lower authority orientation on three variables: DANIEL Q4

Table 3.4
Correlations between Background Variables and Informants' Answers

	Dilemma 1 (Daniel)			Dilemma 2 (James)			
	Pay for Son or Nephew (Q1) nephew=0; both=.5; son = 1	Harmony with Wife or Parents (Q6) parents=0; both=.5; wife= 1	Should Grown Son Obey? (Q4) 0=yes; .5=sometimes; 1=no	Give Money or Refuse? (Q1) 0=yes; 1=no	Does Father Have Authority? (Q5) 0=yes; .5=yes and no; 1=no	Total Daniel[a]	Total James[b]
Education (in Years of Schooling)							
Original Sample	-.0734	.0892	.4812*	-.0109	.2913	.2400	.1227
Augmented Sample[c]	.0316	.0363	.4978**	.2417	.3321*	.3295+	.3079*
Age (in Years)							
Original Sample	.1504	.1009	-.3445+	.1045	-.1956	-.0884	-.0401
Augmented Sample	.0686	.0234	-.3553*	-.2064	-.2783+	-.1652	-.2788+
Religion (1=NonChristian, 2=Roman Catholic, 3=Protestant)							
Original Sample	.4493*	.2482	.2310	.1993	.2209	.3758+	.2408
Augmented Sample	.3482*	.2670	.2099	.4530***	.4070**	.3550*	.5101***
Ethnic Group (1=Kipsigis, 2=Abaluyia)							
Original Sample	.2253	.1443	-.0953	.0260	.3535+	.0211	.2465
Augmented Sample	-.0323	.1544	.0424	.2457+	.3976**	-.0420	.4342**
Social Position (1=Elder, 2=Student)							
Original Sample	-.1373	.0407	.4202*	.1364	.3134	.2054	.1937
Augmented Sample	-.0897	.0649	.4941**	.3395*	.4129**	.2625	.3610*

Note: All tests of significance for Pearson correlations are two-tailed.

$+p < .10$. $*p < .05$. $**p < .01$. $***p < .001$.

[a] The TOTAL DANIEL index consists of the respondents' answers on the three Dilemma 1 questions listed in this table (Questions 1, 4, 6), plus Question 4 (Should Daniel obey his parents in this case? 0=yes, .5=yes & no, 1=no), Question 7 (Would you condemn Daniel if he just moved his wife and children to the city and did not pay for the education of his nephew? 0=yes, 1=no), and Question 8 (Would you yourself expect your eldest children to help their younger brothers and sisters with school fees? 0=yes,1=no) in Table 3.1. TOTAL DANIEL scores could range from 0 to 6, with a *high* score indicating *lower authority orientation.*

[b] The TOTAL JAMES index consists of the sum of the respondents' scores on the two Dilemma 2 questions listed in this table (Questions 1 and 5), plus Question 4 (Who actually has the right to the money, the son or the father? 0=father, .5=both, 1=son), and Question 11 (If a son breaks a promise to his father, is that better, worse, or just the same than if a father breaks a promise to a son? (0=worse, .5=just the same, 1=better) in Table 3.1. Scores on the TOTAL JAMES index could range from 0 to 4, with a *high* score indicating *lower authority orientation*.

[c] To increase the statistical power of this correlational analysis, the original sample of 25 men has been augmented by DANIEL and JAMES data for 10 women interviewed by the Kipsigis and Abaluyia university students as part of Edwards's (1974) dissertation. Furthermore, data for the JAMES dilemma have been added for 12 male community adults interviewed by Sara Harkness, from the Kipsigis community called Kokwet (for details, see Harkness, Edwards, & Super, 1981). This yields a total Augmented Sample, $n = 47$ (22 Kipsigis community adults, 7 Kipsigis secondary students, 10 Abaluyia community adults, and 8 Abaluyia secondary students).

(Should grown son obey?); JAMES Q5; and TOTAL JAMES. In contrast, Age (being younger) correlated significantly with lower authority orientation on DANIEL Q4 only. It is interesting to note that one of the interview variables, DANIEL Q6 (Harmony with wife or parents), did not correlate significantly with any of the background variables.

What about the subgroup factors: Ethnic Group (Kipsigis versus Abaluyia) and Social Position (elder versus student)? Within the augmented sample, JAMES Q5 and TOTAL JAMES correlated significantly with authority orientation: the Kipsigis men were more authority-oriented than the Luyia men. Even when the effects of subgroup differences in age, education, and religion were statistically controlled for (by partialling them out), still the correlation of Ethnic Group with TOTAL JAMES remained significant at $r = .3308$ ($d.f. = 42$, $p < .05$, two-tailed). To many of the Kipsigis informants, it seemed, James's yielding his money to his father was a matter of appropriate respect by a young son; many suggested the father might really be "testing" James to see if he is a good, respectful boy who could be relied upon in future. To the majority of the Luyia informants, in contrast, it seemed that the father's seeking James's money for beer was completely out of bounds, beyond reasonable authority, while the long term educational benefits for James of going to the Nairobi Show were too great to pass up.

Social Position was a more powerful predictor than Ethnic Group. Within the augmented sample, being a student rather than an elder correlated with lower authority orientation on four variables: DANIEL Q4, JAMES Q1, JAMES Q5, and TOTAL JAMES. Even after partialling out the effects of age, education, and religion, the correlations for JAMES Q1 and JAMES Q5 remained significant at the $p < .05$ level (r's = .3257 and .3230, respectively). This suggests that the social role of being an elder (household head, husband, father, someone looked upon as a role model in the community and used to giving advice and counsel) versus being a young, unmarried student may have influenced the men's tendency to side with established paternal authority beyond what was contributed simply by their respective experiences connected to church and school.

CONCLUSION

The moral-judgment interviews of Kipsigis and Abaluyia community leaders and secondary students were examined for what they had to say about concepts of paternal authority and family unity. The thematic analysis revealed that all of the men—young and old, married and unmarried—shared a common vocabulary for talking about the underlying issues and moral conflicts raised by the dilemmas. The core values of respect, harmony, interdependence, and unity were not only alive and well, they were stressed over and over as the central virtues of family living by members of all four subgroups. In a stylistic variation on these themes, the ideal of seeking "reasonableness" in one's thinking and behavior seemed more prominent among the Luyia men, whereas maintaining "respectful" role relations (often defined as reciprocal communication and demonstrated loyalty) seemed to preoccupy the Kipsigis elders and students.

Although the men of all four subgroups shared a common ground for talking about the moral conflicts, they did disagree in the sides they took on various questions, and their choices varied systematically with their ethnic group, social position, age, education, and religion. Not surprisingly, the young, unmarried students—and educated persons in general—tended to take more positions against the side of paternal authority, especially on DANIEL Q4 (Should a grown son obey his parents?) and JAMES Q5 (Does the father have the authority in a case like this?). Perhaps more surprisingly, however, was how strongly religion influenced informants on both James and Daniel dilemmas. According to Harkness and Super (personal communication, 1992), this result makes sense for Kipsigis subjects because the Protestant churches have characteristically made much stronger demands for psychological culture change than have the Roman Catholics in the Leldayet area. Furthermore, the Protestant missions even today have always involved whole families of outsiders coming to live in Kipsigis communities, thereby providing role models of western, nonauthoritarian, monogamous family life, whereas Catholic missions are run by members of a religious order, people without spouses and children. Similarly, for the Abaluyia, Munroe and Munroe (1986), discussing how the Protestant ethic has played itself out among the Logoli of Western Province, have noted that since the turn of the twentieth century the Quakers have preached an individualistic philosophy looking toward achievement in the here and now. This Protestant ethic seems to be mirrored in our Abaluyia informants' emphasis on "reasonableness" as a standard of interpersonal conduct and on autonomy in decision making.

In conclusion, the texts resulting from moral-dilemma interviews have been shown to offer rich information about the content of people's values, in particular, the individual meanings that people construct as they grapple with delicate and important issues concerning family roles and relations. These data offer a different kind of information from that generated by behavioral studies or survey questionnaires, the usual means of studying moral value change. When conducted systematically on a representative sample of people, moreover, the moral dilemma texts offer the possibility of establishing not only what values are shared by a reference group but also how particular experiences and background factors have shaped individuals' perspectives on those values.

NOTE

This chapter is based upon a new analysis of data originally collected during 1972–1973 at the Child Development Research Unit (John Whiting, director) at the University of Nairobi and supported by grants from the National Institute of Mental Health (MH1096–18) and the Carnegie Corporation. A faculty grant from the University of Kentucky, Research and Graduate Studies, supported the reanalysis and presentation of this paper at the international conference, "Changing Families and Ecology in Contemporary Western Kenya," Kakamega, Kenya, August 1992. I especially wish to thank my original research assistants, University of Nairobi students Ezra arap Maritim, Runo Elijah, and Salma Gulamali, who helped in data collection, transcription, and interpretation, and Beatrice and John Whiting, my academic advisors and intellectual guides.

REFERENCES

Cox, F., with Mberia, N. (1977). *Aging in a changing village society: A Kenyan experience.* Washington, DC: International Federation on Aging.

D'Andrade, R. (1992). Schemas and motivation. In R. D'Andrade & C. Strauss (Eds.), *Human motives and cultural models* (pp. 23–44). Cambridge: Cambridge University Press.

D'Andrade, R., & Strauss, C. (1992). *Human motives and cultural models.* Cambridge: Cambridge University Press.

Davison, J., with the women of Mutira. (1989). *Voices from Mutira: Lives of rural Gikuyu women.* Boulder, CO: Lynne Rienner Publishers.

Edwards, C. P. (1974). *The effects of experience on moral judgment: Results from Kenya.* Unpublished doctoral dissertation, Harvard Graduate School of Education.

Edwards, C. P. (1975). Societal complexity and moral development: A Kenya study. *Ethos, 3*, 505–527.

Edwards, C. P. (1978). Social experience and moral judgment in East African young adults. *Journal of Genetic Psychology, 133*, 19–29.

Edwards, C.P. (1979). The comparative study of the development of moral judgment and reasoning. In R. Munroe, R. L. Munroe, & B. B. Whiting (Eds.), *Handbook of cross-cultural human development* (pp. 501–527). New York: Garland.

Edwards, C. P. (1982). Moral development in comparative cultural perspective. In D. Wagner & H. W. Stevenson (Eds.), *Cultural perspectives on child development* (pp. 248–279). San Francisco: Freeman.

Edwards, C. P. (1985). Rationality, culture, and the construction of "ethical discourse": A comparative perspective. *Ethos, 13*, 318–339.

Edwards, C. P. (1986). Cross-cultural research on Kohlberg's stages: The basis for consensus. In S. Modgil & C. Modgil (Eds.), *Lawrence Kohlberg: Consensus and controversy* (pp. 419–430). Sussex, England: Falmer Press Limited.

Harkness, S., Edwards, C. P., & Super, C. (1981). Social roles and moral reasoning: A case study in a rural African community. *Developmental Psychology, 17*, 595–603.

Harkness, S., Edwards, C. P., & Super, C. (1992). Personal Communication.

Kohlberg, L. (1981). *Essays on moral development: Vol. 1. The philosophy of moral development.* San Francisco: Harper & Row.

Kohlberg, L. (1984). *Essays on Moral Development: Vol. 2. The psychology of moral development.* San Francisco: Harper & Row.

Kohlberg, L., Levine, C., & Hewer, A. (1983). *Moral stages: A current reformulation and a response to critics.* New York: Karger.

LeVine, R. A. (1973). Patterns of personality in Africa. *Ethos, 1*, 123–152.

Munroe, R. L., & Munroe, R. H. (1986). Weber's Protestant ethic revisited: An African case. *The Journal of Psychology, 120*, 447–456.

Piaget, J. (1948). *The moral judgment of the child.* Glencoe, IL: Free Press. (Originally published 1932).

Rokeach, M., & Ball-Rokeach, S. J. (1989). Stability and change in American value priorities, 1968–1981. *American Psychologist, 44,* 775–784.

Saltman, M. (1977). *The Kipsigis: A case study in changing customary law.* Cambridge, MA: Schenkman Publishing Co.

Snarey, J. R. (1985). Cross-cultural universality of social-moral development: A critical review of Kohlbergian research. *Psychological Bulletin, 97*, 202–232.

Suda, C. A. (1990). Division of labour by gender and age—Implications for equity. In G. S. Were (Ed.), *Women and development in Kenya* (pp. 39–56). Nairobi, Kenya: Institute of African Studies, University of Nairobi.

Triandis, H. C. (1989). Cross-cultural studies of individualism and collectivism. In J. Berman (Ed.), *Nebraska Symposium on Motivation, 1989* (pp. 41–133). Lincoln, NE: University of Nebraska Press.

Triandis, H. C., McCusker, C., & Hui, C. H. (1990). Multimethod probes of individualism and collectivism. *Journal of Personality and Social Psychology, 59,* 1006–1020.

Wagner, G. (1949). *The Bantu of North Kavirondo, Volume 1.* New York: Oxford.

Were, G. S. (1967). *A History of the Abaluyia of Western Kenya, c.1500–1930.* Nairobi, Kenya: East African Publishing House.

Whiting, B. B., & Edwards, C. P. (1988). *Children of different worlds: The formation of social behavior.* Cambridge, MA: Harvard University Press.

4

Gender, Status, and Values among Kikuyu and Appalachian Adolescents

Susan Abbott

In 1971–1972, I carried out fieldwork in Kenya in a rural Kikuyu community in the highlands of Central Province. My study examined the effects of male labor migration for wage employment on family decision making and on the married women staying in the area to farm and rear their children (e.g., Abbott, 1976, 1980; Abbott & Arcury, 1977; Abbott & Klein, 1979; Weisner & Abbott, 1977; Mitchell & Abbott, 1987).

Beginning in 1987, I embarked on a new research project in rural eastern Kentucky in the United States, also a highland zone, which has a mixed ethnic heritage that is predominantly English, Scotch, and Irish. The eastern Kentucky research is investigating social class differences in child rearing and family life in a predominantly coal mining county.

At an early stage of the research in both studies, the same questionnaire was administered to secondary school students to measure the values, attitudes, and beliefs of young people about to move into full adult status. This chapter presents the results of a descriptive and comparative analysis of questionnaire items pertaining to gender roles and aspects of social stratification as perceived by the students in the two samples. By examining these students' values and beliefs in the context of their contrasting local cultural, social, and economic contexts, I hope to account for the patterns that emerge. I conclude with new questions based on what I observed in the original Kenyan research site during a return visit to Kenya in the summer of 1992 and on comparison with the findings of some of the studies included in this volume.

COMPARISON OF LOCAL CULTURES

Table 4.1 shows some of the cultural differences between the two locations where these data were collected. The kinship systems, marriage practices, composition of households, and inheritance practices all differ in substantial ways, as do language (American Southern Highlands English versus Kenyan English and Kikuyu). Further differences can be seen in the division of labor at the household level. In the rural industrial eastern Kentucky community, women work predominantly as housewives with fewer than the national average working for wages outside the home, while the rural Kikuyu women all work as the primary family farmers who are responsible for feeding themselves and their children and for making a contribution to their husband's food supply while the latter raise cash crops for sale. These patterns are similar to those described by others included in this volume for the Western Province of Kenya, and they are typical of much of sub-Saharan Africa. Finally, the local and national political systems differ, although both systems have been heavily influenced historically by British institutions.

There are other interesting similarities. Both local economies are linked into the international market economy and both produce primary commodities—in the one case coal, in the other case coffee and tea. In both cases the products are destined for domestic use as well as for export markets. Both local communities are affected by international economic forces. Both communities have high levels of unemployment or underemployment. Both communities rely on wage labor of at least some family members. Both local communities support elites whose positions are based in differences in education, occupation, and income; however, the stratification system in eastern Kentucky is an older one. The boundaries between the strata in eastern Kentucky are sharply drawn, and the lifestyles of those differentially located in the structure are more divergent than in rural Kenya in 1971.

The local Kenyan system was still in the process of emerging in 1971–1972. The boundaries were fuzzier, but the direction in which the system was moving was as clear as the growing pile of dressed building stones destined to be assembled into a European-style dwelling by one prosperous community resident who worked in Nairobi, a dwelling as dramatically different from those surrounding it as the coal company superintendent's large Tudor-style house next to the coal miner's clapboard dwelling in Eastern Kentucky (Abbott, 1988, 1992; Abbott & Klein, 1979).

Finally, in both communities Protestant Christianity predominates, although the denominations differ. The Kenyan community still retained some pre-Christian practices and beliefs, and not all eastern Kentuckians belong to, or attend, church.

All the schools from which students were selected to fill out the questionnaire are located in rural areas that are tied to more populous regional towns or large urban centers where certain kinds of shopping, medical care, and government services are available that are not available locally. Both rural locations are peripheral to the cores of their respective regions. And while both areas have some local wage jobs, both have a history of labor migration to other areas to find wage employment, although the pattern of migration differs between the two communities.

Table 4.1
Eastern Kentucky and Kikuyu Local Cultures

Variable	Eastern Kentucky	Kenya
Kinship system	bilateral with Eskimo terminology	patrilineal with Omaha terminology
Marriage system	serial monogamy	polygyny permitted
Postmarital residence	neolocal but tend to settle in kin-neighborhoods	patrilocal
Household composition	strong nuclear family preference	mother/child household; husband occupies own house
Inheritance	sons and daughters equal; adult–child who cares for elderly parents may get more	sons only; daughter entitled to use rights in father's/brothers' land if not needed by them
Economy	extractive industrial and service jobs dominate with high unemployment	subsistence farming with heavy cash cropping for domestic and international markets; wage labor across a range of occupations; high unemployment or underemployment.
Division of labor	men as wage earners, women as housekeepers, but some women work as wage earners though at lower rates than nationally	women are the farmers responsible for feeding family, care for house and children, and primary labor for cash crops; men involved in labor migration as wage earners.
Political system	democracy with local and national elite power structure; marked local stratification based in kinship, education, income, and occupation	traditionally egalitarian with stratification based primarily in gender and age, with councils of male lineage elders working within age grade system; now a limited democracy with universal suffrage; emerging stratification system with elites based in education, income, and occupation
Religion	Protestant Christianity predominant with strong fundamentalist bias, a few Roman Catholics, some belonging to no church and do not attend church	Protestant Christianity—most Anglican, some Roman Catholic, some retention of pre-Christian practice and belief

In this part of Kenya the usual pattern in 1972 involved labor migration of males only; their wives and children stayed on the rural homestead, where the women farmed and ran the home place (Abbott, 1976). This varies from the one family/two households pattern described by Weisner for the Abaluyia community in Western Province, where he has based his research (Weisner & Abbott, 1977). In eastern Kentucky, migration for wage employment more often involves the relocation of the nuclear family unit, although close ties are usually maintained with their home location and return migration is not uncommon (Schwarzweller, Brown, & Mangalam, 1971).

One last point of comparison should be drawn. One sample of students is a highly selected group who have survived an intense national examination system to earn a place in secondary school in a system where at the time these data were collected only 7 percent to 10 percent of rural primary school children completing the last year of primary school achieved a seat in a government secondary school. These youth were buoyed by the expectation that they would do much better in the emerging cash economy and urban society of Kenya than their less fortunate peers, despite the strictures imposed by a 1971–1972 unemployment rate of about 40 percent. The other group is composed of students living amidst a depressed rural industrial economy fallen victim to the usual boom/bust cycles of the coal industry and its recent technological changes and a shifting international division of labor that have together permanently changed the employment picture of the region with official unemployment rates of 17 percent to 20 percent and real unemployment closer to the Kenyans' 40 percent. All these youth are affected by the international economy and must cope with limited local economies, but they live in contrasting local structures and occupy different places in those structures.

METHODOLOGY

The two samples were selected in a similar manner. In the Kenyan study (Abbott & Arcury, 1977; Mitchell & Abbott, 1987), six secondary schools in the vicinity of my ongoing 1971–1972 community study were approached about their willingness to allow their students to fill out the questionnaires during class time. Three of the schools were girls' schools, two were boys' schools, and one was coeducational. Kenyan secondary schools were structured at the time of data collection with grades numbered from Form 1 through Form 4.[1] These grades followed completion of seven years of primary school. The classes selected by the headmistress or headmaster to fill out the questionnaire were all either Form 3 or Form 4, with the exception of a few students who were in Form 2. I supervised the administration of the questionnaire in each classroom. In all, 176 students completed the questionnaire. The mean age of the sample was 17.7 years with a range of from 14 to 25 years. It was fairly common when these data were collected for Kenyans to start primary school somewhat older than in the United States. It was also the case that some of these students probably did not go straight through, because their families sometimes lacked money for school fees, forcing periodic hiatuses in their schooling.

The eastern Kentucky sample (n = 152) was drawn from the three high schools under the jurisdiction of the local county school board. All three were coeducational. The questionnaire was given to all high school juniors (Grade 11) in class on the day on which it was administered. Three seniors (Grade 12) also filled out the questionnaire in one of the high schools. In one high school, I was permitted to oversee the administration of the questionnaire myself. In the other two high schools, teachers administered it after receiving instructions from their respective school principals.[2] The purpose of the questionnaire and the manner in which it was to be administered were explained to the principal by the author. The mean age of the Kentucky sample is 16.6 years and the range is from 16 to 19 years.

The questionnaire was derived from Robert Edgerton's "Culture and Ecology Interview Schedule" (Edgerton, 1971), which was designed for use in a comparative study of personality, values, and behavioral styles of adults from four different East African cultures. It was used with only minor modifications in both settings. The questionnaire was administered in English in both settings. It consists in eighty-two open-ended questions that probe for values and attitudes related to gender, family, interpersonal relations, mental illness and suicide, life goals, and so forth. In addition, two other sections were included in the questionnaire—twelve sentence completions that are a measure of ego-development as conceptualized by Loevinger and her associates (Loevinger & Wessler, 1976) and a twenty-question self-report of symptoms of anxiety and depression, the Health Opinion Survey (Macmillan, 1957; Abbott and Klein 1979; Mitchell and Abbott, 1987; Abbott, 1988). The ten questions analyzed for this paper come from the eighty-two open-ended questions. They were selected for their pertinence to local gender roles and social stratification.

After appropriate procedures were followed for developing codes for the students' responses to the open ended questions, the data were analyzed using a variety of descriptive statistical techniques and tests of association.

COMPARISON OF THE TWO SAMPLES

The two samples are roughly comparable in age and number of years spent in school. The mean age of the Kentucky students was 16.6 (range 16–19, S.D. = 1.17), while the mean age of the Kikuyu students was 17.7 (range 14–25, S.D. = 1.58). The Kentucky students had spent eleven (juniors) or twelve (seniors) years in school; the Kikuyu students had spent ten (Form 3) or eleven (Form 4) years. The students differ in the number of siblings reported, with the Kentucky students having on average 2.46 siblings (range 0–17, S.D. = 2.06) and the Kikuyu students having 6.2 siblings (range 0–14, S.D. = 2.26). The Kentuckians describe a more extreme range than the Kikuyu, however.

I can continue to compare the two samples on other variables of interest by going beyond the information included in the students' questionnaires (Abbott, 1976; Abbott & Klein, 1979). These data represent all married men and women between the ages of thirty and seventy in a community near the schools from which the students were drawn for the study. These data will provide a frame for understanding further differences between the two samples. Although these men and women are not necessarily the parents of the students sampled for the study (since most Kenyan secondary schools are boarding schools and entrance is gained through performance on a national competitive examination, students may or may not be assigned to a school near their home community), I have no reason to believe that the characteristics of the families of the Kikuyu students who filled out the questionnaires fell outside the range of variation that existed in the community where I worked. They were all Kikuyu whose home communities were located within similar rural areas of Central Province.

The Kentucky students were predominantly local: 70.4 percent were born in either the county where they attended school or in a contiguous county, and an additional 5.3 percent were born in another part of Kentucky. Those who were born outside Kentucky, 24.3 percent, came primarily from a neighboring state like Ohio, West Virginia, Indiana, or perhaps Michigan. The mean number of years resident in the county was 13.8, and the mode was 16 (range=1–9, S.D.=5.3). More than 75 percent of the students had lived all or most of their lives in the local area. Judged on the basis of the locations the students identified for their homes, the Kenyan sample was also a predominantly local sample.

The Kentucky sample is heavily working class, although it includes some children of middle class businessmen, managers, and professionals. The students' fathers' mean years of education is 11.6 years (range 0–21, S.D. = 4.08), while their mothers have slightly more education, a mean of 11.9 years (range 3–23, S.D. = 3.58). The adult men and women in the Kikuyu community study had far less education by comparison. The men had a mean of 2.3 years, but a range similar to the Kentuckians' (0–22 years), while the women had a mean of 1 year of education and a more restricted range of 0–6 years. Approximately 50 percent of adult men and women had no formal schooling.

The majority of the Kentucky students come from stable homes: 80.8 percent described their parents as living together. Slightly more than 14 percent described their parents as divorced or separated, and an additional 4.5 percent said one or both parents were deceased. Within the Kikuyu community, divorce or separation was extremely rare; only 3 divorces were recorded among the seventy-four marriages in the community. Nearly 15 percent of the 74 married women in the community shared their husband in a polygynous marriage. This means that some situations that might produce a divorce or separation in Kentucky lead to a polygynous marriage instead in Kenya. Overall, however, polygyny is declining in frequency for both economic and cultural reasons, including the influence of Christianity. A few more parental deaths had occurred in Kentucky than in the Kenyan community, reflecting the dangerous nature of the dominant coal mining occupation.

I have no data for the Kenyans comparable to the data on the Kentucky students' educational and occupational aspirations. These youth are like United States youth as a whole in that they all aspire to at least high school education, but they differ in that fewer aspire to a four year college education. Nationally, about

66 percent of working class youth aspire to four years of college, while only 40 percent of these students say they want a college education (Crowley & Shapiro, 1982, p. 395). Further, although the occupational aspirations of the Kentucky students accurately reflect the occupational structure of the United States as a whole, they are lower than the stated aspirations of American working class youth of the same age, who aspire to high status technical and professional occupations in much higher proportions. Based on national survey data, about 50 percent of American adolescents say they want such occupations, compared to 37.9 percent of this sample. A much lower percentage of the girls said they wanted to be a housewife, only 2.7 percent compared to 24 percent nationally (Shapiro & Crowley, 1982, pp. 35–37). This is a substantial difference and may indicate a significant local shift in girls' aspirations.

RESULTS

I will examine first beliefs and attitudes attached to gender roles in the two samples. Then I will examine the students' attitudes toward those who have been least and most successful in the economic struggle.

The first question the students were asked was "Would people in your community prefer to have sons or daughters?" A summary of the students' answers is presented in Table 4.2. To a striking degree, both eastern Kentucky girls and boys believe that sons are preferred in their community. Sixty-two percent gave that response. Slightly more than 27 percent said that people had no preference, that they wanted both; and only 6.3 percent believed that daughters were preferred.

Table 4.2
Students' Beliefs about Preferred Sex of Children[a]

	Eastern Kentucky		Kenya	
	%	No.	%	No.
Son	62.0	49	38.9	65
Both	27.9	22	52.7	88
Daughter	6.3	5	8.4	14
Unsure	3.8	3	0.0	0

Note: Eastern Kentucky, *n* = 79; Kenya, *n* = 167.

[a] The question as it appeared on the questionnaire was "Would people in your community prefer to have sons or daughters?"

The Kikuyu present a contrast. They reversed the positions of "sons" and "both": 52.7 percent believed that both were preferred, while 38.9 percent felt sons were preferred. The percentage who listed daughters as the preferred category was similar to the Kentuckians: only 8.4 percent saw daughters as preferred. It is notable that youth who have grown up in a system structured by a patrilineal descent system with its explicit male bias, including inheritance rules that bar women from inheriting paternal land, are more likely to say that people value both daughters and sons than youth who have grown up in a bilateral kinship system that lacks gender-aligned descent groups—that is, in a system that treats females and males as equal when counting kin and counts the sexes equal before the law when deciding on inheritance. Suda (1992) describes the same pattern of gender preference expressed by these Kikuyu youth among an ethnically mixed, though predominantly Kalenjin, sample of women in Kericho District. This may indicate that this more gender-balanced pattern is widespread in Kenya. How are we to understand this? Examination of the responses to the next question gives us some help.

The students were asked to describe why sons, daughters, or both were preferred. The Kentuckians said that sons were preferred because first and foremost, "they can work." Next, they are "less worry." Third, they "continue the family line." Fourth, "they are a companion for the father." Fifth, "they can be athletes" and engage in sports. And finally, they just "like boys." When the Kikuyu said sons were preferred, they mentioned such things as "they care for the parents while the daughters leave," they continue the family line and can inherit, they are "more profitable," and finally they can become local leaders. Care of parents and inheritance were also reported as reasons for preferring boys in Suda's (1992) study.

When the Kikuyu were describing the reasons both are desirable, their most common response, they would say "they are both profitable," "they are both useful," and "they are both equal." In contrast, those Kentuckians who gave the "both" response usually followed it with something like, "They don't care what they have as long as they're happy and healthy. People love them both equally." The Kentuckians' responses are more similar in tenor to those Suda reports for her western Kenyan sample than they are to those given by these Kikuyu youth.

Though daughters were the least preferred category, the Kikuyu pointed out that "daughters bring in bridewealth to the family when they marry," that they help with the house and farm work, that they are useful "for reproduction," and that "they give their earnings to their parents." Suda makes a brief reference to a similar recognition among her sample that daughters tend to be more "sensitive and responsive to the needs of their parents than men." The few Kentuckians who felt daughters were preferred said that they could be a companion for the mother, they liked girls, and one believed they were less difficult to deal with than boys.

Notable here is the Kikuyu emphasis on the economic usefulness or "profitability" of children of both sexes, contrasted with the expressive and status enhancement emphasis in the evaluation of children for the Kentuckians. The Kentuckians do note boys' economic usefulness ("They can work"), but the other reasons given for gender preferences reflect different dimensions of interest. Finally, while Suda's predominantly Kalenjin sample shared some of the Kikuyu concern with the value of males in inheritance and the Kentuckians' recognition of their value as workers, they do not seem to be as extreme as the Kikuyu in their emphasis on both genders' profitability.

Responses to other questions also help us understand these students' perceptions of gender roles. Table 4.3 presents a comparison of the students' responses to two pairs of questions: "What kind of man (woman) do people around here respect?" and "What kind of man (woman) does a woman (man) want to marry?" The various responses were grouped for the analysis into two major categories of response. One category coded all responses that reflected an emphasis on individual achievement of status and/or wealth, including traits that are likely to contribute to achievement and status like high levels of education, leadership qualities, intelligence, and so forth. The other category brought together all responses that were reflective of social relational skills and orientations that indicated deference to authority, emphasis on fulfilling traditional role expectations like being a good mother or father, exhibiting moral rectitude, and other personal qualities that enhance social relations like being a loving and caring person.

Comparing the responses to the two questions phrased for men, we can see a dramatic contrast between the eastern Kentuckians and the Kenyans. The eastern Kentuckians, both males and females, place greater emphasis on moral aspects of a person's behavior, attitudes toward authority, and qualities of the person like having a good temperament, being loving and caring, wise and sociable, than do the Kikuyu youth, for whom individual achievement and attaining wealth are apparently paramount. This is particularly striking in their responses to the question about the kind of man a woman wants to marry—over 90 percent of boys and girls gave responses in this category. They are more willing to recognize other values when thinking about the kind of man people respect, but the majority still opt for achievement and wealth.

The eastern Kentuckians repeat their pattern of response for the qualities desired in men in their perceptions of qualities desired in women. The Kikuyu responses have shifted now, and a mixed picture emerges. The Kikuyu students' beliefs about what kind of woman is respected are similar to the Kentuckians' views in this matter—people respect women who demonstrate qualities of moral rectitude, are good mothers, are sociable, and have good temperaments much more than they respect women who are rich and who have achieved high levels of education or other kinds of high status. Although the general pattern is in this direction, there is another interesting aspect to the responses.

The Kikuyu girls and the eastern Kentucky boys are more than twice as likely as the eastern Kentucky girls to believe that women of achievement and wealth are respected (27.4% and 29.7% vs. 12.2%). The pattern becomes even more pronounced when the students are asked to typify the kind of woman a man wants to marry. The Kentucky boys are four and a half times more likely to say a man wants an achieving, high-status wife than the Kentucky girls (34.3% vs. 7.3%); the Kikuyu girls are about four times more likely (29.8% vs. 7.3%); and the Kikuyu boys, who are the most interested in an achieving, high-status wife, are about seven and a half times more likely (55% vs. 7.3%). Within both groups, however, the girls are similar in that they are less likely to believe that a man would want an achieving wife than are their male peers.

Table 4.3

Desirability of Social Relational vs. Individual Achievement Traits for Males and Females, by Student Culture and Gender

		Eastern Kentucky Students				Kenya Students			
		Males		Females		Males		Females	
Question		SR	IND	SR	IND	SR	IND	SR	IND
Kind of man people respect	%	69.4	30.6	80.9	19.1	41.8	58.2	46.6	53.4
	No.	(12)	(11)	(34)	(8)	(33)	(46)	(41)	(47)
Kind of woman people respect	%	70.3	30.6	87.8	12.2	78.1	21.9	72.6	27.4
	No.	(26)	(11)	(36)	(5)	(57)	(16)	(61)	(23)
Kind of man woman wants to marry	%.	71.8	28.2	85.7	14.3	8.2	91.8	9.6	90.4
	No	(23)	(9)	(36)	(6)	(6)	(67)	(8)	(75)
Kind of woman man wants to marry	%.	65.7	34.3	92.7	7.3	45.0	55.0	70.2	29.8
	No	(23)	(12)	(38)	(3)	(36)	(44)	(59)	(25)

Note: SR = Social relational skills, traits, behavioral predispositions like being of good moral character; being a good mother or father; attaining married status; attaining elder status; being obedient to authority; being loving, caring, sensitive; respectful; stable; sociable; good temperament; wise. The Kentucky sample was more likely to mention loving, caring, and sensitivity as desirable traits. IND = Individual achievement, high status, or traits that are likely to contribute to achievement and status. This includes items like high level of education, wealth, high position in society as well as traits like physical attractiveness, leadership qualities, intelligence, etc.

It appears that in both cases there is higher cross-sex agreement regarding gender ideals for males than there is for females. The discrepancy between female and male views for both samples is most extreme for the question about what kind of woman a man wants to marry, and the eastern Kentucky girls are more discrepant in their beliefs overall from their male peers than the Kikuyu girls are from Kikuyu boys.

The gross lumping of responses into the category labeled Social Relational Skills obscured an important difference in the kinds of answers supplied by the two groups of students. While the Kentuckians' most common responses could be classified as representing some aspect of moral rectitude, they also put heavy emphasis on love, loving, and knowing that your prospective spouse loved you and that you loved him or her. The Kikuyu put an emphasis on knowing one's duties and role expectations as a married person and on having an ability to work hard. The ability to work hard was particularly important for women. Further, being physically attractive was most commonly given as a response by the eastern Kentucky girls to the question of what kind of woman a man wanted to marry. It was mentioned by only one of the boys, but several girls mentioned it as a primary attribute (cf. Edwards, this volume; Kilbride & Kilbride, this volume; Munroe & Munroe, this volume; Nasimiyu, this volume; and Weisner, this volume).

Finally, Tables 4.4 and 4.5 give us a glimpse of the students' attitudes toward the poor and the rich. Here I would like to point to the Kentuckians' inclination to say that poor and rich are "the same as others," a response that was absent from the Kikuyu students' repertoire. It is interesting that the Kentucky boys are nearly twice as likely to deny differences—whether of the rich or the poor—than are the Kentucky girls. The literature on the region has often described this tendency to deemphasize differences among people in interpersonal relations, coupled with a marked preference for egalitarian social relationships. The students' responses are also congruent with the value they place on "being nice," loving, caring, and con-

Table 4.4
Students' Beliefs about Community Attitudes toward the Poor[a]

		Eastern Kentucky Students		Kikuyu Students	
		Males ($N = 35$)	Females ($N = 42$)	Males ($N = 81$)	Females ($N = 87$)
Same as others	%	51.1	31.0		
	No.	(20)	(13)		
Pity, should help	%	20.0	47.6	74.4	75.0
	No.	(7)	(20)	(58)	(66)
Worthless, bums, nasty	%	8.6	11.9	20.5	19.0
	No.	(3)	(5)	(16)	(16)
Other	%	14.3	9.5	5.1	6.0
	No.	(5)	(4)	(4)	(2)

[a]The question as it appeared on the questionnaire was "How do people feel about a poor man?"

forming to traditional roles as implied in their ideal gender characterizations described earlier and explicitly stated in their responses to other questions not presented here.

Table 4.5
Students' Beliefs about Community Attitudes toward the Rich[a]

		Eastern Kentucky Students		Kikuyu Students	
		Males ($N = 33$)	Females ($N = 41$)	Males ($N = 81$)	Females ($N = 87$)
Same as others	%	45.5	19.5		
	No.	(15)	(8)		
Jealous, negative	%	24.2	41.5	33.3	33.3
	No.	(8)	(17)	(27)	(29)
Respect, positive	%	18.2	26.8	53.1	58.6
	No.	(6)	(11)	(43)	(51)
Other	%	12.1	12.2	13.6	8.1
	No.	(4)	(5)	(11)	(7)

[a] The question as it appeared on the questionnaire was "How do people feel about a rich man?"

The Kikuyu students were much more likely to respect and feel positively about the rich, a response that is congruent with their positive valuing of wealth and achievement in the earlier questions pertaining to gender ideals. These students were also far more likely than the Kentuckians to feel one should help the poor, though Kentucky girls are more inclined to be helpful than the boys. The Kikuyu are apparently more willing to acknowledge hierarchy and stratification differences. The two groups are not absolutely different, however, since similar proportions in both groups recognize that envy and jealousy are also felt toward the rich, just as there are those who feel the poor are worthless bums and "nasty" (cf. de Wolf, this volume; Håkansson & LeVine, this volume; Kilbride & Kilbride, this volume).

DISCUSSION

The perceived preference patterns for offspring, in combination with gender ideals as reflected in the students' responses to these questions, are reflective of the cultural, social, and economic differences outlined in Table 4.1. Even though Kikuyu culture explicitly privileges males in many ways, it is a culture in which women have real power based in their economic roles as the family farmers; in their role in reproduction, which is highly and explicitly valued; and in the emotional hold they have over their sons, who never leave home. They are an example of a social and cultural arrangement that Peggy Sanday (1981) calls "mythical male dominance."

These Kikuyu students have mothers at home who are proud of their physical strength and ability to do hard physical labor in their gardens, who produce much of the food the family eats through their own labor with help from their children, who haul firewood and water on their backs for the family, who tend coffee trees and milk cows. They have mothers who often see their own interests as different from their husband's interests in marriages that are sometimes congenial and sometimes not, where husbands and wives do not sleep together and often do not eat together. Many students have fathers who live where they have a wage paying job, so far away that they grow up seeing him only every few months for a brief visit—a situation many of their mothers like because it gives them maximum independence in running the farm and rearing their children.

Though most of their families see themselves as Christian, they all know the earlier Kikuyu origin myth that tells a story about a time when women ruled and men were weak. The myth explains how the women were able to stop the men risen in successful rebellion from achieving total symbolic supremacy through changing the feminine names of the nine Kikuyu clans to men's names. The women threatened to kill all their children and said they would refuse to have others if the men changed the clan names. An uneasy truce was achieved, for the women held the ultimate trump card—the men's patrilines cannot continue without the cooperation of nonrelated women, and the women know it (Kenyatta, 1965, pp. 5–10).

This is the cultural context for these Kikuyu students' belief that boys and girls are equally valued and valuable. It is similar in its broad outlines to the other Kenyan cultures discussed in this volume; however, it varies in some of its details in important areas, like women's postmarital retention of membership in their natal patrilineage and women's rights of usufruct in paternal land. Both can have important implications for gender relations in times of marked social change (see Håkansson & LeVine, this volume; Nasimiyu, this volume; Håkansson, forthcoming).

On the other hand, the dominant conservative Christianity of Eastern Kentucky constantly reemphasizes the role of the man as the proper head of the family as prescribed in the Book of Genesis by God, who said to woman, "I will greatly multiply your pain in childbearing; in pain shall you bring forth children, yet your desire shall be for your husband, and he shall rule over you" (Gen.3:16 Revised Standard Version). Farming of any kind is gone today, yet it was a mode of subsistence that gave to earlier generations of women in this area of Kentucky a sense of self-esteem and accomplishment, along with much hard work as they pridefully counted their jars of canned produce from their kitchen gardens and covered their children at night with their skillfully stitched quilts. The county ranks at the bottom of Kentucky's 120 counties in farm productivity. Many people do not plant kitchen gardens each year; many people, especially those living in the remnants of the old coal camps, do not have the ground to garden even if they want to.

The distinctly masculine ethos of the coal industry is pervasive. The local economy, dominated by coal and lean on jobs of any kind, has retarded movement of women into wage-earning jobs. At this time approximately 60 percent of American women with children under 14 work outside the home for wages. Only 40 percent of the mothers of these students have any kind of wage-paying job, and most of those who do work outside the home have low-paying traditional women's jobs as secretaries, clerks, waitresses, and health aides or licensed practical nurses.

It is clear from their responses to other items in the questionnaire that these students continue to believe that a married woman's role is limited to housekeeping, childrearing, and supporting her husband, while they see supporting the family as the primary attribute of the role of husband/father. It is the male economic role that ranks highest among the reasons given for the preference for sons. Within this context it is interesting to note again that very few of the Kentucky girls say they aspire to futures in which they are exclusively housewives.

The discrepancies between the boys' and girls' responses provide another way to view these data. It was noted earlier that overall there is higher cross-sex agreement about gender ideals for males than for females. It was also noted that the Kenyan boys and girls, though discrepant to some extent in their responses to all four questions, were much less so than the Kentucky youth, with the exception of their answers to the question about the kind of woman a man wants to marry. The vast majority of girls in both cultures believe that men want to marry women who conform to the local traditional role for women, a view shared by a much lower proportion of the boys answering these questions. The local roles are not identical; as I've just pointed out, the Kikuyu role provides women with a major role in food production, an attribute shared by western Kenyan traditional and contemporary agricultural societies (Nasimiyu, this volume; de Wolf, this volume) but absent from the Kentucky traditional women's role. Both traditional roles, however, share an emphasis on childrearing, running the home, and taking care of the husband's needs while submerging one's own needs and interests to those of one's children and husband. The husband is given the position of authority in both local traditions.

I can think of two different ways to explain these discrepancies. First, they may have always been there, and all we are tapping in these questionnaire responses are differences in the ongoing male and female versions of the local culture. After all, Kikuyu culture is characterized by a sharp distinction between the world of men and the world of women. Men and women spend very little time with each other outside the domestic setting and not very much time together in that setting. Companionate marriages are not part of their cultural ideal in the traditional scheme of things. This probably gives Kikuyu women a higher degree of emotional independence from their husbands than is typical in the Kentucky marriages. I published an earlier analysis of decision making in families about issues important to the family (Abbott, 1976); in that paper I demonstrated that while they agreed on some issues, men and women are quite discrepant in their views about who should be making decisions in many areas of family life. This can be seen as supportive of the interpretation of separate male and female cultures.

It might be that these Kentucky youth are also simply reflecting an ongoing and long-standing difference in male and female versions of their local culture. There is evidence that some separation exists between males and females in that part of rural Kentucky, though they are less separate in their respective domestic arrangements than the Kikuyu. In most cases these youngsters live in nuclear family households in which their mother and father share a bed and in which the whole family sits down to share at least one, if not more meals each day. The sociable and intimate nature of nuclear family interaction should contribute to greater knowledge about the opposite sexes' beliefs and values on a number of topics, including their preferences for the kind of person they would want for a mate (B. B. Whiting & J. W. M. Whiting, 1975; J. W. M. Whiting & B. B. Whiting, 1975).

Based on this understanding of the differences between rural Kikuyu and rural Kentucky family life and gender roles, I would expect the Kenyan boys and girls to be more discrepant in their beliefs and values than the Kentucky boys and girls. Instead, the reverse is true, with the exception of the question about the kind of mate a man wants, on which the Kentuckians and the Kenyans are equally discrepant. It appears that another explanation is needed.

The second explanation I can offer involves cultural, social, and economic change: Both local communities are undergoing dramatic change that has been fueled by their inclusion in the world economic system and its attendant cultural and social attachments. This change is differentially affecting male and female youth in these two communities, just as it is differentially affecting the two communities, as well as affecting the two communities as a whole.

Prior to the impact of the western world on Kikuyu culture, before the modern nation of Kenya was formed out of the British colonial state, women and men were reared into a set of predominantly ascribed roles, although there was apparently some room for men to achieve some distinction based on their own initiative as warriors and later as elders and through regional trading activities with the Maasai and other groups. That world is gone now, and the old virtues no longer hold. The contemporary Kenyan world places a premium on achieved status based on individual competitiveness (B. Whiting, 1977). Sharon Mitchell and I pointed out in an earlier analysis of the Kikuyu data (Mitchell & Abbott, 1987) that the Kikuyu boys seem to be adapting more readily to these new demands than the girls. We also pointed out that evidence suggested that the girls were under greater pressure in rural areas to continue conforming to the traditional role expectations of Kikuyu women, even if they completed secondary school. The Kenyan data suggest that, in comparison with the boys, the girls are experiencing a great deal of conflict between the expectations and attitudes of their community, which expects them to conform to the traditional female role, while they are being trained in the individualizing, competitive values and attitudes of the new order represented by achievement in school and attainment of a job after school. Differential impact of contemporary change on women and men has been noted for other areas of Kenya (cf. Håkansson & LeVine, this volume; Kilbride & Kilbride, this volume; Nasimiyu, this volume).

Communities in the eastern Kentucky coal fields where these Kentucky youth live are under economic pressure to change a way of life that has been patterned on the labor demands of the coal industry. Thirty percent of these adolescents have fathers directly employed in some aspect of coal mining, and the industry affects every other business in the county. This order seems to have been in place now for about seventy years (Arcury, 1988), so it is about three generations deep. As the grandparents of these adolescents abandoned farming and took up mining, they established a division of labor that required a full-time housekeeper who ran the home and reared the children and maintained the coal miner, who was in the mines twelve hours a day, six and sometimes seven days a week. There were few or no jobs for women outside the home, and there certainly was no role for a woman in the mines.

At the same time, women lost their role as farm wife when they moved into the coal camps. The result was a more constricted role for many women. Now their role is changing again. The coal industry is changing its labor demands; it needs fewer and fewer men to maintain the same levels of productivity. The whole region is struggling to diversify and find alternatives. The county that is home to these students has yet to attract significant alternatives except in the service sector. There are more jobs for women than there used to be, although they are predominantly minimum-wage jobs.

Strong evidence for a desire to change traditional gender roles on the part of the Kentucky girls was pointed out earlier when noting the extremely low number who stated they aspire to an exclusive adult role as a housewife. The discrepancies between the boys' and girls' responses can be seen as a measure of the degree of change currently underway in the local community. It also indicates that change in beliefs and attitudes related to gender roles are changing at different rates among these girls and boys.

CONCLUSIONS

This analysis has provided a comparison of youths' beliefs and attitudes related to some aspects of gender within their respective cultures—rural Kikuyu in Kenya and the eastern Kentucky coal fields' version of rural American culture. In both cases gender roles reflect dominant economic systems and the local division of labor, and they also reflect other aspects of their respective cultures, including the models for gender relations coded in religious beliefs. Neither local culture is static, however, and these data can also be interpreted to reflect ongoing change in both communities, change that is affecting males and females differently.

In August 1992 I returned to Nyeri, Central District, for the first time in twenty years to visit friends in my former research community and to see what changes could be observed. Much has changed, at least on the surface. There has been considerable investment in infrastructure—the main roads are now paved, a major water project has provided piped water to peoples' homes, much more electricity is available and being used, and some people now have telephones. About 20 percent of the homesteads in the community now have stone houses, and many others have replaced their mud-and-wattle houses with timber and concrete dwellings. No thatch roofs remain. Public transportation in all forms is abundant. Many new public buildings have been built, and there are many more schools.

But the population of the country has also increased dramatically in the ensuing years (de Wolf, this volume; Weisner, this volume; Suda, 1992: but cf. Bradley, this volume). The current economic recession coupled with high inflation has created real stress for everyone. An article in the *Daily Nation* on August 1, 1992 (p. 15) estimated that four million school leavers are jobless—a frightening figure. I wonder how students today in the same secondary schools I visited twenty years ago would respond to the questionnaire? Would they still value attaining wealth and the personal traits required to attain it and to get ahead in life in a very competitive, tough economic environment that more and more is going to require an entrepreneurial outlook to be successful? Or have they reacted and adapted as the Kentucky students have to a low-opportunity local economy by emphasizing the expressive role relations in the extended family, the smoothing out of hierarchy, and the denial of stratification differences? Edwards (this volume) presents convincing evidence that core values associated with family living like respect, harmony, interdependence, and unity have remained strong across generations. Her study overlapped mine in time. Would she get the same results today?

And what has happened to their perceptions of gender roles? People I talked with told me that more women are buying land for themselves if they have the resources to do so. There are clearly more secondary schooling opportunities for girls in the area than there were. Women have been the backbone and the heart of many of the development projects and home improvements in the area, getting the men mobilized as well as donating their personal funds and providing labor. Are secondary school girls feeling as much role strain as they were twenty years ago? Do they experience the same pressure as before to conform to traditional roles in the rural areas? I was told that many now refuse to marry, that they would rather just take care of themselves and their children and not have a dependent man to take care of as well. Others in this volume also report a decline in marriage rates, or at least significant delay in time of first marriage, for women, and increases in the numbers of young women having babies outside approved marriages (Bradley, this volume; Kilbride & Kilbride, this volume; Håkansson & LeVine, this volume). So this change extends beyond Central Province.

In continuing the discussion on contemporary life in my former research site, one woman commented that, in many cases, having a man in one's life was like having another child around the house. She held the opinion that many men had become irresponsible and just spent their money on themselves, drinking it up and forgetting their wives and children. A man in the same conversation countered that the problem with many men was the lack of work, not some fundamental flaw in their values and their character. How are these opinions expressed by middle-aged, world-weary adults affecting contemporary youth, for they surely hear them expressed? Are they more cynical about their relationships with their boyfriends and girlfriends, or do they ignore the difficulties they see in their parents' relationships and other men's and women's relationships with each other?

Robert and Ruth Munroe (this volume) argue that strong gender differentiation has been retained among the Maragoli despite some adjustments made to behavioral contingencies, like the need to adjust assignment of childhood chores to meet the new time demands of school. They point out that this emphasis on gender distinction is an identified culture complex in most of traditional Africa, one that demonstrates great tenacity. If this is so, then gender roles will be particularly resistant to change. I have also pointed out the apparent stability of traditional Kikuyu gender roles, at least up to the mid-1970s (Abbott & Arcury, 1977). The changed economic conditions simply act to increase the strain in the social relations of men and women, who are pursuing separate and sometimes contradictory strategies, as Håkansson and LeVine (this volume) outline for the Gusii. One can see this strain in the conversation recounted above. An option some seem to be selecting is to lead even more separate lives, though de Wolf (this volume) hints at a different strategy adopted by many Bukusu, one that involves adoption of a model of closer cooperation within the household.

I have no answers to these questions, but new research among secondary school students across the country can help provide answers. Kenya's youth are Kenya's future. The economic, political, and cultural forces that I have suggested are most important in bringing about change among the Kikuyu in Central Province affect all of Kenya's ethnic groups, as the other chapters in this volume illustrate. They are indeed global forces, as the Kilbrides and I have emphasized by our inclusion of comparative material drawn from American research. Descriptions of Kenyan youths' values and attitudes related to gender, family, and stratification can be used to document current cultural and social change in Kenya and as part of the basic data for writing Kenyan cultural and social history. They can also be used as the basis for social policy recommendations to government. Despite recent publications like Hollos and Leis's *Becoming Nigerian in Ijo Society* (1989) and Worthman's Kikuyu adolescent studies (Worthman, 1986; Worthman & Whiting, 1987), adolescents remain a neglected population for research in Kenya and throughout all of Africa.

NOTES

Funding for the Kikuyu field research was provided by the Carnegie Corporation through the Child Development Research Unit, Harvard University and the University of Nairobi, John W. M. and Beatrice B. Whiting, Directors. These data were collected between August 1971 and December 1972. The eastern Kentucky field research was funded through an Appalachian Studies Fellowship and through two grants from the University of Kentucky Research Committee. The data were collected between February and August 1987. The 1992 trip was funded in part by a travel grant from the University of Kentucky. Data analysis was funded by the University of Kentucky. I want to thank the students and school authorities in both research locations for their cooperation and help in making this research possible. I also want to thank Helen Crawford for her help in manuscript preparation.

1. Kenya followed the British model of school structure when these data were collected. Kenyan schools are now being shifted from the British model to a different model of primary and high schools called the 8-4-4 system.

2. Sixty-six percent of the questionnaires from one of the three high schools were unusable. It was clear from the students' responses that they refused to cooperate in filling out the questionnaire, and more boys refused than girls. I can only speculate on the reasons for that. The questionnaire was given on the last day or two of classes before dismissal for summer vacation, and it is probable that the teachers did not frame the task in a convincing way

to students whose only interest was leaving as soon as possible. There were no difficulties of this kind in the other two schools—in one 100 percent of the questionnaires were usable (the one I directly supervised), and in the other they were 95 percent usable. Because of the problem with the students' attitude toward the task in the first school, the analysis of the values questions for this paper is limited to the subset of questionnaires from the two schools where no difficulties were encountered, although the demographic data are based on the total set of usable questionnaires.

REFERENCES

Abbott, Susan. (1976). Full-time farmers and weekend wives: An analysis of altering conjugal roles. *Journal of Marriage and the Family, 38*, 165–174.

Abbott, Susan. (1980). Power among the Kikuyu: Domestic and extra-domestic resources and strategies. In Lucille Harten, Claude Warren, & Donald Tuohy (Eds.), *Anthropological papers in honor of Earl H. Swanson, Jr.* (pp. 8–14). Pocatello, ID: Idaho State University Museum.

Abbott, Susan. (1988). Symptoms of anxiety and depression among eastern Kentucky adolescents: Insights from comparative fieldwork. *Proceedings of the Third Annual University of Kentucky Conference on Appalachia: Health in Appalachia* (pp. 102–115). Lexington, KY: Appalachian Center.

Abbott, Susan. (1992). Holding on and pushing away: Comparative perspectives on an eastern Kentucky childrearing practice. *Ethos, 20*, 33–65.

Abbott, Susan, & Arcury, Thomas. (1977). Continuity with tradition: Male and female in Gikuyu culture. *Youth and Society, 8*, 329–358.

Abbott, Susan, & Klein, Ruben. (1979). Depression and anxiety among rural Kikuyu in Kenya. *Ethos, 7*, 161–188.

Arcury, Thomas A. (1988). *Agricultural diversity and change in industrializing Appalachia: An ecological analysis of eastern Kentucky, 1880 to 1910* (CDC Development Paper, No. 23). Lexington: University of Kentucky, Center for Developmental Change.

Crowley, Joan E., & Shapiro, David. (1982). Aspirations and expectations of youth in the United States. Part I. Education and Fertility. *Youth and Society, 13*, 391–422.

Edgerton, Robert. (1971). *The individual in cultural adaptation: A study of four East African peoples*. Berkeley: University of California Press.

Håkansson, N. Thomas. (1994). The detachability of women. *American Ethnologist,* 21, 516–538.

Hollos, Marida, & Leis, Philip E. (1989). *Becoming Nigerian in Ijo society*. New Brunswick: Rutgers University Press.

Kenyatta, Jomo. (1965). *Facing Mt. Kenya*. New York: Vintage Books.

Loevinger, Jane, & Wessler, Ruth. (1976). *Measuring ego development* (Vol.1). San Francisco: Jossey-Bass.

Macmillan, A. M. (1957). The health opinion survey: Technique for estimating prevalence of psychoneurotic and related types of disorder in communities. *Psychological Reports, 3*, 325–339.

Mitchell, Sharon, & Abbott, Susan. (1987). Gender and symptoms of depression and anxiety among Kikuyu secondary school students in Kenya. *Social Science and Medicine, 24*, 303–316.

Sanday, Peggy Reeves. (1981). *Female power and male dominance: On the origins of sexual inequality*. Cambridge: Cambridge University Press.

Schwarzweller, H. K., Brown, James, & Mangalam, J. J. (1971). *Mountain families in transition: A case study of Appalachian migration.* University Park: Pennsylvania State University Press.

Shapiro, David, & Crowley, Joan E. (1982b). Aspirations and expectations of youth in the United States. Part II. Employment activity. *Youth and Society*, 14, 33–58.

Suda, Colette A. (1992). *Fertility and the status of women in Kericho District: A cultural interpretation.* Paper presented at the Conference on Ecological Change and Human Development, in Western Kenya, Kakamega, Kenya.

Weisner, Thomas S., & Abbott, Susan. (1977). Women, modernity, and stress: Three contrasting contexts for change in East Africa. *Journal of Anthropological Research, 33,* 421–451.

Whiting, Beatrice B. (1977). Changing life styles in Kenya. *Daedalus, 106,* 211–226.

Whiting, Beatrice B., and John W. M. Whiting (1975). *Children of six cultures: A psychocultural analysis.* Cambridge, MA: Harvard University Press.

Whiting, John W. M., & Whiting, Beatrice B. (1975). Aloofness and intimacy of husbands and wives: A cross-cultural study. *Ethos, 3,* 183–207.

Worthman, Carol M. (1986). Developmental dyssynchrony as normative experience: Kikuyu adolescents. In J. Lancaster & B. Hamburg (Eds.), *School-age pregnancy and parenthood: Biosocial dimensions* (pp. 95–112). New York: Academic Press.

Worthman, Carol M., & Whiting, John W. M. (1987). Social change in adolescent sexual behavior, mate selection, and premarital pregnancy rates in a Kikuyu community. *Ethos, 15,* 145–165.

HEALTH

5

HIV/AIDS Risk Factors and Changing Sexual Practices in Kenya

A.B.C. Ocholla-Ayayo

There were 25,000 AIDS cases worldwide by 1988, and an additional five to ten million people were infected with the human immunodeficiency virus (HIV) (World Health Organization, 1988). Sub-Saharan Africa, with 10 percent of the world's population, had 30 percent of the world's HIV-positive cases (Caldwell, 1989; Bongaarts, 1988, p. 1). It was estimated that the incidence of acquired immune deficiency syndrome (AIDS)–related deaths in Africa would be around twenty-five per thousand by the year 2000 (World Health Organization, 1987). This death rate is comparable to that of the Black Death in fourteenth century Europe or that of the post–World War I influenza epidemic at the height of the outbreak in India (Caldwell, 1989).

Kenya reported 964 AIDS cases in 1987. The national rate was 4.31 per 100,000. Urban areas had 19.94 cases per 1,000 (World Health Organization, 1987). By 1990, Kenya had reported more than 3,500 confirmed cases (National AIDS Control Programme, 1990). By 1991, this had risen to 10,500 confirmed AIDS cases; and by 1992, there were 50,000 cases (Ministry of Planning and National Development, September 1993). Two thirds of these were in urban centers, led by Mombasa, Kisumu, and Nairobi.

The origin and spread of the AIDS pandemic in Africa, and in Kenya in particular, has been the subject of much debate, both academic and political. Scholars such as Caldwell (1989) focused on sociocultural factors particular to Africa and their relationship to the rapid spread of AIDS and HIV in Africa. Caldwell argued that "the African model is more vulnerable to spread of HIV virus than the Eurasian one" (Caldwell, 1989, p. 5). In contrast to western countries, where the population at risk was generally more defined and identifiable—at that time linked primarily to male homosexuality and drug abuse—Caldwell noted, AIDS in Africa is spread more diffusely throughout the heterosexual population. Citing Goody's (1973) comparison of African and Eurasian systems, Caldwell attributed the high incidence of AIDS in Africa to traditional African marriage systems, which included weak conjugal bonds, polygyny, and few sanctions on premarital and extramarital sex and pregnancy. The European and Asian models of marriage had strong conjugal bonds, monogamy, and a high value placed on virginity. Caldwell and Caldwell (1990) later argued that both the high HIV prevalence rate and higher fertility in Africa could be attributed ultimately to these kinds of basic cultural differences.

Some African scholars thoroughly disagreed (Waite, 1988). A variety of responses were published, arguing specifically against the notion that Africans traditionally were more promiscuous than people on other continents (Waite, 1988, p. 36). For example, Waite (1988, p. 1) stated that "most of the stereotypes were based on myths ... there was nothing inherent in African practices to support the allegation that sexual excesses were wide spread." Brokensha (1988) held a similar position. It was noted that prostitution is common and institutionalized in both Europe and Asia (Waite, 1988; Ocholla-Ayayo, 1989). Evidence suggests that premarital relations were prohibited in many African traditional systems. Premarital and extramarital liaisons have only become a way of life in the wake of colonialization and modernization, accompanied by new found individualism and the erosion of traditional norms (Ocholla-Ayayo, 1970, 1976, 1989). In contrast, sexual abstinence has never been quite as firmly anchored on other continents and sanctions against pre- and extramarital sex have weakened everywhere during the twentieth century. It is no accident that when parallels are sought for African adolescent sexuality, the comparable statistics come from contemporary American cities (Cherlin & Riley, 1986; Kilbride & Kilbride, this volume).

These African objections to a model that attributes differences in the spread of HIV to contrasting historical patterns of marriage and sexuality have been largely ignored to this point, and few responses have been published in North America. Caldwell and Caldwell (1990) later replied to these concerns that the objections came from African elites whose values had been transformed by Christianity. They also argued that the original article had not mentioned promiscuity. However, some African scholars continue to feel that the model portrays black Africans as more promiscuous and less moral than Eurasians. In this chapter, data are presented suggesting that current sexual practices in Kenya are largely artifacts of modernization, not elements of traditional Kenyan society.

Other responses to AIDS in Kenya had economic and political implications. In 1988, after the first AIDS cases in Kenya were reported by the foreign press, British sailors docked at Mombasa were not permitted to go ashore. Legislators in Kenya lodged protests with appropriate political authorities over this action, arguing that it was a kind of racism. The Kenya Medical Association may have known that there were AIDS cases in Kenya but have tried to cover up the extent of the problem for the sake of Kenya's tourist industry, the country's most important source of revenue.

British authorities knew that sailors and prostitutes were inseparable and that prostitutes and their customers had among the highest HIV rates worldwide. In Kenya, the lowest status prostitutes had twice the estimated seroprevalence rate of high-status prostitutes (Kreiss, Koech, Plummer, 1986). This led some tour operators to monitor the movements of warships around Mombasa or to provide their clientele with "good-time girls" transported from up-country, where they were more likely to be free of sexually transmitted diseases (STDs) and AIDS (Ocholla-Ayayo, 1991, p. 28).

The paranoia about AIDS among travelers to Africa was underscored by publications in the United States and Europe, which speculated that the HIV virus might have originated in Africa, a debate irrelevant to its spread among travelers. The epidemiology of AIDS in Kenya suggests that HIV spreads from urban to rural areas and that the virus probably came into Kenya from elsewhere. Kenya's major cities are the world's getaway spots. Mombasa is a major gateway from the Indian Ocean. Cross-border migration between Uganda, Tanzania, and Kenya have contributed to its spread. Truck drivers are known to spread the HIV virus into Kenya, especially from Uganda and Tanzania (Bronkensha, 1988). Truck drivers from Rwanda and Burundi cross Tanzania and Uganda before they reach Mombasa. On this journey of several weeks and through several countries, they make many stops, spreading [illegible] HIV virus as they go (Ocholla-Ayayo & Schwarz, 1991).

The spread of AIDS [illegible]a today has multiple causes. These are simultaneously social, econo[illegible]ral. There is a desperate need for sophisticated behavioral, socioeconomic, and sociocultural research on sexuality in Kenya. Such research is likely to reveal behavior patterns and social networks of interactions more intricate and multifarious than we have realized. The data to be presented here will suggest that the individual risk of infection increases in Kenya with the adoption of a modern lifestyle, not the maintenance of a traditional one.

Why is AIDS/HIV more prevalent in Africa than elsewhere? It is true that in Kenya heterosexual partners are involved in a wider variety of marriage forms, including polygyny. Widow inheritance, or leviratic marriage, was a feature of traditional African society that may be disappearing, but divorce and separation have increased with modernization. There is also more sexual freedom, which has come about through the breakdown of traditional authority. Rules of conduct that used to surround sex and reproduction in many Kenyan ethnic groups have eroded. Control over young people has decreased, resulting in high rates of premarital pregnancy, illegal abortion, and high HIV-positive rates among secondary school students in some parts of Kenya. There are more casual prostitutes today than at any time in Kenyan history, perhaps because of unstable economic conditions. In Kenya's major cities, including Nairobi, Mombasa, and Kisumu, street prostitutes wait for motorists to pick them up.

In this chapter I examine several of these risk factors and their relation to beliefs about the nature of sexuality in Kenya, both today and in the past.

THE STUDY

The data reported here come from a larger project titled "Sexual Practices and the Risk of the Spread of HIV/AIDS and other STDs in Kenya." They provide evidence of changing attitudes and behaviors regarding sexuality in Kenya. One of the goals of the larger study was to investigate the determinants of, and beliefs about, indiscriminate and casual sex in Kenya and to provide information that may help in the prevention of AIDS and other STDs. The data presented here focus on beliefs about changing behaviors that may contribute to high HIV and AIDS rates in Kenya.

Most of the data presented here come from a survey of 10,340 respondents in 3,600 Kenyan households. Three or four persons were interviewed in each household.[1] These households were in eight districts (South Nyanza, Kisumu, Busia, Nairobi, Kajiado, Machakos, Nyeri, and Mombasa), and included twenty-nine different ethnic groups. The majority of the respondents were from four major Kenyan ethnic groups: Luo (29%), Kikuyu (20%), Luyia (18%), and Kamba (13%). Focus-group discussions provided additional information to supplement the survey.[2] In this chapter, we focus mainly on the findings from the survey, supplemented by information obtained in the focus groups.

POLYGYNY

One of the explanations proposed for the high incidence of AIDS in Africa is that polygynous marriages promote the spread of HIV. It is argued that multiple marriage partners increase the size of networks through which HIV is spread. In addition, polygyny is thought to promote extramarital sexual relations, as younger women seek sexual satisfaction that their older, weaker husbands cannot provide. If there is competition among the cowives about the number and sex of children, some cowives may seek conception outside marriage. As I will show later in this paper, there is evidence that extramarital liaisons are more likely to happen nowadays than in the past (Kilbride & Kilbride, this volume). The institution of polygyny, which is widespread in Africa and usually not found in the Eurasian system (Caldwell 1989), is undergoing a variety of other transformations in contemporary Kenya. These changes have serious implications for the spread of STDs.

There is some evidence that polygyny rates are actually declining in Africa (Shapera, 1971, for Botswana during the 1960s). Data from Kenya show that polygyny decreases as the level of education increases (Kenya 1979 census, Central Bureau of Statistics, 1984, 1989). The rate of erosion of polygyny in Kenya is difficult to assess. Moslem communities in Kenya continue to have institutionalized polygyny. Mosley, Linda, and Becker (1982) report that in 1979, 33 percent of Kenya women lived in polygynous marriages. Kosminski (1985) found that 59 percent of married women in South Nyanza in Kisumu district lived in polygynous marriages. The highest polygyny rates in Kenya are in Western and Coast provinces. However, polygyny rates differ widely even within these regions.

Other evidence suggests that polygyny is increasing in Kenya (see Ssennyonga, this volume). Ocholla-Ayayo and Makoteku (1989) found that the number of polygynous marriages is higher than expected among the Kikuyu, who were thought to practice less polygyny than other Kenyan ethnic groups. This became evident through data that demonstrated that Kikuyus isolate wives in different parts of the same locality or in different towns throughout the district, resulting in an underestimation of the number of polygynous marriages in the region. Ocholla-Ayayo and Makoteku (1989) also found that girls who drop out of school were more likely to join polygynous marriages. They argue that this trend may maintain polygyny for some time.

In the survey sample for the study we report here, 67 percent of the respondents were married, 24 percent were single, and 5 percent were divorced or separated, and the other 4 percent did not specify their status. Of those who were married, 45 percent were in monogamous unions, but only 10 percent stated they were in polygynous marriages.[3] Polygyny may be underreported in this sample, possibly because Christian churches in Kenya often do not recognize polygynous unions.

EXTRAMARITAL SEXUALITY

In Kenya, economic necessity demands that a high proportion of men in the rural areas go to cities to look for work. The men, as well as their wives left behind in the countryside, may develop new sexual relationships outside the union. The longer the husbands stay away, the more tempting it is to establish sexual relationships that are more covert than premarital sexual relations. These may end up as a second union.

The fertility of monogamously married women in Kenya is generally lower than that of polygynous women. Polygynous marriages may allow for women who have recently given birth to maintain a longer postpartum abstinence period, because the husband can turn to the second wife for sex. This practice would seem to lead to lower fertility. However, extramarital relationships on the part of polygynous women may eventually level out these fertility differences.

Data from the survey show that over 64 percent of the respondents had had sex at least once a week during the preceding four weeks. Most (56%) had sex with their regular partners, while 8 percent had sex with casual partners. In addition, 7 percent had sex with both regular and casual partners. Data on coital frequency from the survey indicate that there is indeed a high level of sexual activity in the population (Table 5.1).

Table 5.1
Coital Frequency in Four Weeks Preceding Survey

Frequency	No. of Cases	Percentage
Once a week	3072	29.7
Twice a week	2009	19.4
More than twice a week	1450	14.4
Don't remember	1492	14.4
Not stated	2317	22.4

Note: $N = 10{,}340$.

Acquah (1958) reports that some school girls in West Africa have sexual relations to pay their school fees, and female employees find in casual sexual relationships another source of income. Kenya is not immune to this practice (e. g., Ocholla-Ayayo & Muganzi, 1987; Ocholla-Ayayo & Ogutu, 1986; and others). Obbo (1987) found that non-elite Kenyan women have sexual relations outside marriage to meet their specific needs. Gomini reports of the Digo of Kenya's coast that "[t]he best opportunity a married woman has for obtaining cash independently from her husband is by committing adultery" (1972, p. 101). Since illicit sexual relations can be conducted secretly, the money the woman obtains can go unnoticed by her husband. Bleek (1976) reports for West Africa that no self-respecting woman would remain in a "friendship" without material compensation. In Kenya, few women would pay the expenses of an evening out with a man, no matter how rich they might be.

The focus-group discussions indicate that people believe that traditional values and norms related to sexual behavior have eroded. Focus group participants felt it was more difficult to enforce traditional norms because of increased intertribal marriage, urban–rural interactions, and interethnic education. Most participants agreed that extramarital affairs are common. One group estimated that up to 25 percent of married people in their area engaged in extramarital sex. They attributed the change to education and to the introduction of western culture, including television, video, cinemas, drinking, pornography, discos, and dancing. A few groups cited increased access to contraceptives as a factor contributing to increased sexual activity. They also argued that wealthier people are more involved in casual sexual liaisons. The most common explanation for women's extramarital affairs were additional income and other material benefits, as well as the desire to become pregnant.

Survey results concur with the focus groups. The majority of the respondents (69%) felt that traditional norms restricting premarital and extramarital sex are no longer applicable in Kenya.Table 5.2 shows survey respondents' opinions about extramarital sex. For the majority of the respondents, extramarital sex is never acceptable, especially for themselves. However, the rationale behind this may not be related to morality. Participants in the focus groups were more concerned about the consequences of premarital sex or sex outside of marriage—pregnancy, STDs, and AIDS—than they were about the morality of the sex act itself.

ADOLESCENT SEXUALITY AND PREMARITAL SEX

Adolescents now constitute 20 percent to 25 percent of Kenya's population. These adolescents will represent a substantial portion of the labor force within the next fifteen years. The prevalence of HIV among some secondary students in parts of western Kenya indicates a seropositive rate of 14 percent to 16 percent. Although this region may have a higher HIV-positive rate among young people than other parts of Kenya, possibly because of an overall higher HIV rate due to the proximity to international truck routes, such data suggest that adolescent sexuality is a clear threat to Kenya's future economic security.

Table 5.2
Distribution of Respondents' Views on Extramarital Sex

Attitude	No. of Cases	Percentage
Just okay other	1266	12.2
Never okay other	2877	27.8
No opinion other	498	4.8
Just okay personal	1223	11.8
Never okay personal	4196	40.6
No response personal	175	1.7
Not stated	105	1.1

The data on adolescent fertility and abortion in Kenya provide a clue to the incidence of premarital sex. Mati and Ngoka (1983) found that adolescent fertility was 18 percent in Nairobi, 10 percent in Machakos, 27 percent in Kisumu, and 9 percent in Mombasa. Bradley (in press) found that 16 percent of young unmarried women in a Maragoli sublocation were living at home with their children. A study by Ocholla-Ayayo and Osiemo (1989, p. 24–28) shows that forty-three districts in Kenya have single mothers with an average of more than four children per woman. In Western Kenya, single mothers may leave their children with parents in the rural areas and move to Kisumu or other urban centers in search of employment, only to return later with a second or a third child (Bradley, in press; Kilbride & Kilbride, this volume). Similar data are available for other districts (see Ocholla-Ayayo, 1992a; Ocholla-Ayayo & Ogutu, 1986; Ocholla-Ayayo, Lema, Obudho, Muganzi, Suda, Njau, & Khasakala, 1991).

Since abortion is not legal in Kenya, many girls who try to end their pregnancies subsequently present at hospitals with septic abortions. This is a problem in both rural and urban settings (Mati & Ngoka, 1983; Aggarwal & Mati, 1983). For example, Rogo (1992) and Lema (1987) report that 28 percent of the cases of induced abortions at Kenyatta National Hospital in 1982 were girls under nineteen years.

The sociocultural and economic changes which have taken place in the last 30 years have deprived many societies of their moral or institutional barriers to premarital and extramarital sex. In western Kenya it is common for elders and parents to decry the incidence of premarital sex by young people, as well as the adolescent pregnancies that follow. Elderly people say they are dubbed "walking corpses by the youth over whom the old people have no power." Husbands blame wives and wives blame husbands for lack of authority over the youth (Muganzi & Ocholla-Ayayo, 1987; Ocholla-Ayayo & Ogutu, 1984–1985).

There is considerable evidence that premarital sex was not condoned precolonially among many Kenyan ethnic groups. Among ethnic groups that circumcised girls, sexual relationships before circumcision were uncommon. Nowadays, it is common for some girls to become pregnant before the age of circumcision. As a consequence, the Nandi circumcise girls early to prevent pregnancy prior to circumcision (Ocholla-Ayayo, 1992b). Among the Luo, many old women and men still point out that premarital virginity was important to fertility. It was seen as a sign of purity that forced a man to treat his wife with honor and respect. A traditional Luo woman who was not found a virgin at the time of marriage would live with that stigma, to be whispered about by her cowives. Her virginity, or lack of it, would even come up during the marriage of her daughter (Ocholla-Ayayo, 1976, 1981). Parkin (1973, p. 324) maintains that "the Luo girls in Kenya were traditionally expected to remain chaste although this is no longer the case." Parkin (1973) and Ocholla-Ayayo (1979, 1985) report that premarital pregnancy is no longer considered a disgrace to the Luo family because it is now so common. Similar statements have been made about the Gusii (Mayer, 1973), Akamba (Kabwegyere & Mbula (1979), Logoli (Wagner, 1949, Bradley, in press), and Bukusu (Bradley, in press).

Focus group participants agreed that, in most traditional societies in Kenya, brides were expected to be virgins and premarital sex was not permitted. These rules were supported by sanctions that included payment to the family of the girl who was violated and, in the case of marriage, either return of the bride found not to be a virgin or reduced bridewealth at marriage.

Premarital sexual liaisons may take place out in the fields, in boarding school dormitories, in open public houses, and in lodges—places out of reach of the authority of elders. Over 60 percent of the survey respondents in this study believe that young people frequent bars, lodges, and brothels. The data also indicate that men are much more likely to go to these places than women. Elders assert that night dances also provide an opportunity for meeting and for gratifying sexual feeling. Increased independence and political freedom were enjoyed by girls and boys in the colonial era. Freedom from traditional sexual rigidity is associated with political freedom and independence. The contemporary notion that not all courtship must lead to marriage is contrary to most traditional and religious expectations.

In Kenya, boys and girls in both rural and urban areas engage in premarital sex, but cultural norms in Kenya, both traditional and Christian or Moslem, have prevented full recognition of the extent to which this occurs. Kiragu (1989, p. 4) states, "Whether we like it or not, the children in the study area [Rift Valley Province] are sexually active and they begin at a very early age." The average age at first intercourse was eleven years. Ocholla-Ayayo and Ogutu (1986) reported that a large number of teenagers are sexually experienced, a fact that Kenyan society is generally reluctant to accept because of its moral implications. Kiragu notes that Kenyans prefer to think that all young people will wait until marriage to have sex, even though few adults were themselves virgins at marriage (Kiragu, 1989, p.6).

Our findings indicate sexual activity among children eleven years old and younger. Table 5.3 presents data on age and sexual activity. Although the most sexual activity takes place in the twenty to twenty-four year age group, there is considerable sexual activity among those who are much younger. Furthermore, teenage sex often involves multiple partners, in that boyfriends or girlfriends are not retained for long periods of time. Girls change boys, boys change girls, and in the course they are both at risk to acquire and spread HIV/AIDS.

Table 5.3
Percentage of Respondents' Sexual Activity by Age

Age Group	No Sexual Activity	Regular Partner Only	Casual Partner Only	Both	ISI[a]
10–14	58.1	35.5	6.5	0.0	6.5
15–19	54.1	30.6	9.7	5.6	15.3
20–24	30.1	52.2	10.2	7.5	17.2
25–39	18.6	67.6	4.2	3.2	7.4

[a] Indiscriminate Sex Index is the sum of percentages of respondents who had sex with casual partners and those who had sex with their regular partners as well as with casual partners.

Over 80 percent of survey respondents felt that less than 10 percent of girls are virgins at marriage. People no longer see virginity as virtue, and the stigma attached to the violation of premarital sexual norms has lost its meaning. We also see in Table 5.4 that the number of respondents who felt premarital sex was acceptable matched those who did not. Obviously, the rules or norms restricting premarital sex do not apply today in Kenya.

Table 5.4
Distribution of Respondents on Their Attitude toward Premarital Sex

Attitude/View	No. of Cases	Percentage
Public Opinion		
Just OK for others	2970	28.7
Never OK for others	3041	29.4
No opinion about others	410	4.0
Personal Opinion		
Just OK for self	1679	16.2
Never OK for self	1936	18.7
No response about self	149	1.4
Not stated	155	1.5

One of the most surprising results of the survey was that many respondents believe girls had sex for money and other economic gain (Table 5.5).

Premarital sexuality is also related to religious affiliation. For example, Arena (1973) found that among the Mto wa Mbu in northern Tanzania, Christian girls were more likely to engage in premarital sex than the Moslem girls and that they were more likely to become barmaids than the Muslim girls. The same could be true in Kenya. Schapera (1971, p. 241) reported of Botswana that even "the most regular church goers among the younger people do not regard it as wrong to indulge in sexual relations, provided that they can avoid conception." In Kenya, many girls of staunch Christian parents have ended up as single mothers with more than one child (Ocholla-Ayayo, 1991; Juma, 1992). Juma (1992), in a study

Table 5.5
Reasons Given by Respondents for Girls Having Sex with Men in Their Community

Reasons	No. of Cases	%
Money (economic)	4635	44.8
Gifts (economic)	989	9.6
Sexual experience	818	7.9
Leisure (social satisfaction)	1128	10.9
Love (socio-psycho-instinct)	1010	9.8
Sociocultural motive	751	7.2
Don't know	1009	9.8

in Nyakach, reported that almost every homestead had a single mother or a girl who was expecting, regardless of religious faith or social status. However, our data show a decline in indiscriminate sexual activity with higher levels of religiosity (Table 5.6). We do not have data on actual religious affiliation, however.

Table 5.6
Respondents' Sexual Activity According to Religiosity

Religiosity	No Sexual Activity %	Regular Partner Only %	Casual Partner Only %	Both %	ISI[a] %
Very important	31.3	57.8	7.1	3.8	10.9
Somewhat important	26.7	55.3	8.3	9.7	18.0
Not important	27.7	40.8	14.4	18.1	32.5

[a] Indiscriminate Sex Index is the sum of percentages of respondents who had sex with casual partners and those who had sex with their regular partners as well as with casual partners.

Although it is obvious that young people in Kenya engage in premarital sex in previously unsuspected numbers, their awareness of AIDS and other STDs is also considerable. The data on knowledge of AIDS and other STDs demonstrates a high level of awareness for both men and women in this sample. Ninety percent of young people under the age of twenty-four knew about AIDS, and nearly as many in other age groups had heard of AIDS. Those who were most educated had the highest level of awareness.

Despite the tendency for Kenyan society to be conservative about acknowledging the degree to which young people engage in premarital sex, focus-group participants felt AIDS education in the schools was very important. The young people were the strongest supporters of increased sex education and access to contraceptives, including condoms, in the school setting. Some focus-group participants suggested that young people should be taken to hospitals to be shown people dying of AIDS. They also felt that parents should be more involved in talking to their children about sex.

Although some focus group participants felt that people have changed their attitudes toward sex with many partners and have reduced the number of partners they have, most felt that adolescents, young people, and prostitutes were less likely to change their behavior. There is widespread recognition that young people learn by experience and that even a school-based education campaign would not be successful in convincing students to change.

OCCUPATION AND INDISCRIMINATE SEX

The indiscriminate sex index (ISI) is the percentage of respondents who had sex with both casual partners and regular partners plus the percentage of the partners who had sex with casual partners (see Table 5.7). The group with the highest ISI is the unemployed, 19.9 percent. The seasonally employed and students are also target groups, with high ISIs of 17.4 percent and 17.1 percent respectively. The most worrisome thing is that there is no safe employment or profession. All are likely to have or spread HIV.

Table 5.7
Distribution of Respondents by Occupation by Chance Survival and Chance Extinction

Occupation	Chance Survival SA%	Chance Extinction ISI%
Farmers	87.2	12.8
Armed forces personnel	86.5	14.7
Drivers	84.0	15.5
Manual workers	85.9	14.1
Sales/Service workers	85.6	14.4
Clinical personnel	87.0	13.0
Professional managers	87.3	12.7
Self employed	84.6	15.4

HOW KENYANS VIEW AIDS

Our focus-group discussions provide considerable insight into how Kenyans see AIDS. As the data have shown, nearly all the respondents knew about AIDS. The main sources of information about AIDS were radio, television, newspapers, and other people (friends). In some groups, participants had seen AIDS victims, and their knowledge about it increased through these contacts. Health workers and teachers were rarely cited as sources.

In Kenya, AIDS is known by a variety of nicknames. These include *ayaki*, *chira*, *slim*, *usaidizi*, *saidia*, *sichola*, *ihira*, and *ukimwii*. Among the older groups, the transmission of AIDS was sometimes associated with violation of cultural norms governing sexual relations—people who got AIDS were those who engaged in premarital and/or extramarital sexual relationships. *Chira* is the disease associated with transgressions due to extramarital sexual relationships.

Although many people had heard of AIDS, the majority of them were not sure of what AIDS actually is. They knew that AIDS is a sexually transmitted disease and that it can also be transmitted through blood transfusions and injections with infected needles. In every group, a number of participants suggested that AIDS can also be transmitted through kissing, shaking hands, contact with an AIDS victim, breathing a victim's air, mosquito bites, and the sharing of glasses or dishes. Some respondents viewed AIDS as an advanced stage of other STDs and the result of incomplete/incompetent therapy. A few participants in each group knew that a person could have AIDS and yet be free of symptoms for an extended period.

Knowledge of the symptoms of AIDS was widespread. The most commonly mentioned symptoms included extreme weight loss, diarrhea, cough, prolonged fever, and scaly or dry skin. Others mentioned loss of energy, fatigue, joint pains, and red lips. Some participants in the rural areas associate women with painted lips with AIDS. Lip painting is less common among or unknown to most rural women.

Most people believed that AIDS was brought to Kenya from outside by foreigners such as tourists and truck drivers. People from America, Europe, Uganda, Tanzania, Zaire, and Rwanda, along with Kenyans returning from abroad were often cited as the source of the AIDS virus. Prostitutes were singled out as major carriers of the disease. Some participants in each group, especially in western Kenya, believed that AIDS is imported in food, used clothes, and medicines. Medical doctors were cited in a few groups as contributing to AIDS transmission. Several individuals said that private physicians interested in maximizing profit reused needles without sterilizing or changing them.

People offered a variety of solutions to the AIDS pandemic in Kenya. They suggested use of condoms, screening of blood, sterilization of syringes, single use of disposable needles, intensification of education on AIDS, and the establishment of special medical facilities for people dying of AIDS. The most common suggestion was that people should limit their partners, a practice referred to as "zero grazing." This term comes from a practice in the more crowded rural areas of feeding cattle in a confined area rather than letting them graze everywhere. This means, in this context, that people should stick with one partner.

Participants in some groups had rather strong suggestions, including testing for all tourists, identification and confinement of all carriers, and closing down of bars and brothels. Some even recommended killing people who had the virus. Participants in several districts recommended that the government pass laws to regulate sexual immorality, particularly prostitution. They also suggested more job opportunities for the unemployed, especially prostitutes and women. In many groups there were some participants who wanted the government to take a hard line with single and married men and women, including those with children, who persist in indiscriminate sexual relations.

CONCLUSION

The data presented in this paper indicate that there have been changes in the way Kenyans view premarital and extramarital sexual relations. Relationships that were unacceptable in the past are now widely practiced in the modern setting. Contrary to Caldwell's models comparing African with Eurasian systems, the extent to which Kenyans engage in premarital and extramarital relations is mostly an artifact of modernization and westernization, not an element of traditional Kenyan society. Although AIDS awareness is high, it is clear that indiscriminate sexual activity has not declined. The degree to which people engage in premarital and extramarital relationships without regard to their own health indicates that the AIDS pandemic in Africa will not be solved without drastic measures.

NOTES

1. Some might argue that individuals within the same household do not constitute independent observations and should thus be separated for statistical analysis. However, given communication networks at the community and national level, as well as intrahousehold tensions (e.g., between cowives, generations of in-laws, or husband and wife), it is not clear that individuals within households are any more "connected" than those between households. This may be especially relevant to Africa. See Watkins (in press) for a discussion of the relationship between gossip and fertility decline in Europe or Kilbride and Kilbride's (1990) discussion of "delocalization" in Kenya and Uganda, for example.

2. The survey population consisted of males and females mostly between the ages of fifteen and forty-nine years, selected by random and cluster sampling. Females constituted 52.8 percent of the respondents. The majority of the respondents (90%) were ages fifteen to thirty-nine, less than 1 percent were ten to fourteen, and 10 percent were over age forty. More than half (54%) had completed secondary school, 36 percent had primary educations, and 9 percent had no schooling. More than half (60 percent) were employed either regularly or seasonally. Two thirds felt that religion was an important part of their lives. We included questions on level of education, ethnicity, marital status, type of marriage, religion, religiosity, and recreational activities.

3. Forty-five percent of those surveyed did not respond to this question.

REFERENCES

Acquah, I. (1958). *Accra survey by West African Institute of Social and Economic Research, 1952–1956*. London: London University Press.

Aggarwal, V. P., & Mati, J. K. G. (1983). *Obstetrics outcome of adolescent pregnancy*. Nairobi: Kenya Medical Report, Ministry of Health.

Arena, W. (1973). Mto wa Mbu, a multi-ethnic community in northern Tanzania. In A. Molnos (Ed.), *Cultural source materials for population planning in East Africa, Vol.3: Beliefs and practices*. Nairobi: Institute of African Studies, University of Nairobi.

Bleek, W. (1976). *Sexual relationships and birth control in Ghana: A study in Rural Town, Amsterdam*. Center for Social Anthropology, University of Amsterdam.

Bongaarts, J. (1988). *Modeling the spread of HIV and the demographic impact of AIDS in Africa* (Working Paper No. 140). New York: Center for Policy Studies.

Bradley, C. (in press). Women's empowerment and fertility decline in western Kenya. In Susan Greenhalgh (Ed.), *The anthropology of fertility: Remaking demographic analysis*. Cambridge: Cambridge University Press.

Brokensha, D. (1988). Social factors in the transmission and control of AIDS in Africa. In N. Miller & R. C. Rockwell (Eds.), *AIDS in Africa: The social and policy impact* (pp. 167–173). Lewiston/Queenston: Edwin Mellen Press.

Caldwell, J. (1989). *Disaster in an alternative civilization: The social dimension of AIDS in sub-Saharan Africa demographic centre.* Canberra: Health Transition Centre, National Centre for Epidemiology and Population Health, Australian National University.

Caldwell, J., & Caldwell, P. (1990). High fertility in sub-Saharan Africa. *Scientific American, 262*(May), 118–125.

Central Bureau of Statistics. (1984). *Kenya contraceptive prevalence survey (KCPS).* Nairobi: Ministry of Planning.

Central Bureau of Statistics. (1989). *Kenya demographic and health survey (KDHS).* Nairobi: Ministry of Planning.

Cherlin, A., & Riley, N. E. (1986). *Adolescent fertility: An emerging issue in sub-Saharan Africa* (PHN Technical Note 86–23). Washington, DC: World Bank.

Gomini, R. (1972). Harlots and bachelors: Marital instability among the coastal Digo of Kenya. *Man 7, 1*, 95–113.

Goody, J. (1973). Bridewealth and dowry in Africa and Eurasia. In J. Goody and S. J. Tambiah (Eds.), *Bridewealth and dowry* (pp. 1–58). Cambridge: Cambridge University Press.

Juma, M. A. (1992). *Adolescent fertility in Nyakach, Kisumu District.* Unpublished master's thesis, Policy Studies and Research Institute, University of Nairobi.

Kabwegyere, T. B., & Mbula, J., (1979). *A case of the Akamba of eastern Kenya.* Canberra: Health Transition Centre, National Centre for Epidemiology and Population Health, Australian National University.

Kilbride, P. L., & Kilbride, J. C. (1990). *Changing family life in East Africa: Women and children at risk.* University Park: Pennsylvania State University Press.

Kiragu, Karungari. (1989). *Adolescent fertility in Kenya.* Preliminary research report, Department of Population Dynamics, Johns Hopkins University.

Kosminski, S. (1985). *Family planning and child nutrition in south Nyanza District.* Department of Community Health, University of Nairobi.

Kreiss, D., Koech, D., & Plummer, E. (1986). *AIDS in Kenya.* Nairobi: Medical Research Institute.

Lema, V. M. (1987). *A study of knowledge, attitude and use of contraception with relation to sexual knowledge and behaviour amongst adolescent secondary school girls in a cosmopolitan city in Africa.* Unpublished Master of Medicine thesis, Department of Community Health, University of Nairobi.

Mati, J. K. G., & Ngoka, W. M. (1983). The Nairobi Birth Survey IV: Early perinatal mortality rate. *Journal of Obstetrics and Gynecology, East and Central Africa*, 2, 129.

Mayer, I. (1973). The Gusii of western Kenya (South Nyanza). In Molnos (Ed.), *Cultural sources for population planning in East Africa* (pp. 97–113). Nairobi: Institute of African Studies, University of Nairobi.

Ministry of Planning and National Development. (September, 1993). *Guidelines for the HIV/AIDS chapter in the 1994–1996 District Development Plans.* Nairobi: Office of the Vice President and Ministry of Planning and National Development.

Mosley, H. W., Linda, W., & Becker, S. (1982). *The dynamics of birth spacing and marital fertility in Kenya* (Scientific Report No. 30). New York: World Fertility Survey.

National AIDS Control Programme. (1990). *AIDS in Kenya*. Nairobi: Ministry of Health.

Obbo, C. (1987). The old and the new in East African elite marriages. In D. J. Parkin & D. Nyamwaya (Eds.), *Transformations of African marriages* (pp. 263–280). Manchester: Manchester University Press.

Ocholla-Ayayo, A. B.C. (1970). *Evolution of man and his culture in Kenya*. Unpublished master's thesis, Prague University.

Ocholla-Ayayo, A. B. C. (1976). *Traditional ideology and ethics among the southern Luo*. Uppsala: SIAS, Uppsala University.

Ocholla-Ayayo, A. B. C. (1979). *Marriage and cattle exchange among the Luo* (Paideuma Occasional Paper). Frankfurt: Forbenus Institute.

Ocholla-Ayayo, A. B. C. (1981). *Female migration and wealth dissipation among the exogamous communities in southern Kenya*. Population Studies and Research Institute, University of Nairobi.

Ocholla-Ayayo, A. B. C. (1985). *Culture and social dynamics of population control in Africa south of Sahara*. Paper presented at the African Regional Youth Workshop on Population Awareness, Nairobi.

Ocholla-Ayayo, A. B. C. (1989). *The impact of kinship ties in the process of urban growth in Kenya*. Paper presented at the International Workshop on Urban Development in Rural Context in Africa, Uppsala, Sept. 14–17.

Ocholla-Ayayo, A. B. C. (1991). *The spirit of a nation: An analysis of policy, ethics and customary rules of conduct for regulating fertility levels in Kenya*. Nairobi: Shirikon Publishers.

Ocholla-Ayayo, A. B. C. (1992a). *A change in sexual practices and the risk of the spread of HIV/AIDS in Kenya*. Paper presented at the workshop on Changing Families and Ecology in Contemporary Western Kenya, Nairobi, Kenya, August 5–7.

Ocholla-Ayayo, A. B. C. (1992b). *The magnitude of indiscriminate sexual practices and the risk of the spread of HIV/AIDS in Kenya*. Paper presented at the workshop on the Socioeconomic Impact of AIDS in East and Central Africa in Kenya, Nairobi, July 8–10.

Ocholla-Ayayo, A. B. C., Lema, V., Obudho, R., Muganzi, Z., Suda, C., Njau, P, & Khasakala, A. (1992). *Final research report on sexual practices and the risk of the spread of AIDS and other STDs in Kenya*. Nairobi: Population Studies and Research Institute, University of Nairobi.

Ocholla-Ayayo, A. B. C., & Makoteku, J. M. (1989). *Marriage pattern and fertility differential in Kenya*. Nairobi: Population Studies and Research Institute, University of Nairobi.

Ocholla-Ayayo, A. B. C., & Muganzi, Z. (1987). *Marriage patterns as fertility determinants with differential effect in Kenya*. Nairobi: Population Studies and Research Institute, University of Nairobi.

Ocholla-Ayayo, A. B. C., & Ogutu, G. E. M. (1984–1985). Preliminary report on the impact of religious and socio-cultural values on rural transformation. Nairobi: Population Studies and Research Institute, University of Nairobi.

Ocholla-Ayayo, A. B. C., & Ogutu, G. E. M. (1986). *A joint study on the impact of socio-cultural values and religion on rural transformation*. Nairobi: Population Studies and Research Institute and Department of Religious Studies, University of Nairobi.

Ocholla-Ayayo, A. B. C., & Osiemo, J. A. O. (1989). Sociocultural dynamics of fertility change and differential in Kenya. *Kenya Journal of Sciences Series C*, 2(1), pp. 15–24.

Ocholla-Ayayo, A. B. C., & Schwarz, R. A. (1991). *Preliminary research report on sex practices and the spread of AIDS and STDs in Kenya*. Nairobi: Population Studies and Research Institute, University of Nairobi.

Parkin, D. J. (1973). The Luo living in Kampala, Uganda, Nairobi and Central Nyanza, Kenya. In A. Malnos (Ed.), *Cultural source materials for population planning in East Africa, Vol. 3: Beliefs and practices* (pp. 330–339). Nairobi: Institute of African Studies, University of Nairobi.

Rogo, K. (1992). *Adolescent sex: Its difficulties and danger. An outline for clinical personnel, parents, and teachers*. Nairobi: Kenya Medical Association and Ministry of Health.

Schapera, I. (1971). *Married life in an African tribe*. Harmondsworth: Penguin. (Originally published in 1940).

Ssennyonga, Joseph. (1978). *Population growth and cultural inventory: The Maragoli case*. Unpublished doctoral dissertation, University of Sussex, Sussex.

Wagner, G. (1949). *The Bantu of Northern Kavivondu, Vol.1*. Oxford: Oxford University Press.

Waite, G. (1988). The politics of disease: The AIDS virus and Africa. In N. Miller & R. C. Rockwell (Eds.), *AIDS in Africa: The social and policy impact* (pp. 145–164). Lewiston/Queenston: Edwin Mellen Press.

Watkins, S. C. (in press). Social integration and social change: The pace of fertility decline in England and France. In Susan Greenhalgh (Ed.), *The anthropology of fertility: Remaking demographic analysis*. Cambridge: Cambridge University Press.

World Health Organization. (1987). The AIDS epidemic in Africa. Vienna: WHO Publications

World Health Organization. (1988). *Guidelines for nursing management of people infected with Human Immunodeficiency Virus (HIV)* (WHO AIDS Series, No. 3, pp. 1–42). Geneva: World Health Organization.

World Health Organization. (1989). *The AIDS epidemic and its demographic consequences*. Proceedings of the UN/WHO Workshop on Modeling the Demographic Impact of AIDS in Pattern II Countries: Progress to Date and Policies for Future, December 13–15, New York.

6

The Social and Cultural Contexts of Food Production in Uganda and Kenya

Michael A. Whyte

In western Kenya—and elsewhere in East Africa—subsistence agriculture has increasingly tended towards "monoculture" of maize and/or cassava; in recent years local food production has not always been sufficient for local needs. Across the border, in southeastern Uganda, maize is merely one of a number of cash crops, and the system of food production that exists today is varied and productive, providing for local subsistence as well as a significant export. In this paper I explore the local social and cultural contexts in which "monoculture" and "multiculture" have developed. I emphasize the economic, social, and above all the cultural factors that have led to this state of affairs.

In 1979 my wife and I were carrying out field research from a base in Marachi Location, western Kenya. We avidly followed the events leading to the fall of Idi Amin on the BBC, supplementing this at times meager source with trips to Busia on the border for firsthand information. By May the road to eastern Uganda was open, and we leapt at the chance to return to Bunyole, where we had made our first field study from 1969 to 1971. That visit was a joyful occasion, a long round of visits and meals and beer and talking. There was food aplenty, millet, potatoes, bananas, and even rice, not to mention groundnuts, beans, and vegetables.

When we left to return to Kenya, friends in Bunyole loaded our car up with all gifts of food, including five chickens and two kilos of freshly pounded sesame packed in banana leaves. We were overwhelmed, and so too were our Kenyan friends when we unloaded our bounty in Marachi. In the village where we were staying, the maize crop was still too green to be picked, and most households had long since run out of last season's supplies. Whole families were living on supplies bought for them by a relative with a job. Some—usually female headed households—were living from day to day on the proceeds of beer selling, trade, or agricultural day-labor. Everybody had been eating only maize porridge and greens for months.

Local residents considered this seasonal food shortage to be the normal state of affairs. All agreed that, in the past, things had been different—but it was not at all clear *when* this self-sufficient past had been. Instead of years, people spoke in terms of crops: "Before the maize came, we had food enough."

It is certainly true that in western Kenya the one-time staples, millet and sorghum, have given way to maize and cassava, with hybrid maize winning increasing popularity (Ongaro, 1988). The process has been gradual; Thompson's glowing description of agricultural bounty and diversity in 1884 is echoed by Gunter Wagner, writing fifty years later. However, by that time *zea mays* (introduced in 1923) had become the dominant grain (Wagner, 1970, vol. 2, p. 19). The variety of subsidiary crops of all sorts seems to have diminished, with maize–cassava dominance having become more absolute (see for example Wagner, 1970, vol. 2, p. 36; Hay, 1972; Ominde, 1971; Republic of Kenya, 1977). Across the border in eastern Uganda, maize had always been a minor crop. By 1979 it was being grown more readily, not least in order to take advantage of seasonal, informal, and illegal markets in Kenya. Today, still more maize is grown in Uganda, primarily as a cash crop. In Bunyole, however, it is still only one of many cash crops: there, as in Uganda generally, maize is still not a food of preference.

This contrast in farming systems was not the point of my Kenyan research, but it had been on my mind for a number of months as the result of a series of conversations with the manager of the only bottled beer bar in the sublocation. He was a Munyole refugee from Uganda and a keen farmer; we spent a great deal of time discussing the state of agriculture in Marachi. My friend insisted that the main problem with farming in Marachi was the Marachi farmer—man or woman. He insisted that they were both bad farmers, technically unimaginative, and (dare I quote him?) lazy, unwilling to work hard enough. The land, he insisted, was even more fertile here than in Bunyole; just as large a variety of crops could be grown. He "proved" his point by acquiring some land and establishing, among other things, a flourishing banana plantation. All sorts of crops grew well for my friend and his wife and, indeed, for a handful of farmers in each Marachi village I came to know who seemed to have a similar attitude toward agriculture. But the vast majority continued to plant their maize, their cassava, and beans—and continued to run short of food months before the next harvest. Of course, the point at issue is not "laziness." The Marachi men and women with whom I lived and worked were certainly not layabouts. They were instead investing time and energy differently; their farming system was the result, not of indolence, but of choices made.

Why should there have been so great a contrast in farming systems? One major difference between eastern Uganda and western Kenya is summed up in the oppositions peasant farmer/migrant laborer (Brett, 1973; Whyte & Whyte 1985). These have been the alternatives presented to Ugandans and Kenyans for the last seventy years. Western Kenya has long been a pool of labor, feeding plantations, farms, industries, and slums. Most of Uganda, certainly most of eastern Uganda, became part of the economy of cash cropping: coffee, cotton, tea, and tobacco. Yet too much should not be deduced directly from such general patterns of political economy. The effects on agriculture of the withdrawal of male labor are clearly significant, but no such logic of production *dictates* the status of the western Kenyan agricultural economy. Cotton cultivation, which structured agriculture and economic life in Bunyole from 1920 to 1975, was profitable only so long as no one had to use the cotton cash for food. But could food self-sufficiency not have been achieved with maize and cassava? Marachi and Banyole today are not simply products of their respective economic histories; they are also actors. Over the generations they have helped to create their economies by pursuing their own ideas and ideals. (For examples from western Kenya, see de Wolf, this volume; Hay, 1972; Kongstad & Mönsted, 1980; Super & Harkness, this volume; and Cohen & Odhiambo, 1989). Abanyole—men and women—take pride in agriculture and express this pride in the variety of food they produce. Today, fifteen years after the collapse of cotton as a cash crop, Abanyole have created a new agricultural economy based on selling food—rice, beans, millet, cocoyams, groundnuts, sesame, sunflower, onions. Relative to the general state of affairs in Uganda, this new, decentralized economy is booming (Whyte, 1988, 1990a, 1990b). Nonetheless, Abanyole appear impoverished even by Marachi standards when it comes to access to things—from semiluxuries such as perfumed soap, bottled beer, or new clothing to bicycles (and their spares), tools and utensils of all kinds, or "inputs" such as fertilizer and insecticide.

The contrast between Abanyole and Abamarachi as peasants and workers pursuing their respective strategies is a useful way to begin to understand the meaning of agricultural diversity—so long as we remember that the very pursuit of these strategies is culturally and socially creative in unintended ways (Barth, 1989, pp. 34–5). In the following discussion I shall contrast material from Bunyole (before and after the Amin coup) and Marachi, drawing on fieldwork and the results of return visits to both places in 1987 and, in Uganda, material collected by Susan Whyte in 1989 and 1990. I examine differences in the culture of agriculture, in terms of (1) local autonomy, (2) gender and culture, (3) the symbolic role of agriculture and, by way of conclusion, (4) some speculations on the role of agricultural skills and knowledge.

First of all, a few ethnographic signposts. Abanyole and Abamarachi speak related Luyia languages and share a number of cultural features. Named, totemic patrilineal clans are central to male and female identity; clan and family provide a framework for most of social life. Marriage is viri-patrilocal, with men owning/controlling land and with women—as daughters, sisters, wives, and mothers—gaining use rights through men. Population density is high in both places: 100–150/km^2 in Marachi (Ominde, 1971) and 114/km^2 in Bunyole (calculated on the 1969 Census [Republic of Uganda, 1971]). Both peoples live in regions of moderate soil fertility; Marachi is well drained by a number of streams and rivers, while Bunyole is altogether flatter, bounded by broad papyrus-choked "rivers" and interspersed with seasonal swamps. There are also a number of more or less subtle differences in cultural practice and social organization; clan and kin terminology differ, as do beliefs and practices concerning the supernatural and the treatment of misfortune (Whyte & Whyte, 1985, 1981). The two groups were never part of a precolonial unity.

LOCAL AUTONOMY AND AGRICULTURAL DIVERSITY

For the last ninety years (at least), Abanyole and Abamarachi have lived in "villages" that are simply areas of dispersed households, each surrounded by its fields and fallow. Both regions were noted for their productive and varied indigenous agriculture. Crop diversity at the household level was thus the rule in both places up through the 1920s, as we have seen. Bunyole households continue to cultivate a wide variety of crops to the present day; cultivation intensity in Marachi has followed the pattern of decline and loss of variety common to western Kenya as a whole. Indeed, Marachi has gone through a number of ups and downs, a final brief florescence just before independence being followed by a steady decline in agriculture generally (Ogutu, 1979).

Crop diversity within a household is, of course, not simply a matter of choosing more plants. Household farming systems are complex, based on a balancing out of factors such as soil fertility, cropping sequences, and intercropping strategies to maximize ground cover while avoiding pests and excessive labor. Such farming systems are integrated solutions to a variety of technical problems (Anthony, Johnston, Jones, & Uchendu, 1979; Low, 1986). Changes in the diversity of household production on the order of what we have seen in western Kenya are apt to represent degradation of a total farming system and not mere simplification.

It is also useful to look at another kind of diversity—at the village level. Just as household diversity is related to farming systems, the degree to which a village's households chose different cropping strategies can be a sign of the larger economic–political system in which farming takes place. Surveys carried out in 1970 in Bunyole and 1979 in Marachi show distinct patterns. In Bunyole, practically everybody in the villages surveyed grew the same mix of cotton and major crops. What variation did exist at this crude level was accounted for by the position of the household in the development cycle. However, had the survey been planned and carried out by Banyole, significant variation at another level would have been recorded. Most larger households included a number of individuals who maintained separate fields and granaries and who pursued slightly different cropping strategies. Furthermore, men and, especially, women were continuously experimenting with and evaluating their food production through the selection of seeds and cuttings as well as through exchanges. Today Bunyole villages contain households as well as individuals who are pursuing more radically different cropping strategies. For some, seasonal cultivation of rice paddy (for sale and consumption) is the focus of activity; for others a more traditional blend of cereals, oil seeds, and pulses is preferred. Every household, however, does sell some food as a cash crop, a major innovation and, given that food crop prices have very nearly kept pace with inflation as a whole, a rather good business. Yet, as already noted, few if any households have chosen to specialize to the point where they were no longer *self-sufficient* in a variety of foods.

In Marachi, diversity at village level is a long-standing pattern. As in Bunyole, it is related to the position of a household in the development cycle, but it is also related to the different "migration cycles" in which households find themselves (cf. Weisner, this volume). Because the personnel of households can change dramatically from season to season (wives or sons' wives leave to join husbands in town, men return home from work in order to "rest" for a season or a year), it is difficult to predict the intensity of agricultural activity from household to household. (Although change in personnel is high in households, older generations do tend to stay in the village and provide continuity.)

Our neighbor (in 1979) had been "resting" from his normal work in the building industry in 1978; the result was a bumper crop of maize and groundnuts. Money earned in 1977 paid for seed, plowing, and fertilizer. In 1979 money was short, our neighbor worked most of the year and had time only on occasional weekends, and considerably less maize was planted that year—without benefit of chemicals. Our neighbor's wives ran short of food and turned to brewing to make ends meet; there was less time to weed and to prepare new fields.

In addition to elaborations on "migrant cycles," Marachi villages often contained one or two households of people who did not migrate, choosing instead to devote full time to their agriculture. Such families approached, in the variety of their agriculture, the Nyole norm. However, much of their economy was based on producing food to sell for consumption and seed to their neighbors. Such households were at times in a position to *buy* newly harvested maize from households with immediate cash needs; four months later, members of the families who had sold maize returned to buy their own crop back again for food or seed. Although many Abamarachi did indeed appear to be indifferent farmers, some were known for their skill and for the variety of seeds they possessed. A well looked after set of fields was a thing to be proud of in Marachi as well as Bunyole, but it was far less common to find someone choosing that particular route to security. In our village survey in 1979, two out of three households had food (maize) deficits in each season; four out of five bought one sack or more of maize; two (out of fifty) had grown and sold maize as a major cash crop.

GENDER CULTURE AND CROPS

Margaret Jean Hay (1972) has provided a detailed economic history of Kowe, another Location in western Kenya. There she shows how gender separation in agriculture increases as men shift their labor from farming to migrant work. Their wives are left literally holding the hoe, and many choose to drop it as quickly as possible in order to take up activities that bring in more cash and provide more independence. It is sometimes suggested that women heads of households in migrant labor regimes do at least gain some measure of autonomy; in western Kenya and with respect to agriculture, they are simply overworked. The loss of agricultural diversity in this region is a mark of autonomy *lost*, as women are increasingly pressed into short-term strategies—trading, brewing, distilling, craft production, or casual labor—designed to insure family reproduction and, in some cases, survival (cf. Nasimiyu, this volume). Their agriculture tends to become simply one more necessary strategy, a means to an end. In Bunyole, on the other hand, women *do* have a degree of autonomy and flexibility. One reason for this is that the farming system itself is more nearly autonomous in terms of marketing and freedom from central control and, most important, in terms of being a significant activity for both sexes. There is no established pattern of male migration, and household decisions about farming are not set against these larger concerns. Because women in Bunyole are not solely responsible for food production, they have more room to maneuver; because they are not the only producers in their households, female agriculture can express and reflect different strategies and abilities. In Bunyole, women have "their" crops—such as cow peas—which are theirs not because men have abandoned cultivation, but because the crop and its rituals expresses something women find important about their femininity.

SKILLS, KNOWLEDGE, AND CROP DIVERSITY

As noted, agriculture in Bunyole and, indeed, in much of Uganda, has changed greatly in the past generation. New crops and new marketing forms have been adopted. Food crops, the special province of women, are now some of the most attractive cash crops. Farmers, both men and women, have drawn on local knowledge of varieties, soil types, and so forth. They have also drawn on their traditions for local, household experimentation with seeds and varieties.

With respect to knowledge and skills, the comparison of cotton and, especially, hybrid maize is instructive. Both crops are "packaged." Seed, together with fertilizers and insecticides and cultivation directives, is bought or distributed each year. "Improvements" are made by research establishments out of sight of the local farm and never as a result of local experimentation. In Uganda, a precondition for cotton cultivation was food self-sufficiency. In this sense, the industrial element in cotton cultivation—"follow the directions"—was counterbalanced by an inspired creativity in food crop production. Food crops, locally consumed, represented a partial—and in the end a real—independence from the national economy. It was the misfortune of maize that it was edible. Unlike cotton, which assumed a complementary subsistence agriculture, maize (with cassava and greens) could be eaten at home as well as sold. Given the other constraints and pressures upon western Kenyans, local agriculture become less complex, less diverse, more maize dependent. The spread of hybrid maize is simply one further step away from autonomous agriculture.

The notion of de-skilling (Braverman, 1974, pp. 424–449), usually discussed in relation to the transformation from industrial craft to mass production, is perhaps relevant here. Skilled labor, in industry and in agriculture, can be defined in terms of worker autonomy, the structuring and disposition of one's labor in terms of experience. Semiskilled or unskilled labor is less autonomous, needing direction and organization; in industrial contexts it is also cheaper, more flexible, and less powerful. De-skilling is then the process of reorganizing production so that control passes from skilled worker to managers and machines. A diverse agricultural economy such as that found in Bunyole is based on local skills and knowledge. Cotton cultivation was an attempt to "semi-industrialize" one part of local agriculture—ignoring local experience and stressing centrally determined "good cotton practices." Yet because the cash cropping of cotton assumed subsistence cultivation of food, the local agricultural skills of farmers were preserved together with food crop diversity. When the Ugandan state began to lose control of cotton marketing and, indeed, of the national economy, farmers in many parts of southern Uganda were in a position to exploit this de facto decentralization, drawing on skills, knowledge, and a lifetime experience with seed selection, evaluation, and experimentation.

In western Kenya it appears that something resembling de-skilling—the loss of producer autonomy—has occurred. Hybrid maize cultivation is a case in point. But more generally the reduction in crop diversity that had begun many years before was a sign of a farming system which was losing its autonomy, becoming one component of a national system of production. Again the contrast with cotton is instructive. In Uganda, men and women cultivated cotton "for the government," but they did so together, at home, as part of a complex farming system that combined food and cash crops. In western Kenya, men were drawn into wage employment away from home, while their wives attempted to maintain a labor-starved agricultural economy at home.

THE MEANING OF FOOD AND CROPS

There is no place here to begin to cover the ritual elaboration of agriculture in any detail. As might be expected, such rituals persist in Bunyole: first fruits ceremonies within the household, neighborhood "food priests" (*abasengi b'emere*) who carry out fertility ceremonies, neighborhood rainmakers who are paid a cess from each household to do the same. At the level of impressions, much ceremony in Bunyole has to do with sacrifice, which is meant to draw attention to prayer and which involves blood and meat but also millet porridge, sesame, and beer. Prayers almost always end with blessings, which have to do with food, plenty, and fertility.

The cotton cultivators of Bunyole grew and consumed a variety of foods, of which millet, cow peas, and sweet potatoes have a special mythological status. The first clans to enter Bunyole are associated with these food crops. Of the three, millet was surely felt to be most important by the Nyole, and power over this crop was the prerogative of the senior Nyole clan, the sign of its preeminence. But the real point of three foods and three clans has to do with cooperation and interdependence, not hierarchy. Just as all three foods (and indeed many more) were combined to form a farming system, so too the three original clans (and eventually more than two hundred others) were also interdependent (see Whyte, 1990a).

From the 1930s to 1975, millet was grown as universally as cotton (and seldom marketed). But millet alone was not enough to live on; just as important was having a variety of foods—not merely from season to season, but also to choose from at any one time. Guests would be offered at least two staples and a number of relishes, and this without straining household resources. This variety of foods is directly related to crop diversity. Variety, because it is satisfying, and diversity, because it is a hedge against disaster, are both explicit goals of producers. Maize, however, was seldom grown and even more rarely eaten by choice.

For Banyole, as for most southern Ugandans as late as the end of the 1970s, maize porridge (*ugali*) was a dish for school children, prisoners, and other institutionalized unfortunates. Even maize beer was in a sense institutional; it was sold only at the weekly markets. In Kenya, on the other hand, maize meal is the national food; it is eaten in villages and towns, by farmers and by workers. To have one's own homegrown maize is good, but a sack of maize from Kitale or Busia will also do. What is important is to have maize enough so that the basic meal can be prepared.

The symbolism of maize is connected to its role as food. *Posho*, the flour that was a part of so many wage contracts, and *ugali*, the food itself, are metonymic of twentieth century life. In this sense maize/*posho*/*ugali*, with its market status, its history as a traded commodity, its status as the food of the workplace and the traveller, connects country households to the economic history of Kenya, to modern life, consumption, and the market. Ugandan disdain is in part directed to this generality. Eating maize—every day—emphasizes too great a connectedness, too little autonomy, too much of a surrender to the "European" categories of the colonial past: beef and potatoes for whites; chapatis, rice, and curries for Asians; *ugali* and greens for Africans. In Uganda, and certainly in Bunyole, value is placed on staple foods produced in a family context. Being self-sufficient in a variety of staples and relishes is what marks the good life.

ONE FOOD OR MANY? A FINAL WORD ABOUT POSSIBLE FUTURES

I began with my friend Mr. Wanjala and his observations on western Kenyan agriculture. I want to close with another "long conversation," one that runs through the year spent in Marachi. Many Marachi men and some women had lived in Uganda for extended periods during the 1950s to the 1970s, working in industry, construction, or the service sector in Jinja, Kampala, and a variety of smaller towns such as Iganga or Mukono. They spoke with some nostalgia about Uganda, and most insisted that, if only the money were worth anything, they would return straight away, despite Idi Amin. At the same time, many were not sanguine about the future prospects for their own country. They feared a coup (not unreasonably in 1979) and the devastation it could bring. We will starve here, they insisted. "We are not like Uganda, where there is lots of food in the countryside. If we [Marachi] are all sent home from work there will not be enough food."

Country life had become harder, more hand to mouth. A young friend provided me with a particularly apt illustration.

> When I was a child [late 1960s–early 1970s] we owned cattle, and we were given milk-tea before we went off to school in the mornings. In that time there were not as many *mabati* houses and people did not dress as well, but my mother had a bag of money buried under

her bed. Today the children here [in this lineage] do not taste milk; there are few cows left and the milk is sold. In the morning before school they may get a bit of *ugali* left from the evening meal. My mother no longer has her bag of money.

Yet it is this very realization of connectedness that may be of utmost importance to Kenya's political as well as economic future. At least in western Kenya, people seem quite clear that there is no way back to local self-sufficiency (cf. Kilbride & Kilbride on "delocalization," this volume). There is also no point in mourning the loss of that farming system that so delighted Joseph Thompson a hundred years ago. At least for the short term, it makes sense to construct a future based on joining more fully an extant national culture and national economy. The other side of de-skilling is, of course, adaptability.

For Banyole, caught in the success of their decentralized food production, autonomy is still the name of the game. Families seek both to exploit the new markets for "nontraditional cash crops" and to avoid buying food themselves. The Nyole "economic miracle" is part of the Ugandan miracle, where mere survival is an achievement of some note. Nyole, in common with other Ugandans, have responded to the collapse of state marketing institutions in a dramatic way, and in so doing they have pointed the way to new relationships between state and local society. Yet here, too, there are challenges, for changes have occurred that are unlikely to be reversed. Banyole in their success have left behind the protective uniformity of the cash and subsistence farming system of the pre-Amin eras. Village diversity is becoming an established norm, as farmers seek to build on their knowledge and experience in order to exploit specific marketing niches. Agriculture, which once provided a kind of mechanical agricultural solidarity, is now "hot"; success in rice or castor beans brings in the capital needed to expand or intensify production. The less successful can make ends meet by providing their labor. It is ironic that success in this new, decentralized economy, where prices are more farmer favorable than ever before, may mean the establishment of the kind of rural class structure that Banyole had avoided since the beginning of the colonial era.

Gender issues have also come to the fore here as in the rest of the country. The Nyole domestic economy, based for so many years on self-sufficiency and cooperation between man and wife/wives, rested on a distinction between cotton, the inedible cash crop, and food, the responsibility of wives and mothers. Nowadays, Mother's sack of rice or millet may be appropriated and "spent" on school fees or some other "good" purpose, playing havoc with husband–wife relations and the domestic economy, where food is both symbol and staff of life. Class and gender conflicts are not insurmountable; my point is simply that they cannot be avoided. Banyole, too, have no way back.

NOTE

A version of this paper was presented at the African Studies Association Annual Meeting, Baltimore, November 2, 1990.

REFERENCES

Anthony, K., Johnston, B., Jones, W., & Uchendu, V. (Eds.). (1979). *Agricultural change in southern Africa*. Ithaca: Cornell University Press.

Barth, Frederik. (1989). The analysis of culture in complex societies. *Ethnos, 54*, 120–142.

Braverman, Harry. (1974). *Labor and monopoly capital*. London: Monthly Review Press.

Brett, E. A. (1973). *Colonialism and underdevelopment in East Africa: The politics of economic change 1919–1939*. London: Heinemann.

Cohen, David, & Atieno Odhiambo, E. S. (1989). *Siaya: The historical anthropology of an African landscape*. London: James Currey.

Hay, Margaret Jean. (1972). *Economic change in Luoland: Kowe 1890–1945*. Unpublished doctoral dissertation, University of Wisconsin.

Kongstad, Per, & Mönsted, Mette. (1980). *Family, labour and trade in western Kenya*. Uppsala: SIAS.

Low, Allan. (1986). *Agricultural development in Southern Africa*. London: James Currey.

Ogutu, M. A. (1979). Agriculture and the development of markets in the western Province of Kenya, 1930–1960. In B. A. Ogot (Ed.), *Ecology and history in east Africa* (pp. 216–242). Nairobi: Kenya Literature Bureau.

Ominde, Simeon. (1971). Rural economy in Western Kenya. In S. Ominde (Ed.), *Studies in East African geography and development* (pp. 216–241). London: Heinemann.

Ongaro, W. A. (1988). Adoption of new farming technology: A case study of maize production in Western Kenya. *Economiska Stidier, 22*. Handelshöjskolan vid Göteborgs Universitet (Sweden).

Republic of Kenya. (1977). *Integrated rural survey, 1974–75*. Nairobi.

Republic of Uganda. (1971). *Report on the 1969 population census*. Entebbe.

Richards, Paul. (1985). *Indigenous agricultural revolution*. London: Hutchinson.

Thompson, Joseph. (1887). *Through Masai Land*. London: Sampson, Low, Marston, Searle & Rivington.

van Zwanenberg, R. M. A., & King, Anne. (1975). *An economic history of Kenya and Uganda 1800–1970*. London: MacMillan.

Wagner, Gunter. (1949/1970). *The Bantu of western Kenya. With special reference to the Vugusu and Logoli, Vols. 1 and 2 (Eonomic life)*. London: Oxford University Press.

Whyte, Michael. (1988). Nyole economic transformation in Eastern Uganda. In H. B. Hansen & M. Twaddle (Eds.), *Uganda now: Between decay and development*. London: James Currey

Whyte, Michael. (1990a). "We have no cash crops any more"—Agriculture as a cultural system in Uganda. In Anita Jacobson-Widding & Walter van Beek (Eds.), *The creative communion: African folk models of fertility and the regeneration of life*. Uppsala: Acta Universitatis Upsalensis.

Whyte, Michael (1990b). The process of survival in Southeastern Uganda. In M. Bovine & L. Manger (Eds.), *Adaptive strategies in African arid lands* (pp. 121–146). Uppsala: SIAS.

Whyte, Michael, & Whyte, Susan. (1981). Cursing and pollution: Supernatural styles in two Luyia-speaking groups. *Folk, 23*, 65–80.

Whyte, Michael, & Whyte, Susan. (1985). Peasants and workers: The legacy of partition among the Luyia-speaking Nyole and Marachi. *Journal of the Historical Society of Nigeria, 12*, no. 3–4, 139–158.

7

Malnutrition and Gender Relations in Western Kenya

Susan Reynolds Whyte and Priscilla Wanjiru Kariuki

Although Kenya has made substantial achievements in providing for the well-being of its citizens, malnutrition in young children remains a matter for concern. National nutrition surveys carried out in 1977, 1979, and 1982 indicate that the situation was particularly severe, and worsening, in Coast, Nyanza, and Western provinces (Republic of Kenya, 1983). Malnutrition has been recognized as a national problem (Republic of Kenya, 1981), whose root causes and treatment must be addressed through planning and interministerial coordination. District Development Plans often mention it. The Ministry of Health defines it as a "family problem" in that the nutrition unit is placed within the Division of Family Health. Yet in practice, childhood malnutrition is a "women's problem" and is treated as such by health authorities, who address their nutrition intervention efforts to mothers.

This means that women's situations and changes in gender relations are particularly important for an adequate understanding of childhood malnutrition. In this chapter we explore some of the gender issues relevant to the problem of child malnutrition. We are not so much interested in isolating causes of malnutrition, as in examining the social situations in which it exists and must be addressed. We will emphasize women's own versions of nutrition problems, which contrast in some important ways with the views of health planners and personnel. While nutrition intervention programs tend to treat women as individual actors, women see themselves as enmeshed in social relationships that affect their ability to care for their children.

In 1987 and 1988, a study (Whyte, 1988) was carried out in western Kenya to examine the impact of the Family Life Training Programme (FLTP), a nutrition intervention program that has existed under the Ministry of Culture and Social Services since 1974.[1] Under this program, mothers with malnourished children are admitted to residential centers for a three-week period of training and intensive feeding of the children. One part of the study consisted of structured data on two categories of women. A community survey was made in six sublocations, which involved interviews with 300 mothers and the weighing of 460 children under five years. Another sample was composed of 151 women (referred to as trainees) and their malnourished children who had been admitted to the Family Life Training Centres (FLTCs) at Ahero, Lwak, and Butula. They were interviewed in their homes and the children weighed three to four months after discharge.

The other part of the study was qualitative. Data collection entailed many open discussions and less structured interviews with mothers and other family and community members. Three university students engaged in participant observation at the centers for three months. Attempts were made to fit the information gathered on malnutrition into a broader framework of culture and society in western Kenya. (This was facilitated by the fact that one of the authors had earlier carried out a year of ethnographic fieldwork in this part of Kenya.) Here we present themes from the qualitative part of the study. The cases we have selected illuminate conceptions and relational patterns that have general relevance for understanding the situations of western Kenyan mothers. Although we mention some figures from our survey results, we have not chosen our cases as representative in a statistical sense. They are exemplary in a way we hope will be useful for discussion and for policy and planning.

The communities studied were located in Siaya and Kisumu Districts, where the populations are mainly Luo speaking, and in Busia District, where Luyia speakers predominate. These areas are strongly patrilineal, with Luo people in particular known for their well developed lineage ideology and male dominance (Parkin, 1978).

MALNUTRITION—A PROBLEM OF FEEDING OR FAMILY LIFE?

We found that 38 percent of the 460 children under five in our community sample were malnourished in that they weighed 80 percent or less of the standard weight for their age. The situation was worst in Busia District, where 42 percent of the children fell into this category. The figure for Kisumu District was 33 percent. In Siaya, 40 percent of the sample was malnourished. A baseline survey had been carried out using the same methodology in the same area of Siaya (Uyoma) in 1983, when 34 percent of a similar sample fell into the malnourished category (Kaseje et al., 1986). Malnutrition in Kenya is recognized by health workers as taking two forms: *marasmus* and *kwashiorkor*. Marasmus is characterized by extreme thinness; the child's weight is very low in relation to its age. Kwashiorkor is characterized by swelling of the limbs, face, and abdomen and by changes in hair and skin color and texture. The child's weight may not be quite so low because of retention of fluid in the tissues. In the view of health workers, the primary cause of malnutrition is poor feeding, especially at the time of weaning and up to the age of five years; efforts are made to teach mothers the principles of a balanced diet and the importance of suitable weaning foods given frequently during the day. Health workers recognize that the roots of malnutrition are actually complex. Sickness, especially measles, diarrhea, and chronic malaria, may precipitate malnutrition. And they realize that there may be factors in the social and economic situation of the household that inhibit good feeding. Still, the overwhelming emphasis in nutrition programs is on feeding practices. Proper feeding of children is both the best prevention and the best cure for malnutrition.

These views contrast with those of the mothers in the communities we studied. Although there were points of overlap, there was a very marked difference in emphasis in the way local people perceived the health problems of young children. When we described the symptoms of marasmus and kwashiorkor, most mothers said that they recognized them. Well over half of the mothers knew of children with these conditions, and about 20 percent said that their own children had suffered from at least one of them. The most common causes to which kwashiorkor was attributed were poor feeding (lack of quantity and variety in food) and sickness with concomitant loss of appetite.[2] Mothers whose own children were malnourished tended to point to sickness as a cause; poor feeding was usually seen as the cause of kwashiorkor in other women's children. For marasmus, sickness and poor feeding were also mentioned by some. But in the Luo speaking areas, the most common explanation was that rules about family relationships had been broken. Extreme thinness was often called by the term *chira*, which suggests a dangerous state of pollution; almost all of the causes of *chira* have to do with the transgression of principles governing sexuality and/or seniority. It can come about because of adultery, contact with an uninherited widow, or disregard of seniority rules, such as those requiring that a senior wife should sow and harvest before a junior one, or that an elder brother should build a house before a younger one (Abe, 1981; Ocholla-Ayayo, 1976; Parkin, 1973, 1978; Ssennyonga, this volume; Thorup, n.d.; Whyte, 1990). *Chira*, or *ishira* as it is called in Luyia languages, can also arise because of carelessness in observing the proper separation of sexuality between generations. Thus many families say that a grandmother who is still sleeping with her husband should not hold her grandchild.

The idea of appropriate separation also underlies the notion of *ledho* or *heru*, another concept used to explain thinness and failure to thrive in very small children. If a breastfeeding mother becomes pregnant, it is thought that the nursing child is in a dangerous relationship to the child in its mother's womb. It is weaned immediately "for its own good"; in explaining this, people did not speak of the quality of the breastmilk (cf. Van de Walle & Van de Walle, 1991) so much as the inappropriate contact between siblings. That it is a matter of separation and not "bad milk" seems to be confirmed by the fact that some mothers even avoid holding the "displaced" child, in order to protect it from *ledho* caused by contact with its unborn sibling.

Some health workers try to explain to mothers that such ideas are wrong—that pregnant mothers should continue breastfeeding and that improper feeding, not wrong relationships, causes malnutrition. Others are less concerned to criticize and concentrate on teaching good childcare practices; their approach seems to be that *chira* concepts do no harm as long as children are also fed well. What we want to stress here is that mothers who talk about *chira* and *ledho* have a fundamental insight that is not always appreciated in nutrition programs: that child health is embedded in a context of family relations and gender relations. The individual mother and child should not be seen in isolation from their social relations to significant others.

THE FAMILY CONTEXT OF MALNUTRITION

The strains to which marriage in western Kenya is being subjected have been reported by a number of researchers (Bradley, this volume; Cattell, this volume; Håkansson, 1988; Håkansson & LeVine, this volume; Kilbride & Kilbride, this volume; Pala, 1980; Potash, 1978; Parkin, 1978; Whyte, 1979/80). Yet despite widespread concern among Luo and Luyia people themselves about the deterioration of marriage as an institution, more than 90 percent of the mothers in our community sample reported that they were married. Marriage is confirmed by the payment (or promise) of bridewealth and, ideally, is permanent. Only two out of the three hundred women in our community sample said that they were divorced. In fact, women do separate from their husbands, but bridewealth is rarely repaid and, in many situations, such women would be considered still married (see Potash, 1978).

Two patterns are especially significant for the marital situations of western Kenyan women. One is polygyny, which means that a man's attention and resources must be shared with another woman and her children. Of mothers in the Luo speaking districts, 37 percent had cowives, in comparison to 16 percent in Luyia speaking Busia District. The other significant pattern of marriage is the absence of husbands due to labor migration. Only 53 percent of the mothers in the community sample had their husbands at home. That is to say, roughly half of the mothers and children we visited were having to manage their daily affairs without a husband and father.

It is unclear whether or not the absence of the father in itself affects the child's nutrition. Kennedy and Cogill (1987) found that, in South Nyanza District, children in female-headed households were actually better nourished than those in male-headed households, and they suggested that this is because such mothers have more control over household income and are more likely to spend it in ways that benefit children's health. In our study, we found that the women who were admitted with their children at the nutrition centers were more likely than others in the community to have no husband or to have a husband who was absent. But this may be because such women were more likely to be referred to a center and were more likely to be able to go. The material from the community sample did not indicate a significant relation between the presence of a father and the nutritional status of the children.

We suggest that figures on marital status and presence of husband tell only part of the story. The real issues have to do with the quality of cooperation between husband and wife and the possibility of support from other family members.

In talking to mothers and their families, it became clear that a number of the children became malnourished or failed to recover in the context of marital conflicts. Many women who said they were married were in fact cooperating very poorly with their husbands. Because of marital discord, women sometimes left home for periods of time, and the children became sickly while in the care of someone else. Sometimes husbands devoted all of their attention and resources to another wife.

The Gender Context of Malnutrition

Elizabeth, married to a man of Nyakach, had been staying with her husband in Nairobi, where he worked. Their firstborn child was staying with her mother, and the new baby was still breastfeeding. When Elizabeth found out that her husband had taken a second wife, who was staying at his home in Nyakach, she was very annoyed, but remained in Nairobi with her husband. One day her mother-in-law brought the new wife to town, and there was a dramatic confrontation in which her husband and five of his clansmen demanded that she return to the country immediately, allowing the new wife to stay with their husband in Nairobi. She said she could not leave until daylight, and they chased her. She laid the baby down and ran. When she returned to the house later that night, the baby, her husband, and in-laws were gone.

She went home to her mother in the country and although she heard that the baby had been taken by her mother-in-law, she did not go to their home to fetch it. The mother-in-law was a trader, so she often left her grandchild in the care of someone else. After two months, she brought the child, now swollen with *kwashiorkor*, to Elizabeth's mother's home. By this time, Elizabeth had gone to stay elsewhere; her father and brother advised against accepting the child, but her mother felt sorry to see it being passed about and agreed to care for it. She bought medicine from a local shop "for swollen belly" and gave the child vitamin pills and tried to give it a good diet. But she did not take it to the mission hospital; she thought that really should be Elizabeth's responsibility. After a period of improvement, the child suddenly took a turn for the worse. The grandmother sent for Elizabeth, who was annoyed to find her mother had agreed to care for the child when it was so poorly. Nevertheless she went to the Family Life Training Centre at Ahero with her child. From there she was sent to New Nyanza General Hospital in Kisumu, where her child died. Her husband's people came and took the corpse for burial at their home. Elizabeth went for the funeral ceremony; according to Luo custom her husband should have come to complete the ceremony with her. But after two weeks he still had not appeared, and she left for good.

This case story illustrates a number of the social factors forming the gender context of malnutrition in western Kenya. There is the movement back and forth between the husband's place of work and the family's home in the country. There is the conflict between husband and wife, not infrequently over polygynous marriages. There is the question of child custody and responsibility in the event of separation or divorce, as well as the role of grandmothers and other care providers in situations where the mother is not caring for her own child.

Many mothers of malnourished children told of difficult relations with their husbands. Some men who were away working neglected their wives and children, not only economically (as we shall discuss in the next section), but also in terms of showing interest, concern, and responsibility. They did not come home for months on end nor send for their wives to visit them. The wives were left to seek support from their in-laws when their children fell ill—and they were not always willing or able to give it.

Even husbands who were at home were not always supportive. Rose of North Wanga came to the Family Life Training Centre with a malnourished child and aching ribs after the most recent beating by her husband. She said he was a heavy drinker and very authoritarian. He would not allow her to use family planning, always checked through her possessions, and always favored his new wife. In this situation it was important to Rose that her own relatives visited her often, that her mother-in-law tried to help her, and that she was a member of an active church women's group.

In their book on Siaya, Cohen and Atieno Odhiambo (1989) point out the problem of unwed mothers and the way in which *kwashiorkor* afflicts the "children of children," who are begotten in the grass. Luyia people speak likewise of the growing number of "children of the unmarried hut" whose fathers refuse to recognize them. These children remain in their mothers' homes, and when the mothers marry or go away to school or work, they are often left in the care of their grandmothers (Bradley, this volume; Cattell, this volume; Kilbride & Kilbride, this volume; Ocholla-Ayayo, this volume). Many Luo and Luyia people think it is inappropriate or even dangerous for a woman to bring her child by another man with her when she marries (Whyte, 1990, p. 106). And if she does so, her husband may not feel obligated to support the child as he does his own biological children.

Grandmothers' Difficulties Caring for Grandchildren

Antonina from Bukhayo was caring for two of her daughter's children—by two different men. The daughter had lived with each for a year, but neither had paid bridewealth, and now she was staying with a third man in Nakuru. When the youngest grandchild became sickly and malnourished, the grandmother took him to the hospital and later to a health center. She said bitterly that the child's father had refused to help her with food or money to take the children for treatment—and yet he was a teacher. "In the old days, girls also got pregnant without being married. Then the elders held a meeting and the girl named the father of the child and he had to marry her or pay something to her family."

Thus one of the problems grandmothers faced was that they did not have adequate support in caring for their grandchildren. Sometimes, too, infants were left with them when they were so young that they should have been breastfeeding. We met one great-grandmother at Butula Family Life Training Centre who had breastfed two grandchildren. Her great-grandchild was left with her when it was only a few months old; the mother had to go back to her studies at a teacher's training college. The old woman did not have enough milk, and the child became malnourished.

There is still another situation in which the health of children is directly dependent upon support from other women. When mothers fall ill and die, their children are cared for by grandmothers, older sisters, and, less frequently, stepmothers, rather than by their fathers (although widowers are occasionally admitted to the FLTCs with their malnourished children). It is often the case that small children become malnourished while their mothers are ill; when the mother dies, the child who is handed into another woman's care is already in poor condition.

Mothers' and Grandmothers' Illnesses Affecting Children

Auma of North Wanga arrived at Butula Family Life Training Centre one day with two grandchildren: seven year old Teresa carrying a shrunken and weak six month old baby. Auma's daughter had become pregnant again immediately after giving birth to her seventh child. Auma (who was trained as a "traditional birth attendant") thought perhaps her daughter had been anemic. She fell ill and was admitted to hospital where she stayed for two months. During this time she was separated from her baby, who was cared for by seven year old Teresa. By the time the mother died, the baby was very severely marasmic and dehydrated.

Sometimes cultural characteristics seem to constrain good care for such motherless children. If a grandmother is still sexually active, she may not want to hold her grandchild for fear of exposing it to *chira*. In the case above, Auma never touched the sickly child, although she clearly cared about the baby and had made the long journey to the FLTC in a desperate attempt to save its life.

Other cultural patterns directly support children whose mothers have died, for example, the custom of a dead woman being replaced by her sister, who marries the widower and cares for the children.

Sororate Customs

We met a very young replacement mother at the Ahero Family Life Training Centre. Shortly after her sister died, she was asked in a dream to care for the surviving infant. At the age of fifteen, she dropped out of school and married her brother-in-law. When the baby became sickly and malnourished, she took it from clinic to clinic and struggled to feed it properly. Her husband is a laborer on a sugar estate, and she stays with him there. She says that her parents-in-law love her very much for having agreed to quit school in order to care for their grandchild.

In general the women admitted to the FLTCs were younger than the average mother of small children in the community (based on our survey of three hundred mothers). But again, this may be a reflection of the greater responsibilities that prevent older women from leaving home for three weeks.

The most striking characteristic of the mothers of malnourished children was that they were poor. This brings us to the issue of economy and gender.

MALNUTRITION AND THE "*GOROGORO* ECONOMY"

The "*gorogoro* economy" is the term Cohen and Atieno Odhiambo (1989) use to describe the western Kenya rural economy in which staples are sold by a standard measure (a *gorogoro*), whose size has steadily decreased while its price has remained the same. Characteristic for this economy is that inadequate subsistence agriculture is supplemented by insufficient, irregular remittances from migrant men. When a home's own crops have been eaten, food is bought by the *gorogoro* to tide the family through to the next harvest.

Practically all of the mothers in our two samples had access to land. The acreages tended to be larger in Busia District, where more than 80 percent said that they farmed more than three acres. In the Kisumu and Siaya samples, less than 15 percent had that much land. The staple crops are maize, sorghum, and cassava, with cassava particularly important in Busia District.

Although almost all women in our sample were farmers, there were very few who were able to produce a nutritionally balanced variety of foods year round. Most families are not even able to produce enough staples to last from one harvest to the next. In some parts of Kisumu and Siaya districts, the second rains are very unreliable, so only a single harvest each year can be counted on. In the dry season there are not many vegetables. Most families do not have their own supply of milk; those who are fortunate enough to have milking cows usually sell at least some of the milk.

Given the difficulties of producing an adequate diet, it is clear that some food must be purchased. The remittances sent home by husbands working on the sugar and tea estates or in towns have to buy food as well as pay for school fees, taxes, medicine, transport, and clothing (see also Bradley, this volume). Both our quantitative material and our discussions with mothers of small children revealed lack of cash as an absolutely central problem for child nutrition.

The communities with the highest rate of malnutrition were those in Busia District, where 45 percent of the mothers reported a monthly income of K.Sh.100 (about US$6.00) or less. In Siaya and Kisumu Districts, 18 percent to19 percent of mothers in the community sample were in this very low income bracket. The mothers of malnourished children admitted to the FLTCs were even more likely to have a minimal income. Thus 77 percent of the Butula trainees interviewed were trying to manage on K.Sh. 100 a month or less; the corresponding figures for Lwak (Siaya) and Ahero (Kisumu) were 57 percent and 38 percent.

Interviews with mothers three months after their training at the centers revealed that they were well aware of what foods they should give their small children, but were often unable to afford them. Only five of the forty-two ex-trainees from Butula FLTC said that they were able to feed their children as they had learned at the center, and even those added "but not always." They explained that they did not themselves produce a sufficient quantity and variety of food and that they could not afford beans, green yams, groundnuts, milk, eggs, fruits, and meat. This fits with our finding that although 81 percent of the malnourished children gained weight during their three weeks at the Butula FLTC, only 34 percent of the same sample gained any weight at all in the three months after discharge.

In this situation a mother's ability to earn a bit of cash on her own is critical. We found considerable variation in the extent to which women in the sample areas had their own income through trade, sale of handicrafts, or day labor. The women in the Busia District sample were much less involved in independent economic activities; the Kisumu and Siaya women, being closer to the lake and to major transport arteries, seemed to have more opportunities—many traded in fish, for example. In an otherwise isolated village in Siaya, women were earning cash by selling firewood to those who smoked Nile perch on the lake shore.

The relation between child nutrition and mother's work has been reviewed by Carloni (1984). She contrasts the view of women-in-development experts, that families benefit from women's income-earning activities outside the home, with the concern of nutritionists that working mothers are unable to care for and feed their children adequately. She concludes that both approaches share the assumption that women's work is the independent variable and the nutritional status of children the dependent one. This cause and effect assumption is oversimplified, she suggests. Both women's work and nutrition may be affected by other variables, and it is more useful to examine closely the household situations of mothers involved in off-farm earning activities. In many cases, women are forced to seek casual wage labor because the family is too poor to survive without their earnings. So many other factors (e.g., landlessness, market dependency, declining employment opportunities, rising food prices, erosion of real wages, poor access to markets) may be responsible for malnutrition that it makes little sense to view the mother's employment as its cause (Carloni, 1984, p. 3).

Our material suggests that the interplay of factors may be even more complex than Carloni proposed. When a child becomes sickly and malnourished, an economically active mother may spend her trading capital on medical care. She may have to discontinue her paid work in order to care for her sick child. It must be borne in mind that malnutrition is usually a long-term condition, often beginning with a serious illness. This means that a mother's work may be disrupted over a considerable period, reducing family income and interfering with subsistence farming.

Mutual Influence Between Women's Work and Child Malnutrition

One mother interviewed upon admission to Ahero Family Life Training Centre was from Oyugis, a trading center between the lake and the Kisii highlands. Her husband was a tea-picker in Sotik, and he was able to send her K. Sh. 100–150 a month. She supplemented that income by trading in *omena* [Swahili *dagaa*; small sardine-like fish that are dried]. She used to go to the lake often, buying fish for 40 K. Sh. and selling in Oyugis for K. Sh. 100. But eight months ago her child got measles and subsequently developed *marasmus* and *kwashiorkor*. Since then she has given up her trading and now lives on her husband's remittance.

Other mothers told similar stories, leading us to see the relation between economic circumstances and malnutrition as one of mutual influence, where a child's ill health is both a result of and a factor contributing to the family's poverty.

WOMEN AS HEALTH CARE PROVIDERS

Research on the causes of malnutrition has pointed to the characteristics of childcare that are crucial for helping children to grow well. The intimate association between disease and malnutrition means that prevention of disease by immunization and improved hygiene and early effective treatment of sickness episodes are absolutely essential. Feeding patterns should include a long period of breastfeeding, avoidance of bottles, and gradual weaning over to a varied diet with high energy in relation to bulk, given in frequent feedings (King et al., 1972). The quality of childcare is also important, and there is apparently a feedback effect here; attention, stimulation, and consistent sensitivity to the child's needs are necessary so that the child becomes active and develops the ability to engage caretakers (Peters & Niemeijer, 1987; Weisner, this volume). Adequate child spacing ensures that children are not weaned too early and that they receive sufficient care during the dangerous first two to three years of life.

Who is responsible for providing this kind of childcare? Mothers are. Mothers must be motivated to bring their children for immunization, mothers wait with their sick children in the long queues at health centers. They nurse and feed the children and grow the food to provide a good diet. They are alert to the child's needs, and they interact most intimately with it. Mothers' bodies are the locus of conception and pregnancy, and they must ensure that babies are properly spaced. The primary role of mothers seems so self-evident that it is rarely questioned.

The view that mothers as individuals are responsible for child health seems to be supported by the consistent finding in Kenya and other developing countries that educated mothers have healthier children (Mosley, 1989; Cleland & van Ginneken, 1989). Although the exact mechanisms by which education influences the mother's ability to provide better childcare are the subject of debate, there seems little doubt that it does so. Our material from western Kenya fits with other findings in that the communities with the highest rates of malnutrition had the lowest rate of maternal education: in the Busia District samples, 54 percent of the mothers of small children had no formal schooling at all, while the figures for Siaya and Kisumu were 17 percent and 23 percent respectively. With the increase in primary school enrolment in Kenya, it seems likely that in the next generation of mothers nearly all will have at least a few years of school, with whatever benefits that brings in health knowledge, attitudes, discipline, self-confidence, and status. But for the present, many unschooled mothers are caring for children, and nutrition programs cannot change that fact.

What they can do is provide responsible mothers with information and try to motivate them in certain directions. Most nutrition intervention and health education programs are based on the assumption that teaching individual mothers to care well for their children will reduce malnutrition.

The question we want to consider is: To what extent should mothers as *individuals* be seen as providers of health care? There is a good argument for treating mothers as autonomous subjects who can learn and make decisions about their children and their lives. A program addressed to individual actors is more tangible than one addressed to a "situation" or to "society" or "the economy" or "the system." Individual mothers must perceive themselves as having control and being able to influence their children's health (cf. Simons, 1989). At the same time, mothers are social beings, who exist within a particular set of relationships to men and other women, within specific economic and cultural contexts. The gender organization of western Kenya sets limits and gives possibilities for child health care. We have already given some examples of how malnutrition is enmeshed within social relations. Now we want to explore further and more specifically the way mothers as individuals and as socially embedded persons provide health care.

Taking small children for immunization and treatment is the responsibility of a mother, unless she is not living with them. (In the case of Elizabeth of Nyakach, remember that her mother wanted her to come home and take the child to the hospital.) The significance of sickness and the consequent need for treatment in western Kenya can scarcely be overemphasized. One study from South Nyanza District found that the average woman and child are ill one out of every four days (Kennedy & Cogill, 1987, p. 42); the Baseline Study for the FLTP carried out in Siaya in 1983 found that 68 percent of children under five had been ill during the two weeks prior to the interview (Kaseje et al., 1986, p. 31).

A father or other family member can go to buy medicine for the child at home, but a mother takes her child to the health facility. What determines whether or not she does? Aside from factors like distance to the health facility and evaluation of the service available there, we should recall the argument about mother's work and how it impinges on child health care. Sempebwa (1988) reports on a study in Kisumu District showing that children whose mothers were away from home more than six hours a day were less likely to be taken for immunization and treatment. A mother's workload, which is a consequence of the gender organization of the economy, may inhibit her ability to take advantage of the health system's facilities. The FLTCs reported that fewer mothers brought children for nutritional rehabilitation during the season of heavy agricultural work. In part, the issue here is what priority the mother as an individual gives to her work in relation to the perceived value of visiting government health facilities. But that evaluation is not made in isolation; it may well be influenced by her husband, relatives, and neighbors. Thus some men did not want their wives to go the FLTC for three weeks, because there was no one else to cook. A young wife who is still cultivating together with her mother-in-law may find it easier to take her child to the clinic, because she is not solely responsible for the domestic and farming work.

Even more important is the role that significant others have in mobilizing the mother to seek treatment. In medical anthropology, the term "therapy managing group" (Janzen, 1978) or "therapeutic support structure" (Janzen, 1990) is used to refer to the people who mobilize and support a sick person in seeking therapy. Our interviews with the women who brought their malnourished children to FLTCs gave some indication of how this process works in western Kenya. The role played by family and others is well illustrated by the story told by Penina, whom we met at Ahero FLTC with her child who was suffering from severe *kwashiorkor*.

A Woman's Therapy Managing Group

My child fell sick four months ago with fever, diarrhea, and vomiting. At first I bought aspirin and aspro—he refused to take chloroquin because that's so bitter. There was a health center near my home, but I didn't go there because I didn't know anyone working there. If you don't know someone you aren't treated well, and besides health centers these days often don't have drugs. So I came here to Ahero where my mother lives; she knows the retired clinical officer who runs a private clinic here. He said my child had measles, and I paid K. Sh. 50 for treatment, but the child was not admitted. The sickness continued, and I saw the child's body swelling. I thought it might be *chira*—maybe my husband was moving with other women. I asked him, and he said maybe it was him, that we should just get treatment. But when the practitioner (*ajuoga*) came, he told us that this was not *chira* because that makes a child thin and ours was swollen. (Our neighbors said this was *akuodi,* which makes the body to swell, the hair to turn brown, and the skin to change.) The practitioner said maybe our child passed where a child with *akuodi* had been washed and that's how he caught it. Soon after, the Aga Khan health workers visited us at home; they suggested we come to the FLTC, and they brought us here the same day.

When we met Penina she was having a visit with a relative who had come to see her. Her husband was living at home; they both made papyrus mats, which she sold in the market, using the money as she saw fit to buy what the family needed. "I just live peacefully with my husband," she said. From the health workers' point of view, Penina's child became malnourished because of measles and also perhaps because, as she told us, she used to feed him on tea and bread, as she sat selling mats in the market. She also saw the measles and the child's swollen body and she acted; but her response was very much shaped and supported by her relations to others. The only treatment attempt in which she seems to have acted on her own was the initial purchase of medicines (cf. Van der Geest & Whyte, 1989).

We have already touched on some of the economic factors that limit a mother's ability to feed her children an adequate diet. The local staff at the FLTCs recognized that many mothers were unable to buy the oil, eggs, milk, and beans that would enrich their children's food. But, they said, even if a mother has very little, she should know how to use it. If she has ten shillings, she should buy dried fish and not fried bread and soda for the child. If she only has porridge made on water, she should at least know to feed the child five times a day. She can go to the butcher and ask him to give her the blood from slaughter animals—that costs nothing. This response emphasizes that mothers as individuals can learn and act to improve the child's diet.

Yet not all mothers actually prepare the food which their children eat; a young wife does not usually form an independent consumption unit until she is allocated land of her own; that is, her husband will assign fields to her only when his father has given him his share of land (although these practices vary in different communities). When she begins to harvest from her own fields, she will get her own kitchen. Until then, she and her children eat from her mother-in-law's kitchen. The position of a daughter-in-law, particularly in the first years of marriage, is one of dependence. She and her children eat what her mother-in-law provides. This situation has been documented by Kryger (n.d.), who gives the example of a young Luo mother who had recently moved into her husband's home, bringing a malnourished child. When asked why she had not given beans and milk to the child, as she had been advised at the nutrition center, she replied that her mother-in-law had not offered them beans or milk.

There are other situations too where a mother might not be cooking herself—if she were staying with relatives, on an extended visit, or if she were sick. A woman who has been staying elsewhere with her husband might also cook with her mother-in-law for a period when she returns to her husband's home. The situation of Mary, whom we met at Butula Family Life Training Centre, provides a dramatic example of how a woman's ability to feed her children might be inhibited by her position in a larger household.

Women's Position in Extended Family Homestead and Child Health

Mary and her husband were from Busia District, but had been living in Kampala where he worked as a charcoal dealer. She had two children and was caring for two other children of her dead cowives. (One of her cowives had been shot in Uganda, the other died of diarrhea, she said.) Her own youngest child became ill in Uganda and failed to recover despite being admitted to Mulago Hospital for three weeks. Finally she brought all the children home, but there her own child's condition worsened and her cowife's child developed *kwashiorkor*. She explained that she had no house of her own in her husband's homestead, and his mother cooked for her and also for her sister-in-law and her children. All the children of the home ate together, and the big ones ate faster so the young ones did not get enough. Mary said that when she asked her mother-in-law to help her carry the sick children to the Family Life Training Center at Butula, the older woman said that everybody had to carry their own burden. If the children were bewitched in Uganda, she should have left them to die there. After admission to the FLTC, one of the children became so critical that it was referred to the district hospital. Mary asked her husband if she could take the child there, and he in turn asked his father, who refused.

Other evidence of the authority of the senior generation in this home came to light when our assistant visited the family and found another grandchild (the child of Mary's sister-in-law) with severe *kwashiorkor*. Although she advised that this child be brought to the FLTC immediately, the mother-in-law refused. She said that she first wanted to see whether the treatment there worked for Mary's children. In the weeks that followed, Mary's children improved at the center, while the other child died. Mary seemed to be on good terms with her husband, who visited her almost every day while she was at the center. But she was very unhappy with her mother-in-law and hoped that her husband would put up a house for her so she could cook for her own family when she completed her stay at the center.

The quality of child care is another aspect of health care provision that is assumed to be the responsibility of the individual mother. We have already touched upon the issue of whether a mother's work prevents her from caring for her child properly. Here again it is important to look more closely at the actual social situations of mothers. All mothers have to be away from home some of the time, if only to fetch water and firewood and work in their gardens. We asked the three hundred women in our community sample who cared for their small children when they had to leave home. The most common answer was that other children did so—either young children who were not yet in school or older ones when they came home after school. Although practically no small children were left alone, it is clear that the care provided by a five year old, or even by a nine year old who has been in school all day, may not be as attentive as that provided by an adult. In the Siaya and Kisumu District samples, where large extended-family compounds are common, small children are also left in the care of other adults, usually their paternal grandmothers. Hardly any mothers (only 4%) said that they always took their children with them when they went out. By contrast, one third of the Busia District mothers said that they did not leave their children with others, but always took them with them. Thus an appreciation of the actual patterns of child care in western Kenya suggests that both older women and school children should be involved in the kind of child health education currently aimed at mothers.

One of the factors that most markedly affects the quality of care a mother provides is child spacing. The picture of a mother with a chubby, happy infant and a miserable, malnourished one-and-a-half year-old was all too common. As we have mentioned above, local concepts about *ledho* emphasize the need to wean a child abruptly as soon as the mother realizes she is pregnant again. Health workers teach that a pregnant mother can continue breastfeeding as long as she eats well. But here they are going against a local conception that seems to be confirmed by the common experience that "displaced" children become sickly. Here too, health education needs to reach other members of the family, teaching them to provide extra care and attention to a young child whose mother is pregnant. The study on the relationship between malnutrition and the home environment in Coast Province (Peters & Niemeijer, 1987) states that it is not clear whether a malnourished child generates a lower level of stimulation on the caretaker's part or whether lack of stimulation should be seen as causal, leading to increased risk of malnutrition. It seems logical that there is no one-way cause and effect here, but a mutual influence in which passive, unhappy children get less attention. If one adds to that situation a new breastfeeding baby, it is apparent that the "displaced" child is at even greater risk.

Family planning as a method of spacing is an obvious solution, but it was very little used in western Kenya at the time of our studies. Only 4 percent of the mothers in the community sample were using modern methods of family planning (pills, injections, or IUD) at that time, although as Bradley (this volume) and others now are documenting, contraceptive use is increasing, pronatalist values are changing, and fertility rates are beginning to fall. This very low utilization rate at the time of 4 percent, despite official promotion of family planning, is partly due to poor services. But it is certainly also due to the strong pronatalist attitudes in this part of Kenya. Most people do not distinguish child spacing from child limitation, and they did not want to limit the number of their children, at least not until after the first eight. Here again, it is important to see the individual mother's position in a social context. In discussing family planning with mothers, we found that many expressed an interest. But often they said that their husbands were opposed to the idea or that they feared even to raise the topic, and they also feared to use family planning without their husbands' permission. We did indeed encounter many men who spoke vehemently against birth control. Yet we suspect that many women are ambivalent about it, and it is somewhat convenient to blame their husbands for being antagonistic to family planning. Some health workers told us that polygyny promoted fertility in that cowives, consciously or not, competed with one another as to children. Through their children they make claims on their husband's attention and resources, so that it is disadvantageous to limit births if their cowife does not.

CONCLUSION

The significance of women's position for the health of their children has been recognized by a number of scholars. In this chapter we have contrasted the assumption that women as individuals care for children with the view of western Kenyan women that they do so as socially connected persons. A consideration of the concept of autonomy may help to summarize our argument.

Caldwell argues that female autonomy (which he suggests is enhanced by education) is an important factor in mortality decline: "When a woman's morality and behaviour in the widest sense are primarily her own responsibility rather than that of her male relatives, then she will assume broader responsibilities, including those of deciding early and with certainty that children are sick and need rest and treatment; she will not worry about waiting to consult her husband or his mother or brothers (Caldwell, 1989, p. 215)."

Our case material provides detailed examples of how lack of autonomy may inhibit a woman's ability to care for her children: the young bride who must feed her malnourished children whatever her mother-in-law provides and the mother who must have her husband's or father-in-law's permission to take a child to hospital. Women's highly dependent economic position is a consequence of the genderized political economy of western Kenya, with its combination of male labor migration and patrilineal, virilocal access to resources.

However, our material also suggests that the value of female autonomy is conditional; we need to specify what we mean by autonomy and how it might be expressed in particular local settings. If autonomy is defined as individualism and lack of mutual obligation, even educated women cannot be, and may not want to be, autonomous. Social support networks are probably even more important to health in developing countries than in western settings. The difficulty is in distinguishing what is supportive from what is oppressive.

Western Kenyan women are enmeshed in social relations, and their children are enmeshed with them. As Bledsoe (1990) has recently asserted, childcare is never simply a question of the relation between child and adult; it is always also a matter of relationships among adults. Children are treated as symbols of adult relationships. A good example of this point was the way Elizabeth of Nyakach refused to go to her husband's rural home to collect her breastfeeding baby because she was angry at her husband and his family. Among cowives, envy easily arises if a father is more concerned with the children of one wife, because treatment of the children is seen to reflect the relationship to their mother. The tendency for parents to invest more care in the children of unions that have current value for them, pointed out by Bledsoe for the Mende of Sierra Leone, was even more pronounced in western Kenya, where mothers do not usually take children of a previous union with them into a new one. Those children are left to the care of grandmothers, and often neither the father nor the mother provides much support. Even educated mothers hand their children into the care of grandmothers; in fact, this is the common pattern when school girls get pregnant and try to continue their education after delivery (again, practices which vary across western Kenya).

Such examples illustrate the negative consequences that adult relationships and interests may have for childcare. But children are also symbols of adult relationships in the positive sense that solidarity with the mother is expressed in concern for the child. Neighbors and relatives who help a mother to get treatment for her child, relatives who care for orphans, and siblings who babysit while their mother is working make survival possible. Women without support networks are very vulnerable, as are their children. Feierman (1981) documented this point some years ago in a study from northwestern Tanzania. The children in her sample who died were children of mothers who were socially isolated. Perhaps they were autonomous in some sense, but they had no social resources to help them meet their children's health crises.

This brings us to the point that female autonomy is valuable if it is defined as the ability to mobilize relevant resources, both social and economic—if it means the capacity to take initiatives and the knowledge to decide when they are necessary. It is irrelevant if it means independence in the sense of the ability to manage without the help of others. That kind of independence is possible only for people with a stronger economic situation than most women have in western Kenya (see Bradley, this volume; Nasimiyu, this volume).

The mothers in our study wanted support more than independence from their husbands and families. They need assistance in the form of cash and help with agricultural labor; sometimes husbands are unable to help more than they do, but many women felt that husbands did not use the resources they had sensibly, thus forcing wives to try to manage independently in very difficult circumstances.[3] Mothers also need support in terms of concern for the welfare of their children. Some women complained that their husbands wanted many children but showed no interest in caring for them, because they saw that as a woman's job. We noticed that men were quick to criticize women for failing to care for children properly, but they seldom took an interest themselves in what children were eating or whether they had been vaccinated. When men were attentive to a child's health problems, mothers appreciated it as a sign of concern for the mother as well.

These considerations have implications for child health programs in general and for nutrition programs in particular. It is important to teach individual mothers and to strengthen their perception of themselves as autonomous agents who can influence their children's health. But it is also necessary to recognize that mothers like those in western Kenya must have enlightened support in caring for their children. We say enlightened because it became clear to us in the course of our study that older siblings, mothers-in-law, grandmothers, and especially husbands need to be aware of the same messages that health educators are aiming at mothers. In a gender system of the type we have examined here, mothers and children do not form isolated dyads. Perhaps they do not do so anywhere, but their social embeddedness is particularly clear in western Kenya.

NOTES

We wish to acknowledge the support of the Danish International Development Agency as well as that of the Danish Council for Development Research for the preparation of this chapter. We would like to thank Ms. Rose Adero, Ms. Roselyn Lwenya, and Ms. Merita Oduor for their assistance at the centers and in the field. The Family Life Training Programme staff at headquarters in Nairobi and especially at the three centers in western Kenya were extremely helpful, and we want to thank them as well.

1. The program consists of fourteen residential centers to which mothers and their malnourished children are admitted for a period of three weeks. The mothers are trained in principles of good nutrition and family health, and they are helped to feed their children intensively using local foods. The program is currently being supported by the Danish International Development Agency.
2. On the basis of research in Samia Location, Olenja (1988) found that *kwashiorkor* was often attributed to sorcery. Swelling of parts of the body often provokes suspicion of sorcery in East Africa. But in our study, we found only a few examples of sorcery as an explanation for *kwashiorkor*.
3. Recent work by Holmboe-Ottesen and Wandel (1991a, 1991b) in Rukwa, Tanzania, emphasizes the importance of marital relations and particularly the significance of male contributions to the household economy for the nutritional situation of children.

REFERENCES

Abe, Toshiharu. (1981). The concepts of *chira* and *dhoch* among the Luo of Kenya: Transition, deviation and misfortune. In N. Nagashima (Ed.), *Themes in socio-cultural ideas and behaviour among six ethnic groups of Kenya* (pp. 127–139). Tokyo: Hitotsubashi University.

Bledsoe, C. (1990). Differential care of children of previous unions within Mende households in Sierra Leone. In Caldwell et al. (Eds.), pp. 561–583.

Caldwell, J. C. (1989). Routes to low mortality in poor countries. In J. C. Caldwell & G. Santow (Eds.), pp. 1–46.

Caldwell, J. C., & Santow, G. (Eds.) (1989). *Selected readings in the cultural, social and behavioural determinants of health.* Canberra: Health Transition Centre.

Carloni, A. S. (1984). *The Impact of maternal employment and income on the nutritional status of children in rural areas of developing countries*. Geneva: United Nations Administrative Committee on Coordination—Subcommittee on Nutrition.

Cleland, J. G., & van Ginneken, J. K. (1989). Maternal education and child survival in developing countries: The search for pathways of influence. In J. C. Caldwell & G. Santow (Eds.), *Selected readings in the cultural, social and behavioural determinants of health* (pp.79–100). Canberra: Health Transition Centre.

Cohen, D. W., & Atieno Odhiambo, E. S. (1989). *Siaya: The historical anthropology of an African landscape*. London: James Currey.

Feierman, E. (1981). Alternative medical services in rural Tanzania: A physician's view. *Social Science and Medicine, 15B*, 399–404.

Findley, S., Caldwell, J., Santow, G., Cosford, W., Bised, J., & Broers–Freeman, D. (Eds.) (1990). *What we know about health transition: The cultural, social and behavioural determinants of health.* (Vol. 2). Canberra: Health Transition Centre.

Håkansson, T. (1988) *Bridewealth, women and land. Social change among the Gusii of Kenya.* Uppsala: Almqvist & Wiksell.

Holmboe-Ottesen, G., & Wandel, M. (1991a). Wife, today I only had money for pombe. In K. A. Stølen and M. Vaa (Eds.), *Gender and social change* (pp. 93–119). Oslo: Norwegian University Press.

Holmboe-Ottesen, G., & Wandel, M. (1991b). Men's contribution to the food and nutritional situation in the Tanzanian household. *Ecology of Food and Nutrition*, 26, 83–96.

Janzen, J. M. (1978). *The quest for therapy: Medical pluralism in lower Zaire.* Berkeley: University of California Press.

Janzen, J. M. (1990). Strategies of health seeking and structures of social support in Central and Southern Africa. In S. Findley, J. Caldwell, G. Santow, W. Cosford, J. Bised, & D. Broers–Freeman (Eds.), *What we know about health transition: The cultural, social and behavioural determinants of health, Vol. 2* (pp. 707-719). Canberra: Health Transition Centre.

Kaseje, D., Thuo, M., Mukabana, M., Thorup, H., & Kryger, S. (1986), *A nutrition baseline survey* (report to the Family Life Training Programme, Lwak Centre). Nairobi: Ministry of Culture and Social Services.

Kennedy, E. T., & Cogill, B. (1987). *Income and nutritional effects of the commercialization of agriculture in southwestern Kenya* (Research Report 63). International Food Policy Research Institute.

King, M., King, F., Morley, D., Burgess, L., & Burgess, A. (1972). *Nutrition for developing countries.* Nairobi: Oxford University Press.

Kryger, Susanne. (n.d.). *Social and cultural aspects of childhood malnutrition in Siaya District.* Unpublished manuscript, Institute of Anthropology, Copenhagen.

Mosley, W. H. (1989). Will primary health care reduce infant and child mortality? In J. C. Caldwell & G. Santow, G. (Eds.), *Selected readings in the cultural, social and behavioural determinants of health* (pp. 261–294). Canberra: Health Transition Centre.

Ocholla-Ayayo, A. (1976). *Traditional ideology and ethics among the Southern Luo.* Uppsala: Scandinavia Institute of African Studies.

Olenja, J. M. (1988). *Malnutrition and infant mortality among the Samia of Busia District, Western Kenya: Methodological and conceptual issues.* Paper presented at the workshop on Research and Intervention Issues Concerning Infant and Child Mortality and Health, International Development Reseach Centre, Ottawa, August.

Pala, A. O. (1980). Daughters of the lakes and rivers: Colonization and the land rights of Luo women. In M. Etienne & E. Leacock (Eds.), *Women and colonization* (pp. 186–213). New York: Praeger.

Parkin, D. (1973) The Luo living in Kampala, Uganda, Nairobi, and Central Nyanza, Kenya. In A. Molnos (Ed.), *Cultural source materials for population planning in East Africa,* Vol. 3 (pp. 330-339). Nairobi: East African Publishing House.

Parkin, D. (1978). *The cultural definition of political response: Lineal destiny among the Luo.* London: Academic Press.

Peters, C., & Niemeijer, R. (1987). *Protein-energy malnutrition and the home environment: A study among children in Coast Province, Kenya* (Report 22). Food and Nutrition Planning Unit, Ministry of Planning and National Development, Nairobi and African Studies Centre, Leiden.

Potash, B. (1978). Some aspects of marital stability in a rural Luo community. *Africa, 48*, 380–397.

Republic of Kenya. (1981). *Sessional Paper No. 4 of 1981 on National Food Policy.* Nairobi: Government Printer.

Republic of Kenya. (1983). *Third rural child nutrition survey,1982.* Nairobi: Central Bureau of Statistics.

Sempebwa, E. (1988). *The relationship between mother's availability and infant and child health.* Paper presented at the workshop on Research and Intervention Issues Concerning Infant and Child Mortality and Health, International Development Research Centre, Ottawa, August.

Simons, J. (1989). Cultural dimensions of the mother's contribution to child survival. In J. C. Caldwell & G. Santow, G. (Eds.), *Selected readings in the cultural, social and behavioural determinants of health* (pp. 132–145). Canberra: Health Transition Centre.

Thorup, H. (1988). *Underernæring...sygdom eller straf?* [Malnutrition...sickness or punishment?]. Unpublished magister thesis, Institute of Cultural Sociology, University of Copenhagen.

Van der Geest, S., & Whyte, S. R. (1989). The charm of medicines: Metaphors and metonyms. *Medical Anthropology Quarterly, 3*, 345–367.

Van de Walle, E., & Van de Walle, F. (1991). Breastfeeding and popular aetiology in the Sahel. *Health Transition Review, 1*, 69–81.

Whyte, S. R. (1979/1980). Wives and co-wives in Marachi, Kenya. *Folk, 21–22*, 133–46.

Whyte, S. R. (1988). *Kenya's Family Life Training Program: An impact study.* Copenhagen: DANIDA.

Whyte, S. R. (1990). The widow's dream: Sex and death in western Kenya. In M. Jackson & Ivan Karp (Eds.), *Personhood and agency: The experience of self and other in African cultures* (pp. 95–114). Uppsala: Almqvist & Wiksell.

AGING

8

The Discourse of Neglect: Family Support for the Elderly in Samia

Maria G. Cattell

FAMILY SUPPORT OF AFRICAN ELDERLY

Caring for African Elderly

There is a growing professional and public debate on "the African family" in Kenya today, and an important focus of this debate is the family support of the elderly. Some, emphasizing failures, argue that the idea of the protective extended family is a myth or refer to its disintegration or disappearance. Growing numbers of aged Africans have serious problems because they are widowed, childless or sonless, without family, and/or destitute. Old people may be excluded from formal development projects and their income generating opportunities. Others are resident aliens or refugees living their final years in a foreign country because of labor migration, war, or political instability. Some—usually very frail elderly who no longer contribute to their families—suffer neglect or abuse (Colson & Scudder, 1981; Cox & Mberia, 1977; Folta & Deck, 1987; Guillette, 1992; Hampson, 1982, 1990; Khasiani, 1983; Menya, 1985; Nyanguru, 1987; Okojie, 1988; Potash, 1986; Sangree, 1987, this volume; Treas & Logue, 1986).

However, in sub-Saharan Africa, there is rarely any alternative to family support (Cattell, 1993). Most of the available evidence indicates that extended families, though overstretched and often with inadequate resources, continue to be the primary support system for vulnerable members, including children (Kilbride, 1986, 1992; Kilbride & Kilbride 1990, this volume; Weisner, this volume) and the elderly.

For example, in large scale surveys conducted in the 1980s in four West African nations, Peil (1985, 1988) found that families, while providing varying levels of support, remain strong in both urban and rural areas. About 80 percent of her respondents (aged sixty and over) were receiving help from children, grandchildren, and siblings. Elsewhere, Peil and her colleagues state that "assumptions that societal changes are leading to disintegration of family life are premature" (Ekpenyong, Oyeneye, & Peil, 1986, p. 17).

Indeed, families are the chief support of the elderly everywhere (Cattell, 1992a; Kendig, Hashimoto, & Coppard, 1992; Kosberg, 1992; Shanas, 1979). In nonindustrial or less developed nations, sons and daughters are the primary caregivers for elderly parents (Nydegger, 1983; Rubinstein & Johnsen, 1982); in developed countries children rank second to spouses in providing elder care, as in the United States (Chappell, 1990).

Among the Samia, a Luyia subgroup in western Kenya, family support networks of the elderly center on parent–child exchanges but include others, notably wives (for men) and persons connected through the key parent–child dyad, especially daughters-in-law and grandchildren. Support of the elderly involves extended families whose mutual obligations are acted out over entire lifetimes, as will be shown in this chapter. I will argue in this paper that elderly and non-elderly Kenyans alike share in a "complaint discourse" about their problems. The elderly focus on neglect of their needs and lack of attention and respect. The younger focus on all the heavy demands on their very limited resources to help the elderly. This discourse can be seen as a way of reinforcing or attempting to recast and justify changes in social norms regarding the social contract of caregiving obligations.

The Meaning of Family: Families as Exchange Networks

In kin-based subsistence systems, the interdependent extended family has been the major support network for all its members, with older persons counting on their children for security in old age. Even with this century's radical social, economic, and political shifts in Kenya, exchange-oriented family ideology ("family morality" [Caldwell, 1982]) continues to provide the cultural context and moral force for family support of the elderly and others. This is so despite some individualistic tendencies such as household formation and stress on individual achievement and the consequences of universal education and westernization, which are essential to wealth flows reversals and fertility decline (Bradley, this volume). The reasons for this are partly ideological, related to cultural values (cf. Weisner, Edwards, de Wolf, this volume), partly practical in terms of household organization and family risk management (Cain, 1985; Caldwell & Caldwell, 1987; Frank & McNicoll, 1987; Nugent, 1985).

In this chapter "family" sometimes refers to residential units, for example, in the rural homestead or compound, called in the Samia language *edaala* (plural, *amadaala*). *Amadaala* commonly have three generations sharing the compound (Cattell, 1989a; Nangina Hospital, 1986). In 1985 I carried out a survey of old people (age fifty and over) of Samia in western Kenya: 200 women and 216 men. Of these 416 elders, 75 percent lived in multigenerational *amadaala*, most often with daughters-in-law and grandchildren present. Those present in the homestead are, of course, the ones most likely to provide routine, ongoing help and personal care when needed and other necessities, including social interaction.

I also use family to refer to the wider extended family whose members are geographically dispersed (by school attendance, marriage, and employment) into "duolocal" or "multilocal" families (Weisner, this volume), which straddle rural and urban locations and growing wealth and social class differences. For example, nineteen of the elders in my 1985 survey of older Samia had no living child, three hundred and sixty-seven of the rest had children living away from the home area, and half reported contacts weekly or several times a month with children living "outside." Only eight elders said they never saw outside children.

Created in part by their attachment to place (especially the rural home place) and shared residence, families are also created through choice and negotiation, conflict and struggle, visits and exchanges (Fapohunda & Todaro, 1988; Moore, 1978). In this view families are not rigid units determined by the boundary hedges of an *edaala*, nor by immutable kinship based on birth and marriage. Rather, families have a contingent nature arising from kin ties, which are either ignored or kept active through a variety of contacts and exchanges. Families are "dense centers of exchange relationships" (Guyer, 1979, p. 5). Family exchanges include persons, labor, goods, money, affection, advice, and other material and nonmaterial benefits (Knowles & Anker, 1981; Rempel & Lobdell, 1978; Ross, 1975; Ross & Weisner, 1977). Through exchange, families become support networks for their members (Kendig, 1986).

Intergenerational Contracts

In an exchange perspective, family relationships are conceived as "implicit contracts" (Fapohunda & Todaro, 1988). Family contracts involve shared ideas about relationships and appropriate exchanges between kin dyads such as parent and child, in-laws of different generations (for example, mother-in-law and daughter-in-law), siblings, and grandparent and grandchild. All these (and others) are relevant to family support of the elderly, but the focus here is the parent–child contract.

Throughout sub-Saharan Africa, respect for elders and care of the elderly are important indigenous values, with parents and children at the center of family exchange relationships. In this tradition, wealth (or benefits) flow up the generations—from children to parents (Caldwell, 1982). In Caldwell's view, these "wealth flows" are transactions of material goods and other benefits such as labor, leisure, and advice. The time frame is that of a lifetime. The ideal is that children care for elderly parents, just as parents once cared for them (LeVine & LeVine, 1985). This "intergenerational contract" does not come from written law but is implicit in shared cultural understandings: "the values, the habits, the conventions of behaviour which give one generation an expectation of certain actions on the part of another" (Thomson, 1989, p. 372). Their fundamental underlying principle is reciprocity, or the expectation that in the long run everyone is treated fairly (see also Bradley, this volume).

Under the stresses of modern life, especially the geographic dispersion of families (Kilbride & Kilbride, 1990; Weisner, 1976) and the impoverishment of many

Figure 8.1
Samia and Bunyala Locations, Busia District, Kenya

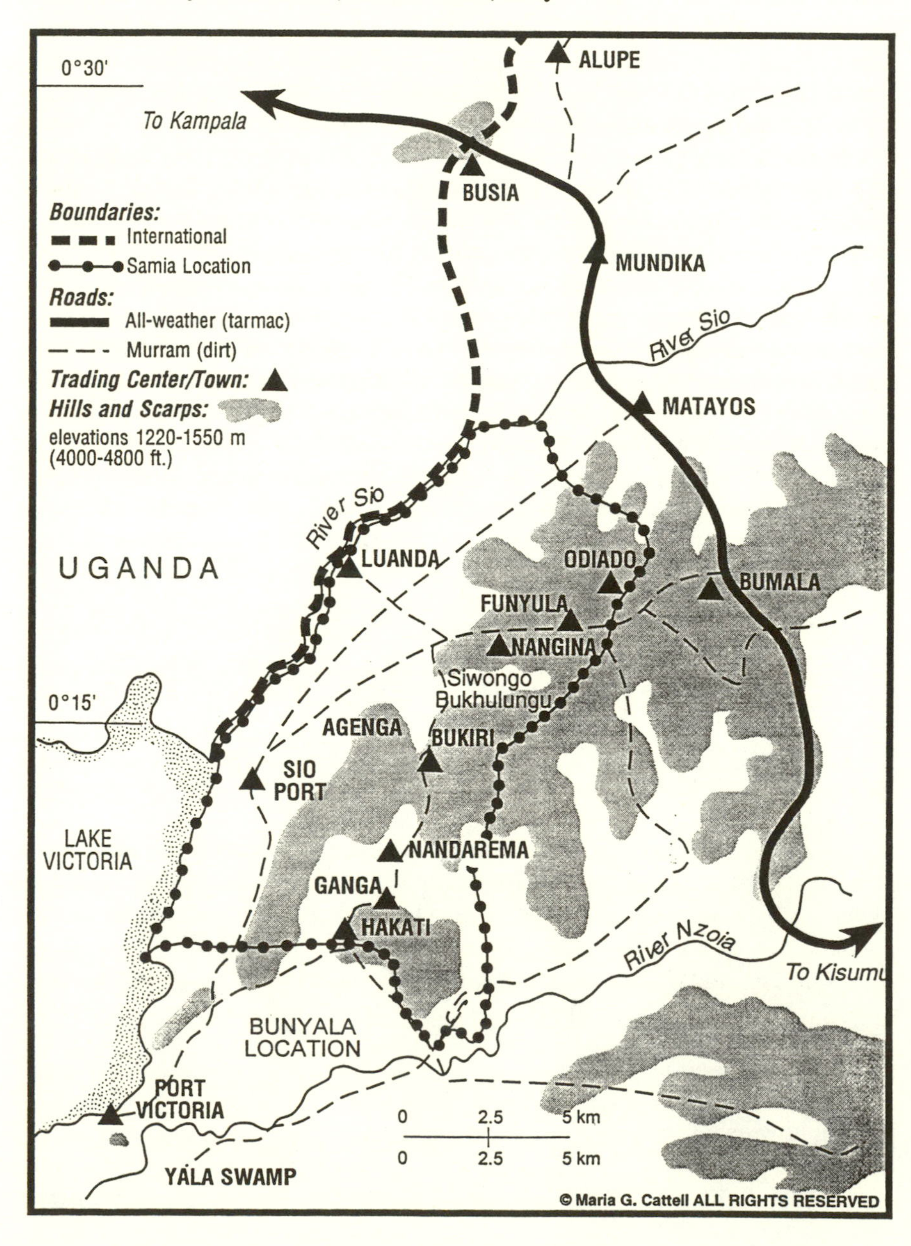

Africans (Illiffe, 1987), combined with demographic aging (Albert & Cattell, 1994; Thomson, 1989), this intergenerational contract is the subject of much debate in Kenya at both national and local levels—in the media, in professional discourse, and in everyday conversations (and in other parts of the world, too, e.g., Bengtson & Achenbaum, 1993). Frequently one reads or hears that "families are neglecting their old people." The remainder of this chapter deals with the issue of family support of the elderly from the perspectives of both discourse, or talk about the matter, in Kenya and in Samia, and practice, or what people in Samia are actually doing about it.

RESEARCH SITES AND METHODS

Data for this chapter were obtained from ethnographic fieldwork among Abaluyia people in western Kenya, primarily in Samia Location, but also in Bunyala Location, south of Samia, and among Abaluyia in the city of Nairobi. The research extended over two years, from November 1983 through November 1985, with visits of four to six weeks in 1982, 1987, 1990, 1992, and 1993. The map of Samia Location (Figure 8.1) shows the western Kenya research area, where I spent most of my time at Nangina, Siwongo, and Bukhulungu. Research methods included participant observation; informal and structured interviews with people of various ages, including seventh- and eighth-grade school children, mature adults, and the elderly; biographical narratives of older Abaluyia; and, in 1985, a survey of 416 older Samia (200 women, 216 men) carried out in four sublocations ranging from Odiado and Luanda to Sio Port and Bukiri (for more details, see Cattell, 1989a).

A CENTURY OF CHANGE IN SAMIA

The Samia (*Abasamia*) are a Luyia subgroup dispersed through the hill country surrounding the northern shores of Lake Victoria in Kenya and in the lakeside community of Sio Port, Kenya (Figure 8.1); many Samia also live across the international border in Uganda.

In the late nineteenth century, Samia was a small scale society of self-sufficient agropastoralists with a barter economy (Kitching, 1980), local money (livestock, grain, Samia hoes), and locally made products (Burt, 1980). Political systems were kin based (Seitz, 1978), and culture was policy, as Ronald Cohen (1984) puts it. Because of cattle raids and attacks on homes, people lived in *engoba* (singular: *olukoba*), walled villages of ten to twenty households (Soper, 1986)—as was the case throughout western Kenya (Thomson, 1885; Wandibba, 1985). Strangers were regarded with suspicion and hostility. Most people stayed close to home during the day. At night they came in from their fields with their cows and secured the *olukoba* gates. The major reference point for individuals was extended family clusters of fathers and sons, that is, patrilineages (*enyumba*). Intergenerational relationships were played out over lifetimes lived in clearly defined spaces, where family caregivers were likely to be readily available and enforcement for deviations (through social sanctions such as public opinion and elders' reprimands) could be immediate and difficult to evade.

During the twentieth century this relatively isolated world changed radically under an onslaught of outside influences and externally motivated social, economic, and political development: colonialism and nationhood, urbanization, and the introduction of money, cash cropping, wage labor, and various European ideologies and practices including Christianity and formal education. Power and control of resources shifted to a considerable degree from local elders to outsiders and to the young (Cattell, 1989a, 1989b, 1992b, 1994). Now, in the late twentieth century, homes (*amadaala*) in Samia are spread out over the Samia hills, and many families have members who live in other rural areas in Kenya, in cities, and abroad. These geographically extended families spread out subsistence risks by allowing members to participate in a variety of opportunities in both the rural (peasant) and urban (wage labor) economies (Cattell, 1988; Ross, 1975; Wandibba, this volume).

Growing Old among Kin

Despite this century of complex and profound change, many individuals live their lives in what Moore (1978) calls "lifeterm social arenas" of relatively constant social networks. Rural-dwelling family members visit their city kin and stay for lengthy periods. Urban-dwelling family members engage in circular migration, coming home for visits to maintain their rural ties for immediate and long-term benefits to themselves (LeVine & LeVine, 1985; Ross, 1975; Weisner, 1976). Many retire or plan to retire to their rural homes. Even longtime urban dwellers regard the rural area as home and source of personal and social identity, among Abaluyia as among Luo, as was brought out dramatically in the controversial burial of a Luo attorney, S. M. Otieno (Egan, 1987; Cohen & Odhiambo, 1989; Obudho & Aduwo, 1989).

Among the Samia today, even with the high prevalence of multilocal families, most people grow up in a strongly kin oriented context. Clans, patrilineages, and extended families are salient in the lives of most Samia in both rural and urban areas. In spite of extensive male participation in labor migration through the century, mostly elderly Samia have lived out their lives among close kin in a lifeterm social arena. Of the 200 older women surveyed, 7 percent had been labor migrants, 93 percent had lived "many years" (since marriage) in the same home. Of the 216 men, 87 percent had worked (and lived) outside Samia, but 73 percent said they had lived in Samia "all their lives"—a reflection of the subjective and practical reality that even when you live elsewhere, the land is home, and home is also where your kinspeople are.

DISCOURSE: "OUR OLD PEOPLE ARE BEING NEGLECTED"

African parents continue to look upon children as their best old-age security, generally with good reason, as pointed out above. Persistent cultural beliefs about family relationships continue to guide people's behavior, albeit in settings pervaded by influences from the world market economy, the national government, formal schools, and other imported institutions and extrafamilial ideologies. The indigenous ideology of the parent–child intergenerational contract remains powerful, but there is unease at all levels about the current situation and future prospects of the growing numbers of African elderly (Okojie, 1988; cf. Shuman, Stanford, Harbert, Schmidt, & Roberts, 1993)—an unease that has sparked a widespread professional and folk discourse about family support of old people. The debate is sometimes directed toward alternatives such as pensions and old people's homes, but most often it focuses on family support.

Beyond that, the discourse is also about being African in an Africa that has changed radically during the past century. It is about keeping the best of "African tradition," or "our African culture," as it is often called in the Kenya press, about forging an African identity, as discussed by writers from Maquet (1972) and Taban lo Liyong (1969) to Ngugi (1981), Were (1982, 1985), and many authors in Ojwang and Mugambi (1989).

The commentary on family support of African elderly often takes the form of complaints, dire predictions, and exaggerated claims of family neglect of old people. Over and over one encounters such remarks as "The extended family is falling apart." "We're forgetting our African traditions." "Old people don't get respect and care as they used to." "Our old people are being neglected."

Such comments call attention to families' struggles in today's world. They indicate concern about maintaining the integrity of families and defining the role of the family in modern life. They attempt to reinforce culturally valued standards of behavior, or "cooperation-reinforcing" norms, which are threatened by the forces of modernization and new ideas and values concerning family exchange and elder care (Nugent, 1990). While government policy can help to reinforce family cooperation (Nugent, 1990; Okojie, 1988), norm reinforcement is an ongoing process of everyday life (Cohen, 1984). In the long run, it may result in renegotiation of the terms of intergenerational contracts.

As discussed above, the professional literature on aging in Africa contains contradictory themes on family support of the elderly: laments for the demise of the extended family and increasingly abundant evidence of the paramount role of the extended family in the care of elderly Africans. The same themes are expressed in Kenya at workshops and conferences, in professional publications (e.g., Kenya NGO Organising Committee, 1985), in newspapers, and in conversations on the streets of Nairobi and the footpaths of rural Samia. There are numerous anecdotes about neglectful families (especially sons and daughters) and abandoned elders. There is much discussion of the way things were, the way things are, they way they should be. Almost everyone engages in this discourse, from the poor and illiterate to President Moi.

Given the extent of this discourse, a few examples of how this discourse is conducted at the national level will situate the Samia discourse in a wider cultural context.

The Discourse of Norm Reinforcement in Kenya

Rosenberg (1990) describes "complaint discourse" as the means by which elderly !Kung of Botswana call attention to their needs. !Kung exaggerate and fabricate to suggest what could happen if families neglect their old people—like the old man who told a "big story" about having been abandoned by his people when he was injured, when in fact they had given him solicitous care. Rosenberg interprets the old man's big story as a restatement of "the social contract of caregiving obligations" by a negative example (1990, p. 26).

Kenyans also engage in complaint discourse as a way of reinforcing social norms. For example, when they talk about families in the abstract, they lament that "the family is disappearing" and "our old people are being neglected." But when they are asked, "How is everyone at home?" they complain about the demands their families put on them, report their struggles to provide for children and "my old mom," and tell the listener how they are contributing to a brother's "dowry" (bridewealth) or that a sister or cousin is staying with them in order to attend a better school or provide help in the home, or that they have to go home for a family funeral.

At a HelpAge Kenya "Seminar on the Aged," a government official said that the African extended family had "completely died off and some traces of it can be found only in rural areas" (quoted in Tout, 1989, p. 84, and HelpAge Kenya, 1988, p. 22). The recognition that "traces" of the extended family still exist in rural areas seems grudging and most probably contravenes the experience of the official who made it and the experience of most Kenyans. Those who succeed in the modern sector and have salaried employment are particularly likely to be deluged with requests for assistance from family members. They know very well that there is more than a trace of the extended family around.

Kenya's daily newspapers report on and thus popularize various local publications and the speeches of politicians, government officials, and other prominent Kenyans. But the newspapers also have their own voice—often a complaining voice, but sometimes one presenting more positive aspects of aging. I will give a few examples.

On the positive side, during 1985 there were a number of full-page features on elderly Kenyans. Some of these elders (men), such as ex-senior chiefs, were widely known; others (women) were persons of local fame, such as a traditional dancer, a midwife, a "tree-climbing grandma" who harvested lemons and oranges and took them to a Nairobi market, and a banana hawker. The articles emphasized the past accomplishments and present vigor of these old people. Every one of the twelve that I read described the person as living in a family setting.

Many newspaper articles fell into the complaint category, such as "When old age becomes a heavy burden" (1984, p. 11). In this full-page article the reader's eye is caught by a large picture of an old man bent beneath his possessions, which he has rescued from his slum home, just destroyed by police. The text warns that "[w]ith the disintegration of the extended family system, the mutual obligation of caring for family members has been eroded and even in the rural areas, the problem is beginning to get out of hand." The article deals primarily with destitute urban elderly, "most of whom have lost their roots," that is, they are without family, they have no connections in the rural area. Institutional solutions such as homes for the aged, daycare programs, and pension schemes are presented. Whatever the accuracy of this portrayal of Nairobi's old people, the article is a vivid commentary on what could happen to all Kenyans. It is a warning, a danger signal.

Some news items called up visions of an African society in which the extended family worked smoothly and intergenerational obligations and expectations were fulfilled. For example, at a wedding, the president of Kenya advised the newlyweds not to follow western lifestyles but to welcome their parents into their homes and care for them in their old age, in accordance with African tradition ("Moi urges couples to live in peace," 1984, p. 3). In another item, Professor Mutungi railed against homes for the aged as "unAfrican" and called for a government program which would enable aging people to be cared for within their families ("Homes for the aged . . ." 1984).

In a humbler rebuke, a journalist described a visit to her grandmother, who served her bread instead of the eggs she had expected—eggs being a favorite gift of grandmothers to visiting grandchildren. This provoked nostalgia about the traditional foods her grandmother used to serve during week-long visits, and no doubt resounded in the memories of many Kenyans who have fond memories of visits with a grandmother and the "sweet" foods she gave them (Ngunjiri, 1985).

The *Kenya Times* had a regular page of poems written by its readers. One poem by Kenneth Gituna (1984), speaking in the voice of an elder, expresses central elements in the intergenerational contract: parents' struggles to educate their children and the return they get—in this case, rejection. The elder complains that when the young get education and success,

> They forget their senescent parents
> Back at home
> Who made the sacrifices
> Who raked in their cravings
> to educate them.
> They slap them on the face.

In these and other ways the discourse on intergenerational relationships and obligations, on the role of the extended family in the lives of modern Kenyans, is carried on in the public arena at the national level. It is also heard in Samia.

Discourse about Old Age in Samia: "I Am Suffering"

In Samia, the discourse goes on along the footpaths, in other public places, in homes. Here it has local meanings but is, at the same time, part of the wider discourse on intergenerational relations. Kenya's newspapers are sold in rural shops and brought back by travelers; their content enters local communication streams, which are almost entirely oral, especially among older persons, the majority of whom cannot read and write.[1]

From eighth graders to ancients, the Samia people expressed themes of reciprocity and familial interdependence, recognizing them as fundamental principles in social relations and survival strategies throughout life (Cattell, 1988). Older people said, "I can still take care of my people. I still work. I still feed my family." Younger people, even primary school pupils, combined personal ambition with family responsibility, hoping for a good education so they can get employment and help their family. One eighth-grade schoolgirl wrote in an essay that she wanted to help her family "because I saw the suffering they have had with my school fees."

In this family context, the parent–child dyad is central. Key Samia metaphors of parenthood are giving birth and feeding: parents are those who gave birth to you (said of men as well as women) and fed you, with mothers especially defined by food-giving. Therefore children owe their parents, especially their mothers, not just in an existential sense, but quite concretely, for nutrition, health, and many kinds of parental caregiving. A mother can say, "I fed you with this breast. I sent you to school. How can you refuse me?" The Samia intergenerational contract is clear; its terms are understood by both young and old. Children should help parents, be obedient to them, show them respect throughout their lives. When parents are too old to work, they should be fed by their children—just as those children had been fed when they were too young to work. Lastborn sons in particular should care for their mothers so they do not suffer in old age.

The obligation of child to parent does not wait for the parent to become old; it is lifelong. By the time children are a few years old they should begin to "reward" their parents by minding a younger child or doing errands. Throughout their lives children should give their parents their labor (work) and the fruits of their labor (gifts and money) along with respect, obedience, and deferential behavior. Even a person who becomes "useless," who can no longer work or even give advice, should be taken care of by children and other family members. "After all," people say, "my parents fed me and cared for me when I was young." This clear statement of a conception of lifetime intergenerational exchange was often repeated in conversations.

Many older people (63% of those in my survey) said there is "no goodness" in old age, and a word repeated many times was *okhusanda* (to suffer), a favored phrase being "I am just suffering." But many also said, "Old age is good if you have children to help you; then you can just sit and eat." This vision of "sitting and eating," of basking in the sun or sitting before a fire and waiting for food to be brought, was used by young people also. It is in fact a key metaphor for the proper conclusion of the intergenerational contract when an old parent becomes too frail to work.

With so much agreement about the way things should be, what else is there to say about it? For one thing, old people had many complaints about the young.

(Older Abasamia are experts in complaint discourse. Many young people said to me, "Oh, old people always complain. That's the way they are.") In conversations and interviews elders recalled "our days," when children respected their parents, when men and boys ate together at the evening fire (*esiosio*) and girls and younger boys were with their mothers in the kitchen and later in the evening in the grandmother's house (*esibinje*). Such reminiscences often included a counterpoint, a direct contrast with the situation today: "Young people nowadays don't want to walk (or sit/eat/talk) with old people." In the survey, such comments were made by many to explain responses to closed-end questions such as one that asked if there is a gap today between old and young—with 90 percent agreeing with the statement. Many comments focused on schools and generational differences created by education (e.g., speaking English, turning to books for information) as the cause of this gap.

Elders have other things to complain about than the young, however—and even those who are well off by local standards, who are able to "sit and eat" because they are taken care of by their families, even they complain, as in the following case studies.

Opiyo: A Frail Old Man "Sits and Eats" While Complaining

In 1985 Opiyo of Siwongo village was about eighty years old. He no longer went to dig or visit kin and friends, nor did he go to market or chief's meetings, not even to funerals. He stayed in his modest compound where one day was much like another. Opiyo got up from bed about 7:30, when the sun's rays were warming the compound, and went outside to sit on his stool. Here the frail old man sat, chin in his hands, until noon. Then he ate lunch, prepared by his wife or daughter-in-law, rested a bit in his house, and sat on his stool again until the evening chill sent him into the kitchen to keep warm by the fire. After eating, he went to bed. He did not complain about his care but was unhappy about his loss of strength and inability to walk or do any work. "Old age is just too much. I have no strength; I am useless." Asked how he saw his future, Opiyo (a saved or born-again Christian; see Cattell, 1992b) said, "I only think about God." Advised by local hospital personnel to have a blood transfusion, Opiyo refused: "Let me just be this way. Will I put off death?" Was he consulted by young people? "How can I advise those who do not come?" he complained. "When they pass here, do they even greet me?" Frail as he was, Opiyo lived until December 1986.

Mzee Oyioma: Health, Wealth, and Complaints

Mzee Oyioma lives in a prosperous *edaala* in the village of Bukhulungu. His home has several large houses and five granaries. Even the latrine has a metal door and plenty of headroom. Several of Mzee's well educated children have good jobs. Mzee Oyioma was in his late sixties in 1984. He was tall and thin but vigorous; he carved wooden canoe paddles and biked many kilometers to Port Victoria to sell them. Whenever I visited him, he dressed up in a shirt with buttons, trousers, and jacket—all clean with no patches or tears. His family (wife, son, daughter-in-law, grandchildren) always treated him with respect. But in spite of his obvious prosperity and the respect and care of his family, Mzee Oyioma had complaints: "If I had been educated and could have had other [more] educated children, then I couldn't be suffering now. When I was younger, I had strength and money from my fishing business. It was a life of happiness. Now all that I had, I don't have that now. Now I am suffering." Nearly a decade later, in 1993, he was thinner and frailer, but still with his family, still taking his paddles to Port Victoria—and still complaining.

This generation of old people grew up in a Samia that was just beginning to be affected by changes that would transform their society in the twentieth century. They remembered the respect and care given their own parents and grandparents; they themselves had been instructed by their elders at *esiosio*, the men's fire, or in *esibinje*, the grandmother's house—institutions now defunct (cf. Cohen, 1985; Bradley, in press). Even allowing for the common human tendency to idealize the past, their memories very likely represent a time when older Samia had more control of their world and its resources, material and human, received more respect and care from the young, and had more opportunities to educate and advise (Cattell, 1989b, 1994; cf. Wanjala, 1985). Their complaints expressed justifiable disappointments about their expectations for a good old age.

Elders' complaints revealed difficulties in adjusting to aging bodies. Indeed, when you become old, life is not as good as it used to be, as both Opiyo and Oyioma said. It is not good to lose strength, to reduce work, to be unable to care for your family or participate fully in exchanges, to wonder if you will be able to sit and eat when your time for that comes. Even when family support is exemplary, old people may express a subjective or inner reality that seems out of keeping with the "objective" reality of being able to sit and eat (cf. George, 1993).

Elders' complaints also served as reminders or even exhortations to potential caregivers about the way things should be done. By their complaints Mzee Oyioma, Opiyo, and many other elderly Samia upheld and reinforced norms of family care for aged parents, reminding their children of filial duty. Old people do this in many cultures, and their complaints seem to be "a conscious or unconscious strategy to ensure or maximize support" (Foner, 1985, p. 392). Thus it seems likely that discourses on reinforcement of intergenerational contracts are nothing new in Samia, but it is also likely that they are particularly intense now because of the radical changes that have occurred in the lifetimes of today's old people. It is even more poignant that these elders themselves helped bring about the changes as innovators through labor migration, becoming Christians, sending their children to school, and in other ways.

I also heard many instances of complaint discourse from local health care and social work professionals and from younger Samia. Many bewailed the passing of the old ways, today's lack of respect for the elders, the neglect of old people by their families. There was contradictory evidence in their own behavior and, often enough, in their own words, even in casual remarks such as those of the girl in a shop who explained her presence by saying, "I've come to buy soap for my granny." Nevertheless, their comments reflect modern stresses on families and struggles to live up to their own ideals (see also Cattell, forthcoming).

PRACTICE: SAMIA FAMILIES AND THEIR ELDERLY

Family Support of Elderly Samia

Do Samia children meet their obligations to their parents? Yes, in many cases they do, qualified by factors such as proximity, resources available, and other demands on them. However, some elderly have no living children (childless elderly are not absent altogether, as Sangree [this volume] found in Tiriki). Some have just one child, who gives little or no help; they must depend on others whose motivations may be less strong than those of sons and daughters. Some elderly suffer neglect, abandonment, and even abuse.

Manyuru: A Woman without a Son "Sits and Eats"

The old widow Manyuru's only daughter lived a day's walk away. She came to see her mother once or twice a year to repair her house and do other work; occasionally she sent a small sum of money. Manyuru lived in Bukhulungu village in her husband's compound (he died in 1964) with two younger (but not young) cowives. Each woman had her own house. The cowives' big houses were built by their sons, but Manyuru, her only son dead, lived in small houses built for her by community health workers or by a stepson. In 1985, Manyuru, then about 85 years old, no longer had strength to cultivate. Her cowives sometimes shared the food they grew, but on most days Manyuru hobbled to a stepson's home for a meal. Grandchildren took firewood and water to her house. By 1987, blind from cataracts and untreated eye infections, unable to walk, she just stayed in her house. She continued to receive necessities through her extended family resources until her death in a house fire in 1992.

Even in Death: A Father Abandoned by His Son

A widowed old man had not seen his only son for many years. The son was employed in Kisumu, about sixty miles from Samia. When the old man died, the son was notified, but he did not come home even then. Neighbors and other kin who came to bury the old man did not know what to do, as burial was properly the son's duty. No one could explain why the son didn't come. Finally the old man's decaying body was buried when a social worker from Nangina Hospital accepted the responsibility. The son never came.

A Hidden Old Woman: Her Family Conceals Their Shameful Neglect

An old woman, no longer able to walk, was kept by her family in a house off the main path. She was kept there to conceal her so anyone passing the house and visitors to the home would not realize that the family, though possessed of the means, was neglecting the old woman, not providing her with sufficient food, water, clothing, and firewood.

The quality of care may vary with the quality of salient relationships. Conflict between the generations is found in many if not all societies (Foner, 1984). Among the Samia, an older woman's well-being can be crucially affected by her relationship with her daughter-in-law, who is often her son's surrogate in her support and care.

Late-Life Conflict: A Mother-in-law Suffers

Cecilia, strong and active all her life, was a farmer and potter. She had educated her children through money earned from making pots, including giant beer pots taller than herself. But by 1985 Cecilia, then aged about seventy-six, was becoming frail and depended on the family in her *edaala*. Everything was fine until one son, working some kilometers distant, took his wife and children to live with him. The other son's wife had never gotten along with her mother-in-law. So Cecilia often waited "too long" for the daughter-in-law to bring water and food. Even the grandchildren were not allowed to help their grandmother by bringing her water or clay for making the small pots she could still manage to produce. Things were still this way in 1993.

Such neglect was not the usual pattern, however. In most homes I visited where *abakofu* (old persons) lived, families were trying to meet their obligations to their elderly and to see that they had adequate housing, food, and clothing. In the 1985 survey, interviewers judged that most older persons' houses were in as good condition—or even in better condition—than other houses in their *edaala*, in contrast to the situation of the old woman neglected by her family. A number of elderly, asked about their daily routines in focused interviews, described eating patterns similar to those of the population as a whole (Nangina Hospital,1986). On weekdays the old people (like younger adults) often wore torn, dirty clothes, because you don't wear nice clothes for digging in the fields and doing other work; on Sundays, when they came to church, *abakofu* sported "Sunday best" like everyone else.

A few general questions about family support were asked in the 1985 survey. As shown in Table 8.1, most (89%) said they were receiving at least some assistance from sons and daughters and often from grandchildren (53%) and other kin as well. This was true regardless of the elders' age or functional ability. If these 416 old people are typical of Samia elderly (as I have no doubt they are), then most elderly in rural Samia are receiving assistance in the form of services, gifts, and money from sons, daughters, and other family members.

Of those with living children, nearly all of the 189 women (96%) and 208 men (91%) said they were getting some assistance from children. There are some striking gender differences in the patterns of assistance. For example, when it comes to work, more daughters help their mothers, more sons help their fathers. Daughters are more likely to give gifts (often food or clothing), while sons are more likely to give money. In general, women receive more assistance from their children than men, which fits the cultural expectation that children must be most assiduous in providing care for elderly mothers. These gender differences in patterns of family support are probably related to a variety of factors including work roles, residential patterns, marital situations, ages of children and grandchildren, gender differences in economic resources, affective aspects of parent–child relationships, and the needs (real or perceived) of the parents.

In practice, sons' obligations, especially personal care, often are met by their wives and children. Indeed, as everywhere in the world (Albert & Cattell, 1994),

Table 8.1
Sources of Support for Old People of Samia[a,d]

	Women (N = 200)		Men (N = 216)	
Characteristic	N	%	N	%
Help from child/children[b]	182	91	189	88
Get some help from sons	153	77	161	75
Son(s) give				
gifts	108	63	71	36
money	77	45	72	36
work	65	38	94	47
Get some help from daughter(s)	161	81	147	68
Daughter(s) give				
gifts	128	71	91	46
money	48	27	45	23
work	93	50	92	43
Help from grandchild/grandchildren[c]	130	65	92	43

[a] Missing values are not noted. Percentages are rounded.
[b] Of the 45 who receive no help from a child, 19 (11 women, 8 men) have no living children.
[c] 93% of the women, 87% of the men have at least one grandchild; of those being helped by grandchildren, 26% of the women and 39% of the men said their grandchildren were too young to work.
[d] The following were not asked about directly but were mentioned as sources of support in responses to open-ended questions:

Daughter-in-law 54 (number of homes in which daughter-in-law stays = 244)
Spouse provides necessities 30
Spouse helps with problems 18
Other family (e.g., brother) 9
Nonfamily (e.g. religious group, work group) 42

Everyone was asked who provided their food and water; because of little variation, these responses were not tabulated, but nearly all men said their wives prepared food and carried water for them.

women in Samia provide most hands-on care to the elderly, while sons are more likely to provide financial help (cf. Sangree, this volume).

Consolata: A Daughter-in-Law's Tender Loving Care

In 1984 and 1985, Consolata, in her late fifties, was an active woman, rarely at home because she was always going somewhere: to church or prayer group, to market to sell a chicken or buy soap or salt, to the mill to have her maize ground into flour. But in 1987 she was dying of breast cancer. Her family had taken her to the hospital, but it was too late for medical treatment. She spent her final months sitting on the veranda of her house in Siwongo village, cared for by her daughter-in-law Mary (not by her husband, who was still with her). Mary had left her husband at his job in Mombasa and come home to care for her mother-in-law. For months, Mary cooked and served food to Consolata, washed her body and her clothes, talked with Consolata as she worked. During the day people passing the house called out greetings or stopped to chat. The nights were long and lonely with little to distract Consolata from her pain. When she died she was buried in her husband's compound.

Wives provide much care of elderly men, as with Opiyo, as they provide many essential services for husbands throughout their married lives. Almost all the men surveyed (92%) had at least one wife (one-third had two or more wives). Of the two hundred women surveyed, 56 percent were widowed and had to depend primarily on their children and other extended family members, including daughters, daughters-in-law, and grandchildren. In any case, like Consolata, women would not receive personal care from husbands; that is not men's work.

Though daughters move to their husbands' homes when they marry, the mother–daughter bond often remains strong. Daughters return home to be with their mothers, sometimes for extended visits and also because they continue to be members of their father's patrilineage and need to be present for certain ritual and family decision making occasions. Thus, even though they are living away from their parents, many daughters continue to assist their mothers with work. Even Manyuru's daughter, herself in her sixties, did what she could. Daughters also give gifts to their mothers directly or through their children.

Because women go to live in their husbands' homes when they marry (patrilocal residence), any children live in homes with their paternal grandparents, whom they see daily. They also visit their mothers' parents, especially during school holidays. The visiting grandchild always takes a gift (food or other items such as clothing and blankets) and usually receives gifts (especially food: eggs, a chicken) in return. While visiting, the grandchild helps with work; and for both grandchild and grandparent, warmth, good humor, and happiness are likely to be elements in the affectional exchange (Cattell, 1994). Women receive more assistance from grandchildren than do men because they are more likely to have grandchildren old enough to help, since women become parents at much younger ages than men and also because most men get the same kind of help from their wives.

Many sons and daughters living in urban areas come home at least several times a year, with some visiting several times a month. Often these visits are of several weeks' or a month's duration. Visitors usually come with gifts, and they do not sit idle for long. As the Samia saying goes, "A visitor is a visitor for three days; then you put a hoe in their hand."

Family care of the elderly is not accidental, however, nor is it simply the result of cultural beliefs. People prepare for old age throughout their lives by investing in kin, especially their children, but also daughters-in-law and grandchildren (cf. Stucki, 1992).

Maua and Ndimu Invest in Children and Grandchildren: Ready to "Sit and Eat"

In 1977, when he was in his mid-fifties, Maua retired from employment with Kenya Railways and returned to Samia to farm the land inherited from his father. For a few years he worked as a night watchman, but stopped because he did not want people to think his children were not providing for him and Ndimu, his wife. Maua had not gone to school, because his father, a man wealthy in cows, believed cows were the best investment for his sons' future. However, Maua, who today owns only one cow, and Ndimu invested heavily in the education of their five children. "It is important to educate your children," said Maua, "for a good child who has gone to school and has a good job will send a money order or clothes or something to his parents." In 1985, though he was a vigorous, active man, Maua complained of poor health and lack of strength. A few years later he was chosen to be village *luguru* (headman) in Siwongo, a post he still held in 1993. Over the years Ndimu has cared for grandchildren born outside of marriage and the sons of divorced cowives. Sometimes she helps her married daughters with childcare, such as daily care for several weeks when one daughter had an emergency need. In 1993 one granddaughter was staying with her in order to attend a nearby school. All their children are well educated, have salaried employment, and help their parents in various ways such as building a house, giving them clothes and money, and helping with farm and domestic work. Maua has already distributed his land to his sons, who are developing their plots. Ndimu and Maua are ready when it is their time to sit and eat.

Nayari Invests in Her Children and "Sits and Eats"

Nayari had been a famous singer (she once sang for President Kenyatta) and a community activist, promoting schools, community health, and her church. She and her husband helped develop a local primary school and sent all their children to school, even their three daughters, who all married well. Two sons became school heads; the third has a prosperous medical clinic in Kisumu town, one hundred kilometers from Nayari's home in Bukiri. After her husband died in 1973 Nayari continued her many activities. She was one of the first to be trained in Nangina Hospital's Community Health Worker program. But by 1987 Nayari, then in her mid-seventies, was so frail that she could no longer leave her home. Once always on the go, she reluctantly accepted her "sit and eat" status. She received excellent and loving care from two coresident daughters-in-law, with whom she had excellent relationships. Nayari also enjoyed the company of a flock of grandchildren living within a few hundred meters of her house and frequent visits from one daughter who lived two hours' walk from her. This woman's lifetime investments in her children made her old age a comfortable one until her death in 1991.

Family Support by Samia Elderly

Old people do not just take—they are actively involved in exchange relationships as long as they are able (cf. Kendig, 1986). In my 1985 survey, 29 percent of the women and 41 percent of the men said they help others—often their own dependent children (more true of men, who may have children with younger wives into their sixties or even seventies) and grandchildren, many born outside of marriage (*abaana besimba*) and cared for by the maternal grandmother (cf. Ingstad, Bruun, Sandberg, & Tlou, 1992; Kilbride, 1992; Kilbride & Kilbride, 1990). In a survey subsample ($n = 252$, women and men combined), 29 percent said they were responsible for at least one grandchild.

Older people also exercise their quintessential capacity of giving advice, especially about farming, Samia customs, and kinship. They also complain that young people "don't want to hear what we old people have to tell them, they just go to books." Nevertheless, many schoolchildren reported (in a survey, $n = 155$) that their grandmothers and grandfathers told them about the past and about Samia customs.

However, as people grow frailer, they produce less, they have less to give. They reduce their activities, both productive and social. Their blood becomes "cool," their brains become "weak," and their advice may no longer be sought. As they sit and wait to eat, wait for someone to bring them food, these frail elders depend not on direct exchanges but on the expectations of care based on the intergenerational contract that assumes lifetime reciprocity between parents and children and, by extension, daughters-in-law and grandchildren.

CONCLUSIONS, THEORETICAL AND PRACTICAL

Theoretical and Methodological Considerations: Families and Exchange

In this chapter, quantitative data give a general picture of elderly Samia in western Kenya. Qualitative data, especially case studies, indicated various ways specific individuals prepared for old age and, as elders, negotiated support and care. This multimethod approach reveals the diversity of experiences and situations among old people living in a relatively homogeneous sociocultural setting—a homogeneity that extends beyond Samia to embrace Abaluyia throughout western Kenya, albeit with a good deal of intracultural variation, as suggested by other chapters in this volume.

A historical dimension, achieved through a combination of published historical sources, biographical interview materials, and my own long term participant observation research, shows the persistence of family morality based on principles of reciprocity and exchange. Even in the contemporary situation of delocalization and family disruption, this cultural model provides the moral force for family support of elderly Samia in the 1980s and 1990s, as it did in the earlier years of the twentieth century.

The value of the exchange framework used here is that it shows families as interactive units over time and space. An exchange perspective reveals the contingent nature of families, the dynamics of families as continually created and recreated, and the processual nature of family support networks. It shows how experiences of old age develop from earlier life events, and how old age security is a continually evolving process. An exchange analysis also highlights the bidirectionality of wealth or benefit flows, in which older people, even the very oldest, participate as long as they are able.

Research Issues: Old People of Sub-Saharan Africa

The following suggestions for future research apply not just to the Samia of Kenya but also to the elderly throughout sub-Saharan Africa. We need to know more about the dynamics of family exchange. Research on the specifics of transactions would show more clearly the strengths and weaknesses of families and ways they do or do not provide support for their older members. In addition, intergenerational contracts are only a subset of an array of implicit family contracts. To understand the full picture of elder support, data on exchanges within as well as between generations (as among spouses or siblings) are needed, and on sources of support beyond the family, especially locally available support such as that from religious groups and mutual aid societies.

Also valuable would be research directed toward categories of elderly individuals who are at greatest risk, for example, the childless or sonless, those living alone, those without family, destitute elderly, the frail and infirm. Retirement, until recently a phenomenon of the industrial world, is another little-known aspect of old age among Africans. In addition, research on aging in Africa needs greater sensitivity to rural–urban, ethnic or cultural, and gender differences and more attention to the impact of AIDS. The AIDS pandemic is a growing threat to elders' security, with currently an estimated 800,000 HIV-positive Kenyans, primarily those aged fifteen to forty-nine (*Weekly Review*, October 1, 1993) who are most likely to be caregivers to the elderly, whose illness often requires care from older family members, and whose deaths leave the elderly alone to bring up grandchildren.

Practical Applications: Western Kenya

In spite of the loosening of family bonds and geographic dispersal of families, in spite of (perhaps also because of) widespread and growing poverty, the extended family in Africa remains the primary support network in western Kenya, as observed in this chapter and others in this volume. Our joint conclusion is that families cannot meet all the needs of all their members but are likely to remain the most important social support/social security system for many years to come.

However, cultural models and practices are not static. They respond to conditions ranging from the macroeconomic to local topography, soil fertility, and land tenure arrangements, as some of this volume's authors discuss in detail (see especially de Wolf). The people of western Kenya have been profoundly affected by delocalization (discussed by the Kilbrides) and by imported values and behaviors interacting with the indigenous. The current family crisis in western Kenya is certainly the result of a century and more of changes that have disrupted indigenous adaptive strategies. The crisis has sparked renegotiation and redefining of various aspects of family relationships among the Luyia and other Kenyans, as is amply demonstrated in this volume.

A number of chapters deal with various categories of family members. Several concern aspects of intergenerational relationships, particularly from the perspective of older persons: the "emerging social contract" regarding the role of grandparents in the modern problem of premarital pregnancies (Kilbride & Kilbride, this volume; see also Håkansson & LeVine, this volume), changes in the status and roles of Tiriki elders in their families and communities over the past four decades (Sangree, this volume), and my own discussion of family support of elderly Samia. Weisner, in his review of the Luyia cultural model of "socially distributed nurturance," focuses on children. Bradley considers the effects on fertility decision making of the empowerment of adult women. This diversity of interests and approaches reveals the complexity and intertwining of family relationships and reminds us that shifts in one dimension, or alterations in one cultural model or family contract, have multiple effects throughout families and communities.

Complexity need not deter efforts at remediation, however. One major thread in many of these chapters is the importance of local knowledge, local values, and local solutions—and the importance (if not necessity) of revitalizing indigenous ideals in contemporary adaptive strategies.

In practical terms regarding the elderly, in Samia and elsewhere in western Kenya, the question is how to strengthen individuals' lifetime ability to be self-supporting and participate in family exchanges as long as possible and thus improve their chances of receiving family care in old age as the ultimate benefit of intergenerational exchange. This will require, among other things, empowering women (Bradley, forthcoming; Chaney, 1990; Rix, 1991; Udvardy & Cattell, 1992) and the elderly (Ageing International, 1993) plus achieving economic development, which reduces the poverty of Africans generally and of women and the elderly in particular.

The strongly positive cultural view of old age and the elderly, currently the subject of much debate, could be encouraged among young people even though modern life has eroded the authority of old people and the respect given to their knowledge. Old people themselves can be important cultural resources in reinforcing cultural norms and the intergenerational contract. Their traditional advisory and teaching roles could be encouraged in modern settings such as schools. Schools—populated almost entirely by young people (teachers as well as students)—often are source and symbol of intergenerational division and conflict. They could also be places where the young are encouraged to seek the knowledge of the old, learn about their cultural heritage, and be reminded of the obligations between the generations through assignments requiring conversations with older family members. Old people themselves could confront the new world on its own terms by coming into classrooms to "advise" the young about local history, customs, and folk culture—also reminding the young of their obligations to the elderly.

Practical Applications: Sub-Saharan Africa

The foregoing discussion of practical applications for western Kenya would also apply to much of sub-Saharan Africa, though it would be important to take into account local cultures and conditions.

In addition, there is the question of what formal institutions are doing or could be doing for the elderly. While pension schemes are sometimes suggested, they are not a realistic solution for the majority in sub-Saharan African nations, many being among the world's poorest nations. But governments can take other, less costly measures, for example by ensuring that modern inheritance laws do not disrupt elders' ability to encourage old age assistance through manipulation of resources that their sons (rarely daughters) hope to inherit and by discouraging the privatization and individualization of tastes, which are a counterforce to family joint interests and mutuality of actions (Nugent, 1990).

Changing attitudes toward the elderly, especially in regard to their value in socioeconomic development, and promotion of income generating activities by them would seem to be a sensible course, though not easy to achieve (Treas & Logue, 1986). Nor would even the most aggressive incorporation of older persons into development projects benefit those most in need: the very old and frail who can no longer engage in productive work. It is unlikely that residential institutions, pensions, and other formal supports will be a major resource for the majority of African elderly any time soon. Family based and community based solutions offer the most viable alternatives and have the advantage of developing from indigenous values and lifeways.

NOTES

I am grateful for the invaluable help over the past decade of my Abaluyia field assistants, especially John Barasa "JB" Owiti from Samia, who has been with me throughout and, since 1985, Frankline Teresa Mahaga from Bunyala. Others who helped in the research include Margaret Rapando Ochieno, Rosemary Okello Apeli, Patrick John Katende, Teresa Mudimbia Makokha, Seline Nafula, Julian Auma Odaba, Pamela M. Ogara, and Pius Wanyama Okomba, all from Samia, and Lynette Makhino and Benson Wandabwa of Bungoma. Thanks also to the Medical Mission Sisters at Nangina, Holy Family Hospital (Nangina), Nangina Girls Primary School, and Samia officials, among others; and to my husband Bob Moss. Above all, *mutio muno* to the many people of Samia and Bunyala who allowed me to share their lives in various ways.

Research funds were provided by the National Science Foundation (grant BNS8306802), the Wenner-Gren Foundation (grant 4506), and Bryn Mawr College (Frederica de Laguna Fund grant). I was a research associate at the Institute of African Studies, University of Nairobi, in 1984 and 1985.

Earlier versions of this chapter were presented at the annual meetings of the American Anthropological Association and the African Studies Association in 1990, as well as at the Conference on Ecological Change and Human Development in Kakamega in 1992.

1. In my survey, 94 percent of the women and 60 percent of the men never attended school. Only fifteen men had gone further than fourth grade; these are close to figures for Busia District as a whole (Republic of Kenya, 1979).

REFERENCES

Adamchak, Donald J., Wilson, A. O., Nyanguru, A., & Hampson. J. (1991). Elderly support and intergenerational transfer in Zimbabwe: An analysis by gender, marital status, and place of residence. *Gerontologist, 31*, 505–513.

Adeokun, Lawrence A. (1984). *The elderly all over the world: Nigeria.* Paris: International Center of Social Gerontology.

Albert, Steven M., & Cattell, Maria G. (1994). *Old age in global perspective: Cross-cultural and cross-national views*. New York: G. K. Hall/Macmillan.

Andretta, Elizabeth H. (1983). Aging, power and status in an East African pastoral society. *Studies in Third World Societies, 23*, 83–109.

Apt, Nana Araba. (1986). Sources of support and care for the elderly in Ghana. *Zeitschrift fur Gerontologie, 19*, 90–95. Tr. David J. S. Gleaton and Mariluise Weber.

Apt, Nana Araba. (1987). The role of grandparents in the care of children in Ghana. In Patrick A. Twumasi (Ed.), *Problems and aspirations of Ghanaian children: Implications for policy and action* (pp. 264–291). Project Report for the Ghana National Commission on Children. Accra: Government of Ghana.

Apt, Nana Araba. (1992). Family support to elderly people in Ghana. In Hal Kendig, Akiko Hashimoto, & Larry Coppard (Eds.), *Family support to the elderly: The international experience* (pp. 203–212). Oxford: Oxford University Press.

Bamisaiye, A., & DiDomenico, C. M. (1983). *The social situation of the elderly in Lagos, Nigeria* (Research report). London: Help the Aged.

Bengtson, Vern L., & Achenbaum, W. A. (Eds.). (1993). *The changing contract across the generations*. New York: Aldine de Gruyter.

Bledsoe, Caroline, & Isiugo-Abanihe, U. C. (1989). Strategies of child fosterage among Mende grannies in Sierra Leone. In Ron Lesthaeghe (Ed.), *Reproduction and social organization in Sub-Saharan Africa* (pp. 442–474). Berkeley: University of California Press.

Bradley, Candice. (1995). Women's empowerment and fertility decline in Western Kenya. In Susan Greenhalgh (Ed.), *Situating fertility: Anthropology and demographic inquiry* (pp. 157–178). Cambridge: Cambridge University Press.

Brown, Charles K. (1985). Research findings in Ghana: A survey on the elderly in the Accra region. *African Gerontology, 4*, 11–33.

Brown, Charles K. (1990). *Aging and old age in Ghana*. Tampa, FL: International Exchange Center on Gerontology.

Brown, Charles K. (1992). Family care of the elderly in Ghana. In Jordan I. Kosberg (Ed.), *Family care of the elderly: Social and cultural changes* (pp. 17–30). Beverly Hills, CA: Sage.

Burt, Eugene C. (1980). *Towards an art history of the Baluyia of Western Kenya*. Unpublished doctoral dissertation, University of Washington.

Cain, Mead. (1985). Fertility as an adjustment to risk. In Alice S. Rossi (Ed.), *Gender and the life course* (pp. 145–159). New York: Aldine.

Caldwell, John C. (1966). The erosion of the family: A study of the fate of the family in Ghana. *Population Studies, 20*, 5–26.

Caldwell, John C. (1982). *Theory of fertility decline*. New York: Academic.

Caldwell, John C., & Caldwell, Pat. (1987). The cultural context of high fertility in sub-Saharan Africa. *Population and Development Review, 13*, 409–437.

Cattell, Maria G. (1988). *Family support for the aged in rural Kenya: Intergenerational exchange and old age security*. Paper presented at the annual meeting of the Society for Cross-Cultural Research, El Paso, Texas.

Cattell, Maria G. (1989a). Old age in rural Kenya: Gender, the life course and social change. Unpublished doctoral dissertation, Bryn Mawr College.

Cattell, Maria G. (1989b). Knowledge and social change in Samia, Western Kenya. *Journal of Cross-Cultural Gerontology, 4*, 225–244.

Cattell, Maria G. (1990). Models of old age among the Samia of Kenya: Family support of the elderly. *Journal of Cross-Cultural Gerontology, 5*, 375–394.

Cattell, Maria G. (1992a). *Informal systems of old age support in developing countries: Anthropological perspectives* (Seminar discussion paper). Washington, DC: World Bank.

Cattell, Maria G. (1992b). Praise the Lord and say no to men: Older Samia women empowering themselves. *Journal of Cross-Cultural Gerontology, 7*, 307–330.

Cattell, Maria G. (1993). Caring for the elderly in sub-Saharan Africa. *Ageing International, 20*(2), 13–19.

Cattell, Maria G. (1994). "Nowadays it isn't easy to advise the young": Grandmothers and granddaughters among Abaluyia of Kenya. In Jeanette Dickerson-Putman & Judith K. Brown (Eds.), Female age hierarchies [special issue]. *Journal of Cross-Cultural Gerontology, 9*, 157–178.

Cattell, Maria G. (forthcoming) Old people and the language of complaint: Examples from Kenya and Philadelphia. In Heidi Hamilton (Ed.), *Old age and language*: Multidisciplinary perspectives. New York: Garland Press.

Chaney, Elsa M. (Ed.). (1990). *Empowering older women: Cross-cultural views. A guide for discussion and training*. Washington, DC: American Association of Retired Persons.

Chappell, Neena L. (1990). Aging and social care. In Robert H. Binstock & Linda K. George (Eds.), *Handbook of aging and the social sciences* (3rd ed.) (pp. 438–454). New York: Van Nostrand Reinhold.

Cohen, David William. (1985). Doing social history from Pim's doorway. In Olivier Zunz (Ed.), *Reliving the past: The worlds of social history* (pp. 191–235). Chapel Hill: University of North Carolina Press.

Cohen, David William, & Odhiambo, E. S. Atieno. (1989). *Siaya: The historical anthropology of an African landscape*. London: James Currey.

Cohen, Ronald. (1984). Age and culture as theory. In David L. Kertzer & Jennie Keith (Eds.), *Age and anthropological theory* (pp. 234–249). Ithaca: Cornell University Press.

Colson, Elizabeth, & Scudder, Thayer. (1981). Old age in Gwembe District, Zambia. In Pamela T. Amoss & Steven Harrell (Eds.), *Other ways of growing old: Anthropological perspectives* (pp. 125–154). Stanford, CA: Stanford University Press.

Cox, Frances M., & Mberia, Ndung'u. (1977). *Aging in a changing village structure: A Kenyan experience*. Washington, DC: International Federation on Aging.

Dorjahn, V. R. (1989). Where do the old folks live? The residence of the elderly among the Temne of Sierra Leone. *Journal of Cross-Cultural Gerontology, 4*, 257–278.

Draper, Patricia, & Harpending, Henry. (1994). Cultural considerations in the experience of aging: Two African cultures. In B. R. Bonder & M. B. Wagner (Eds.), *Functional performance in older adults* (pp. 15–27). Philadelphia: F. A. Davis.

Egan, Sean (Ed.). (1987). *S. M. Otieno: Kenya's unique burial saga*. Nairobi: Nation Newspapers.

Ekpenyong, Stephen, Oyeneye, Olutunji, & Peil, Margaret. (1986). Nigerian elderly: A rural–urban and interstate comparison. *African Gerontology, 5*, 5–19.

Fapohunda, Eleanor R., & Todaro, Michael P. (1988). Family structure, implicit contracts, and the demand for children in Southern Nigeria. *Population and Development Review, 14*, 571–594.

Folta, Jeannette R., & Deck, Edith S. (1987). Elderly black widows in rural Zimbabwe. *Journal of Cross-Cultural Gerontology, 2*, 321–342.

Foner, Nancy. (1984). *Ages in conflict: A cross-cultural perspective on inequality between old and young*. New York: Columbia University Press.

Foner, Nancy. (1985). Caring for the elderly: A cross-cultural view. In Beth B. Hess & Elizabeth W. Markson (Eds.), *Growing old in America: New perspectives on old age* (3rd ed.) (pp. 387–400). New Brunswick, NJ: Transaction Books.

Frank, Odile, & McNicoll, Geoffrey. (1987). An interpretation of fertility and population policy in Kenya. *Population and Development Review, 13*, 209–244.

George, Linda K. (1993). *Financial security in later life: The subjective side*. Philadelphia: Boettner Institute of Financial Gerontology, University of Pennsylvania.

Gituna, Kenneth. (1984, May 5). Poor lads. *Kenya Times*, p. 7.

Gracia, Mathieu. (1985). Research findings in Cameroon: Older persons in villages in the District of Dibombari. *African Gerontology, 3*, 25–39.

Guillette, Elizabeth A. (1992). *Finding the good life in the family and society: The Tswana aged of Botswana*. Unpublished doctoral dissertation, University of Florida.

Guyer, Jane I. (1979). *Household budgets and women's income* (Working Paper No. 28). Boston: Boston University, African Studies Center.

Hampson, Joseph. (1982). *Old age: A study of aging in Zimbabwe*. Gweru, Zimbabwe: Mambo Press.

Hampson, Joseph. (1989). Social support for rural elderly in Zimbabwe: The transition. In John M. Eekelaar & David Pearl (Eds.), *An aging world: Dilemmas and challenges for law and social policy* (pp. 201–210). Oxford: Clarendon Press.

Hampson, Joseph. (1990). Marginalisation and rural elderly: A Shona case study. *Journal of Social Development in Africa, 5*(2), 5–24.

HelpAge Kenya. (1988). Situation Report. Nairobi.

"Homes for the aged 'alienate inmates.'" (1984, November 6). *Daily Nation*. Nairobi.

Iliffe, John. (1987). *The African poor: A history*. Cambridge: Cambridge University Press.

Ingstad, Benedicte, Bruun, Frank, Sandberg, Edwin, and Tlou, Sheila. (1992). Care for the elderly, care by the elderly: The role of elderly women in a changing Tswana Society. *Journal of Cross-Cultural Gerontology, 7*, 379–398.

Kendig, Hal L. (Ed.). (1986). *Ageing and families: A support networks perspective*. Sydney: Allen & Unwin.

Kendig, Hal L., Hashimoto, Akiko, & Coppard, Larry (Eds.) (1992). Family support to the elderly: The international experience. Oxford: Oxford University Press.

Kenya NGO Organising Committee. (1985). *Women and Ageing*. Nairobi.

Khasiani, Shanyisa A. (1983). The effectiveness of the family and other organizations in meeting the social economic needs of the aging population in Kenya. Nairobi: Kenya National Council of Social Service.

Kilbride, Philip L. (1986). Cultural persistence and socio-economic change among the Abaluyia: Some modern problems in patterns of child care. *Journal of East African Research and Development, 16*, 35–51.

Kilbride, Philip L. (1992). Unwanted children as a consequence of delocalization in modern Kenya. In John J. Poggie, Jr., Billie R. DeWalt, & William W. Dressler (Eds.), *Anthropological research: Process and application* (pp. 185–203). Albany: State University of New York Press.

Kilbride, Philip L., & Kilbride, Janet Capriotti. (1990). *Changing family life in East Africa: Women and children at risk*. University Park: Pennsylvania State University Press.

Kitching, Gavin. (1980). *Class and economic change in Kenya: The making of an African petite-bourgeoisie*. New Haven: Yale University Press.

Knowles, J. C., & Anker, Richard. (1981). An analysis of income transfers in a developing country. *Journal of Development Economics, 8*, 205–226.

Kosberg, Jordan I. (Ed.). (1992). Family care of the elderly: Social and cultural changes. Beverly Hills, CA: Sage.

LeVine, Sarah, & LeVine, Robert A. (1985). Age, gender, and the demographic transition: The life course in agrarian societies. In Alice S. Rossi (Ed.), *Gender and the life course* (pp. 29–42). New York: Aldine.

lo Liyong, Taban. (1969). *The last word: Cultural synthesism.* Nairobi: East African Publishing House.

Malan, J. S. (1990). *The aged in Lebowa and Venda.* Pretoria: Human Sciences Research Council.

Maquet, Jacques. (1972). *Africanity: The cultural unity of black Africa.* London: Oxford University Press.

Masamba ma Mpolo. (1984). Older persons and their families in a changing village society: A perspective from Zaire. Washington, DC: International Federation on Ageing and World Council of Churches.

Menya, Martha J. (1985). Medical and social welfare of the elderly in Kenya. *African Gerontology, 4*, 35–47.

Moi urges couples to live in peace. (1984, December 30). *The Sunday Times*, pp. 1, 3. Nairobi.

Moller, Valerie, & Welch, Gary John. (1990). Polygamy, economic security and well-being of retired Zulu migrant workers. *Journal of Cross-Cultural Gerontology, 5*, 205–216.

Moore, Sally Falk. (1978). Old age in a life-term social arena. Some Chagga of Kilimanjaro. In Barbara G. Myerhoff & Andrei Simic (Eds.), *Life's career–Aging: Cultural variations on growing old* (pp. 23–76). Beverly Hills, CA: Sage.

Nair, Kay. (1989). Attitudes of Indians towards caring for the aged in the home environment. In Monica Ferreira, L. S. Gillis, & Valerie Moller (Eds.), *Ageing in South Africa: Social Research Papers* (pp. 178–188). Pretoria: Human Sciences Research Council.

Nangina Hospital. (1986). *Survey of client population of Nangina Hospital, Samia Location (Kenya).* Unpublished report. Samia Location: Nangina Hospital.

Ngugi wa Thiong'o. (1981). *Decolonising the mind: The politics of language in African literature.* Nairobi: Heinemann Kenya.

Ngunjiri, Waruguru. (1985, Jan. 27). New food tastes no longer sweet. *Nairobi Sunday Nation.*

Nugent, Jeffrey B. (1985). The old-age security motive for fertility. *Population and Development Review, 11*, 75–97.

Nugent, Jeffrey B. (1990). Old age security and the defense of social norms. *Journal of Cross-Cultural Gerontology, 5*, 243–254.

Nyanguru, Andrew Chad. (1987). Residential care for the destitute elderly: A comparative study of two institutions in Zimbabwe. *Journal of Cross-Cultural Gerontology, 2*, 345–358.

Nydegger, Corinne. (1983). Family ties of the aged in cross-cultural perspective. *Gerontologist, 23*, 26–32.

Obudho, R. A., & Aduwo, G. O. (1989). The rural bias of Kenya's urbanisation. In J. B. Ojwang & J. N. K. Mugambi (Eds.), *The S. M. Otieno case: Death and burial in modern Kenya* (pp. 65–75). Nairobi: Nairobi University Press.

Ojwang, J. B., & Mugambi, J. N. K. (Eds.). (1989). *The S. M. Otieno case: Death and burial in Modern Kenya.* Nairobi: Nairobi University Press.

Okojie, Felix A. (1988). Aging in Sub-Saharan Africa: Toward a redefinition of needs research and policy directions. *Journal of Cross-Cultural Gerontology, 3*, 3–20.

Peil, Margaret. (1985). Old age in West Africa: Social support and quality of life. In John H. Morgan (Ed.), *Aging in developing societies: A reader in third world gerontology, Vol. 2* (pp. 1–21). Bristol, IN: Wyndham Hall Press.

Peil, Margaret. (1988). *Family support for the Nigerian elderly*. Paper presented at annual meeting of the African Studies Association of the United Kingdom.

Peil, Margaret.(1992). Family help for the elderly: A comparative study on Nigeria, Sierra Leone and Zimbabwe. *Bold, 2*(3), 2–4.

Peil, Margaret, Bamaisaye, Anne, & Ekpenyong, Stephen. (1989). Health and physical support for the elderly in Nigeria. *Journal of Cross-Cultural Gerontology, 4*, 89–106.

Potash, Betty. (Ed.). (1986). *Widows in African societies: Choices and constraints*. Stanford, CA: Stanford University Press.

Prather, Johnnie. (Ed.). (1993) The possibilities of empowerment [Special issue]. *Ageing International, 20* (1).

Rempel, Henry, & Lobdell, Richard A. (1978). The role of urban-to-rural remittances in rural development. *Journal of Development Studies, 14*, 324–341.

Republic of Kenya (1979). *Kenya population census 1979*, Vol. 1. Nairobi: Central Bureau of Statistics and Ministry of Economic Planning and Development.

Rix, Sara E. (1991). *Older women and development: Making a difference*. Paper presented at Expert Group Meeting, Integration of Ageing and Elderly Women into Development, Vienna.

Rosenberg, Harriet. (1990). Complaint discourse, aging, and caregiving among the !Kung San of Botswana. In Jay Sokolovsky (Ed.), *The cultural context of aging: Worldwide perspectives* (pp. 19–41). Westport, CT: Bergin & Garvey.

Ross, Marc Howard (1975). *Grass roots in an African city: Political behavior in Nairobi.* Cambridge: MIT Press.

Ross, Marc Howard, & Weisner, Thomas S. (1977). The rural-urban migrant network in Kenya: Some general implications. *American Ethnologist, 4*, 359–375.

Rubinstein, Robert L., & Johnsen, Pauline T. (1982). Toward a comparative perspective on filial response to aging populations. *Studies in Third World Societies, 22*, 115–174.

Sangree, Walter H. (1986). Role flexibility and status continuity: Tiriki (Kenya) age groups today. *Journal of Cross-Cultural Gerontology, 1*, 117–138.

Sangree, Walter H. (1987). The childless elderly in Tiriki, Kenya and Irigwe, Nigeria: A comparative analysis of the relationship between beliefs about childlessness and the social status of the childless elderly. *Journal of Cross-Cultural Gerontology, 2*, 201–223.

Seitz, Jacob R. (1978). *A history of the Samia Location in Western Kenya, 1890–1930*. Unpublished doctoral dissertation, West Virginia University.

Shanas, Ethel. (1979). The family as a social support system in old age. *Gerontologist, 19*, 169–174.

Shuman, Tarek, Stanford, E. P., Harbert, A. S., Schmidt, M. G., & Roberts, J. L. (Eds.). (1993). *Population aging: International perspectives*. San Diego: University Center on Aging, San Diego State University.

Soper, Robert (Ed.). (1986). *Kenya socio-cultural profiles: Busia District*. Nairobi: Ministry of Planning and National Development/University of Nairobi, Institute of African Studies.

Stucki, Barbara (1992). The long voyage home: Return migration among aging cocoa farmers of Ghana. *Journal of Cross-Cultural Gerontology, 7*, 363–378.

Teitelbaum, Michele. (1988). Singing for their supper and other productive work of African elderly. In Enid Gort (Ed.), *Aging in cross-cultural perspective: Africa and the Americas* (pp. 61–68). New York: Phelps–Stokes Fund.

The strong impact of AIDs. (October 1, 1993). *(Nairobi) Weekly Review*, p. 20.

Thomas, Samuel. (1992). *Old age in Meru, Kenya: Adaptive reciprocity in a changing rural community*. Unpublished doctoral dissertation, University of Florida.

Thomson, David. (1989). The intergenerational contract—Under pressure from population aging. In John M. Eekelaar & David Pearl (Eds.), *An aging world: Dilemmas and challenges for law and social policy* (pp. 369–388). Oxford: Clarendon Press.

Thomson, Joseph. (1885). *Through Masai Land*. London: Edward Arnold.

Togonu-Bickersteth, Funmi. (1989). Conflicts over caregiving: A discussion of filial obligations among adult Nigerian children. *Journal of Cross-Cultural Gerontology, 4*, 35–48.

Tout, Kenneth. (1989). *Aging in developing countries*. New York: Oxford University Press/ HelpAge International.

Treas, Judith, & Logue, Barbara. (1986). Economic development and the older population. *Population and Development Review, 12*, 645–673.

Udvardy, Monica, & Cattell, Maria G. (1992). Gender, aging and power in sub-Saharan Africa: Challenges and puzzles. *Journal of Cross-Cultural Gerontology, 7*, 275–288.

Wandibba, Simiyu. (1985). Some aspects of precolonial architecture. In S. Wandibba (Ed.), *History and culture in Western Kenya: The people of Bungoma District through time* (pp. 34–41). Nairobi: Gideon S. Were Press.

Wanjala, Chris L. (1985). Twilight years are the years of counsel and wisdom. In Simiyu Wandibba (Ed.), *History and culture in Western Kenya: The People of Bungoma District through time* (pp. 78–91). Nairobi: Gideon S. Were Press.

Weisner, Thomas S. (1976). The structure of sociability: Urban migration and urban–rural ties in Kenya. *Urban Anthropology, 5*, 199–223.

Were, Gideon S. (1982). Cultural renaissance and national development: Some reflections on Kenya's cultural problem. *Journal of East African Research and Development, 12*, 1–12.

Were, Gideon S. (1985). Ethnic and cultural identity in African history: A myth or reality? In Simiyu Wandibba (Ed.), *History and culture in Western Kenya: The People of Bungoma District through time* (pp. 5–10). Nairobi: Gideon S. Were Press.

"When old age becomes a heavy burden." (1984, Feb. 24). *Daily Nation*, p. 11. Nairobi.

9

Pronatalism and the Elderly in Tiriki, Kenya

Walter H. Sangree

Tiriki is situated in the southeastern corner of Western Province. It is populated predominantly by members of Abaluyia clan lineages whose forebears, since precolonial times, have been incorporated into the age group system of the Kalenjin Nandi-speaking Terik, who were also living in some of the area that is now Tiriki Location. Incorporation into the Terik/Tiriki age group system was and still is brought about by secret initiation rites, which involve circumcision of the adolescent (nowadays preadolescent) males. Aside from this incorporation into Terik/Tiriki age groups, the majority of Tiriki are virtually identical, culturally and linguistically, to the Idaxo and Isuxa who live just north of them; those Tiriki living in the southwesterly areas of the location meld right in culturally and linguistically with the Maragoli bordering them to the west.

Within the space of a lifetime, the score or so of culturally related but politically noncentralized distinctive societies of Western Province have moved from the economic self-sufficiency and political autonomy of small peasant communities to become the second-largest ethnic entity in Kenya. Furthermore, most communities in the densely populated southern portion of the province are now totally dependent for economic and political survival upon their earnings in the growing urban and rural labor markets elsewhere in Kenya (see Weisner, this volume). Kenya as a nation is, of course, also rapidly increasing its interdependency with the larger economic-political domain of the modern industrialized world.

One can now find evidence at every turn of Tiriki's connectedness with contemporary industrialized world culture, and many attributes of western industrialized society are as commonplace in Tiriki as they are in less urbanized areas of Europe or America. These attributes include the ubiquitousness of Christianity (Islam has only a few followers in Tiriki), western medical and public health practices, British- and, more recently, American-type schooling and specialized training for the young, "western" clothing styles, transistor radios and tape recorders, and motorized transport, not to mention the pervasiveness of a money market economy. Nevertheless, many attributes of Tiriki local life remain very different from contemporary Europe and America. Among the most striking of these differences is the high status and respect generally accorded the elderly. In this chapter I shall explore why this is so.

My research in Tiriki, covering the period between 1954 and 1982, clearly reveals that the social roles of Tiriki elders have been greatly affected by the modernization process, but that the status of the elderly has remained high as this "third world tribal" society has become incorporated into the modern industrialized world. Cowgill's "Modernization Model" of social change, which postulates the inevitable loss of power and status by elders as a traditional society becomes urbanized (Cowgill, 1974; Foner, 1984, p. 197), is of questionable validity or utility, indeed appears to be misleading, in the Tiriki case. It will be seen that the social and cultural factors in Tiriki that have fostered the continuation of a very high fertility level there for a full generation after the inception of a family planning program in western Kenya are dynamically linked to the continuing high status of the elderly.

In this paper I shall portray some of the changes that the winds of modernization have brought to the Tiriki, particularly the elderly Tiriki. Although the role the elderly play in the community's formalized judicial and religious affairs has markedly diminished in recent decades, both seniority as a status-conferring principle and the traditional interrelationships between grandparenthood and elderhood remain very strong. It will be seen that the growing responsibility grandparents have assumed, particularly in the local domestic economy, including much of the childcare for their younger grandchildren, affords them a major contemporary power base that helps assure, although it does not alone account for, their continuing high status in rural Tiriki (see Kilbride & Kilbride, this volume).

In the introduction, I shall note Tiriki's principal traditional social structural features and also briefly contrast Tiriki concepts of time and aging with those prevalent in the west. In the first section, I outline the Tiriki male initiation and graded age group system, and also the ancestor cult. These two institutions together traditionally ascribe high judicial and religious status and related special social duties and responsibilities to Tiriki male elders, *basaxulu*. In the conclusion of that section, I explain why grandparenthood has always played a crucial role in establishing both men's and women's seniority and thus their credentials as elders. Indeed, people who fail to become grandparents have never been able to enjoy the status and power of elderhood in this strongly patrilineal society. The social pressure to fulfill the cultural ideal of having many children and then grandchildren has been a potent factor in bolstering and maintaining the average fertility level in Tiriki of around eight children per woman well into the 1980s.

In the following section I present an overview and brief analysis of changes in Tiriki that have impinged upon the traditional status of elders since the coming of colonial rule in 1902. Some aspects of the elders' authority, particularly those based on their control of traditional knowledge, formerly of high value to the society, have been considerably weakened by the modernization process. Tiriki elders, however, have achieved a new power base that reinforces their traditionally high status in both family and community affairs and thus secures them the continuing respect of their juniors. Two by-products of westernization have become important contemporary underpinnings of the Tiriki elders' current high status and respect. These are, first, the increasing shortage of arable land arising from an explosive population growth, and second, the growth of the urban centers and the practice in western Kenya of younger adults' gaining their livelihood primarily from months and years spent in those centers as migrant wage workers or salaried employees (see Weisner, 1976). This section concludes with a summary description and analysis of the current power base of the Tiriki elders living in the tribal areas.

The conclusion is a brief commentary on what might be called the "secularization" of the elders' status during the last eighty years, the Tiriki elders' own view of their current condition, and a speculative statement about their future status.

INTRODUCTION

Tiriki: A Brief Overview

Tiriki had a population of approximately forty thousand in 1954 when I began my twenty months of fieldwork there (Sangree, 1965, 1966). Today (1992), so far as I can estimate, about twice that many people call Tiriki Location their home, and many more now living permanently elsewhere recognize their Tiriki ethnic origin. Tiriki is one of a score or so of Abaluyia Bantu-speaking peoples in Western Province that now form the second largest ethnic group in Kenya. Traditionally these societies subsisted in this tropical highland region with very fertile volcanic soil, primarily from hoe cultivation of cereal crops and secondarily from tending cattle, smaller livestock, and fowl (Wagner, 1949).

The British effectively imposed *pax britannica* in Tiriki in 1902, and the colonial administrators quickly set up so-called tribal boundaries and implemented tribal chieftaincies in the region. Prior to this, Tiriki and neighboring societies were politically "noncentralized," with no one clan or political group having special authority over all the others (Wagner, 1940). Tiriki male initiation procedures and associated graded semigenerational age groups were not only central to the Tiriki's tribal identity and solidarity but also reinforced the judicial and mystical power of the elders, extending it, on occasion, from lineage and clan to community and tribal affairs. Tiriki clearly can be labeled as a "gerontocracy," because both seniority as an authority-bestowing principle and the relatively high status of elders in both local and tribal affairs have traditionally been central features of its social organization and remain so to this day in local community affairs.

Tiriki elders in 1954–1956 told me that prior to *pax britannica,* young men in Tiriki occupied themselves primarily with cattle herding and cattle raiding; women, assisted by their older unmarried daughters and younger daughters-in-law, did nearly all the farm work on fields assigned them by their husbands. Tiriki men traditionally were circumcised and initiated shortly after puberty into the age group occupying the initiate warrior age grade. Then, during a period of bachelorhood usually lasting a decade or more, initiated sons tended their fathers' herds and participated, together with other members of their age group military division (*ibololi*), in cattle raids against herds of other communities. Every young man, with his father's and brothers' help, thus acquired and tended the cattle needed for his bridewealth. Clan exogamy was strictly enforced, and wives often came from outside the local community or even from non-Tiriki Abaluyia communities against whom cattle raids were occasionally fought. As Tiriki elders reported it to me, "We often married our enemies!" A bride, under the supervision of her mother-in-law, initially helped cultivate her husband's father's fields. Once the couple had three children it was traditional for the husband's father to grant him fields for his exclusive use, which he then assigned his wife to farm.

Both elders' accounts and early mission and administration records indicate that, even prior to the advent of the World War I, men in the initiation and warrior age grades had started working for European settlers as wage laborers, viewing this as an alternative to herding and a substitute for cattle raiding. They were able thereby to amass the cash not only to pay the British imposed annual poll tax but also to purchase cattle for bridewealth as well as manufactured goods. Such goods very soon became available, both in a growing number of rural shops owned and operated by immigrant East Indians and at weekly multitribal open air markets supervised by the local multitribal British District Administration.

Tiriki Concepts of Elderhood

The Tiriki traditionally, in common with most proletariat societies, had no formalized chronological concept of age calculated by reference to a dating system (Fortes, 1984). The closest they had to this was their men's circumcision ascribed age group (*lixula*) system. Soon after the coming of the British, who immediately fostered the establishment of Christian missions, local converts to Christianity began to have their children's birth dates recorded in mission records. When I did my first fieldwork in Tiriki in 1954–1956, I found that most illiterate pagans, as well as literate Christians, knew the year, if not the exact date, of each of their children's births and were beginning to have them recorded in the tribal rolls. Chronological age, however, still did not have much personal significance, and people were not yet celebrating birthdays.

Every Tiriki male, so far as I could ascertain, has always been very cognizant of both his own age group and that of every other man with whom he interacts. A man's formal and informal status, and his responsibilities in most community and tribal affairs were and still are largely ascribed by his age group and its relative seniority in the age grade system. For example, all members of the same age group traditionally are welcome to participate together in beer drinks, which, until very recently, were held frequently throughout the community; but a man does not usually drink or socially relate informally with members of an age group senior to his own unless explicitly invited by them.

Ordinal age reckoning is also important in other Tiriki social domains. The agnatically seniormost man present in a lineage gathering, for example, has the right to preside. A man's oldest son has special duties and privileges vis-à-vis his father and all his younger siblings; youngest sons also have special responsibilities, and a woman's last born (*muxogosi*), whether male or female, has a unique social role and a special relationship with her or his mother (Sangree, 1981).

Women's lives are generally less affected by seniority than men's, but traditionally a man's first wife had significant authority over all his successive wives. Generational seniority is important for both men and women. One's generation is defined for every individual first by being in the generation succeeding one's parents, then by the birth of one's first child. The attainment of matronhood is necessary for a woman's acceptance as a peer by other young matrons and gains her new respect from those not yet parents. Grandmothers similarly claim and receive deference from those not yet grandparents. Men who are initiated need not be fathers to be considered adults, but sometime during his adulthood a man must achieve parenthood, indeed he must have one living child, in order not to find himself a pariah by the time he reaches the age when most of his peers are becoming grandparents. We shall see the reasons for this later in this chapter.

When I was in Tiriki in 1982 I found a small but significant minority of relatively affluent middle-aged men who had returned from the urban areas to live in Tiriki, after having held positions in the Kenya military, Civil Service, or the private sector where retirement at age fifty-five is usual. For them, of course, chronological age was instrumental in bringing about a very real change of life, namely, a return to residence in Tiriki; thus they escaped from the relative anonymity of retiree-elderhood in contemporary urban Kenya to the high status of tribal elderhood. With some money saved and invested to bring them income and/or their government pensions, these retirees are able to maintain in the tribal environment a standard of living, economically speaking, considerably higher than most of their Tiriki age peers who have never held salaried jobs.

TIRIKI MALE INITIATION, GRADED AGE GROUPS, ELDERHOOD, AND GRANDPARENTHOOD

Terik/Tiriki Initiation and Graded Age Groups

The Tiriki are unique among Abaluyia groups in having become fully integrated, long before *pax britannica*, into the male initiation and graded age group system of the Kalenjin Terik who directly border them to the southeast (LeVine & Sangree, 1962; Sangree, 1965, 1966). We shall see that the power of the elders in Tiriki is reinforced in the family, lineage, and clan and greatly augmented in community and tribal affairs by these male initiation procedures and the related formalized graded semigenerational age groups. Although I am writing in the present tense, it should be noted that this summary of Tiriki initiation practices is based principally on information I was given in 1954–1956 (Sangree, 1965, 1966). I know that these practices continue into the 1990s, but undoubtedly in somewhat altered form.

Male Initiation

It is forbidden for a youth to be initiated into the age group immediately junior to his own father's; in practice, a boy generally enters whichever age group is open to initiation at the time he and his age peers reach physical maturity, which is usually two, and less frequently three, age grades junior to his father's. Initiation of Tiriki youths into the age group then open for initiation is held every three to five years at multivillage ceremonials. Traditionally this involved the initiates being secluded for six months. Back in the late 1940s, however, a time when most Tiriki who got any schooling did so in their early adolescence, the seclusion period was shortened to fit into the six week summer school vacation period; in recent years the age of initiation has been reduced to that of primary and intermediate school attenders, that is, roughly age seven to twelve, thus lessening conflicts for those with vacation time employment and for those going away to boarding school for secondary education.

Initiation begins with initiands being induced to confess and pay fines to the elders for all sexual activity they have engaged in heretofore. Then they are circumcised in the seclusion of a sacred initiation grove (*shibanda* or *gabunyonyi*), which only others already initiated or awaiting circumcision may enter. Informants reported that bravery under the circumcision knife is one basis for judgment of a peer's strength of character, but that an even more important test of an initiated person's worth is his steadfastness in never revealing to noninitiates any of the mysteries or goings-on during the initiation, including the bravery or cowardice of anyone else he has seen initiated.

During the convalescent and postconvalescent seclusion period, nearly all aspects of the initiands' lives, especially sleeping, eating, and bathing, are strictly regimented by counselors from the immediately senior warrior-grade age group. At one point during the seclusion period the initiands are mystically "put to death and reborn" in the circumcision grove by the presiding ritual elder circumcision chiefs. Later, in a special hilltop initiation grove (*gabogorosiyo*), initiands learn about tribal mysteries, including a curse that the ritual elders can employ, which causes those cursed to "swell up and die badly."

Boys, prior to being initiated, generally do not socialize with initiated men, the most striking exception being grandfathers' playful interaction with their young grandchildren of both sexes. But after emerging from initiation, their daily lives are quite transformed; they eat, drink beer, take their leisure with other initiated men, and generally eschew the social company of women and children; they may now have lovers so long as they do not violate clan- and lineage-based incest/exogamy (*bwixo*) rules. Women and children are regarded as socially inferior to all initiated males and as jural dependents of senior initiated male relatives. Tiriki men explicitly attribute their superior status to having been through the circumcision–initiation procedures.

TERIK-TIRIKI GRADED AGE GROUP SYSTEM

The traditional Terik–Tiriki graded age group system consists of seven named age groups, each embracing an approximately fifteen-year age span (Sangree,

1965, 1966, 1986). A man who lives to be old progresses through five distinctive age grades. Youths are initiated into the group occupying the juniormost age grade.

The changeover of the age groups from one grade to another is held every fifteen to sixteen years. Traditionally this is marked by a great Terik-Tiriki bicultural ceremonial that precedes the initiation of a new group of adolescent youths into the newly formed juniormost age group. This precipitates an upgrading of all the more senior age groups. The former initiate group moves up into the warrior age grade. The former warriors become elder warriors, whose principal concerns traditionally are their individual family affairs and the supervision of the warriors' activities. The former elder warriors move into the junior elder grade, where judicial matters, such as community and clan dispute settlement and lineage inheritance mediation, become their major traditional community tasks. The former junior elders in turn assume senior elder status; traditionally they then take over mystical and religious matters relating to the clan ancestor cults, control of witches and witchcraft, and the beneficent use of sorcery; certain death-dealing mysteries that men first learn about when initiated and the supervision of initiation rites also become primarily the concern and responsibility of the ritual elders. The erstwhile ritual elders at this point retire from their age graded responsibilities in a formal sense, but in fact remain active and influential among the ritual elders for as long as they feel so inclined and their strength permits.

The ceremonial closing of one initiate age group and graduating of each age group to the next more senior age grade was prohibited after 1902 by the British colonial administrators, who believed this would help discourage intertribal cattle and vengeance raids. Informally, however, the initiation elders have continued to close the current initiation age group and open the next age group to initiation approximately every fifteen years, with each group informally thereafter being described and addressed in terms appropriate to the next higher status. To this day, age group members show deference towards those in age groups senior to their own and expect to be shown similar deference by more junior age group members.

Initiation, Age Groups, and Community Solidarity

Tiriki villages, typically ranging from three hundred to five hundred people in size, comprise several dozen agnatically organized family households or homesteads (*inzu*), each surrounded by its own farmland. I never found a Tiriki village (*lidala*) that didn't have families of several different clans living in it. Traditionally villages were separated by uncultivated areas left fallow and used for grazing, but in recent decades land has become very scarce, and boundaries between villages are no longer marked by any break in the farm settlement pattern. Somewhere within each village is a grove of shade trees where people can comfortably gather. Nowadays, often a few small retail shops and "hotels" serving bottled beverages and tea are found near these village gathering places on small plots laid out and leased by the Administration.

Several villages cooperate for circumcision. All the boys belonging to the same sub-tribal district (*lusomo*), comprising perhaps a half dozen villages, are circumcised and then secluded together at the sacred groves and initiate seclusion areas maintained for that purpose by the circumcision elders who come from various villages in their district. Elders of all the Terik-Tiriki districts exchange visits fairly regularly; thus they are able to schedule these initiation ceremonials so that they occur simultaneously throughout the entire network of Bantu Tiriki and Kalenjin Terik initiation districts. I was told that prior to *pax britannica* all the initiates from a particular circumcision district, together with the men of more senior age groups who were initiated in that district, formed a single military division (*ibololi*) and fought as a unit in the not infrequent cattle and vengeance raids mounted against non–Terik-Tiriki groups.

I found in 1954–1956 and 1961 that almost every afternoon people of the same age group, regardless of clan affiliation, seated themselves around a single giant beer pot, or two or three big pots if the gathering was large, each drinking from the communal pot through his own long reed tube (Sangree, 1966). The venue of these drinks shifted from one village to another within a district, a core of elders from different villages being on hand for virtually every drink. This was where recent decisions at the district subchief's court were rehashed. Current disputes in the village or between neighboring villages were usually discussed at these beer drinks and frequently successfully arbitrated without being taken to the subchief's court. In any event, since the elders' testimony was usually the principal factor in the subchief's decisions in matters brought to his court, these were the forums in which most local disputes were, in effect, settled.

Changing Age-Graded Social Roles

The age-group initiation practices, in addition to establishing a special set of age group bondings, help maintain a general status hierarchy vis-à-vis more senior and more junior age groups. The five traditional age grades (initiate, warrior, senior warrior, judicial elder, and ritual elder) socially reify four or five successive social roles through which one moves during one's adult life span together with one's age group peers; but they probably have never limited in a rigid manner any particular social role to one and only one age group at a time. By 1956, work as a laborer away from tribal lands had replaced the decade or more of bachelor warriorhood devoted principally to cattle raiding and cattle herding that Tiriki elders in 1955–1956 said had characterized initiate and junior warrior age grade life when they were young.

Tiriki Elderhood: The Traditional Ancestor Cult

The traditional religious system of the Tiriki, in contrast to the local and tribal political systems, is rooted in their patrilineally organized ancestor cult of remembrance and supplication. A prevailing traditional Abaluyia and general Bantu notion is that spirits of the deceased have a pervasive influence over the fortunes of the living. This belief found ceremonial expression in Tiriki when lineage elders evoked and eulogized their deceased clan, subclan, and grandparental forbears. The lineage elders typically gathered to do this at one or another of the ancestral shrines, which were found beside the granary belonging to the senior man of each extended family homestead. These shrines consisted of a branch of the tough rot-resistant tree *lusiyola* (*markhamia platycalyx*) stuck vertically into the ground, where it was surrounded by two or three small stones. One stone was said to represent the elder's father, another the elder himself. The third stone was not added until after the family head's eldest son had at least one child of his own, making the family head a grandfather and thus truly a lineage elder. Remembrance of the ancestors (*baguga*) at the ancestral shrine (*lusambwa*) was believed to motivate the ancestral spirits (*misambwa*) to strengthen and spiritually protect their descendants who thus honor them (Sangree 1965, 1966, 1989). We saw earlier that the Terik-Tiriki graded age group system both affirms and reinforces the appropriateness of ascribing high status to seniority. The ideological foundations, however, of the Tiriki elder's social responsibility and power are derived principally from the ancestor cult and from the related importance of grandparenthood.

Grandparenthood: A Necessary Prerequisite for Elderhood

The core traditional status and the principal power-mediating activities of every elder Tiriki, both male (*musaxulu*) and female (*mushele*), are grounded primarily in religious ceremonials and domestic and social responsibilities either carried out on behalf of one's own grandchildren or undertaken on behalf of other more junior members of the lineage and clan. Only after having first carried out such activities for a grandchild of his own is a man accepted as a presiding elder in his lineage's or clan's affairs, and only then is his wife (the infant's grandmother) first regarded as an elder (*mushele*).

Two traditional beliefs and practices, maintained by draconian sanctions, make having no living progeny a terrible calamity for an elderly Tiriki; indeed as late as 1992, they usually prevented childless elder men and women from ever living out their old ages in the communities where they spent their reproductive years (or what should have been their reproductive years).

Although they have always fostered children of deceased or absent relatives, Tiriki traditionally never adopted nor claimed fostered relatives or children of nonrelatives as their own children; this interdiction was reinforced by the prevalent belief that such actions would offend the ghosts or the ancestral spirits of the children's true begetters or bearers, which would then take vengeance on the adopters and their kinspeople. Legitimate paternity is viewed by the Tiriki as rightfully falling to the man who actually impregnated the mother. Fatherhood (and thus grandfatherhood and lineage and clan membership) depend for affirmation upon the marital sexual fidelity of the infant's mother at the time of conception or, failing this, on her naming the genitor at the time of the baby's birth. It is believed that in any adulterous union the true father of the infant will be confessed prior to its birth because Tiriki women are told that they will probably otherwise die during labor.

I was told that during initiation Tiriki youths learn about a form of sorcery believed to make the victim sterile, but which has the side effect of also rendering the employer of the sorcery sterile. Thus, a childless older man is treated with great circumspection because it is feared envy may motivate him to use this sorcery against fertile relatives and neighbors. Informants told me that men with no living offspring before they get very old either die or leave the community for places unknown (they "get lost, gorrrr!").

The same is true of older childless women. They may be accused of being witches (*baloji*) who bring death to other women's children. Indeed, I found no childless old men or women living in the two Tiriki villages where I made censuses in 1955 (see Cattell, this volume, for information on the childless elderly in another Abaluyia society).

In contrast to the absence of the childless elderly in Tiriki communities, there is no shortage of elderly parents (both postmenopausal women and older men—some rumored to be impotent from old age) with living offspring. No one fears that elders with children will use sterility-producing sorcery on younger people, because people believe that the victims' elder kinspeople would then retaliate by utilizing the same type of sorcery against the users' own children and grandchildren (Sangree, 1987).

The interconnectedness of the generations, particularly of alternate generations, is reinforced by Tiriki naming practices. In addition to a clan name, and nowadays a Christian name, every child, within a few days of birth, is assigned a personal name by the grandparents or elder relatives of the grandparental generation. Typically the infant is given the name of a deceased grandparent, great-grandparent, or great-great-grandparent, but never the name of a living relative (Sangree, 1987). Married people with children often address and refer to each other teknonymously, the name of a person's eldest child typically being used as the teknonym. It is noteworthy that I did not even become aware of the Tiriki use of teknonyms until 1961 when I returned to Tiriki as a parent for the first time and found I was frequently addressed as "Dada Beth," Beth being the name of my firstborn.

The Tiriki believed, and still believe, that one can only achieve full acceptance as an elder through having children of one's own, whose destinies over the years, in turn, become as intertwined with their parents' destinies as their parents' are already with their own parents and with their patrilineal forbears (Sangree, 1974, 1987). Nowadays Christian beliefs and ceremonials and western medical practices have largely supplanted traditional ancestor supplication rites, but the ideology of parenthood and social pressures on both men and women to have many children are so diffuse and pervasive that parenting many children and taking great pride in the birth of numerous grandchildren continued until recently in rural Tiriki (Sangree, 1987).

I gained my clearest insights as to why Tiriki continued to have many children both from observing and experiencing, in 1982, the sorts of opprobrium from peers and elders that people were subjected to who appear to be falling behind in the goal to parent six or more children, including two surviving sons. Those with at least two sons but fewer than six children received expressions of mild condolence together with reassurances that it may not be too late to parent a few more children. I shall give just two examples of the sorts of social pressure I observed and experienced in this regard.

In 1982 I became reacquainted with one of my age peers who seemed to have done very well for himself since I had last seen him in 1961. With a position of major responsibility in the District Civil Service, which paid a good salary, he had been able to build himself a substantial home of cinder blocks, invest in a shop and a "hotel" (restaurant) at the local market, and devote nearly a quarter of his inherited two hectare farm to growing coffee. He was anticipating with pleasure his retirement in another year, which would enable him to devote more of his time to these enterprises and also to take on additional responsibilities in the local church where he already served as a Deacon. His wife, a District Public Health Officer, had another decade before reaching the mandatory retirement age of fifty-five; thus they foresaw no difficulty in living comfortably and paying the school fees for their eight children, who ranged in ages from five to fifteen, on the combination of her salary, his substantial retirement pension, and prospects for increasing profits from his retail shops and coffee bean crops. This man was one of several well-to-do men in his village; he was the only one, however, about whom I heard deprecating remarks repeatedly from his age peers, both wealthy and poor, and also from those who were his age juniors. I was cautioned by several men of his village "not to take his opinion seriously on anything." I remember all too well one occasion when he spoke up at a public meeting at the marketplace, hecklers from his own age group yelled for him to sit down and be quiet. One of them, nodding in agreement with the other hecklers, said in a stage whisper, "Who wants to hear the opinion of a man with only one leg!"

Later, when I was talking this over with some other Tiriki friends they told me the Tiriki have a saying: "One's sons are one's legs." They pointed out that this man had eight healthy children—seven daughters, but only one son! Thus, I began to realize that having fewer than two sons by the time you reach elderhood definitely rendered you a social cripple in Tiriki.

During that same 1982 visit to Tiriki, when my age peers first learned I had only two daughters and no sons, at first they were effusive with their condolences and assertions that I should and would soon have more children. Later, when people began to take seriously my repeated assertions that I had enough children and intended to have no more, first my friends and then age peers who knew me less well began to come up to me and comment quietly, "You are not as tall as you were when you were younger; indeed you seem to be getting very short!" Finally I realized that people were making allusions to my sonlessness, which, of course, metaphorically rendered me "legless," and thus very short!

By 1982 everyone in Tiriki, both illiterate and educated, had come to accept the fact that an educated, well-to-do, Christianity-professing elder such as myself, and the Tiriki friend I have just described, might need and want to maintain the public appearance of being a monogamous family man with no extramarital sexual or paternal commitments. What most older Tiriki of my age group could not accept, however, is that a person of means who did not have at least two sons by his wife would not also contrive to have one or more sons by extramarital alliances, who would step forward at their father's funeral to proclaim their true paternity and claim a share of their father's estate. Extramarital sons (or their mothers if they are still minors) may try to substantiate such a claim through obtaining the testimony, at the funeral, of their father's age peers in whom he had earlier confided these activities. Eventually I realized that my Tiriki age peers were repeatedly taunting me with "becoming shorter" to induce me to reveal to them how many sons I had by extramarital alliances. In their judgment I was clearly wealthy enough to be able to afford a mistress or two and extramarital sons. I also came to realize that people despised my well-to-do Tiriki friend for being such a doctrinaire Christian that he had not to their knowledge produced at least one more son extramaritally!

For women who are approaching the end of their reproductive years without having borne a minimum of three children, the matter is much more serious than simply the withdrawal of her age peers' respect. Tradition demands that a woman's husband's lineage provide her with land on which to grow her food, with shelter including her own cooking hearth, and with food and care if she is not well, for so long as she lives—but they feel obliged to provide this only if she has borne her husband at least three children, regardless of the children's sexes. Even then, however, she can expect only grudging care if her reproductive success has been only the minimal three children. Furthermore, a woman has good reason to worry that unless she has borne her husband at least six children, including two or more sons, he will almost inevitably succumb to male peer group pressure to take a junior wife, or nowadays, if he is a Christian, a fertile mistress. A Tiriki man is obliged by custom to provide land equitably for each of his married sons regardless of their mother's marital status. If a junior wife or acknowledged mistress bears sons for her husband or lover, those sons will share an equitable portion of the land their father received from his father. This will deprive the senior or Christian wife's sons of that portion and thus may make her sons disinclined to provide her with anything more than a rudimentary level of shelter and food in her old age (Sangree, 1987).

It is noteworthy that younger parents are very reticent to speak publicly about the number or well-being of their children, fearing this might make them targets of malevolent sorcery sent from envious, less-fortunate peers. Grandparents, however, perhaps feeling they have the power to deal successfully with any such threat from the envious, relish opportunities to sing the praises of their grandchildren, especially if they have many of them.

CHANGES IMPINGING ON TIRIKI ELDERHOOD

Mission Influences

Evangelical Friends (Quaker) missionaries founded Kaimosi Mission in Tiriki right after the establishment of *pax britannica* in 1902 (Sangree, 1966). By the time I first started my research in Tiriki in 1954, they had successfully converted most Tiriki women to active participation in scores of village congregations throughout the community. Tiriki men, from the outset of mission activity, were excoriated by missionaries for being polygynists and, above all, for participating in "devilish" initiation rites. Men and women alike were also strongly admonished by the Quakers and other evangelical Protestant missionaries not to drink beer (*malwa*), which traditionally had been brewed by wives for their husbands and was very important in men's ceremonial and social life but of little importance to the women, who simply drank as a beverage what was left over by the menfolk. Indeed, therein lies the key to Tiriki women's mass conversion to Christianity in the mid 1930s. This occurred, we were told, after an evangelical Christian convert who had been appointed by the British as Tiriki tribal chief, decreed that no Christian woman could be forced by her husband to brew beer. Quickly thereafter, Tiriki elders recounted, women flocked to join evangelical Protestant churches, thereby escaping the wifely drudgery of brewing beer consumed almost entirely by their menfolk (Sangree, 1962).

By 1954, Christian prayers and religious practices, usually led by younger men and women with some western schooling, had replaced the traditional ancestor rites in most households. Government dispensaries and the well-equipped Kaimosi Mission hospital staffed by younger Kenyan personnel with technical training had supplanted traditional herbal and mystical treatment for most severe illnesses. Thus many of the ritual elders' former responsibilities had been rendered of minor significance. Nevertheless, in spite of the early interference of the British administrators with the age group changeover ceremonies and the protracted onslaught of the missionaries against Tiriki initiation practices, the initiation and age group system remained (and remains to this day) alive and well, with the ritual elders still commanding pinnacle roles in these activities. Tiriki men of the judicial elder age grade were still the principal arbitrators and judges in marriage and inheritance disputes in 1954–1956.

I shall let these brief comments suffice to cover the sorts of changes that occurred in the elders' status during the first fifty-two years of the colonial period; for the rest of this section I shall comment on what I observed and gained commentary about firsthand, namely, changes occurring between 1954 and 1982.

The Elders' Changing Status and the Formation of the Tiriki Historical Committee, 1954–1956

In 1954–1956 Tiriki elders repeatedly complained to me that younger Tiriki didn't show them the respect that they had given the elders when they were young. They told me that their literate children and grandchildren often discounted and sometimes despised them because they had no schooling and only knew about "out-of-date beliefs and practices" (see Cattell, 1989, for a similar situation in another Abaluyia community). I heard most of these complaints from the elders while serving as the official recorder in a special historical committee that the government-appointed chief of Tiriki, chief Hezron Mushenye, had set up in 1954 shortly before my coming to Tiriki. Indeed, its existence was a factor in my choice of Tiriki for research. I had already decided to do my research in an Abaluyia community, and when I heard from a British District Officer that the Tiriki had formed their own Historical Committee it seemed the perfect venue for my initial inquiries, so I chose to take up residence there rather than in some other southern Abaluyia community (Sangree, 1966).

Chief Mushenye was a former intermediate school teacher, a Christian since childhood, who several years before he was appointed chief had been expelled from church membership for becoming a polygynist. He nevertheless remained very much a force for modernization, strongly favoring rapid local development of western type schooling, more medical dispensaries, the development of a public water supply, and the like. Most of the Christians, who also fancied themselves modernists, reluctantly supported the chief because he favored these things. The traditionalists, including most of the judicial and ritual elders of the community, initially had felt estranged from the chief because of his Christianity and his schooling. His taking of a second wife, however, his consequent expulsion from the church, and subsequently his taking of a third and then a fourth wife, had done much to increase his standing with the elders by the time I arrived in late 1954. Chief Mushenye, who established the historical committee on his own initiative, was genuinely worried that as more and more children attended school and consequently came to spend much less time hearing about times past from their grandparents, genealogies and other historical information about Tiriki clans might be lost to posterity. He also used these meetings as opportunities to inform the elders about, and solicit their support for, new sanitary regulations requiring every homestead to build its own pit latrine. During most of 1955 the Tiriki Historical Committee met fortnightly at various prearranged community meeting spots. After each meeting, free beer was served to the attending elders, and it was during this beer drinking that the elders did most of their complaining to me about the erosion of their former high status and respectful treatment.

The elders gave me a lot of information about the clans at these historical committee meetings, which I dutifully recorded, at first in English with the aid of an interpreter and later primarily in Luluyia. Many of the elders also aided chief Mushenye to implement sanitation innovations he was promoting by subsequently speaking in favor of them at village level meetings. It wasn't until 1956, however, after this series of historical committee meetings was over, that I began fully to perceive the strong Christian-literate–traditionalist-illiterate factionalism that had existed up to that time in Tiriki tribal politics; then I also came to realize what an astute political move the formation of the historical committee and Chief Mushenye's use thereby of the elders (and of me) had been in helping heal this split.

The elders approved of the establishment of the historical committee, feeling it was high time that they received public recognition as experts in Tiriki traditions (*biima Bidiliji*) by the literate younger members of the community. Several elders told me they were most pleased that I, an educated "European" (that is, a white person) (*musomi Musungu*), was recording their words "straight"—correctly, honestly ("*udenyanga handiga bulunji maxoba geru*")—so that Tiriki progeny (*biibuli*) in future generations could read it and would not forget them, that is, the contemporary tribal elders. A minority of elders expressed skepticism about the announced objective of the historical committee, commenting that only the rich would be able to buy any book that might result and that most people probably wouldn't read it even if they could afford it; they also noted that I, an outsider, rather than they or their offspring, stood to profit from any book sales. These skeptics nevertheless appreciated the free beer. Not surprisingly, I noted a marked upswing in the pagan elders' support of schooling for their grandchildren during the course of my research in 1954–1956.

All in all, I was struck in 1954–1956 by how little the elders' status seemed to have diminished since the coming of the British and also by how much people still seemed to fear the mystical consequences of incurring the elders' wrath. I assumed, however, that this respect and high status would soon rapidly diminish because of the tremendous increase in schooling, especially at the primary level, that was finally getting under way.

Although I much favored a decrease of the fear of the mystical prowess of the elders, my regrets about the probable future erosion of their status was one of two factors that led me to dedicate my monograph on Tiriki "*Xu Basaxulu Badilijio* 'the Tiriki Elders'" (Sangree, 1966, p. v). The other factor was my real appreciation for the help many Tiriki elders had indeed given me in learning about their society and culture.

In 1954–1956 most men of the initiate and warrior age grades (Sawe and Juma age groups) were "off community (*mulugulu*)" working as laborers in the growing urban areas or on "white highland" farms. The Mau Mau emergency was in effect at that time, and resultant restrictions on using Kikuyu labor in urban areas had greatly increased the employment opportunities for illiterate or minimally schooled Tiriki and other Western Province Abaluyia peoples. The Tiriki, who had lagged behind neighboring Abaluyia groups in embracing western schooling, came to realize for the first time that the more schooling a person had, the better his prospects were in the growing urban labor market. Happily, the rise in demand by parents for schooling for their children coincided with boosted efforts by both missions and the colonial administration, including the chief of Tiriki, to increase the number and quality of schools at all levels.

Changes between 1956 and 1961

I returned to Tiriki in 1961 and organized a recensus of the two villages where I had carried out detailed demographic and social surveys in 1955–1956. Literates in Swahili, let alone English, had been a small minority in 1955, even in the younger age groups. In 1961, however, I found that almost all Tiriki children roughly between ten and fifteen years old had fair facility in speaking, reading, and writing English as well as Swahili. A substantial minority of families had children in intermediate level classes (grades five through eight), and most parents my assistants and I talked with hoped that one or more of their children would complete secondary school and be able to go on to either the university or a teacher's or technical college.

Another striking development between 1956 and 1961 was the colonial government's lifting the ban on Africans planting coffee and tea on their own farms. Many Tiriki men soon started planting these as cash crops, usually on fields of a half acre or less, often on steep slopes not previously cultivated, which they terraced for this purpose. These plantings, in contrast to plantings of maize, millet, and other subsistence crops tended by wives, were being taken care of primarily by casual laborers, generally recruited from older men no longer working out of the community, and by school-aged children. I was told in 1961 that these new plantings would first be harvestable two or three years thence, and that the owners had hopes then of being able to retire to Tiriki and live off the cash these harvests would bring in.

Another fact my 1961 recensus substantiated, one I found very disquieting, was that the birth rate in Tiriki, which had already risen to over eight live births on the average per woman in the 1950s, showed no signs whatsoever of decreasing; at the same time, population pressure on already overcrowded tribal lands (over 1,000 persons per sq. mile in 1956) was being exacerbated by a mortality rate that had declined dramatically during the previous three decades (Sangree, 1987). Postpartum sexual taboos had been abandoned before the 1950s, thanks to early missionaries' preaching that bathing with soap made sexual contact with a nursing wife safe for the husband's health. There was no need to become a Christian to take this precaution, and pagan as well as Christian families also had access to and profited from government public health efforts and mission and government dispensary medical services. Consequently, between World War I and 1954 the fertility rate among pagan and Christian women increased substantially, and the mortality rate decreased, particularly for infants and young children. The resultant population explosion continued unabated in 1961.

In conclusion, it is noteworthy that the help the Tiriki historical committee elders had given me in 1955 in learning about their culture culminated in 1961 when I returned to Tiriki for two weeks. On that occasion several of the elders who had served on the historical committee in 1955 were prevailed upon by the Tiriki chief to attend several special meetings to help me evaluate and correct the draft of the monograph I had written in English and brought with me. Tiriki school teachers were called in, who simultaneously translated and read it aloud to these elders. The corrections the elders gave were noted and I then incorporated them into the final draft of the monograph (Sangree, 1966).

Tiriki Elderhood in 1982: Shifts in Age Grade-Associated Social Behavior

When I next returned to Tiriki in 1982 for a stay of six weeks, I was surprised to find that the elders still were highly respected and important to village life. This may be in part because, as of 1982, only a very small portion of those Tiriki who had completed secondary school were old enough to be in the elder age grades;

thus most younger Tiriki with more than primary schooling, who might have belittled these elders for being so poorly educated, were absent—away studying or working out of the community. Since my detailed firsthand information on Tiriki really extends only to 1982, I shall for the remainder of this paper use the present tense to refer to things as they were that year.

Nineteen eighty-one saw the opening of Golongolo age group to initiation and, thus, the elevation of Juma age group to the judicial elder age grade. Juma age group members now range roughly from fifty-two to sixty-seven years of age. A substantial minority of them can read and write basic Swahili and some English, because, as I have already noted, primary education was beginning to be generally available and valued in Tiriki during the 1950s, when many of them were still of school age. Only a few dozen members of this age group, however, completed their secondary education, and so far as I could ascertain, less than half of these went on to complete college or technical school and joined the growing ranks of the salaried professionals or wealthy entrepreneurs who form the new Kenya bourgeoisie.

Several of this new Tiriki bourgeoisie in the Juma age group are now retired and living in the relatively spacious cement block homes they had built in Tiriki while they were still away working. They, in effect, form a new, distinctive elder gentry who already have come to dominate the ownership of local enterprises such as small market stores and the little "hotels" that serve bottled beer, soft drinks, and tea. They generally leave the running of such establishments, however, as they do the tending and marketing of their small tea or coffee plantings, to less-educated local employees, who are often their kinspeople. Elder members of this new gentry have become leading figures in the management of local churches and parent–teacher associations. The elected local member of Parliament is one of this group.

The less affluent members of Juma age group, that is, the vast majority of elderly Tiriki men, find themselves very busy running both their own and their married absent sons' farms. They are supervising and helping their overburdened wives and those of their absent sons' wives who are not away working (but who are often pregnant or nursing an infant) eke out the greatest yield possible from farms, which nowadays commonly are only one or two hectares in size. Utilizing labor intensive farming procedures, and generally assisted by some of their schoolboy and schoolgirl grandchildren still living at home, they raise two major crops a year of maize or sorghum intercropped with squashes and also legumes, which facilitate continuing soil fertility. The household sweet banana patch has always been the older men's responsibility, but now, in addition, any cattle, sheep, and goats belonging to household members are also tended, or their care is supervised, by the elderly. To summarize, most judicial elders find themselves very busy these days doing the sorts of household chores and supervisory tasks that in the 1950s were done by men in the elder warrior age grade who had already returned home permanently from employment outside the community (see also Kilbride & Kilbride, this volume).

Nowadays, most men of Sawe age group (who are currently in the elder warrior age grade) are obliged to stay away from the community much of the time working for cash at seasonal or short-term jobs or, if they are fortunate, at more steady wage employment; they find they must do this to make enough money to pay the school fees and meet the other expenses of supporting their large number of dependents. In short, most Sawe age group members are employed as laborers and wage workers outside of the community in order to earn necessary cash that the family farming activities simply can no longer supply.

As of 1982, family size in Tiriki had not yet tapered off from 1961, but the infant mortality rate probably had also declined; indeed the Tiriki women now typically bore seven or eight children who reached adulthood (Sangree, 1987). It has become common for young wives to seek employment outside the community, and the incidence of employed married mothers sending children home for their parents to care for has increased strikingly (see Kilbride & Kilbride, this volume). Quite a few Tiriki households have had their numbers further swelled by orphaned children of relatives, such as surviving children of Tiriki families who migrated to Uganda in the 1960s, when offered land to homestead there by the first Obote government, only to be massacred a few years later during the Amin administration.

The remarks I have made about members of Juma age group, who now occupy the judicial elder age grade, apply generally also to members of Mayina age group, who now range from approximately sixty-eight to eighty-two years of age and are the current ritual elders. There are only a handful of the Mayina age group in Tiriki, however, who have achieved what might be labeled a "middle-class" or "bourgeois" lifestyle. Mayina elders, of course, are now generally less physically robust than members of the more junior age grades and more preoccupied with their own health needs. I found that it was the women elders—the wives of Juma and Mayina—who have assumed most of the nursing care both for their husbands and for each other; they also make efforts to care for any unwell males and females of all ages in their family, church parish, and village who don't have spouses or other close family members who can nurse them.

Christian worship has now completely supplanted the traditional ancestor cult practices, with younger bible-college graduates fulfilling the principal pastoral responsibilities. Similarly, herbal and magical medical procedures traditionally carried out by the elders have now been largely supplanted by the services of relatively young employees at mission and government district medical dispensaries trained in western medical procedures.

Notably missing from the contemporary village scene are the elders' beer drinks. Several years ago, Kenya's President Moi, motivated I am told primarily by a desire to quell the increasing rowdiness associated with locally brewed beer drinking parties in urban and peri-urban areas, promulgated a nationwide ban on "native beer." Individuals may still brew beer for their own household, but it can be brewed for multihousehold gatherings and for events such as circumcision ceremonials only if a permit is obtained from the administration in advance, a procedure that, I am told, may take weeks. These restrictions effectively preclude the holding of the traditional informally organized elders' community beer drinks, and the average Tiriki elder simply doesn't have the cash needed to substitute legal bottled beer as an alternative focus for elders' get-togethers. A growing problem in Kenya, probably exacerbated in places such as Tiriki by these recent restrictions on brewing traditional beer, is the illegal distilling and consumption of maize spirits. Drunkenness and associated rowdiness, especially among younger unemployed men, are now major problems in Tiriki, whereas in the 1950s drunkenness was infrequent, and rowdiness was usually effectively controlled by the local judicial and ritual elders (Sangree, 1962).

Disputes in the 1950s and early 1960s that could not be resolved within the household were, as noted earlier, hashed out by the judicial and ritual elders over the beer pots, where they were often successfully mediated without ever being taken to the subchief's courts. Nowadays, however, with elders' community beer drinks a thing of the past, local altercations routinely find their way directly to the tribal and multitribal district courts presided over by younger administrators and magistrates, who have qualified for these positions through specialized schooling.

Although the elders have experienced the erosion of virtually all their traditional religious roles during the last eighty years and most of their community judicial duties in recent years, their role in maintaining the continuity and everyday functioning of the family homestead clearly has expanded in recent decades. Also, responsibility for equitable partition and inheritance of land still rests primarily in the hands of lineage elders, with every man looking to his own father for the land that his wife and later his sons' wives will farm. Today, as in the past, Tiriki men generally keep one portion of the farmland they obtained from their fathers until they die, the rest being bequeathed in equitable portions to each son sometime after he marries, usually by the time he begets three children.

Customarily the youngest son works the father's portion for him and inherits it upon his death. If a man's own father is dead, the senior adult son normally takes over responsibility for land distribution, and elders of the patrilineage appoint someone to fill in for the senior son if he is not yet of age or is away from the community. In the case of major disputes, age group ties assure that elders of both the judicial and ritual age grades of other clans living in the local village will step in to serve as arbiters.

An increasing proportion of younger men now have the land they receive from their fathers or lineage guardians surveyed and registered in the district court; thus they gain the legal right under current Kenyan law to sell that land to whom they choose. Informants we talked with in 1982, however, expressed great reluctance to obtain or dispose of land within the tribal boundaries, which is getting increasingly scarce and valuable (as is all farmland in Kenya), except in the traditional manner. They repeatedly cited as the reason for their conservatism in this regard several well-known instances of land deals where one or both parties had circumvented the elders' traditional control in such matters; not only did protracted and expensive litigation in the district court ensue, but also bitter and long-festering animosities between clan brothers, or village neighbors, resulted.

New Family Caretaker Dimensions of the Elders' Authority

Nowadays, elders are assuming prolonged caretaker responsibilities for the lands they have already passed on to their sons who are working away from the community, and they are also looking after these sons' school-aged children. Thus, the current involvement of elders in the lives of their grandchildren is very different in detail from former times when the sorts of domestic supervisory tasks now carried out by elderly were normally carried out by their sons and daughters-in-law, who had by then returned permanently to Tiriki. Children in Tiriki generally feel at ease with their grandparents—indeed, they are often on more familiar terms with both their grandfathers and grandmothers than with their parents. Reserve and formal respect were and remain a major element in children's behavior towards parents, particularly towards fathers and paternal uncles. The traditional warmth between alternate generations is still evident in the informal ease with which small children lounge and play around their grandparents, in contrast to the constraint they display when with their parents, especially their fathers. It is interesting that elders have been able to maintain this continuity of familiarity with their grandchildren even after assuming more everyday roles of authority towards them. Perhaps this is because they often give orders to and, when necessary, discipline their grandchildren through younger intermediaries, rather than asserting their authority directly.

As I earlier noted, the elders' role in maintaining Tiriki male identity through initiation still goes on; furthermore, the initiates are exposed to the heavy drama and symbolism of initiation under the direct supervision of the circumcision elders at a younger, more impressionable age than ever before. The ritual elders' continuing role as overseers of boys' initiation is rendered certainly different in emotional tone from former times (perhaps more impressive, perhaps less) because of their increased involvement in overseeing the care and supervision of these boys throughout most of their preadolescent childhood.

Elders' roles as controllers of witches and sorcerers and a widespread fear of their power to deprive younger people of their reproductive capacity remain of considerable significance in Tiriki rural life; many people are still very cautious about angering or openly questioning the opinions of more senior elders because of continuing beliefs about the power of their curse.

A great deal of formal deference is still shown elderly Tiriki men and women in many little ways, such as precedence in speaking, in receiving front seats in public meetings, in leading prayers from the congregation in church services, in being politely greeted at the marketplace, or in a marked disinclination for younger people directly to question or dispute with the elders. I was surprised and pleased to see that the elders seem usually more at ease and more secure with their own children than they were thirty years ago. Nowadays, young adults, regardless of their educational level, generally recognize and speak with gratitude about the crucial responsibilities the elders have assumed in the maintenance of their farmlands and in the care of their younger grandchildren. In a nation where population growth is far outstripping economic growth, these homestead farms often remain the most feasible arena in which to raise and care for young children; and for many families they afford the only available, albeit often insufficient, social and economic support system for sick or feeble family members (see Weisner, this volume).

CONCLUSIONS

Tiriki still measure not only their own generativity but indeed the personal and social worth of their own and others' lives primarily by their number of progeny. In precolonial times, the Tiriki believed that their own and their descendant's generativity was dependent upon maintaining the spiritual favor of their deceased clan forebears. Today, no one worries much about the mystical power of deceased forebears; Christian prayer and worship have entirely supplanted any concern about the importance to the living and future generations of ancestral spiritual beneficence. Nowadays, concern about forebears typically ends with the elders who are still alive; in a very real sense concern about the future also begins with these elders, that is, with the roles they have assumed for their grandchildrens' care from the time they are weaned right up to (and sometimes through) secondary school. Formerly, toddlers were tended by children too young to help their mothers with the farm work (see Weisner, this volume). Nowadays, these children attend school much of the time; consequently, not only much of the farm work formerly done by their daughters-in-law but also a good deal of this childcare now falls upon the grandmothers; and grandfathers not only oversee the well-being of the household but also on occasion actively help with these activities.

Tiriki elders enjoy perhaps a higher overall status today than they did when my wife and I first got to know the community in 1954–1956. I think it is also safe to say that they retain responsibilities as central to the continuation of tribal life, even though the nature of these responsibilities has shifted. I heard no comments from elders, as we did in 1954–1956, about feeling neglected or unappreciated by the younger people who could read and write. But the major complaint we did hear from elders in 1982, both male and female, was that they were too busy and too poor—that they had too much to do in trying to run the farm and care for their grandchildren, especially with an ever dwindling supply of both land and cash!

In closing, it is noteworthy that the Tiriki ever since, indeed long before, my wife and I first got to know them in 1954–1956, have been modifying the social roles ascribed to members of each age grade and have been revising the cultural attributes of elderhood. But throughout all these changes they have preserved seniority as a basic legitimizing principle of their authority system (Rosenmayr, 1988). Although the Tiriki have frequently responded to outside pressures and utilized new resources in this process, the changes in the social roles for the elderly in large measure have been in part initiated, and generally supported actively, by the Tiriki elders themselves.

I am troubled by one demographic consideration. Up to now the elderly in Tiriki have remained a relatively small proportion of the population. A marked decrease in infant mortality and an increase in the birth rate in recent decades have, in effect, precluded any recent increase in the proportion of the elderly that might have otherwise resulted from the decreasing morbidity rate among the young adult and middle age cohorts. In the near future, however, barring some horrendous Malthusian scenario or massive emigration (which is increasingly difficult and unlikely), the birth rate will decrease rapidly (see Bradley, this volume), and thus the proportion of the elderly in the population will start to increase markedly. Will the elders then remain, in sum, a social and economic asset for the society as a whole, or will they be in competition more and more with the younger age cohorts for scarce resources? This is a question that is pertinent to all of Kenya; there remains little unused arable land in the country, and all the major tribal groups are experiencing both a population explosion and a land shortage comparable to that of Tiriki (Frank & McNicoll, 1987). Furthermore, seniority, even though it has lost much of its traditional religious significance in recent decades, remains an important status-ascribing principle in every Kenya ethnic group I know of (see Edwards, this volume).

All things considered (including my forecasts in 1956 and 1961 about the imminent demise of the elders' authority, which proved to be wrong), I hesitate to predict or even hazard a guess as to whether the Tiriki elders' status will remain high or become markedly debased during the next few decades. Clearly, the management of the extended-family homestead farm and the care of resident grandchildren are nowadays important arenas in which the elders manifest their authority and affirm their continuing high status in the local community.

Is there is any reason to believe that the sociocultural importance of seniority is dependent upon the continuing existence of the extended family homestead farm? The data I have presented do not point to any such basic interconnection. Instead they suggest that seniority as a status-conferring principle is an important cultural norm that has strongly influenced and shall continue in the future to influence the individual, nuclear, and extended family choices of Tiriki as they respond and accommodate to a changing world (Carter, 1988). Nowadays the management of the extended family farms and the care of the resident grandchildren that the elderly provide are the important services through which they affirm their traditionally high status. If the elderly in Tiriki can in the future continue to find and fill social roles of manifest importance to their extended family members, both those living locally and those living and working in urban areas, their culturally bestowed high status as elders will continue to endure; otherwise it may become just a rapidly fading memory.

NOTE

This paper is a revision and adaptation of Sangree (1993). Special thanks to Lucinda Sangree, Ph.D., for her aid in gathering and interpreting the field research in 1954–1956 and 1982 on which so much of this paper is based.

REFERENCES

Carter, Anthony T. (1988). "Does culture matter?" The case of the demographic transition. In Daniel Scott Smith (Ed.), "Does Culture Matter?" An Exchange. *Historical Methods*, *21*(4), 160–188.

Cattell, Maria G. (1989). Knowledge and social change in Samia, Western Kenya. *Journal of Cross-Cultural Gerontology*, *4*, 225–244.

Cowgill, Donald O. (1974). Aging and modernization: A revision of the theory. In Jaber F. Gubrium (Ed.), *Communities and environmental policy* (pp. 124–146). Springfield, IL: Charles C. Thomas.

Foner, Nancy. (1984). Age and social change. In David I. Kertzer & Jennie Keith (Eds.), *Age and anthropological theory* (pp. 195-216). Ithaca, NY: Cornell University Press.

Fortes, Meyer. (1984). Age, generation and social structure. In David I. Kertzer & Jennie Keith (Eds.), *Age and anthropological theory* (pp. 99–122). Ithaca, NY: Cornell University Press.

Frank, Odile, & McNicoll, Geoffrey. (1987). Fertility and population policy in Kenya. *Population and Development Review*, *13*, 209–243.

LeVine, Robert A., & Sangree, Walter H. (1962). The diffusion of age-group organization in east Africa: A controlled comparison. *Africa*, *32*(2), 97–110.

Rosenmayr, Leopold. (1988). "More than wisdom." A field study of the old in an African village. *Journal of Cross-Cultural Gerontology*, *4*(1), 21–40.

Sangree, Walter H. (1962). The social functions of beer drinking in Bantu Tiriki. In David J. Pittman & Charles R. Snyder (Eds.), *Society, culture and drinking patterns* (pp. 6–21). New York: John Wiley & Sons.

Sangree, Walter H. (1965). The Bantu Tiriki of Western Kenya. In James L. Gibbs, Jr. (Ed.), *Peoples of Africa* (pp. 41–80). New York: Holt Rinehart & Winston.

Sangree, Walter H. (1966). *Age, prayer and politics in Tiriki, Kenya*. London: Oxford University Press.

Sangree, Walter H. (1974). Youths as elders and infants as ancestors: The complementarity of alternate generations, both living and dead, in Tiriki, Kenya, and Irigwe, Nigeria. *Africa*, *44*(1), 65–70.

Sangree, Walter H. (1981). The 'last born' (*Muxogosi*) and complementary filiation in Tiriki, Kenya. *Ethos*, *9*(3), 188–200.

Sangree, Walter H. (1986). Role flexibility and status continuity: Tiriki (Kenya) age groups today. *Journal of Cross-Cultural Gerontology*, *1*, 117–138.

Sangree, Walter H. (1987). The childless elderly in Tiriki, Kenya, and Irigwe, Nigeria: A comparative analysis of the relationships between beliefs about childlessness and the social status of the childless elderly. *Journal of Cross Cultural Gerontology*, *2*, 201–223.

Sangree, Walter H. (1989). Age and power: Life-course trajectories and age structuring of power relations in east and west Africa. In David I. Kertzer & K. Warner Schaie (Eds.), *Age structuring in comparative perspective* (pp. 23–46). Hillsdale, NJ: Lawrence Erlbaum Associates.

Sangree, Walter H. (1992). Grandparenthood and modernization: The changing status of male and female elders in Tiriki, Kenya, and Irigwe, Nigeria. *Journal of Cross Cultural Gerontology*, *7*, 331–361.

Sangree, Walter H. (1993). Grand-parenté et statut des vieux à TIRIKI (Kenya). In Pierre Cornillot & Serge Lebovici (Eds.), *Vieillir en Afrique—Champs de la santé* (pp. 213–249). Paris: La Collection des PUF.

Wagner, Günter. (1940). The political organization of the Bantu of Kavirondo. In M. Fortes & E. E. Evans-Pritchard (Eds.), *African political systems* (pp. 197–238). London: Oxford University Press for the International African Institute.

Wagner, Günter. (1949). *The Bantu of North Kavirondo* (Vol. 1). London: Oxford University Press for the International African Institute.

Weisner, T. S. (1976). The structure of sociability: Urban migration and urban–rural ties in Kenya. *Urban Anthropology, 5*, 199–223.

10

Stigma, Role Overload, and Delocalization among Contemporary Kenyan Women

Philip L. Kilbride and Janet C. Kilbride

INTRODUCTION

Weakening intergenerational interdependence among family members in North America is aptly illustrated in a book entitled *Habits of the Heart* (Bellah, Madsen, Sullivan, Swidler, & Tipton, 1985). This widely read book, based upon interviews Bellah and associates conducted with middle class affluent North Americans on quality of life questions, presents the following characterization of North American values about child–parent relationships:

> Many Americans are uneasy about taking responsibility for children. . . . For highly individuated Americans, there is something anomalous about the relations between parents and children, for the biologically normal dependence of children on adults is perceived as morally abnormal. We have already seen how children must leave home, find their own way religiously and ideologically. . . . This process leads to a considerable amnesia about what one owes to one's parents. The owner of a car dealership speaks of himself as a self-made man, conveniently forgetting that his father established the business. (1985, p. 82)

Bellah et al. found that self-reliance and individualism also characterize parents' attitudes toward their own dependency needs. They state, for instance: "Francis Fitzgerald found that most of the retirees in Sun City Centre had quite remote relations with their children and above all dreaded any dependency on them . . . clearly the meaning of one's life for most Americans is to become one's own person, almost to give birth to one's own person, almost to give birth to one's self (1985, p. 82)."

Extreme individualism (what Hsu [1983] refers to as rugged individualism) is an Anglo-Saxon Protestant derived value of long standing that has become exaggerated in the general U. S. culture and character to the point of material and emotional selfishness. Rugged individualism presently interacts with unfettered capitalism of an extreme sort reminiscent of the "new right" economic agenda of the Reagan–Bush political-economic policy. For instance, on the basis of survey data on more than one thousand North American grandparents, A. Kornhaber argues that rugged individualism has fueled a "new social contract" in the emotional experience of many contemporary grandparents. He writes, "A great many grandparents have given up emotional attachments to their grandchildren...have turned their backs on an entire generation" (1985, p. 189).

In a similar vein, Guttmann (1985) speaks of the new North American "hedonic" grandparent, one who seeks freedom from responsibility. He believes that previous generations of North American grandparents valued individual autonomy which, when it did occur, was for reasons of self-sufficiency. He sees contemporary "hedonism" as the product of "deculturation" or value nonsharing due to a recent breakdown of collective social experience in family or community. "In our families, we sunder the three generation family, split grandparents from grandchildren, and trundle our aged parents off to retirement or nursing homes; and in our politics, even our aged presidents have to deck themselves with the cosmetics and manners of youth" (1985, p. 173).

While the "new social contract" and "hedonism" are now part of the North American national experience, it is probably more accurate to conclude that deculturation has resulted in a wide range of grandparenting styles ("hedonistic," "intimate at a distance," "negotiable," etc.) depending on, for instance, geography, ethnicity, gender of grandparent, and marital status of the parent, to name four major causative factors in modern North American grandparenting relational practices (cf. Bengtson & Robertson, 1985). Nevertheless, "rugged individualism" is "culturally" reinforced and is psychologically inconsistent with interdependent intergenerational bonds, which are arguably a prerequisite for healthy family life.

In our home community of Delaware County, Pennsylvania, for example, many grandparents are striving to counteract parental neglect due to drug and alcohol abuse by joining together in a grandparental support group. This group is seeking financial, educational, and emotional guidance from the larger community as it seeks to provide child care for grandchildren. There are daily accounts in United States newspapers about various aberrations of family life such as incest, child prostitution and pornography, and the battering of women and children (and sometimes men), ranging in age from the infant to the elderly. There is also an increasing incidence of homeless families. This breakdown in family life has accompanied a decline in the three generation household in which extended family members once served as "moralnets," a term coined by Naroll (1983) for social support networks.

PURPOSE

Through a cultural critique (Marcus & Fisher, 1986) of our own society in juxtaposition with Kenya, we have come to support a national policy of "reculturation" in America (Guttmann, 1985). By reculturation Guttmann means that, in the face of the decline or absence of a national cultural tradition resulting from deculturation, North Americans must now reinvent a common extended-family-focused cultural ideology.

Kenya has much to teach us about intergenerational relations, as will be shown below. At the same time, however, a cash economy, land shortage, and the migration of men to cities have all profoundly impacted on family structure, child welfare, and female power in Kenya (see Bradley, this volume; de Wolf, this volume; Freeman, 1988; Nasimiyu, this volume). "Delocalization" of the economy in the twentieth century has involved a shift from local crops grown exclusively for subsistence, largely through female labor, to a monetary national and international economy based on cash crops grown primarily by men for sale outside the community (J. Kilbride, 1992). This has made many women, particularly those without education, arguably economically worse off than their counterparts in the past. In the modern cash economy, children likewise have become less economically valuable than in the past (see Bradley, this volume; Caldwell, 1982). Nowadays children are not always a source of joy or what can be called, in reference to African traditions, "children of value" (P. L. Kilbride & J. C. Kilbride, 1990).

In western Kenya, traditional cultural values and modern socioeconomic circumstances have interacted over historical time to produce, as it were, a new Kenyan social contract, one where grandparents, particularly grandmothers, are increasingly taking on the role of economic provider for their grandchildren. Traditionally, of course, the provider role was the responsibility of the father and mother. These days, however, modern premarital teenage pregnancies, in particular, are having a serious effect on intergenerational relations, as grandparents now assume new support functions, often under economic hardship. In a related process involving gender imbalances in modern life, many teenage girls are often under duress as they seek to manage social stigma arising from their unwanted pregnancies (P. L. Kilbride, 1991). In this chapter we want to consider the situation of both grandmothers and pregnant teen girls to illustrate our theoretical position. At the same time, we want to argue that both North Americans and Kenyans have much to gain from traditional Kenyan family values for the purpose of reculturation (North American) or preservation and reinforcement (Kenyan).

FAMILY, GRANDPARENTS, AND CHILDREN: ETHNOGRAPHIC CONTEXT

Our previous fieldwork has been among Luyia communities in western Kenya, where modern rural life still retains many of the social features prevalent in the precolonial era of about a century ago (P. L. Kilbride, 1980, 1986; Wagner, 1949, 1956). The majority of people continue to be oriented to an agrarian lifestyle and depend, for the most part, on their own labor for subsistence foods and cash crops. Women and children are, as in the past, the most important source of farm labor. For this reason large families are still desired by both men and women, and polygamy is seen as a means of increasing family size and thus providing additional free labor. In one of our studies, for example, when asked, "What do you like most about your child?" most of the twenty-five mothers interviewed mentioned work activities, although "obedience" and "respect for elders" were not uncommon responses. For example, one mother said of her nine-year-old daughter, "She is very much willing to help me. She does not feel comfortable when she sees me working when she is playing; she has to come and help me." Another mother noted admiringly about her nine-year-old son, "He helps in planting and weeding flowers and vegetables; he can also wash things and sweep the home." Rural family life is still very much a collective enterprise, constituting an interpersonal, interdependent system where kinship, age, and gender roles are clearly utilitarian and reciprocal (Kilbride, 1986).

In general, rural children are still highly valued, serve important economic roles in family life, and are the responsibility of extended-family members in situations where parents are unable to provide care (see Munroe & Munroe, this volume; Weisner, this volume). Children are a great source of joy and happiness for most community members (P. L. Kilbride & J. C. Kilbride, 1990), and mothers are conscientious in their child care responsibilities. All twenty-five mothers interviewed in the study cited previously reported accurately where their children were and what they were doing, as discovered by subsequent observational follow-ups by our research assistant.

At the community level, Luyia grandparents or elders played important roles as counselors in affairs of family, clan, and community. We learn, for example, from Aswani that "Abanyore [Luyia] literature is full of folk tales because of the old woman's love of pleasing children. Old women . . . would sit down by the fireside and tell as many stories as they could think of before the children became sleepy" (1972, p. 1). Stories told to children were concerned with pending adolescent life and were for entertainment. Aswani continues:

> Sometimes stories were about domestic life, with married women and their husbands as the major characters. Stories of this type were told to the adolescent and adult audiences. They were meant to warn both boys and girls what they were to expect of their respective partners when they married. . . . The stories were also meant to teach the young men how to behave in crises which might arise in family life. (1972, p. 2)

Idealized themes in these stories stressed morals concerning, for example, sincere love, avoidance of pride, caution, and avoidance of laziness.

To provide some data for our own studies of modernization we gathered systematic information about grandparents. In one of our surveys, with the help of our research assistants, we asked respondents in Samia Location ($n = 62$, 34 females, 28 males) and Nzoia Location ($n = 69$, 37 females, 32 males) to provide their ideal beliefs about the three most important characteristics of a good grandmother and a good grandfather. As we can see from the data presented in Table 10.1, the grandparent ideal as described above is still very much in place. Moreover, in the arguably more traditional Samia areas, grandfathers even at present play a significant role in land dispute resolution. The expectation that grandparents are and should be properly involved in cultural transmission through storytelling, teach-

Table 10.1
Characteristics of Good Grandparents*

Characteristics	Grandfather		Grandmother	
	Samia	Nzoia	Samia	Nzoia
Storyteller, teacher, advisor, transmitter of custom	22	13	26	13
Takes care of grandchildren	2	0	8	5
Gives present to grandchildren	3	2	10	1
Settles family disputes (e.g., land)	9	4	1	0
Loves grandchildren	5	20	4	29
Peace-loving, not quarrelsome, helpful, kind	8	14	5	7
Sociable, friendly, cheerful, free, trusted	3	9	4	12
Good Christian	2	0	1	0
Curer, magician	3	0	2	0
Miscellaneous	5	6	1	1
No response	0	1	0	1

* Adapted from Table 13, Kilbride & Kilbride (1990, p. 188). *N* (Samia and Nzoia) = 131; 71 female, 60 male.

ing, and advising is common. In so doing, they should be sociable, friendly, loving, helpful, and not quarrelsome—in short, the type of person that one can enjoy being with and with whom one can feel close and free to discuss life's joys and sorrows. In the less traditional area of Nzoia, grandparents are involved in cultural transmission, and in some cases grandfathers resolve family disputes.

Of concern here is the finding that in both areas grandmothers more than grandfathers are expected to take economic care of grandchildren. Quite significantly, it is not believed that grandparents should ideally assume total economic support for grandchildren, but there is nevertheless cultural support for the notion that grandparents are and should be involved in asymmetrical exchanges with their grandchildren. Grandparents should ideally give presents, food, and goodwill (traditionally grandchildren sometimes sleep at the house of grandparents, where they can be "spoiled"). These same grandchildren, as adults, are expected to care for their elderly grandparents. In part, however, the major provider role was that of the child's father. Because of delocalization of the economy, many fathers are now unavailable, unable, or unwilling to provide for their children, a responsibility that is falling all too often on the shoulders of caring grandparents. To refuse a grandchild is to go against both cultural convention and psychological sentiment and contentment.

ADOLESCENT PREGNANCY AND ETHICAL DELOCALIZATION

In the 1930s Wagner, writing about Abaluyia of western Kenya where we have worked, noted the importance of having children for both men and women. So strongly was fertility emphasized that a young girl could increase her chances of marriage by becoming pregnant. A man usually welcomed and adopted his "illegitimate" child, who was often thought by his siblings to be their father's favorite child. Overall, the general picture that emerges from Wagner's description is one in which women and men both enjoy prestige and have social power as a consequence of significant economic roles and as producers of children and as performers of other instrumental activities. Men, however, were given greater power than women through ownership of the land, their children, and economic control of their wives.

Hand in hand with economic delocalization is a process of ethical or moral delocalization (P. L. Kilbride, 1991, 1992). By moral delocalization, we mean the erosion of traditional, localized moral codes and ethical practices in favor of modern derived legal, religious, and educational norms and values. In modern East African society, for example, sexual knowledge, practice, and moral responsibility have been delocalized. It can be argued that this process works primarily against the interests of women. Localized East African sexual practices had been embedded in a system of moral obligations, which maximized female and male sexual pleasure and social responsibility (cf. Kisekka, 1976). Worthman and Whiting (1987) document that the pool of unwed mothers appears to be increasing in the Kikuyu community, particularly among those who have significant amounts of formal education (i.e., the more modern). The modern school and associated moral values have replaced the traditional *gweko* rituals as a major peer socialization setting. The *gweko* custom (Kenyatta, 1984) was a form of lovemaking involving an apron used by women to protect their private parts. Sometimes sexual relief was experienced, but "petting" would appear to have been the ideal. Worthman and Whiting state that boys were ostracized from further participation in *gweko* by their peers if they broke the rules. The Church of Scotland mission disapproved of *gweko*, so that most of the educational functions of the practice have been lost in favor of European derived sexual values and inhibitions, what we call would call moral delocalization. They conclude:

> By means of a sacred ceremony, the parental generation transferred to youth the responsibility for regulating premarital sex and initiating the process of mate selection. When this system had been secularized by edict and the introduction of western schooling, both the regulations of premarital sex and mate selection appear to have been destabilized; at least temporarily. We suspect that this effect of modernization is not unique. (1987, pp. 163–164)

Indeed, present-day premarital sexuality does frequently result in unwanted teen pregnancies. Were (1990) discovered, for example, that in the Kakamega district there were some primary schools where as many as four girls per term leave school due to pregnancy. Cattell, who has also worked in Western Province concurs. "A high incidence of premarital pregnancy is not peculiar to Samia and is probably a relatively new phenomenon, since in the early part of the 20th century when today's old people were marrying, female virginity at marriage was expected, tested and rewarded" (1989, p. 510).

Cattell also reports that responsibility for these grandchildren (*abaana besimba,* 'children of the *esimba'* often falls to the maternal grandmother. This is especially the case if the child's mother marries a man who is not the father of the child. In one of Cattell's surveys, she found that of 252 respondents, 29 percent had at least one dependent grandchild and 11 percent had three or more dependent grandchildren. *Abaana besimba* constituted the majority of grandchildren in Cattell's sample. Similarly, P. L. Kilbride and J. C. Kilbride (1990) report that thirty-three of sixty-five Luyia homes in Nzoia had at least one resident grandchild.

In P. Kilbride's own ethnographic research, girls or young women who were impregnated often reported to him that their parents were angry with them. In one known case, a young woman was heavily caned (beaten with a stick). Until recently, regulations required that schoolgirls who got pregnant must leave school; for most, readmission is precluded on practical grounds. Some of our female informants stated that after marriage they would "just leave" their child with their mothers. It is believed by both females and males that an illegitimate daughter has a better chance of later being accepted by her mother's future husband since she can bring bridewealth, whereas a boy, who will need to be given a *shamba* (land), may be less welcome in today's land-scarce circumstances.

A young woman of nineteen represents the current dilemmas regarding care. Her child was conceived with a fellow student when she was in Form 2 (ninth grade under the old British thirteen-year system). She was not using birth control because she "did not understand then." She was "in love," and he was her first boyfriend. He refused to accept responsibility for the pregnancy. The headmaster called his parents, but they also refused to accept responsibility since he was "still young" and would not concede that he was the father. She plans to marry one day, but her daughter will stay with her mother if her future husband refuses the child. Her father died in 1980, but there are about ten acres of land, and the home is a relatively prosperous one. Nevertheless, the grandmother is worried about her ability to support her granddaughter and about what would happen to the girl if she should die.

The Kenyan press has reported instances of schoolgirls throwing their newborns into pit latrines. During our research, one such instance occurred, in which the infant did not die. One day in May 1985, we observed a large crowd gathering at a local secondary school. Joining the crowd, we arrived just in time to see a newborn infant being lifted out of one of the school's pit latrines. The infant's mother, Sarah (a pseudonym), who had attempted the infanticide, was being hustled into her dormitory for interrogation by local officials and nurses while we observed the proceedings and the crowd continued to grow outside. Through observation and interviews, we followed this incident and its aftermath for several weeks, sometimes with the assistance of a female research assistant. Visits occurred in school, hospital, jail, and home situations. Discussions were conducted with the young woman herself, various members of her family, police, school officials, and many other members of the general public.

This sixteen-year-old Sarah became pregnant by a man she hardly knew, a married man visiting the rural area from the city. Until this incident, she had been an average student in matters of school rank and attendance. She comes from a polygynous family but has been raised by her stepmother and her father. Her mother and father were divorced some time ago. The young woman and her maternal family members revealed that she did not get along well with the stepmother and seems to be, in the opinion of her brother, the victim of a broken home. He also believes that lack of money for school fees for her was a factor in her troubles, that is, she hoped to receive money from the man to support her school fees. Sarah did not report her pregnancy to anyone because of fear. According to her, she did not even realize she was pregnant until she was seven months pregnant. She waited about thirty minutes after giving birth before deciding to kill her baby. During this time, she considered such things as "Where will I take the baby?" and "How can I get my school fees back for this term?"

In the days and weeks after she attempted infanticide, her mother and her maternal relatives proved to be a key resource group as they visited her in the hospital and jail. In particular, her maternal uncle, at considerable cost and time, looked after his niece and her newborn during this time of duress. In 1990, Sarah's mother had assumed full responsibility for her grandson, who calls her "mother." He does not know that Sarah is his mother, a circumstance made easier by Sarah's residence elsewhere in a large town where she now attempts to build a new stigma-free life for herself (P. L. Kilbride, 1991). Delocalization and the loss of traditional institutions and supports to assist this woman and the father led to this situation.

GRANDPARENTS: DECULTURATION "ROLE OVERLOAD"

Grandparents suffer the undesirable consequences of ethical delocalization. For example, consider the dilemma of this woman in her fifties, one of three co-wives. Still living at home are a total of twenty-four children among the three co-wives. Two sons live in the compound with their families. Problems associated with school fees and clothing are acute in this compound, since the husband is not a wealthy person. Our informant, in addition to her nine resident children, also supports two grandsons of eight and ten years of age. Her daughter left them behind when she married into another community. She had been made pregnant by two different men, one a teacher. These men disappeared long ago. The daughter's husband forbids her to visit these sons, and she sends no help. She has had three children with her present husband. Her father, already hard-pressed, has paid school fees for these grandchildren (now in Primary 4 and Primary 2), but clothing and bedding are a big problem.

Another grandmother in her fifties has been living with her two sons and a granddaughter in Sisal since 1982. She is divorced and has another son, who lives elsewhere. The latter son is the father of her granddaughter, who is ten years old and a student in Primary 2. The granddaughter has a scar on her forehead where she was beaten with a cooking stick by her stepmother three years ago. Her father had lived in Mombasa in the 1970s, where he had three children (two are now dead) with a woman labelled as a prostitute. He subsequently married another woman, with whom he has had a son and a daughter. This woman became jealous on those occasions when he would "sleep out" and would beat her husband's "outside" child. When interviewed, the child said she was beaten about four times a month but never when the father slept at home. She got along well with her siblings, but she was the only one who was ever beaten. Her father would beat her stepmother whenever he discovered that she had beaten his daughter. The stepmother was remorseful after beating the child, as indicated by her taking the child to a hospital for treatment. The child now lives with her grandmother, who was happy to take her because she had no daughters. Her stepmother sometimes brings clothes, but neither she nor the father provides any other assistance. Her mother frequently visits but is closely monitored by the grandmother for fear that she will steal the child.

Our third grandparent is a man. He provided us with good insight into the stresses experienced not only by himself but by his wife as well. This fifty-two-year-old man lives with his wife, six sons, and a daughter. Two other sons and two other daughters have married and live elsewhere, but one daughter-in-law lives at his home with her three children. Two children of the other daughters-in-law also live with them. He has, however, a total of seven grandchildren living with him, because each of the two daughters who have married out left behind a child obtained before her marriage. These two grandsons, who call him father, were not accepted by their mothers' husbands. In each case, the alleged father denied in court his paternity. One was fined K.sh. 3000, but he never paid. These two children often call their grandfather "father," and he loves them as his own children. One of these is in Form 3 (tenth grade), and the other is in Primary 5 (fifth grade). He is concerned, however, because he feels that his wife does not love these two children. She gives them less food and lots of work to do compared to other children in the homestead. He has told his wife to treat them better, but he feels that most grandmothers are like that and look down on such unwanted grandchildren. It should be noted that these grandparents still have seven of their own children living with them. Nevertheless, they do not appear to be experiencing extreme financial hardships in that they are not among the poorer residents of the community.

Our research did reveal, as shown above, that grandparents do often experience what can be referred to as decultured *role overload*. That is, many grandparents continue to perform traditional grandparenting duties in addition to parenting duties of their own children and grandchildren. The concept of overload has been applied in America to the situation of African American women who, because of adolescent pregnancies, sometimes become grandparents at an early age, sometimes as early as their late twenties (Burton & Bengston, 1985). In Kenya, role overload typically means that grandparents assume the function of economic provider for their grandchild, a responsibility that, according to our survey research on family roles, is ideally thought to be a father–husband obligation (P. L. Kilbride & J. C. Kilbride, 1990). The provider function is now often passed along to grandparents by fathers of premarital children and also by mothers if circumstances so dictate (e.g., marrying a man who will not accept her child). As in the new social contract in America discussed above, Kenyan grandparents sometimes do not welcome their new grandparenting obligations, in part because of a change in wealth flow direction (Bradley, this volume; Caldwell, 1982). In this view, children are now often economically expensive relative to those benefits that previously flowed "up," in generational erms, from children to adults (in agricultural or pastoral labor).

CONCLUSION: THEORETICAL

Overall, our material can be interpreted as still another example of socially negative consequences associated with the process of economic change in East Africa that began in the nineteenth century. While having many obvious social benefits, this process caused numerous disruptions in the social lives of East African peoples. It has been shown that socioeconomic change (what we have called economic delocalization) is responsible, for instance, for a "hungry season" in some areas of Kenya, because of the commercialization of maize, the staple crop (Cohen & Attieno Odhiambo, 1989); for child exploitation in some modern labor practices (Kayongo-Male & Walji, 1984); and for increased rates of child abuse and neglect (Bradley, 1995; Onyango & Kayongo-Male, 1983). Moreover, only women are legally responsible for illegitimate children (Kabeberi, 1990) and have been alienated from land use rights prevailing in precolonial society.

In fact, it can be argued that Kenyan women have, overall, experienced a decline in social power and economic prerogatives in the modern economy as compared to the precolonial past (cf. Obler, 1985; Håkansson; 1988; Suda, 1990; P. L. Kilbride & J. C. Kilbride 1990; Nasimiyu, this volume; Bradley, this volume). In our own work in East Africa, we have tried to show how, in modern times, women occupy stigmatized social roles such as barmaids, or unwed teenage motherless girls, such as Sarah, who are criminalized for attempted infanticide (P. L. Kilbride & J. C. Kilbride, 1990; P. L. Kilbride 1991). This is so even though their behavior is rational or "smart," in one sense, given their economically powerless status. But their behavior is also socially improper and therefore socially deviant or stigmatized (see Freilich, Raybeck, & Savishinsky, 1991). Most pregnant teen girls choose not to attempt infanticide; Sarah's behavior is a case of "hard" deviance (i.e., both culturally improper and not socially smart). Sarah's behavior is clearly improper by cultural standards, while her attempted infanticide, although seemingly personally smart, is not more generally socially smart, as it is not a common or socially approved means to resolve an unwanted pregnancy.

Grandmothers who must assume full economic responsibility for unwanted children are not considered deviant. This behavior is not entirely proper in ideal terms, even though, as our table indicates, grandmothers more than grandfathers can take on the provider role. Typically, however, the father is expected to be a child's primary provider. It can be personally smart to take in a grandchild and also socially "smart" to do so, since it can be a means to acquire bridewealth or other benefits. Nevertheless, while these grandparents' behavior is not considered deviant, there is ambiguity in the status of grandparent childcare provider. It is not quite culturally normative nor always smart. This contributes to the stressful nature of the resultant role overload grandparents face. Whether deviant or stressful, this overload leads to troublesome social lives for modern Kenyan women as compared to women in the past.

Grandmothers are under special duress because of their gender. From colonial times on, women have assumed a particularly harsh cultural and economic burden (see Etienne & Leacock, 1980). Of course, Kenyan men too are experiencing difficulties in maintaining traditional family ideals in modern times; grandfathering as reported here is a case in point. Elsewhere, we have considered the institution of polygyny, where both men and women often experience difficulties in caring for their children (J. Kilbride, 1992; see also Nasimiyu, this volume; Ssennyonga, this volume). Gender role content and power are very sensitive to socioeconomic conditions. Economic factors certainly are mediated by a process of ethical delocalization; nonetheless, we argue that material conditions overrule the ideational as a causative factor in social change in this instance.

Beyond material conditions, however, there clearly is also a process of moral delocalization closely paralleling that of economic delocalization, which can be observed in Kenya. Powerful modern religious, educational, and legal institutions in Kenya, sometimes supported by international organizations, declare that polygamy is "wrong," abortion is absolutely "illegal," "unnatural" birth control is "sinful," and only women are legally responsible for "illegitimate" children. Many believe that women should be punished for premarital pregnancies. This moral climate is historically derived from outside Kenya and, arguably, serves to reinforce macroeconomic patterns associated with the world capitalist system, whose local manifestation is economic delocalization (cf. Wallerstein, 1974). Today's publicly approved morality would have seemed quite foreign to previous generations of Kenyans, as indicated in the work of Wagner (1949, 1956). Wagner writes: "When I asked some elderly pagans whether pregnancy or the birth of an illegitimate child would decrease a girl's chances to find a husband they seemed genuinely surprised at my question . . . they merely insisted that such a girl would marry soon as she would no longer care to reject suitors" (1949, p. 381). In the circumstances where a man suspects he is responsible for a pregnancy, we learn that "While courting her he will as a rule deny being responsible for her condition until after the child is born . . . he would have to pay the full amount of marriage cattle if the girl died in childbirth. He therefore wants to see if everything goes well. When the child has been born he will be quite willing to marry the girl as he had been before" (1949, p. 437). We also learn from Wagner that "even a son begotten by a man in his *esimba* ('bachelor hut') before he married his first wife and by a different girl has the full status of a firstborn son and inherits accordingly" (1949, p. 121).

Although a world systems perspective is assumed here, micro (i.e., national, regional, village) units are themselves also implicated as agents in shaping social and economic relations in economically marginal nations, populations, and regions. As Stonich (1992), for example, in the course of her research in Central America has remarked: "In their worst presentations, these paradigms proposed an all-powerful metropolitan capitalism as the explanation for underdevelopment in the periphery—in effect denying that local initiative and local response had any significant role in the making of history" (1992, p. 138). As de Wolf (this volume) shows, variations in ethnic group values and social organization are significant intervening variables in Western Kenya and throughout East Africa. Not all ethnic groups respond to economic change in the same way nor are they as adversely affected by it. Nevertheless, the general drift of delocalization described here is, in the main, evident throughout East Africa, and no ethnic group is entirely free of its negative consequences, particularly for women and children.

CONCLUSION: PRACTICAL

On the optimistic side, it is fortunate that Kenya has a rich cultural heritage, one where extended-family roles (including, as we have seen here, the grandparental one) were, and to a considerable extent still are, richly elaborated. One can only hope that all of us, both Kenyan and North American, who seek to improve the quality of life of our children and the elderly will heed the advice of the Kenyan (Bukusu) elders, who as funeral orators or "counsellors of wisdom" provide ethical commentary for the public. Wanjala writes:

> Those people who are currently engaged in issues of conduct will be surprised by what there is to learn from *Baswala Kumuse*. These elders teach respect among the youth, who are expected to respect their parents. . . . the ideal man is not the man who plays his own trumpet . . . but he is the man who looks after orphans and widows. . . . They criticize young working people who do not clothe their parents . . . the child–parent relationship is a pervasive theme. . . . *Baswala Kumuse* comment on the pervasive individualism of the present day Kenyan societies. (1985, 88–89)

There is in Kenya a problem of adolescent pregnancy and illegitimate children that challenges the extended-family ideology. This can be seen in the difficult responsibility that the grandparents have in caring for children. At the same time, the extended family on the whole continues to be, for most East Africans (including grandparents), a meaningful support group and a firm symbolic anchor for numerous ceremonial, ritual, and other culturally meaningful events and activities. We have indicated above the ideal roles associated with grandparenting, which stress love, family harmony, and other socially positive attributes. While survey data in the United States sometimes show that North American grandparents are also thought to be "generous," "a source of advice," and sources of "emotional support" (Robertson, 1976), much research suggests that such ideals are in need of widespread cultural reinvention in America. Support for extended family structures, along the lines of traditional African society, would serve to improve the quality of life for many children in America, children who now, in increasing numbers, suffer from such problems as abuse and neglect, homelessness, and adolescent suicide, to name but a few. Nevertheless, we agree with Bellah and his associates who state:

> We should not forget that the small town and the doctrinaire church, which did offer more coherent narratives, were more often narrow and oppressive. Our present radical individualism is in part a justified reaction against communities and practices that were irrationally constricting. A return to the mores of fifty or a hundred years ago, even if it were possible, would not solve, but only exacerbate, our problems. Yet in our desperate effort to free ourselves from the constrictions of the past, we have jettisoned too much, forgotten a history that we cannot abandon. (1985, p. 83)

It should by now be evident that we hold in high regard traditional Kenya patterns of childcare. In the example from Sisal (and probably in other rural areas), the lifestyle represents a mixture of Kenyan and western-derived cultural elements. It seems clear that it is not advisable (nor is it possible) to fully reinstate society as it was before the colonial era. Nor is it advisable (but it is possible) to proceed in the direction of the west, where individualism and depersonalization have produced social-relational pathologies such as child and elder abuse (see Henry, 1963, for a still applicable critique of society in the United States from a cultural perspective).

This chapter underscores a practical suggestion made earlier by Akong'a (1988) in his report on research on adolescent fertility and its policy implications in Kenya. He writes: "It is our strong submission that since the various customary laws which prohibited and inhibited adolescent sexuality and pregnancies out of wedlock can no longer be enforced as [they were] in the past, a law similar to the repealed affiliation ordinance should be reintroduced as a matter of national importance and urgency" (p. 22). Assertion of the legal responsibility of men for their children born out of wedlock, as previously legally mandated in the affiliation law (Kabeberi, 1990), is particularly needful, as "there is a tendency to blame and punish girls while nothing happens in the lives of the men responsible to make them to feel they have done something wrong" (Akong'a, 1988, p. 23).

We do not wish to imply that Kenyan women have not, overall, experienced significant gains along with some of the negative consequences of modernization we have noted here (and for the most part documented by Kenyan women themselves). Kenyan women can say best which aspects of modernity are to be seen as gains or losses when modernity is contrasted with traditional practices (Bradley, 1995; Khasiani, 1992). We would, for example, consider advances in medicine, education, and gender equality associated with worldwide modernization to be gains for all people, male and female, and North Americans and Kenyans alike.

What we suggest here is that those interested in addressing the issue of family problems in Sisal and elsewhere in Kenya pursue a strategy of intervention that seeks to incorporate or revitalize Kenyan traditional ideals. Why not borrow from a tradition where children are valued? Grandparents should be assisted financially in their crucial role of raising unwanted children. Should they not be able to raise such children properly, the costs to society will be immense. Associations of grandparents could be formed at district, location, and local levels, supported by sources, such as churches, sympathetic to family solutions to childcare. In China, for example, grandparents have been assigned important socialization duties while parents work (Korbin, 1981). Such policy has contributed to a dramatically reduced rate of child abuse there. In a Kenyan NGO workshop on "Women and Aging," July 18, 1985, in Nairobi, there was recognition that the contribution grandparents continue to make in helping to raise their (or even others') grandchildren would also serve to alleviate the loneliness and uselessness felt by an increasing number of elderly Kenyans.

REFERENCES

Akong'a, J. (1988). *Adolescent fertility and policy implications in Kenya* (Seminar Paper No. 183). Institute of African Studies, University of Nairobi, Nairobi, Kenya.

Aswani, H. (1972). Luhyia (Bunyore) oral literature. In Taban lo Liyong (Ed.), *Popular culture of East Africa* (pp. 2–23). Nairobi, Kenya: Longman.

Bellah, R., Madsen, R., Sullivan, W., Swidler, A., & Tipton, S. (1985). *Habits of the heart: Individualism and commitment in American life*. Berkeley: University of California Press.

Bengston, V. L., & Robertson, J. F. (Eds.). (1985). *Grandparenthood*. London: Sage.

Bradley, Candice. (1995). Women's empowerment and fertility decline in western Kenya. In Susan Greenhalgh (Ed.), *The anthropology of fertility: Remaking demographic analysis* (pp. 157–178). Cambridge: Cambridge University Press.

Burton, L. M., & Bengston, V. L. (1985) Black grandmothers: Issues of timing and continuity of roles. In V. L. Bengston & J. F. Robertson (Eds.), *Grandparenthood* (pp. 159–173). London: Sage.

Caldwell, J. C. (1982). *Theory of fertility decline*. New York: Academic Press.

Cattell, M. G. (1989). *Old age in rural Kenya: Gender, the life course and social change*. Unpublished doctoral thesis, Bryn Mawr College.

Cohen, D. W., & Atieno Odhiambo, E. A. (1989). *Siaya*. Athens: Ohio University Press.

Etienne, M., & Leacock, E. (1980). *Women and colonialization: Anthropological perspectives*. New York: Praeger Publishers.

Freeman, C. (1988). Colonialism and the formation of gender hierarchies in Kenya. *Critique of Anthropology, 7*(3), 33–50.

Freilich, M., Raybeck, D., & Savishinsky, J. (Eds.). (1991). *The anthropology of deviance*. New York: Bergin & Garvey.

Guttman, D. (1985). Deculturation and the American grandparent. In V. L. Bengston & J. F. Robertson (Eds.), *Grandparenthood* (pp. 173–183). London: Sage Publications.

Håkansson, T. (1988). *Bridewealth, women and land: Social change among the Gusii of Kenya* (Uppsala Studies in Cultural Anthropology, No. 10). Stockholm: Almqvist and Wiksell International.

Henry, J. (1963). *Culture against man*. New York: Random House.

Hsu, F. L. K. (1983). *Rugged individualism reconsidered*. Knoxville: University of Tennessee Press.

Kabeberi, J. (1990). The child: Custody, care and maintenance. Nairobi, Kenya: Oxford University Press.

Kayongo-Male, F., & Walji, P. (1984). *Children at work in Kenya*. Nairobi, Kenya: Oxford University Press.

Kenyatta, J. (1984). *Facing Mount Kenya.* Nairobi: Heinemann Educational Books.

Khasiani, S. A. (Ed.). (1992). *Groundwork: African women as environmental managers.* Nairobi, Kenya: ACTS Press.

Kilbride, J. (1992). *He said-, she said-, she said-, she said-, she said: A look at delocalized polygyny from an interactive ethnographic perspective.* Paper presented at the Annual Meeting of the Society for Cross-Cultural Research, February, Santa Fe, New Mexico.

Kilbride, P. L. (1980). Sensorimotor behavior of Baganda and Samia infants: A controlled comparison. *Journal of Cross-Cultural Psychology, 11*, 131–152.

Kilbride, P. L. (1986). Cultural persistence and socioeconomic change among the Abaluyia: Some modern problems in patterns of child care. *Journal of Eastern Africa Research and Development, 15*, 35–51.

Kilbride, P. L. (1991). Female violence against related children: Child abuse as a modern form of deviance in Kenya. In M. Freilich, D. Raybeck, & J. Savishinsky (Eds.), *Deviance: Anthropological perspectives* (pp. 115–133). New York: Bergin and Garvey.

Kilbride, P. L. (1992). Unwanted children as a consequence of delocalization in modern Kenya. In J. J. Poggie Jr., B. R. Dewalt, & W. W. Dressler (Eds.), *Anthropological research process and application* (pp. 185–203). Albany: State University of New York Press.

Kilbride P. L., & Kilbride, J. C. (1990). *Changing family life in East Africa: Women and children at risk.* University Park: Pennsylvania State University Press.

Kisekka, M. (1976). Sexual attitudes and behavior among students in Uganda. *Journal of Sex Research, 12*(2), 104–116.

Korbin, J. E. (1981). *Child abuse and neglect: Cross-cultural perspectives.* Berkeley: University of California Press.

Kornhaber, A. (1985). Grandparenthood and the new social contract. In V.L. Bengston & J.F. Robertson (Eds.), *Grandparenthood* (pp. 159–173). London: Sage. Publications.

Marcus, G. E., & Fisher, M. J. (1986). *Anthropology as cultural critique: An experimental moment in the human sciences.* Chicago: University of Chicago Press.

Naroll, R. (1983). *The moral order.* Beverly Hills, CA: Sage Publications.

Obler, R. S. (1985). *Women, power and economic change: The Nandi of Kenya.* Stanford, CA: Stanford University Press.

Onyango, P., & Kayongo-Male, D. (Eds.). (1983). *Child labour and health: Proceedings of the first national workshop on child Labour and health, Nairobi, Kenya, December 2–3, 1982.* Nairobi: Acme Press.

Robertson, J. F. (1976). Significance of grandparents. *Gerontologist, 16*, 137–140.

Stonich, S. C. (1992). Society and land degradation in Central America: Issues in theory, method, and practice. In J. J. Poggie Jr., B. R. Dewalt, & W. W. Dressler (Eds.), *Anthropological research process and application* (pp. 137–159). Albany: State University of New York Press.

Suda, C. A. (1990). Division of labour by gender and age—Implications for equity. In G. S. Were (Ed.), *Women and development in Kenya* (pp. 39–56). Nairobi, Kenya: Institute of African Studies, University of Nairobi.

Wagner, G. (1949). *The Bantu of North Kavirondo, Vol. 1.* London: Oxford University Press for International African Institute.

Wagner, G. (1956). *The Bantu of North Kavirondo, Vol. 2.* London: OxfordUniversity Press for International African Institute.

Wallerstein, I. M. (1974). *The modern world system.* New York: Academic Press.

Wanjala, C. (1985). Twilight years are the years of council and wisdom. In S. Wandibba (Ed.), *History and culture in western Kenya: People of Bungoma District through time* (pp. 78–91). Nairobi: G.S. Were Press.

Were, G. S. (Ed.). (1990). *Women and development in Kenya.* Nairobi: Institute of African Studies, University of Nairobi.

Worthman, C. M., & Whiting, J. (1987). Social change in adolescent sexual behavior, mate selection and premarital pregnancy rates in a Kikuyu community. *Ethos, 15*, 145–165.

Mr. Joseph Makindu and Mrs. Makindu inside their Igunga compound. Mr. Makindu was once a chief in Maragoli, an appointed office in post-colonial Kenya. When this picture was taken (late 1989) he had suffered two strokes and was in a wheelchair. He was supported and cared for by his grown children, all of whom had professional degrees. The iron sheet fence was erected by his married daughter to shelter her parents from the stares of jealous neighbors.

Two young Logoli women. It is commonplace for women in Maragoli to give birth before their marriage agreements are finalized. (c. 1990)

Logoli children at Chavakali market running errands. The girl is carrying maize on her head, and the boy and younger girl are carrying chickens. A bookstore ("Vitabu" sign) is in the background. (West Maragoli, c. 1989)

A Logoli schoolgirl sells maize and beans on the road through Igunga Sublocation. Such shops are a common source of work and income for families. (c. 1990)

Bukusu girls near Bungoma town. One girl is holding up some sugar cane she is eating. Two girls in center are wearing school uniforms. (1990–1991)

Bukusu girls on errands. Bungoma town is visible in the background. One girl is carrying a basket that probably contains maize. Another is carrying her younger sibling. A field of newly-planted maize is on the right. (1990–1991)

A family, members of an African evangelical church, Kisa Location, 1970, on their way to worship followed by dancing and singing throughout the community. This family struggled to find sufficient income for school fees, food, travel, and other needs, and the father had attempted unsuccessfully to find work in Nairobi and other cities.

Boys grazing sheep and goats and moving together in a group around their sublocation. It is common for boys and girls to travel separately in such groups after ages 5–7.

Street scene in Kariobangi Housing Estate, Nairobi, 1970. Each steel-sheet–roofed dwelling includes four rooms, a toilet and wash area, and is owned by an African Kenyan grantee (or was bought from a grantee). Most rooms are rented out to a family or several men sharing the room, and are about 12 by 14 feet each, with an average density of 4.2 persons per room.

The Child Development Research Unit opened a field office in Kariobangi Housing Estate, Nairobi in 1969–1970. It was used for fieldwork, interviewing and observations of children in the rural-urban studies reported in Weisner, Chapter 2. John Mbiya Muyesu and Charles Imbwaga Litsalia (standing left and right) were research assistants for these studies. Three men in the rural-urban network are kneeling in front.

An extended family homestead in Kisa Location, 1970. Note the steel-sheet and thatch roofs. The husband in this family homestead had intermittently worked in Nairobi and was currently without wage work.

Four boys in a cabbage field, Ngeca, Kikuyu District, Central Province. Boys are often moving around their community in such companionship groups. Ngeca was a site for settlement of Kikuyu who were moved off of European-expropriated lands. Note the densely settled village housing in the background—unlike the dispersed homestead settlements in Kisa Location and nearly every other community described in this book.

GENDER AND REPRODUCTION

11

Why Fertility Is Going Down in Maragoli

Candice Bradley

This chapter explores the causes of the decline of fertility in a Maragoli sublocation in Western Province, Kenya. Maragoli, the homeland of the Logoli, is a densely populated highland farming region with a long history of high fertility (1995a). The research on which this chapter is based took place between December 1988 and January 1991. It was a restudy of a community that was the focus of a well-known development film, "Maragoli," and the 1974–1976 fieldsite of the University of Sussex–trained Ugandan anthropologist Joseph Ssennyonga, a contributor to this volume. The current study, which follows Ssennyonga's (1978) research by thirteen years, anticipated a decline in fertility in Maragoli and sought to determine whether such a decline, if present, could be attributed to transformations in the structure of gender and intergenerational relations consistent with J. Caldwell's (1982) wealth flows theory of fertility decline. The evidence from this Maragoli sublocation lends some support to the wealth flows hypothesis, but does not rule out alternative explanations.

This chapter begins with a discussion of fertility decline in Kenya and its larger demographic context. I examine competing theories of fertility decline and their critiques. I continue with a discussion of fertility in the Maragoli sublocation of Igunga and conclude with data from Igunga Sublocation on changes in gender and intergenerational relations related to the wealth flows hypothesis.

FERTILITY DECLINE IN KENYA

Up to the early 1980s, Kenya's population growth rate was among the highest in the world. Population was expected to double in seventeen years, and the average rural woman in Kenya could expect to bear 8.4 children in her lifetime (Omurundo, 1989).

In September 1989, the Kenya government announced that fertility decline had begun in Kenya. The announcement was based on data from the 1989 Kenya Demographic and Health Survey (KDHS). These data, considered reliable by outside observers, were touted as evidence of "the first significant decline in fertility in Africa ever," which "should help demonstrate that Africa is not the 'hopeless case' that many demographers suggest it is" ("Birth Control," 1989; see also National Council for Population and Development, 1989; van de Walle & Foster, 1990; Brass & Jolly, 1993).

These data were indeed encouraging. For the second time in ten years, survey results showed evidence of declining fertility and increasing contraceptive use. The 1989 KDHS data supported earlier, less conclusive evidence of declining fertility. The total fertility rate (TFR) for Kenyan women in 1984 was 7.7 births.[1] In 1989, the TFR was 6.7 births. This downward trend was supported by evidence of increased use of modern birth control, with contraceptive use going up more than 50 percent during the five-year period between the surveys. The 1993 KDHS confirmed this trend, with the TFR declining to 5.4 births and contraceptive use increasing to 33 percent. These statistics prompted demographers to conclude that Kenya had begun the process of fertility decline (van de Walle & Foster, 1990; Brass & Jolly, 1993; Central Bureau of Statistics, 1984; National Council for Population and Development, 1989).

CLASSIC DEMOGRAPHIC TRANSITION THEORY

Classic models of fertility decline may be categorized under the rubric of demographic transition theory. Demographic transition is the process by which a nation state moves from high fertility and high mortality to low fertility and low mortality. Earlier models usually conceptualized fertility decline in three stages and were based on the 19th century European and Northern American experiences. In the first stage, both fertility and mortality were high. The second stage was believed to come about in the wake of modernization and improved medical care, which in turn reduced mortality. In the second stage, mortality declined but fertility did not. The third stage was defined by a decline in fertility, and both fertility and mortality were low (Caldwell, 1982; Notestein, 1945).

Classic models of demographic transition emphasized macro-level changes, especially modernization and changes in levels of per capita income. These models were rational, in that individual fertility behavior was thought to be an outcome of rational decision-making processes, as exemplified by Becker's (1965) New Home Economics or by theories of the economic value of children (Nag, White, & Peet, 1978). Finally, these models presupposed a one-time process that was universally applicable (Watkins, 1993).

Anthropologists have criticized classic models of demographic transition for a variety of reasons. One of the best known criticisms is that the European and North American model does not work for contemporary developing countries. For one, the process of development in peripheral nations of the modern world economy have been strikingly different from those of European nations in the throes of industrialization. In Africa, fertility decline had a notoriously slow start, and industrialization was experienced as a component of colonization and marginalization. As such, the three stage model based on the European experience may not be a good template through which fertility in Africa might be understood. The notion that there is a single, well-defined model of fertility decline has therefore been all but abandoned (Caldwell, 1982; Handwerker, 1986; Shannon, 1989; van de Walle & Foster, 1990; Wallerstein, 1974).

COMPETING MODELS OF FERTILITY DECLINE

Caldwell's (1982) wealth flows theory of fertility decline was developed in response to the failure of classical models to account for the persistence of high fertility, despite modernization and improvement in health care, in such places as Africa. Unlike classical demographic transition theories, Caldwell proposes that there are two stages to fertility transition: one in which individuals do not gain economically from restricting fertility, and a second in which it is preferable to restrict fertility. He calls societies in the first stage "pre-transitional" and those in the second "post-transitional."

Wealth flows are "labor and services, goods and money, and present and future guarantees" (Caldwell, 1982, p. 459). High fertility would be found where wealth flows upward from younger to older members of the society. These relationships are usually kin-based. Market economies and mass education reverse the traditional upward flow of wealth and emphasize non-kin-based relationships. Concurrent with these effects are changes in the moral structure of the family (Caldwell, 1980).

In each phase, individual behavior is economically rational. Caldwell's wealth flows theory asserts that societies with low levels of fertility differ from those with high levels in the "net value of intergenerational wealth flows" (Caldwell, 1983, p. 459). In pre-transitional societies, high fertility is economically rational because it is consistent with socially defined economic goals. In these societies there is "no net economic gain accruing to the family (or to those dominant within it) from lower fertility levels" (Caldwell, 1982, p. 157).

Wealth flows theory incorporates elements of cost/benefit models of fertility, including perspectives that argue that children have economic value. These models presuppose that people are rational actors who weigh the costs and benefits of adding an additional child to the household. The benefits of children are, among other things, the work they do, the value of remittances sent home, the pleasure of having children, and the protection large families may provide against enemies. The costs of children are such factors as food, clothing, education, time, stress, and opportunity costs. There may be a net gain to having large families in societies where children do a lot of work (Nag, White, & Peet, 1978; Turchi & Bryant, 1979).

Like classic models of fertility decline, wealth flows theory assumes rationality. However, it also takes into account various noneconomic factors that may contribute to fertility decision making. For example, Ssennyonga (1975) and Ocholla-

Ayayo (n.d.) have argued that there are spheres of African culture that are not necessarily rational in the economic sense. One such sphere may be the value of children in traditional religious systems. There is pressure among some Kenyan ethnic groups, including the Luyia, to have enough children that they may be named after older relatives or relatives who have died. Both Ssennyonga and Ocholla-Ayayo ask whether these beliefs about immortality may be weighed on a cost–benefit continuum. Economists such as Easterlin (1975) might view such values within a rationality model as tastes for children. Wealth flows theory includes the obvious monetary values of children, as well as noncommodified wealth that contributes to power differences by age and sex. Caldwell and Caldwell (1990) later argue that veneration of ancestors is an important factor in understanding high fertility in Africa.

Caldwell (1982) lists three advantages of children that help explain stable high fertility in peasant communities:

1. Families gain economically by having many children. They may also gain political clout and status.
2. Children may be regarded as future investments for potential old age support. However, they can also protect the family's investments. For example, large families may be no worse off than small families, but their sheer size may prevent relatives outside the community from soliciting assistance. Large families are also beneficial where land rights are based on usufruct; the more farmers, the more land and wealth.
3. Some family members may be more privileged by age and gender with regard to work, consumption, and decision making power. Caldwell calls this "situational advantage." Situational advantage includes gender and age roles, power in decision making situations such as consumption, production, budget, and reproduction, and changes in these factors that may bring about changes in fertility.

Like classic models of fertility decline, wealth flows theory is modernization theory at its core. Modernization theorists conceptualize the world as having two types of nation-states: the modern and the modernizing. Countries that are not modern are thought to be moving inevitably toward modernization as long as they adopt new technology and abandon traditions that keep them from full participation in a capitalist market economy (Bradley, 1996).

Caldwell's (1982) description of pre- and post-transitional societies is comparable to modernization theorists' conceptualization of societies. Pre-transitional societies are traditional; they are based on kin relations and transmit power along traditional gerontocratic lines. Caldwell also argues that pre-transitional societies are characterized by a traditional family morality that dictates that children work hard, demand little, and respect the old. Wealth flows upward, and high fertility is beneficial.

For Caldwell, the introduction of universal national education is the prime mover behind fertility transition. A traditional family morality cannot survive the changes brought about by national education programs that promote individualistic and nationalistic values and have agendas that differ from those of the parents. For example, schoolbooks showing pictures of nuclear African families eating at kitchen tables, with appliances and radios in the background, inculcate children with new values and goals. Education also decreases the child's potential as a worker, both within and outside the home, making the child a future rather than a present producer. Thus, education increases the cost of children and makes them dependent on the household for support (Caldwell, 1980).

Thus, as in modernization theory, the change to a post-transitional society is considered inevitable and involves the introduction of values common to capitalist societies, such as individualism, rejection of tradition, and identification with the nation-state. Pre-transitional societies are not modern; post-transitional societies are modern.[2]

Caldwell's assertions about the effects of education on fertility decline have been challenged by Handwerker (1986). Handwerker argues that education does not always lead to a change in values in the expected direction. In fact, some systems, such as Ireland, indoctrinate for high fertility. Handwerker argues that fertility decline comes about through changes in material constraints, in particular from "changes in opportunity structure that increasingly reward educationally acquired skills and perspectives" (1986, p. 402). The core proposition of Handwerker's resource access theory is that women begin to reduce fertility when they have other opportunities besides childbearing for the attainment of adult status, prestige, and wealth. These opportunities are more readily available to educated women. Handwerker's data from Antigua and Barbados show that educational attainment works through women's empowerment to decrease fertility (Handwerker, 1989, 1991, 1993).

Handwerker argues that resource access theory is not about modernity. However, it is very difficult to isolate the empowerment of women from other factors, such as wealth or modernity. For example, women's empowerment may result from larger political and economic changes. These changes, in turn, may come about in the wake of incorporation into the capitalist world economy, the proliferation of information about contraception and other ways of living, improvements in maternal and child health that lighten anxiety about child survival, and the destruction of traditional values that kept women in their place (Nasimiyu, this volume; Bradley, 1995a; Watkins,1993; Hammerslough, 1990, 1991; LeVine, LeVine, Richman, Tapia Uribe, Sunderland Correa, & Miller, 1991).

LeVine et al. (1991) tested a series of hypotheses about the relationship between fertility and education in two towns in central Mexico. On the basis of their findings they argue that there may be multiple mechanisms through which education results in lower fertility. These may be both psychosocial and status related. Women with more schooling have greater aspirations for both themselves and their children, more exposure to the media, and more egalitarian families with fewer expectations of returns from children. These women spoke to their children and utilized child health and prenatal services. LeVine et al. argue that their findings support Caldwell's (1979, 1982) wealth flows theory and are "consistent with the notion that schooling influences individual attitudes in the direction of modernity and individualism as embodied in Western ideologies" (LeVine et al., p. 485).

In this model, the effects of modernization, changes in wealth flows, and empowerment of women are not disaggregated:

> Our exploratory studies of the processes intervening between maternal schooling and demographic outcomes indicate that increased practice of contraception and use of health services were facilitated and complemented by a wide range of psychosocial changes—in mothers' ideational makeup and infant care practices, in their literacy and language skills, and in their exposure to the mass media. The evidence can be interpreted as providing support for theories of status enhancement, modernization, and changing intergenerational economic relationships—theories that variously conceptualize schooling as altering the motives, values, and ideologies of those who attend. (LeVine et al., p. 491–492)

The confounding of wealth flows theory with modernization theory and the economic value of children perspective makes it difficult to compare the efficacies of these theoretical perspectives in a village study. Reversals in intergenerational relationships may be interpreted entirely as effects of modernization. For example, pictures of nuclear families in schoolbooks, the proliferation of radios, newspapers, and paperback books, and extensive contact with Nairobi and other big cities through wage-labor migration all bring modern ideas home to Igunga sublocation (see Watkins, 1993). These modern ideas might include the notion of small family size, individualistic values that result in rejection of gerontocratic authority, and a desire to use contraceptives. At the same time, reversals in wealth flows imply that the costs of children have gone up.

The data from Maragoli presented in this chapter include village level ethnographic evidence about changes in wealth flows as well as a statistical test of various factors predicting contraceptive use. Both suggest that women's empowerment and education are linked to declining fertility, but do not lend support to models that give primacy to modernization, wealth, and education in the absence of various forms of empowerment. Before turning to these discussions, however, I begin with a description of the focal community.

Igunga Sublocation, the focus of the research discussed here, is in the Maragoli region of Western Province. Maragoli is the homeland of the Logoli people, one of seventeen subnations of the Kenyan Abaluyia. The name Maragoli, derived from the clan ancestor, Mulogoli, is incorporated into the names of several administrative locations in this part of Kenya. Igunga sublocation is in West Maragoli Location, Sabatia Division, in Western Province's Vihiga District. About one million Lulogoli speakers live in Kenya, most of them in Vihiga District. In 1989, nearly four thousand people lived in Igunga Sublocation.

Maragoli is a highland farming area located halfway between Kakamega town and Kisumu. Like other Luyia groups, the Logoli are patrilineal, patrilocal horticulturalists. The important subsistence crops are maize, beans, bananas, cassava, sorghum, and sweet potatoes. Most plots are intercropped, with maize and beans grown together almost universally. Plows and tractors are rare because farm plots are generally too small to turn a plow around on. The average plot size in Igunga is .73 ha. Although people often use such inputs as hybrid seeds and pesticides, there is virtually no irrigation except for a few vegetable plots near rivers. Women provide most of the farm labor, but men may assist with tasks at any phase in the agricultural cycle. Women come together in formal and informal work groups for time intensive tasks such as planting potatoes. Schoolchildren also work in the fields. Small plot size and lack of grazing land make large herds of cattle impractical, and the average Igunga household owns less than one cow. Marriages often involve payment of bridewealth in cattle as well as in shillings. Because of clan exogamy, brides often come from neighboring sublocations or ethnic groups. Between 6 percent and 12 percent of Logoli women, and 12 percent of Igunga women, are polygynously married (Wagner, 1949; Moock, 1976; Ssennyonga, 1978).

Even before the 1930s, when Wagner (1949) did his research, western Kenya had already been seriously impacted by colonialism (Karp, 1978; Kilbride & Kilbride, this volume; Leo, 1984; Nasimiyu, this volume; Wagner, 1949, p. 32–35; White, 1990). Major changes took place around the turn of the century, when *pax Britannica* ended most of the tribal warfare in the region, hut taxes were first levied to stimulate wage labor participation, and the Uganda Railway reached nearby Kisumu. In 1906, the Friends African Mission was established at the Maragoli town of Vihiga, the Luyia Bible was written in Lulogoli, and the Logoli people were among the first of the Luluyia-speaking peoples to recognize, with great enthusiasm, the commercial value of education.

The Luyia were involved in wage labor migration from the turn of the century, both to compensate for shrinking farm size and to get cash for taxes. Wagner (1949) notes that during the 1930s, both Luyia adults and children were employed by Europeans in such activities as picking tea on plantations in the highlands of Kericho. For the Logoli, involvement in wage labor migration came earlier than it did for many other Luyia groups, encouraged by high population density and Maragoli's proximity to the growing port city of Kisumu. Gold was discovered in Maragoli in the 1930s, followed by land confiscation (Wagner, 1949, pp. 10, 32–35). As Nasimiyu (this volume) points out, land shortage was a problem throughout the region because of the creation of African reserves, increased cash cropping, and the effects of various land policies. All of these changes put greater strain on already overworked plots and forced people to look for outside employment.

Maragoli, like much of western Kenya, continues to be a labor-supplying region. It has been described as a rural neighborhood by various researchers because of the combination of small plot size with houses close to one another and because it supplies labor to Kenya's urban areas. Igunga is a sort of bedroom community, with little industrial infrastructure nearby that might provide jobs. The factories and industrial agriculture of Bungoma District are absent here. Small-scale trading, civil service, and day labor are the usual sources of outside income in Maragoli. People continue to look to the outside for employment, part of the process Kilbride and Kilbride (this volume) call delocalization.

During the 1950s, over 70 percent of adult males in the nearby Vihiga area were absent. Ssennyonga found that 47 percent of the Igunga households he surveyed were female headed (Ssennyonga, 1978; Moock, 1976). In 1989, 56 percent of the households here were headed by women. In half these households, the husbands work and have their primary residence elsewhere in Kenya.

Since Kenya's independence in 1963, Western Province suffered from marginalization while other areas of the country were developed. Political favoritism in the early postcolonial days left much of Western Province short on paved roads, electricity, and clean piped water. The long term effects of this legacy of underdevelopment are evident today. Although improvements have been promised to Igunga and Viyalo sublocations for over a decade, there are still no paved roads or electricity, and only a few of the wealthiest homes have telephones (Leo, 1984; Lavrijsen, 1984).

Nasimiyu (this volume) argues that land policies instituted during the colonial era increased social stratification among Abaluyia. In Igunga, differences in economic status are evident in roof materials (thatched, iron sheet, and tile), plot size, the numbers and types of cattle people own (zebu, grade, or mixed), and the proximity of homes to the *murram* road running through the middle of the sublocation. Ssennyonga (1977) referred to the wealthier group as the roadside elite, while the poorer people (those living downhill) were forced, often through unfortunate circumstances, to sell roadside plots and to buy or move onto marginal lands near the river. This is similar to the process Nasimiyu describes for the Bukusu.

Historically, the Luyia have had very high fertility. Population density is much greater in the southern part of the Luyia region, where the Logoli, Kisa, Bunyore, and Tiriki live, and less dense in the north among the Bukusu. Wagner, the earliest European ethnographer in Western Province, commented on what he saw during his fieldwork in the 1930s:

> As we approach the southwestern corner of the district the density of population steadily increases. In the chieftaincy of Bunyore it reaches the remarkable figure of 1,137 persons to the square mile. In these parts the native homesteads stand close together; every inch of arable soil is exploited to the utmost, and pasture land is so scarce that not only sheep but also cattle are tethered while grazing or even stable-fed. But even the extraordinary fertility of the soil and the two full crops which it yields every year cannot sustain such a dense population. Clear symptoms of overpopulation begin to show. (1949, p. 15)

Population density for Sabatia Division, where Igunga sublocation is located, is currently estimated at over eleven hundred persons per square kilometer (Ministry of Planning and National Development, 1989).

FIELDSITE AND METHODS

Maragoli's population problem was brought to international attention during the mid-1970s with the release of an acclaimed development film called "Maragoli" (Nichols, 1978). This film was based on Ssennyonga's 1974–1976 fieldwork in what is now Igunga Sublocation. Igunga, then the eastern portion of Viyalo Sublocation, was one of eight fieldsites in a comparative project undertaken by the

University of Sussex, where Ssennyonga was a graduate student (Epstein & Jackson, 1975, 1977). The film dramatized Ssennyonga's and Nichols's shared perspective on the relationship between population and poverty (Nichols, 1990).

Ssennyonga conducted a census of 1,544 people in Viyalo and surveyed 398 women between the ages of fifteen and forty-nine. He also had a focused sample of twelve households, where he collected a range of socioeconomic and fertility data in addition to conducting intensive interviews. The people in many of these households are featured in the "Maragoli" film. Twelve years later, Ssennyonga introduced me in eleven of the households, and these became the core of my own focused sample of twenty-five households.[3] My census of 3,487 people covered all of Igunga Sublocation, an area about twice as large as Ssennyonga's census area. Between 1989 and 1991, a University of Nairobi graduate student and I surveyed 303 women between the ages of fifteen and forty-nine (see Ndege, 1993; Bradley and Ndege forthcoming). The results reported in this chapter include both quantitative and qualitative findings of Ssennyonga's and my work, along with Ndege's, and represent a longitudinal study of a single sublocation in the throes of fertility decline.

This study uses a multimethod approach, which is essential to anthropological demography. Many kinds of data must be collected, including the census and survey data discussed above. These larger scale surveys provide information on fertility, mortality, contraceptive use, education, and socioeconomic status. These data confirm fertility decline in Igunga Sublocation and are used to test hypotheses about the relationship between contraceptive use and other factors that may help us to understand fertility decline.

However, anthropological demographers argue that the kinds of ethnographic data needed to describe changes in intergenerational relations must come from small, focused samples in which the dynamics of relationships between and within households may be understood (Caldwell, 1982; Caldwell, Reddy, & Caldwell, 1988; Greenhalgh, 1990; Hammerslough, 1990, 1991; van de Walle and Foster, 1990). In this study, ethnographic data come from the twenty-five households in the focused study. Data collected in the focused study's households include a time allocation study using randomized spot observations across an entire agricultural season, weekly household budgets, weekly health and medical questionnaires, focused interviews on such topics as bridewealth payments or contraceptive decision making, farm yield data, school and church attendance records, anthropometric assessments of child health, and direct observation of children's eating habits.

FERTILITY DECLINE IN IGUNGA

In 1976, an average of 8.6 children were born to a married woman during her lifetime, and fewer than 1 percent of married women used any form of contraception (Table 11.1) (Ssennyonga, 1978). This was in spite of the fact that there was a family planning clinic within the sublocation. Ssennyonga (1977) argued that the roadside elite had little reason to plan their families, while the downhill people used large families as a survival strategy. A small, growing faction of elite Igunga young people had begun using family planning methods in the 1970s. By 1986, when the sublocation was visited by a *Science86* reporter named John Tierney, contraceptive use seemed to be on the increase. Tierney called the resulting article "Fanisi's Choice" to dramatize the decision of one particular woman to use a modern contraceptive. Fanisi had been pregnant with twins during the filming of "Maragoli."

Table 11.1
Fertility Related Population Statistics, Igunga Sublocation

	Ssennyonga 1977 ($N = 398$)	Bradley 1989 ($N = 303$)
Dependency Ratio	134.0	118.3*
Crude birth rate (per 1000)	49.4	44.5
Crude death rate (per 1000)	14.3	12.2
Total fertility rate	8.6	7.1[a]
Percent contracepting	1.0	31.0[a]

[a] January,1991, data
* $p<.05$.

By the end of 1989, Fanisi's decision had become the choice of 31 percent of the 303 women Ndege and I surveyed. The total fertility rate (TFR) in Igunga, like that at the national level, had dropped, and in 1990 was as low as 7.1. Other statistics from Igunga support the conclusion that fertility is declining (Table 11.1).

Table 11.2 shows the methods of choice and mean years of formal schooling for the ninety-six contraceptors in the survey. Injections of Depo Provera are popular because they are taken every three months, do not interrupt the sex act, and free the woman from having to remember daily pills. Some women like injections because they may be taken without the knowledge of a husband or mother-in-law. Note that the five condom users in the sample have the highest mean education.

By 1989, the family planning clinic within the sublocation had shut down, but Igunga had a resident community health worker. She was an energetic thirty-year-old woman whose briefcase overflowed with condoms, packages of pills, and oral rehydration salts. She knew every woman in both Igunga and Viyalo sublocations and closely monitored their contraceptive decisions. This woman would personally escort her clients to clinics for injections. If a woman told her on a Sunday that she wanted a tubal ligation, the community health worker would escort her to a clinic in Vihiga (five kilometers away) to have the operation performed that very day, lest the woman change her mind. She strongly urged women, as well as sexually active unmarried girls, to take precautions, but she did not coerce them. Christian values made provision of contraceptives to unmarried women unpopular in Igunga and throughout much of Kenya. Girls would therefore visit her quietly, and she would keep their secret.

Table 11.2
Family Planning Methods of Choice and Mean Years of Formal Schooling for 96 Contraceptors, Igunga, 1989–1990

Method	Number	Percent	Years of Schooling
Injection	24	7.9	6.46
Pill	18	5.9	7.35
Rhythm	13	4.3	6.15
Traditional	13	4.3	5.54
I.U.D.	11	3.6	8.55
Tubal ligation/Vasectomy	10	3.3	7.30
Condoms	5	1.7	8.60
Abstinence	1	0.3	7.00
Other (foam, tablets, etc.)	1	0.3	7.00
All methods	96	31.6	7.06

Note: Mean education for the 207 nonusers is 6.10 year.

In August 1989, when an NBC news crew visited Igunga in search of a story about population and impending ecological disaster in Africa, we were unable to find a single person who would give them the story they wanted about people resisting family planning (Bradley, 1991).

Taken together, these data for Igunga Sublocation show that fertility is declining and contraceptive use is increasing. These conclusions are consistent with national level data (Brass & Jolly, 1993).

CHANGES IN INTERGENERATIONAL AND GENDER RELATIONS IN IGUNGA

The central goal of this study was to determine whether a decline in fertility in Igunga could be attributed to transformations in the structure of gender and intergenerational relations consistent with Caldwell's (1982) wealth flows theory. In conjunction with wealth flows theory, alternative hypotheses are also considered. These are modernization theory, the economic value of children model, and Handwerker's resource access theory.

Much of the literature on Maragoli is about change. Change was the stated focus of Wagner's volumes (1949, 1956). Wagner was interested in identifying changes associated with colonialism and contact. By the time Ssennyonga and I were in Maragoli, many of the changes Wagner had documented were already a century old. The changes I discuss in this section of the paper probably occurred within the past ten to twenty-five years, since independence, and in a climate of shifting economic opportunity.

Situational advantage is a key element of wealth flows theory (Caldwell, 1982). It means that some family members—usually older men—control more resources, have more privileges, and wield more power than other family members.

Wagner (1949, pp. 52–53) outlined several of these kinds of inequalities for Maragoli during the 1930s: (1) preference for male offspring over female, (2) the authority of the father over grown and married sons and daughters, (3) the authority of the eldest son over the youngest, (4) inequalities between husband and wife, (5) the inferior legal status of the wife relative to the husband, and (6) patrilineal inheritance of land and cattle by sons only. I will examine some changes in these situational advantages as well as others. I will begin by discussing universal education, the key element in Caldwell's argument.

The advent of a national education program is the engine behind fertility decline in Caldwell's (1979, 1982) conception of wealth flows theory. It is also the focus of its major anthropological challenger, resource access theory (Handwerker, 1986). According to these theories, universal education means free (or almost free) compulsory, enforced education for both males and females. This excludes systems in which education is compulsory but not enforced for one or both sexes (Caldwell, 1980).

In 1978, economic differences between Igunga households affected who went to school (Ssennyonga, 1978). The cost of schooling, which was compulsory then as it is now, included shoes, uniforms, books, and materials, as well as fees and *harambee* (fundraising) donations. Although education was considered free in Kenya (teachers are paid by the national government), even the most reasonable fees and donations were prohibitive for poorer households. Ssennyonga (1978) often came upon secondary school girls from poor Igunga households hoeing or collecting water during school hours. Then, as now, it was common for Maragoli parents to turn to relatives for school fees or to rely on sibling occupational–educational chains, in which older siblings who have been educated and hold jobs send younger siblings to school (Weisner, this volume). Such kin networks lessen education's impact on large or poor households (Caldwell, 1980, 1982; Nag, White, & Peet, 1978). While I was in Kenya, the national government put a ceiling on the amount that could be charged for school fees; however, local leaders in Igunga continued to ask for so called *harambee* donations, often using coercive tactics.

Western Province now has one of the highest school attendance rates in Kenya. Fifty percent of primary school children are girls (Ministry of Planning and National Development, 1989). This is not necessarily the case for other regions of the country (e.g., Coast Province [Eshiwani, 1990]). Gender equity at the secondary school level in Kenya is less encouraging. In 1987, national level statistics show a ratio of 107 boys attending primary school for every 100 girls. At the secondary school level, this ratio dropped, with 144 boys attending for every 100 girls. However, universal education at both the primary and the secondary school levels seems to have been achieved in Igunga.

During 1989, with the exception of one household, all school-age children in my focused household sample of twenty-five attended school. Data collected on outstanding school fee debts for nursery, primary, and secondary school for these twenty-five households show no difference between fees paid for boys and those for girls. Data obtained from the local primary school on absenteeism show that boys were absent slightly more often than girls. People told me this was because both boys and girls are sent to school, but boys play hooky. Similarly, both boys and girls were kept home from school equally when fees were lacking. I rarely encountered school-age girls working during school hours. This contrasts with Ssennyonga's earlier finding that girls were at a disadvantage relative to boys when it came to education.

I asked thirty-four men and women in my household sample to rank nineteen common Igunga activities according to their relative importance. I selected the nineteen tasks from time allocation records collected in the focused sample, choosing the most common tasks that had been recorded in biweekly spot observations over a six-month period. I tested their rankings of the activities by administering a Lulogoli language triads test, using a balanced incomplete block design (BIB) (Weller & Romney, 1988; Kirk & Burton, 1977).

Table 11.3
Ranking of 19 Common Activities by 34 Igunga Residents

Rank	Activity	Logoli Term	Mean Score
1	fetching water	*okuleta amazi*	12.74
2	attending church	*okusia muganisa*	13.79
3	attending school	*okutsia muskulu*	13.85
4	cooking	*okudeka*	15.17
5	childcare	*okulela umwana*	16.17
6	going to shops	*okusia m'maduka*	16.53
7	eating	*okula*	16.62
8	resting while sick	*okusosa novee mulwaye*	16.70
9	grinding maize	*okusia*	17.18
10	preparing soil	*okulima*	17.35
11	planting	*okutaga*	17.44
12	harvesting	*okugesa*	18.82
13	attending funeral	*okusia m'maliga*	19.15
14	weeding	*okusembela*	19.35
15	fetching firewood	*okutenya*	19.56
16	grazing cattle	*okwaya zing'ombe*	20.71
17	marketing (selling)	*okuguliza*	22.00
18	visiting	*okugenika*	23.50
19	resting	*okusosa*	25.15

Table 11.3 shows the rankings and mean scores of the nineteen activities for all thirty-four individuals. Education is ranked third. The seventeen women in the sample, when scored separately, ranked fetching water and attending school equally as the most important activities. Water is carried in buckets or pots from boreholes at the bottom of ravines or from outdoor taps on the compounds of better-off homes. This is an adolescent or adult woman's activity, as well as a common child's chore; respondents stated that no other activity could be undertaken

until water was brought. But one twenty-five-year-old man stated, "[I]t's better to go to school first before doing anything because education is the most important key to life."[4]

Several arguments could be made about the relationship between the high valuation of education and theories of fertility decline. For one, education is a modern activity, as are attending church and going to shops to buy food. These are valued over more traditional activities, such as attending funerals, grazing cattle, marketing, and agriculture. Igunga is clearly modernizing; however, it is also moving from pre- to post-transitional status. The economic value of children model is also supported and is inseparable from the other two models.

Using as an outline Wagner's (1949) list of inequalities he observed in Maragoli during the 1930s, I now discuss other changes in situational advantage that may indicate wealth flows reversals in Igunga.

Preference for Male Offspring over Female

As the educational data indicate, preferences for male over female children in Igunga are no longer as common as they once were. Furthermore, the Igunga survey data show that, if they could select the sex of their next child, an equal number of women would desire female children as would want male children. Using child tracking methods, I found that girls and boys also eat the same amount of food, despite beliefs among the people of Igunga that boys get more to eat than girls (Bradley, 1989). At one time, boys, rather than girls, were allowed to eat eggs and the preferred parts of the chicken, for example. When we tracked Igunga boys and girls in the focused sample, we found children of both sexes eating fruit while perched in trees, licking bowls, and sneaking food, despite a belief in the sublocation that boys licked more bowls and stole more food. I posted some of my field assistants at local shops for several days in 1989 to record the numbers of boys and girls coming in to buy snacks for their own consumption. Although the boys snacked from one shop and the girls from another, they bought equal quantities of junk food (e.g., candy, gum, and *mandazis* [a sweet, fried dough]) and somehow had the change to pay for it. Children running errands for their mothers to the shops took advantage of the opportunity to buy themselves snacks.

The Authority of the Father over Grown and Married Sons and Daughters

The authority of elders, both male and female, has declined. I discuss four aspects of this decline in authority: the decline in bridewealth, declining respect for mothers-in-law, increasing neglect of the aged, and remittances.

Bridewealth has declined in Igunga over a thirty-year period (Bradley, 1995a). This decline has been even more severe for those married within the last two decades. Where there are bridewealth agreements, there has been a decline over a thirty-year period from an average of seven cows promised to an average of six. However, the number of women with bridewealth agreements has also declined. Every woman married between twenty and thirty years ago had a bridewealth agreement, whereas fewer of the younger men have actually sat down with their wives' fathers to make an agreement. The decline in the proportion of marriages with bridewealth agreements begins with couples married in 1969 and continues to marriages from the early 1980s, when it drops sharply. Thus, the decline in bridewealth is really more severe than one would think when looking only at those who had agreements. Numbers of shillings promised is positively correlated with numbers of cows promised, confirming a concomitant decline in the shilling portions of bridewealth agreements. Håkansson and LeVine (this volume) and Håkansson (1988) report a similar decline in bridewealth for the Gusii. I suspect that bridewealth is declining in other Kenyan ethnic groups, challenging Frank and McNicoll's (1987) statement that bridewealth agreements in Kenya have remained fairly stable over time.

In the past, the fluidity of marriage in Maragoli meant that people often moved in together before they actually sat down with male elders to make agreements. Wagner (1949, 1956) argued that even couples who eloped paid some bridewealth. However, the length of time between marriage and agreements has extended, as has the length of time between marriage and the transmission of bridewealth cattle. The authority male elders once had over marriages has accordingly declined, and with it the control over bridewealth cows that they could use to marry off a son or take a second wife. The decline in bridewealth is most severe for households in the lowest economic strata in Igunga.

There is additional evidence of declining respect for elders. One of the most dramatic betrayals is the growing frequency of neglect of older people (see Kilbride & Kilbride, this volume; Cattell, this volume; Håkansson & LeVine, this volume). At one time, children were afraid to neglect their aging parents for fear of being cursed, but Igunga young people now view curses as "superstition." In Igunga, there is increasing evidence of married people neglecting their aging parents, even to the point of death. This is the perception of sublocation leaders who lecture the throngs at funerals (see Kilbride & Kilbride, this volume). Abuse and neglect of old people is counter to the identities and traditional values of western Kenyan agricultural communities and is met with great alarm both in the community and in Nairobi. Evidence of growing awareness of the problem is the frequency of its discussion in the Kenya national press.

Another example of declining power of older people is the mother-in-law/daughter-in-law relationship. Igunga is in many ways a matrifocal community, and a typical household may include a mother-in-law and one or more daughters-in-law as well as grandchildren. Traditionally, a young wife ate in her mother-in-law's house until a ceremony took place in which cooking stones were set up in her own house. Women may eat with their mothers-in-law for years, nowadays also cooking for them. It is more and more common for a daughter-in-law to set up the stones for her own cooking area, whereupon the in-laws lose authority over the younger woman and her labor and their control over the food from her farm, which would go into a bigger pot.

A finding that is less clear in terms of wealth flows theory is that of remittances. One of the important arguments in the value of children literature is that parents benefit from large families once the children are working and can send money and gifts home (e.g., Caldwell, 1982). Ssennyonga noted that several Igunga families benefited from educated children in this way.

In 1989, remittances were recorded for all twenty-five households and ranged from an average of K.Sh. 21 per week (about $1.00) to an average of K.Sh. 510 per week (about $24.00). Children who were successful and who had good jobs were able to send more money home. Thus, the four richest households have children who have attended college and are now doctors, businessmen, and teachers. The people downhill could not afford college and have children who work as maids and security guards. With the exception of a widow with several devoted daughters, the highest remittances came to the richest households. The large family strategy paid off in the long run only for the roadside elite.

Inequalities between Husband and Wife and the Inferior Status of Wife Relative to Husband

There is evidence from Igunga that some wives have achieved considerable autonomy relative to their husbands. Ndege (1993) reports that educated Igunga women are more likely than less educated women to communicate with their husbands about important matters such as contraception. Bradley (1995a) found that Igunga women have achieved considerable gains, but there has been an increase in domestic violence in Igunga, which may result from increased tension between the genders. For example, Igunga women now have a formal village-level leadership structure which was not present during the 1970s. Some Igunga women own their own land and their own cattle (see Nasimiyu, this volume). It is very common for Igunga women over thirty to engage in trade in their own right. Women also belong to cooperatives, where they sometimes save money and get loans. Some Igunga women hire their own laborers and rent additional land where they grow their own cash crops. All of these changes are positive, but are balanced on the negative end by the fact that more than 60 percent of Igunga women report having been beaten by their husbands. The frequency of domestic violence in Kenya, present historically at high rates in many ethnic groups (LeVine, 1959; LeVine & LeVine, 1981; Kilbride & Kilbride, 1990), is a problem often discussed in the national press. Wamalwa (1989, p. 71) argues that spouse abuse in Kenya is on the increase, attributing it to the breakdown of the social system, which is no longer able to control the behavior of men.

In addition to these declines in situational advantage, the high cost of living in Igunga, as throughout Kenya, contributes to higher costs of children (see Brass & Jolly, 1993). Education is one way children become more expensive and less of a short-term benefit. Even if they grow up to send money home, the cost of living in Igunga is high. The monetary needs of Igunga households are similar to those of urban areas. For example, the maize harvest of late 1989 yielded so little in eight of the twenty-five households that people were again buying maize one week after the harvest. The harvests are small because there is insufficient land. During the same farming cycle, the bean harvest was poor or failed completely because of excessive rains.

In a good season or a bad one, people buy food. In addition to maize meal, the staple, they buy milk, tea, sugar, vegetables, meat, and fish, as well as soap, matches, paraffin for lanterns, medicines, and cooking fat. They pay for medical care from private doctors, traditional doctors, and mission hospitals because public hospitals often have no medicines. They pay for transport to and from doctors, and they pay their children's educational costs. And then there are costs above and beyond the costs of everyday living, such as the tin of maize levied by churches, the arbitration fees charged by village leaders, costs of funerals and birth celebrations, local fundraising charges, and fines of shillings and chickens for minor infractions. It is expensive to live in Igunga and to raise children there.

EDUCATION, MODERNITY, AND EMPOWERMENT

Wealth flows theory incorporates the assumptions of modernization theory and the economic value of children perspective, arguing that education teaches western values, raising the costs of children and resulting in reversals in the flow of wealth and power between the genders and generations. Handwerker's resource access theory challenges a basic assumption of wealth flows theory, arguing that education by itself does not lead to fertility decline, but rather that education must be combined with women's empowerment to have any affect on fertility. LeVine et al. (1991) demonstrate one way in which women's empowerment leads to fertility decline, with modernization and westernization as supporting explanations.

To test the relationship between education, power, modernity, and contraceptive use, I created variables that indicate modernity, wealth, and three kinds of empowerment. For this analysis, I use the Igunga survey of 303 married women ages fifteen to forty-nine.

Empowerment

Empowering activities are defined as those activities in which a woman acts in her own right (agency). A woman who is empowered may control or influence social, political, and economic decision making, both within and beyond the household (Bradley, 1995a). I used eight dichotomous empowerment variables, clumped into three groups. Activities are grouped by how women have accessed these activities historically, as well as from the results of a factor analysis.[5]

The first group of variables are contemporary, or modern, forms of empowerment. These are whether a woman hires her own laborers, whether she banks in her own name, whether she belongs to a formal cooperative in her own right, and whether she has credit in her own name. These are activities women have only recently been able to access and are essential to women who wish to own land (Nasimiyu, this volume). Although women participated in informal or work cooperative activities in the past, formal cooperative membership was closed to women during the colonial era. Women's access to credit and agricultural training were limited even recently (Staudt, 1976, 1979). These activities are all related;

women who belong to the cooperative are able to bank and get credit, for example. These four variables form a single indicator.

The second indicator is traditionally masculine forms of power and includes two variables. These are whether the woman rents land in her own right and whether she owns her own cattle. As Nasimiyu (this volume) argues, it was especially difficult for women to gain access to land or cattle both precolonially and during the colonial era. In patrilineal African systems, women have usufruct rights in land and cattle but cannot alienate them. In contemporary Kenya, women may own and inherit land and cattle.

Two additional variables form the third indicator: trading and making crafts for sale. Women who trade may also sell their own crafts, such as pots or products made of banana fibers. These are activities women did precolonially and that they engage in now. These are traditional forms of power.

Wealth

Good indicators of wealth in Igunga are the number of cows owned by a household, the size of the plot, and the distance from the road, since roadside land is more expensive. Houses on the road could eventually have access to electricity and telephones, although no electricity is available in Igunga and telephones are rare. These variables load on the same factor in a factor analysis and are combined into a single indicator.

Modernity

Roof materials, wall materials, and whether a vehicle may be driven onto the compound, are fair indicators of modernity in Igunga. Iron sheet roofs are on the primary houses of 49 percent of the sample. I have been told that a village elder may not become a chief or assistant chief unless he has an iron sheet roof. Walls are usually mud (96%), but some houses have semipermanent walls, which are inexpensive compared to brick or block walls. The few houses in Igunga with tile roofs and brick walls are not in the sample. Like the move from round to square houses during the earlier part of the century (see Comaroff & Comaroff, 1992), more ambitious and forward looking households have semipermanent houses and iron sheet roofs. Households that engage in cash cropping or who often have visitors from the city who drive vehicles will have made arrangements for a driveway (54% of the sample). Having a driveway is an indicator of connectedness to the outside world. These variables are combined into a single indicator, modernity.

Modernity loads on a different factor than the wealth indicator, and the correlation between them is low (.10, see Table 11.4). Like many indicators of modernity, this one is imperfect. This may be because modernity is something that is best measured at the macro level. However, the variable is valuable to the analysis.

The correlation matrix (Table 11.4) shows that the power, modernity, and wealth scales have the desired low correlations. Other variables in the regression analysis are age, years of education, and years married. Years of education, years married, and births are highly correlated with age. Although the correlations for births are given, contraceptive use is the dependent variable in the logit analysis.

Table 11.4
Pearson Correlation Coefficients for 10 Variables from the Igunga Survey

Variable	1	2	3	4	5	6	7	8	9
Age									
Years married	.91								
Years educated	-.42	-.43							
Births	.80	.82	-.36						
Contracepts	.12	.12	.12	.07					
Modernity	.05	.06	.21	.05	.00				
Wealth	.01	.00	.14	-.03	.06	.10			
New Power	.04	.03	.29	-.06	.21	.19	.10		
Masculine Power	.22	.23	.00	.14	.15	.00	-.04	.37	
Traditional Power	.14	.14	-.12	.17	.13	.08	.02	.18	.10

I present two models from the logit analysis.[6] The first is a standard modernization model and includes modernity, wealth, age, and years of education (Table 11.5). Only years of education and age seem to influence contraceptive use. If we resolve the equation for just these two variables, the *t* statistics remain high and the probabilities low. This tells us that age and years of education appear to have something to do with being a current contraceptive user.

Table 11.5
Logistic Regression Analysis of Predictors of Current Contraceptive Use: Standard Modernization Model

Variable	Parameter Estimate	Standard Error	*T*	*P*-value
Constant	-1.973	1.641	-1.202	0.229
Modernity	-0.191	0.169	-1.132	0.258
Wealth	0.002	0.004	0.534	0.593
Years Educated	0.161	0.055	2.896	0.004
Age	0.065	0.020	3.216	0.001

Note: $N = 293$.

However, when we look at the fit between this model and the actual data, we find that these two variables, as they stand, do not predict current contraceptive use very well. The Hosmer-Lemeshow statistic tests the null hypothesis that the observed data are not significantly different from the logistic regression predictions. The probability of .035 tells us that this model predicts values that are not the same as what we see in our data.

Previous research has suggested that education influences contraceptive use when combined with empowerment. Table 11.6 shows what happens when we express this interaction. The Hosmer-Lemeshow statistic for this model yields a high probability of .71. Women who are educated *and* participate in such activities as coops, banking, and credit are more likely to contracept. In addition, women who are older are more likely to contracept, probably because they have reached their family size goals. The wealth and modernity scales and masculine or traditional forms of power, do not contribute to contraceptive use.[7]

Table 11.6
Logistic Regression Analysis of Predictors of Current Contraceptive Use: Age and Women's Empowerment

Variable	Parameter Estimate	Standard Error	*T*	*P*-value
Constant	-2.339	0.578	-4.148	0.000
Age	0.041	0.017	2.407	0.016
Years Educated x New Forms of Power	0.072	0.018	3.940	0.000

Note: $N = 293$. Hosmer-Lemeshow statistic: 5.460 *p*-value: 0.708 *df*: 8.

These results support resource access theory and are virtually identical to Handwerker's findings from Antigua and Barbados (1989, 1991, 1993). Education explains contraceptive use only when combined with other empowerment and life cycle variables. A woman is more likely to contracept if she has more education, is older, and accesses new forms of power. Education by itself does not predict whether a woman will contracept. As Handwerker (1993) has pointed out, education must lead to other opportunities in order for a woman to choose smaller family size. These findings also lend support to LeVine et al.'s (1991) results from central Mexico, demonstrating one of the mechanisms through which education works to reduce fertility.

CONCLUSION

There is a growing consensus about the relationship between education and fertility decline. This consensus is developing mainly from small-scale studies using anthropological methodologies, such as those reported by LeVine et al. (1991) and Handwerker (1989, 1991, 1993). The accumulation of findings from these studies points to the mechanisms through which education leads to lower fertility. Caldwell (1979, 1982) argued that education leads to fertility decline by inculcating western values and changing the economic value of children. The data from the focused household study indicate that there have been reversals in the flow of wealth and power in Igunga, changing relationships between the generations and between men and women. The data from the survey demonstrate some of the mechanisms through which these changes take place.

Education may make women more interested in, or capable of, using credit, banking, participating in a cooperative, and hiring laborers. Thus they may be empowered to resist the demands of relatives to have more children or be more rewarded by these activities than by having many children. Cooperative participation may further expose women to information about family planning and to networks of women who discuss family planning (Hammerslough, 1990, 1991; Watkins, 1993). Women involved in these ways are more likely to limit family size.

Resource access theory is, so far, the best model through which to understand fertility decline in Igunga. As a correction on wealth flows theory, it points to the mechanism though which shifts in wealth flows operate to lead to contraceptive use. Igunga women who contracept are more likely to be involved in activities that I view as contemporary forms of power. There may be something different about these women that might be regarded, by some theorists, as *individual* modernity. They may be more individualistic or ambitious than other women or more concerned with the world outside western Kenya. We have not tested these attitudes in the logit model.

It is easy to see how a desire to limit family size is linked to individualistic values. Young people's desires for status and prestige, both with reference to Igunga and to the larger national context, are linked to their desires for a small number of healthy, well fed, and educated children reared in nuclear family settings. The attitudes of young people in Igunga are reflected in a campaign poster, produced by the Nairobi office of Family Planning Private Sector, showing a westernized African family with two well-dressed children carrying schoolbooks, while the large family is thin, ragged, and shoeless. Ambition and small family size are ideologically connected.

There have been few technological improvements in Igunga over a twenty-year period. Aside from a few telephones in the homes of the elite, services such as clean water have become less available. Modern methods of family planning have been available since before 1974. Mortality has dropped, however, probably a result of somewhat improved access to medical care, lending some support to the classic three stage model of fertility decline.

Individuals who are educated and bank or belong to cooperatives may be in some ways more ambitious and connected than others. However, this does not mean that modernization theory, as a theoretical perspective, is the best route through which to understand fertility decline in Igunga. As world system and dependency theorists have eloquently pointed out, modernization theory does not take into account the ways in which people at the edges of the world economy may lose ground or fail to develop in the face of capitalism (see Bradley, 1996; Smith, Collins, Hopkins, & Muhammad, 1988; Ward, 1984, 1985, 1988). Igunga remains an impoverished place, where land, cattle, food, and basic services are inadequate. Kenya's struggling economy in the face of rampant inflation has further marginalized western Kenya, making it difficult for young people to obtain higher educations or jobs in cities and raising the cost of food and other commodities while dependency on store-bought items grows ("49,000 to miss," 1992; Brass & Jolly, 1993). Thus, people in Igunga may turn to contraception because they can no longer afford to raise so many children.

NOTES

This research was funded by the National Science Foundation (BNS 8709773 and BNS 9011986), a Fulbright–Hays grant, the Wenner–Gren Foundation (Gr. 5076), and the Ford Foundation through the Population Studies and Research Institute (PSRI) of the University of Nairobi, where I have been a member of staff since 1988. This research would not have been possible without the support of the PSRI, especially Prof. H. W. O. Okoth-Ogendo, Prof. A. B. C. Ocholla-Ayayo, Prof. John Oucho, and graduate students James Onyango Ndege and John Kwendo Omurundo. Maragoli field assistants/collaborators were Phyllis Keith, Edith Manono, Cubic Mugera Mudiri, Lillian Mwasiagi, Josephine Mwasiagi, Anne Nyangasi, and Rose Nyangasi. Much input came from friends, colleagues, and mentors in the United States, Kenya, and Europe, including Michael Burton, Daniel Byrne, Frank Cancian, Scarlett Epstein, Anne Fleuret, Eugene Hammel, Charles Hammerslough, W. Penn Handwerker, Brian Hodgkinson, Allen Johnson, Ivan Karp, Philip Kilbride, Robert L. Munroe, Ruth Munroe, Sandra Nichols, Joseph Ssennyonga, Thomas Weisner, and Beatrice Whiting.

1. A total fertility rate (TFR) is a measure which represents an estimate of the average number of children born to women at the end of their reproductive lives (Nag, 1980). TFRs are not always strictly comparable, since they may be computed differently, or represent different age groups (Handwerker, 1989, 1991; Ottieno et al., 1988; Omurundo, 1989). Ottieno et al. argue that differences in statistical analyses provide only small differences in TFR rates for Kenya.

2. Although Caldwell's later papers include discussions of cultural factors which may explain higher fertility in Africa, the basic principles of wealth flows theory are unaffected. In addition, several African countries have begun the process of fertility decline since Caldwell first laid out wealth flows theory; these other papers were written after the transition had begun.

3. The remaining 14 households were selected randomly.

4. Stanley Sahani, interviewed August 8, 1989, by Rose Nyangasi.

5. I used a factor analysis to explore how eight empowerment variables were related for the 303 women in the Igunga survey. Data were collected on two additional variables which had little variance and are not included in this analysis. The component loadings for the eight variables on the first three factors are as follows:

	Component Loadings		
Employment Variables	1	2	3
Hires her own land	.49	.49	-.28
Owns her own cattle	.47	.48	.04
Hire her own laborers	.74	.30	-.18
Trades in own right	.21	.10	.69
Makes crafts for sale	.37	-.21	.63
Belongs to co-op	.59	.05	.22
Banks in own name	.70	-.45	-.18
Obtains credit in own name	.50	-.66	-.22

6. W. Penn Handwerker provided assistance with the logistic regression and its interpretation.

7. There is always the possibility that years of education and new forms of power exert main effects, independent of the interaction. The log likelihood test for main effects says that they do not; the chi-squared probability is .411.

REFERENCES

"Birth control making inroads in populous Kenya" (1989). *New York Times International*, September 10.

Becker, Gary S. (1965). A theory of the allocation of time. *Economic Journal, 229*(75):493-517.

Bradley, Candice. (1989, November). *The value of girls in Maragoli*. Paper presented at the 87th Annual Meetings of the American Anthropological Association, Washington, DC.

Bradley, Candice. (1991, October). Creating an NBC news story. In Presenting Anthropology to the Public [Special issue]. *Anthropology Newsletter*,.

Bradley, Candice. (1993, November). *Altered promises and changed expectations: Fertility and the decline of bridewealth in Kenya*. Paper presented at American Anthropological Association meetings, Washington, D.C., November.

Bradley, Candice. (1995a). Women's empowerment and fertility decline in western Kenya. In Susan Greenhalgh (Ed.), *Situating fertility: Anthropology and demographic inquiry* (pp. 157–178). Cambridge: Cambridge University Press.

Bradley, Candice. (1995b). Luyia. In John Middleton & A. Rassam (Eds.), *Encyclopedia of world cultures. Vol. 9, Africa and the Middle East* (pp. 202–206). New York: G. K. Hall–Macmillan.

Bradley, Candice. (1996). World-system theory. In David Levinson & Melvin Ember (Eds), *The encyclopedia of cultural anthropology* (pp. 1377–1380). Lakeville: Henry Holt, Inc.

Bradley, Candice, & Ndege, James Onyango. (forthcoming). Fertility decline in a Maragoli sublocation. In J. Akong'a, A. B. C. Ocholla-Ayayo, & S. Wandibba (Eds.), *Ecological and cultural change and human development in western Kenya and Western Province*. Nairobi: G. S. Were Press.

Brass, William, & Jolly, Carole L. (Eds.). (1993). *Population dynamics of Kenya*. Washington, DC: National Academy Press.

Caldwell, John. (1979). Education as a factor in mortality decline: An examination of Nigerian data. *Population Studies, 33*, 395–413.

Caldwell, John. (1980). Mass education as a determinant of the timing of fertility decline. *Population and Development Review, 6*, 225–255.

Caldwell, John. (1982). *Theory of fertility decline*. London: Academic Press.

Caldwell, John. (1983). Direct economic cost and benefits of children. In R. Bulatao and R. Lee (Eds.), *Determinants of fertility in developing countries*, Vol. 1. New York: Academic.

Caldwell, John, & Caldwell, Pat. (1990). Cultural forces tending to sustain high fertility. In G. T. Acsadi, G. Johnson-Acsadi, & R. A. Bulatao (Eds.), *Population growth and reproduction in sub-Saharan Africa* (pp. 199–214). Washington, DC: World Bank.

Caldwell, John, Reddy, P., & Caldwell, Pat (1988). *The causes of demographic change: Experimental research in South India*. Madison: University of Wisconsin Press.

Central Bureau of Statistics. (1984). *Kenya contraceptive prevalence survey. First report.* Nairobi: Ministry of Planning and National Development.

Comaroff, Jean, & Comaroff, John L. (1992). *Ethnography and the historical imagination: Selected essays*. Boulder: Westview Press.

Easterlin, Richard A. (1975). An economic framework for fertility analysis. *Studies in Family Planning, 6*, 54–63.

Epstein, T. S., & Jackson, D. (1975). *The paradox of poverty*. Delhi: Macmillan.

Epstein, T. S., & Jackson, D. (1977). *The feasibility of fertility planning*. Oxford: Pergamon.

Eshiwani, George. (1990). *Implementing educational policies in Kenya* (World Bank Discussion Papers: Africa Technical Department Series No. 85). Washington, DC: World Bank.

"49,000 to miss university places." (1992). *The Standard*, July 16, pp. 1–2.

Frank, Odile, & McNicoll, Geoffrey. (1987). An interpretation of fertility and population policy in Kenya. *Population and Development Review, 13*, 209–243.

Greenhalgh, Susan. (1990). Toward a political economy of fertility: Anthropological contributions. *Population and Development Review, 16*, 85–106.

Håkansson, Thomas. (1988). *Bridewealth, women and land: Social change among the Gusii of Kenya* (Uppsala Series in Cultural Anthropology 10). Uppsala: Uppsala University.

Hammerslough, Charles. (1990). *Community determinants of demographic behavior in Kenya: First report*. Unpublished manuscript.

Hammerslough, Charles. (1991). *Women's groups and contraceptive use in rural Kenya*. Unpublished manuscript.

Handwerker, W. Penn. (1986). *Culture and reproduction: An anthropological critique of demographic transition theory*. Boulder: Westview.

Handwerker, W. Penn. (1989). *Women's power and social revolutions*. Newbury Park, CA: Sage.

Handwerker, W. Penn. (1991). Women's power and fertility transition: The cases of Africa and the Caribbean. *Population and Environment, 13*, 55–78.

Handwerker, W. Penn. (1993). Empowerment and fertility transition on Antigua, WI: Education, employment, and the moral economy of childbearing. *Human Organization, 52*, 41–52.

Karp, Ivan. (1978). *Fields of change among the Iteso of Kenya*. London: Routledge and Kegan Paul.

Kilbride, Philip, & Kilbride, Janet. (1990). *Changing family life in East Africa*. University Park: Pennsylvania State University Press.

Kirk, L., & Burton, M. L. (1977). Meaning and context: A study in contexual shifts in meaning of Maasai personality descriptors. *American Ethnologist, 4*, 734–761.

Lavrijsen, J. S. G. (1984). *Rural poverty and impoverishment in western Kenya*. Utrecht: Department of Geography, University of Utrecht.

Leo, Christopher. (1984). *Land and class in Kenya*. Toronto: University of Toronto Press.

LeVine, Robert. (1959). Gusii sex offenses: A study in social control. *American Anthropologist, 61*, 965–990.

LeVine, R. A., LeVine, S. E., Richman, A., Tapia Uribe, F. M., Sunderland Correa, C. S., & Miller, P. M. (1991). Women's schooling and child care in the demographic transition: A Mexican case study. *Population and Development Review, 17*, 459–496.

LeVine, Sarah, & LeVine, Robert. (1981). Child abuse and neglect in sub-Saharan Africa. In Jill Korbin (Ed.), *Child abuse and neglect: Cross-cultural perspectives*. Berkeley: University of California Press.

Ministry of Planning and National Development. (1989). *Kakamega District development plan 1989–1993*. Nairobi.

Moock, Joyce. (1976). *The migration process and differential economic behavior in South Maragoli, Western Kenya*. Unpublished doctoral dissertation, Columbia University.

Nag, Moni. (1980). How modernization can also increase fertility. *Current Anthropology*,

Nag, Moni, White, Benjamin, & Peet, Creighton. (1978). An anthropological approach to the study of the economic value of children in Java and Nepal. *Current Anthropology, 419*, 293–306.

National Council for Population and Development. (1989). *Kenya demographic and health survey (KDHS)*. Nairobi: Central Bureau of Statistics.

National Council for Population and Development. (1993). *Kenya demographic and health survey (KDHS) preliminary report*. Nairobi: Central Bureau of Statistics.

Ndege, James Onyango. (1993). *Correlations and determinants of interspousal communication about family planning in Kenya: A case study of Sabatia Division, Kakamega District*. Unpublished master's thesis, University of Nairobi.

Nichols, Sandra. (1978). The making of Maragoli. *Populi, 5*, 28–31.

Nichols, Sandra. (1990). Personal communication.

Notestein, Frank W. (1945). Population—The long view. In Theodore W. Schultz (Ed.), *Food for the world* (pp. 35–57). Chicago: University of Chicago Press.

Ocholla-Ayayo, A. B. C. (n.d.) *Sociocultural environment and family planning in Kenya*. Unpublished manuscript, University of Nairobi.

Omurundo, John Kwendo (1989). *Infant/child mortality and fertility differentials in Western Province: A divisional level analysis*. Unpublished master's thesis, Population Studies and Research Institute, University of Nairobi.

Shannon, Thomas Richard. (1989). *An introduction to the world-system perspective*. Boulder: Westview.

Smith, Joan, Collins, J., Hopkins, T., & Muhammad, A. (Eds.). (1988). *Racism, sexism and the world-system*. New York: Greenwood Press.

Ssennyonga, Joseph. (1975). Cost/benefit analysis versus parental immortality: Family size in rural Kenya. In T. S. Epstein (Ed.), *The Paradox of poverty*. Delhi: Macmillan.

Ssennyonga, Joseph. (1977). Traditional cultural inventory versus the elite roadside ecology. In T. S. Epstein (Ed.), *The feasibility of fertility planning*. Oxford: Pergamon.

Ssennyonga, Joseph. (1978). *Population growth and cultural inventory: The Maragoli case*. Unpublished doctoral dissertation, University of Sussex.

Staudt, K. (1976). *Agricultural policy, political power, and women farmers in western Kenya*. Unpublished doctoral dissertation, University of Wisconsin, Madison.

Staudt, K. (1979). Rural women leaders: Late colonial and contemporary contexts. *Rural Africana, 3*, 5–21.

Turchi, Boone A., & Bryant, Ellen S. (1979). *Rural development activities, fertility, and the cost and value of children*. Research Triangle Institute & South East Consortium for International Development, Triangle Park North Carolina.

van de Walle, Etienne, & Foster, Andrew (1990). *Fertility decline in Africa: Assessments and prospects* (World Bank Technical Paper Number 125). Washington, DC: World Bank, African Technical Department Series.

Wagner, Gunter. (1949). *The Bantu of western Kenya, with special reference to the Vugusu and Logoli, Vol. 1*. London: Oxford University Press.

Wagner, Gunter. (1956). *The Bantu of western Kenya. Economic life, Vol. 2*. London: Oxford University Press.

Wallerstein, Immanuel (1974). *The modern world-system*. New York: Academic Press.

Wamalwa, Elizabeth Nafuna. (1989). Violence against wives in Kenya. In Mary Adhiambo Mbeo & Oki Ooko-Ombaka (Eds.), *Women and the law in Kenya* (pp. 71–78). Nairobi: National Law Institute.

Ward, Kathryn B. (1984). *Women in the world-system: Its impact on status and fertility*. New York: Praeger.

Ward, Kathryn B. (1985). The social consequences of the world economic system: The economic status of women and fertility. *Review, 7*, 561–593.

Ward, Kathryn B. (1988). Female resistance to marginalization: The Igbo Women's War of 1929. In Joan Smith, J. Collins, T. Hopkins, & A. Muhammad (Eds.), *Racism, sexism and the world-system* (pp. 121–135). New York: Greenwood Press.

Watkins, Susan Cott. (1993). *From provinces into nations: Demographic integration in western Europe, 1870–1960*. Princeton: Princeton University Press.

Weller, Susan, & Romney, A. Kimball. (1988). *Systematic data collection*. Newbury Park, CA: Sage.

White, Luise. (1990). *The comforts of home*. Chicago: University of Chicago Press.

12

Gender and Life-Course Strategies among the Gusii

N. Thomas Håkansson and Robert A. LeVine

INTRODUCTION

In Gusii society not only is the road toward an ideal old age different for men and women, but the ways in which each gender achieves the ideal are mutually contradictory. As in many other African societies, the family provides security and comfort in old age. However, principles of separation and authority based on gender, generation, kinship, and affinity, which define relationships between Gusii family members, differentially affect the life course goals of men and women. These principles are expressed in the division of labor, resource control, and rules of avoidance (*chinsoni*). Our objective in this chapter is to explore the material and social consequences for the elderly of the structurally opposed life-course strategies that result from intrafamily dynamics in contemporary Gusii society.

Analyses of intergenerational relations in African societies have produced two distinct, if not necessarily opposed, perspectives on old age. From one perspective, social support for a secure and comfortable old age is the reward for one's earlier contributions to the welfare of others, and local models of reciprocity generate the expectation that elderly parents in particular will benefit from having nurtured their children (Moore, 1978; Cattell, 1990). From the other perspective, the intergenerational hierarchy of "traditional" African societies always operates to the benefit of parents: through the labor contributions of their immature children when they are young adults, and through the filial support of their adult children when they are old. In this view, wealth (i.e., net economic benefit) flows "upward" toward the older generation, and children become the beneficiaries of this flow only when they become parents themselves (Caldwell, 1982; see also Bradley, this volume).

This chapter presents the case of old age among the Gusii of Kenya, suggesting that neither of these analytic perspectives adequately represents the processes through which adults strive to provide for old age. Our study shows that (a) actions directed toward old-age security are based on both short-term considerations in the local context of adult lives and on long-term strategies designed to maximize lifetime "returns" on "investments"; (b) these actions are influenced by culture specific norms that differentiate the Gusii from other African societies; and (c) they are further differentiated by gender specific norms and contexts. The impact of variations by local culture and gender relations on how aging adults organize their lives must be taken into account in any effort to generalize about old age in Africa.

Attention to the developmental cycle of the domestic group (Fortes, 1958) combined with a processual analysis of change at the local level provides a culture sensitive framework for our description. The shared norms and values that provide structural regularities to the developmental cycles of domestic groups generate socially defined life courses for men and women (cf. Fortes, 1958, pp. 9, 12). However, rapid culture change affects how people over the course of their lives work out their solutions for old age, and the working out of these solutions in turn changes the cultural models for intergenerational expectations and ideal old age.

A closer look at the intrafamily relationships reveals the struggles and divisions that factionalize family members in a changed socioeconomic environment. These struggles reveal norms and values and ideas that inform action and propel changes in life course achievements. Gender inequalities lead to asymmetry of resource access and control, which creates different pathways for women and men towards the ideal old age (Udvardy & Cattell, 1992).

Women's life-cycle strategies are geared toward investment in their children's capacity to provide them with social and economic returns in old age. A husband's desire to marry additional wives is accurately perceived by women as a threat to their future welfare. A second marriage means that less land will be available for the first wife as well as less money for the payment of her children's school fees.

Prescriptions about proper interpersonal behavior in the family preclude men from close association with their sons and daughters-in-law. Men are therefore dependent on marital relationships for labor and services and aspire to polygyny. According to Guyer's (1994) terminology we can say that women pursue a lineal life course strategy, investing in their children for future gains, while men have a partially lateral strategy of investing in wives for current as well as future gains.

THE GUSII FAMILY

The Gusii are Bantu speakers who inhabit a hilly, highland area in western Kenya, fifty kilometers east of Lake Victoria. Their territory comprises present-day Kisii District, which is one of the most productive cash crop areas in Kenya, because of the abundant rainfall and very fertile soils. In 1979, the population density of Gusii Land was 395 persons per square kilometer (Government of Kenya, 1979). Until recently, the population has been among the most rapidly growing in the world, increasing 3 percent to 4 percent per year, and is currently over one million. High population density has forced the Gusii to utilize every available space for agriculture, and many families today are unable to produce enough food for subsistence needs. Thus, in addition to farming, many Gusii engage in employment or business, either locally or in the large urban centers.

Women's access to subsistence and income has been reduced through the emphasis on cash crop production and the increased male control over resources (Håkansson, 1988). The increasing population density in Kisii District has produced very small family holdings. Farms owned by young families comprised two to four acres in the beginning of the 1980s. On these small holdings both subsistence and cash crops are grown. Agricultural studies in some areas of the district show that on average, one third of the total acreage is taken up by such cash crops as coffee, tea, and pyrethrum (Kongstad & Monsted, 1980).

The decreased viability of agriculture as a source of subsistence and income is also encouraging parents to invest heavily in western style education in the hope that their children will obtain salaried employment. It should be stressed that although many have the ambition to send their children, especially sons, to secondary school, less than half of Gusii children actually manage to attend (Government of Kenya, 1979).

Indigenous Social Organization

Indigenous Gusii social organization was first described in detail in the 1940s by Philip and Iona Mayer (I. Mayer, 1975; P. Mayer, 1949, 1950). These norms and values still regulate and inform much of Gusii behavior and ideas about gender, marriage, and kinship (Håkansson, 1988; LeVine, 1982). Indigenous political and social organization is contained within a segmentary lineage system. The nesting segments are defined according to a genealogical grid with an eponymous ancestor at the top. To a great extent, land is both controlled and inhabited by members of territorial clans and lineage segments, which makes physical distance isomorphic with social distance.

Traditionally marriage could be established only through the payment of bridewealth, in the form of livestock, by the husband's family to the wife's. This act established a socially sanctioned marriage through which a woman and a man became socially defined a mother and a father. The wife became the founder of a matrisegment in the patrilineage, and the husband acquired social paternity to all children which his wife gave birth to, irrespective of their biological paternity. The husband had wide-ranging authority over his wife with respect to labor tasks, reproduction, and movement and might also beat her if he so wished. It was men who owned and controlled both movable property and land. Women were legal minors who could neither own property nor act on their own behalf in jural matters. Only through marriage did women obtain socially accepted status and secure access to land.

The family was still organized according to the house–property principles found in many patrilineal societies in eastern Africa (cf. Gray & Gulliver, 1964; Håkansson, 1989). Each wife and her children constituted a house, *enyomba*, an economically and, according to customary law, jurally independent unit. This independence did not mean that a woman could exercise any property rights of her own. She was a trustee and manager of her house's property for her sons, and it was not until her sons had reached maturity that she could engage in independent decision making in daily affairs. Sons inherited only the cattle and other assets that belong to their own house. Each house grew through the marriage of its daughters, whose bridewealth cattle were ideally used by its sons for their marriages. The wealth of the house was livestock, children, and land, which are its inalienable *etugo*. *Etugo* is derived from the verb *ogotuga,* which means 'to rear or to feed' (P. Mayer, 1950, p. 63).

This description of family structure is not provided only as a traditional background against which modern changes can be assessed. On the contrary, we maintain that its structure enters into and affects the course of processes of change. The very constitution of the Gusii family in the form of ascribed rights and obligations and the evaluative content of relationships provide different life course strategies for husbands and wives. The increasing incompatibility of these strategies for gaining security and respect in old age have become increasingly evident during the rapid social and economic changes of the last forty years.

WOMEN AND OLD AGE

The ideal model for a woman's old age is based on the successful development of her sons' families. It is only within the context of marriage that a woman can control property and dependents through whom she builds up a relative independence, prestige, and security for her old age. As her sons marry, a woman becomes to a great extent independent from her husband. By that time, a polygynous man's land is demarcated for each wife as patrimony for her sons. The adult sons defend her against her husband and, together with their mother, protect their interests against other households in the polygynous family. Gusii boys are very close to their mother and can, in extreme cases, even beat a father if he abuses her. Hence, if a woman manages to accumulate dependents in the forms of sons, daughters-in-law, and grandchildren, her independence increases vis-à-vis her husband and other kin and in-laws. Power and influence are built by both women and men throughout the life course. The life course is a social process of accumulating relationships of structurally inferior persons. The more people a person has authority over, the more independent she or he is vis-à-vis others.

Through her sons' wives, a woman acquires dependents who have to show her respect, obey her, and assist her in daily routines. When a woman's sons marry she removes herself more and more from her husband's sphere of authority. She ceases to have sexual intercourse at the onset of menopause. She becomes a member of a son's household and expects to receive services from her son and daughter-in-law and grandchildren. Finally, in her old age, the youngest son and, more particularly, his wife take care of her. She farms together with the daughter-in-law and is assigned grandchildren as helpers with all kinds of chores, such as cooking, house cleaning, and the washing of clothes.

With increasing age, women expect to have daughters-in-law and grandchildren working for and with them. Grandchildren do such heavy chores as fetching water and fuel wood, help with cooking, and run errands. But it is not only the assistance with labor, food, and money that define a good old age. The role as a guardian of tradition and teacher of proper behavior is an integral aspect of being a grandmother. Grandparents usually have a relaxed and informal relationship with their grandchildren, which allows them to discuss topics such as sexuality that cannot be mentioned to parents.

MEN AND OLD AGE

In contrast to women's lineal investments in their own children, men pursue a lateral strategy that aims at plural marriages. While women expect to receive services and goods from sons and their families, men rely on the opportunity to obtain many wives. The value of polygyny for men is multidimensional and cannot be reduced to investment in production and children, as is stressed by many scholars (Goody, 1973; Schneider, 1979; White & Burton, 1988). The focus on production and reproduction in the literature on polygyny obscures the fact that marriage for men is also a way of obtaining control over a dependent person who provides services. Indeed, polygynous marriages are no longer associated with wealth or influential position and must be seen in the light of the model of life course fulfillment. The extreme gender inequalities in Gusii society allow men to use polygyny, and especially their marriage to a younger woman, as a means for gaining access to a multitude of services.

Men are dependent on the marital relationship for labor, household services, and regular sexual intercourse. When they marry additional wives, less land is available for the first wife and less money for the payment of school fees. This is accurately perceived by women as a threat to their future welfare. Nevertheless, many Gusii wives withdraw from an intimate relationship with their husband after menopause. By doing so, a wife deprives her husband of domestic as well as sexual services and thus motivates him to become a polygynist. Elderly grandfathers often mention such aspects of wifely care as cooking, cleaning the house, nursing them when they are sick, washing clothes, and keeping them warm with a fire. The varieties of services that a husband can obtain from his wives are numerous. LeVine even encountered one old man who with great pleasure declared that his new wife shaved him in the morning!

The wealth flow from children to fathers as they grow older entails both goods and services. Older men do receive money, clothes, and other gifts from their children. Of great importance is the fact that children often provide money for such emergencies as hospital bills. Services are performed by women and children. However, the supply of services, care, emotional support, and the like is not an undifferentiated flow from young to old. Behavior is structured by the content of family relationships and shaped by the culturally defined expectations of love, respect, restraint, and authority. While a mother receives assistance from her daughter-in-law and grandchildren, a man cannot count on reliable and continuous assistance from a daughter-in-law. Not only does she direct her effort towards her own husband, his mother, and her children, but she and her father-in-law also must avoid each other.

Principles of Avoidance

As was the case with women, men's life-cycle strategies must also be seen in the light of expectations, rights, and obligations between family members. The possible relationships between Gusii family members are defined by principles of separation and authority, based on gender and generation. These principles are expressed in the division of labor and in rules of avoidance and respect. Women, as we have seen, are responsible for most of the production and preparation of food and for household chores. A man of the older and middle age generations cannot envision doing such things himself. To cook and clean for himself would reduce him to a boy, an unmarried man, which is an absolute diminution in the eyes of the Gusii. These services are performed by a man's wife.

A number of rules, including *chinsoni*, regulate behavior according to gender and age. These rules are important in the everyday personal association between members of a family and affect the ways in which men and women can organize their care in old age. Daughters-in-law and fathers-in-law must practice avoidance of each other. They may not come into bodily contact nor see one another's genitals or other parts of the lower body nor observe any activities related to bodily functions, such as washing and going to the lavatory. A father may not share a room or lavatory with a daughter-in-law. Although he can eat food prepared by her, they may not eat food from the same container. This precludes any direct involvement by the daughter-in-law in an old man's care. *Chinsoni* rules also regulate father–son interaction in a similar manner, making close and frequent contact awkward and potentially dangerous. These rules also prohibit touching everyday domestic objects belonging to either person, such as beds, stools, beer pipes, and clothing, and precludes entering certain parts of the house. Thus, continuous access to female labor and domestic services can be obtained only through a wife.

SOCIAL CHANGE AND CHANGING LIFE COURSE INVESTMENT

The long-term social investments made by individuals are increasingly producing contradictions and conflicts between family members. During the 1940s and 1950s the emerging scarcity of land, market economy, and cash income started to expose the underlying contradictions in the house–property system of the polygynous family. For the late 1950s, LeVine (1964) notes that:

> Although the wives have their allotted fields and the products from them, as well as livestock associated with their respective houses, the husband has control, through his wages and the unallocated reserve fields and livestock, over the surplus resources of the homestead. His distribution of luxuries such as meat, sugar, tea, and clothing becomes the object

> of invidious distinction among the wives, and serious inequalities in the distribution lead to bitter hostility among the wives. . . . The mother . . . is deeply involved in this because she will be dependent on her sons in old age and wants to see them favored by the homestead head. (p. 77)

This independence of houses and house property as the basis of a woman's life course, old age care, and prestige has continued until today. However, economic and social changes have caused an increase in conflict between husbands, wives, and cowives. Today, the acquisition of further wives by husbands is regarded by women as a veritable threat to their future well-being.

By the 1970s the land shortage had begun to make farming unprofitable, and education of children became a vehicle for reaching wealth. Hence, parents began to invest an increasing share of their resources in school fees for their children, first for sons and nowadays, albeit still to a lesser degree, also for daughters. Hence, monetary resources generated by family members are crucial for investment in children, who are in turn supposed to share their earnings with their parents and provide for them a comfortable old age.

The investment pattern in children's education differs between men and women. A woman provides directly for her own children's subsistence and education and has a direct interest in maximizing their future earning capacity. Polygynous men's economic interest in children is considerably more diffuse. They do not have to invest equally in all childrens' education in order to secure at least some future benefits from a few employed sons and daughters who may have different mothers (cf. Frank & McNicoll, 1987, pp. 217–218).

Women Investing in Children

The increasing land scarcity and the importance of education are crucial factors that impinge on women's life-course strategies and the quality of old age. Women who married before the 1950s could rely on the agriculturally based family in which it was important to ensure that the sons established viable families through marriage as early as possible.

Secure and comfortable old age is intimately connected with being a grandmother, a status that women reach when they are still active farmers and household managers. These women are still struggling with building up their current and future social and economic assets. While their expectations and their model of a successful life course remain similar to their older sisters', their experiences and strategies are quite different today.

In present-day Gusii Land, women raise their children in a situation in which the nation state and western cultural ideals impinge upon their strategies for the establishment of a viable resource base for their family as well as for future resources for their old age. To provide their children with high school and further education has meant hard farm work and struggles with their husbands over available cash resources. Since a woman lacks control over the fruits of her own labor, she must not only convince her husband to share his wage and farm earnings, but also to allow her to use the proceeds from cash crops and other income produced by herself. This does not mean that men are not interested in providing school fees for their children. While men in general emphasize the importance of education, their effort is usually not extended to all their children. Fathers contribute money to school fees for one or two children and expect their wives and employed children to pay for the rest. Men also strive to use family resources for other investments and consumption, such as further marriages, the building of new houses, business, and drinking.

Women have a more circumscribed access to entitlements than men and must work harder to receive them (cf. Udvardy & Cattell, 1992). The strength of a husband's and father's privileges extend to the use of bridewealth from his first daughter. To a certain extent, a father can also demand cash from his children without bearing much of the costs involved in their education.

The resources available to women come from two sources: whatever they save from income-earning activities and their daughters' bridewealths. As already explained, a woman's ability to accumulate savings is limited by her reliance on cultivation and by the fact that her husband controls most of any income she may earn.[1] Cultivation is usually not remunerative unless her husband allows her to use the income from coffee and tea for school expenses. Another possibility is the brewing of beer and the distillation of alcohol for sale. These activities, although illegal, can sometimes provide an income for women to pay for school fees. With the importance of schooling, women are now trying to ensure that their children receive enough education to obtain qualified employment. If the efforts result in one child's obtaining employment (e.g., as a teacher or clerk), she or he will then contribute to the siblings' further education and thus provide a reasonable future both for the children and for the mother in old age.

One of the few entitlements available for women to use for educational investments is their daughters' bridewealth. Compared to farming women's regular cash earnings this is a considerable source of income. The use of bridewealth for education rose from zero in the early 1950s to 50 percent in the 1970s (Håkansson, 1988, p. 172). Before the 1970s this bridewealth was commonly used for sons' and husbands' marriages. Today, it is diverted to land purchase, business investments, various form of consumption, and education. However, as average bridewealth payments have declined in value in recent decades, the worth of this source of wealth has diminished. Finally, the period between the onset of cohabitation of a couple and the transfer of bridewealth to legitimize the union has increased in duration, today encompassing two to ten years. In addition, bridewealth has decreased radically in value while school fees have increased (Håkansson, 1988, 1990; see also Bradley, this volume).

A husband's marriage to a second wife directly threatens the welfare of the first wife and her children. Not only does the marriage deflect resources from the education of her children, but a second wife means that the husband's land will have to be divided into two parts, reducing the first wife's land. Furthermore, two families will make increased demands on the husband's off-farm income. A woman's prospects of having all her children provided with secondary school education diminishes, and her sons will inherit smaller pieces of land. Both these factors will reduce the wealth of her family and her sons' ability to support her in old age.

In order to elucidate the effects of polygyny on women's and men's ability to invest in their children's education and future earnings, we selected eighteen women from Håkansson's interviews (see Håkansson, 1988). These were the women whose marriages took place between 1945 and 1962. The rationale for choosing these women was to examine those cohorts who grew up during a time period when secondary school education became important for obtaining salaried employment, that is, from the middle 1960s. These constitute a nonrandom, opportunistic sample of interviews with farming families. Families in which the husband had long-term employment requiring training and education and significant business investments are not included. The husbands in the families selected had been or were employed at the time of the study in unskilled wage employment, and their wives were farmers. They were fairly representative of the average economic standard of a rural Gusii family.[2]

These families have children of varying ages, which made it necessary to compare only those children who had already completed compulsory primary school education at the time of the study. The results show that of nine polygynously married women, only one had been able to send half or more of her children of age to secondary and/or further education. Of the nine monogamous families, eight had put the majority of their children of age through secondary school and beyond.[3] Thus, women in monogamous families today may face a more secure old age in terms of potential assistance from income earning children than those in polygynous unions.[4] In the monogamous unions the wives had been able to utilize more of their own income from farm production and more of their husbands' incomes for their children's education. The reasons for success in paying school fees was in some cases that the husband was dead or that the husband had decided not to divert income for a second marriage.

Men and Constraints on Polygyny

Although polygyny has continued to be prestigious among men, its importance as a means for political and economic advancement has declined. As will be discussed, the role of polygyny as an ideal and a practice, its causes and consequences, and the motivations behind it are complex and contradictory. The continued prestige of marrying polygynously is expressed as "becoming an important man in the clan." According to some male informants, local government-appointed *etureti* elders are normally polygynists. Having many wives, it is thought, shows that they can control many people and are therefore equipped to solve disputes in their communities.

While younger men in their thirties and forties are not immune to the sense of eminence it confers in rural areas, there is a sense that polygyny is not economically and socially practical in today's world. In the 1950s, to be a monogamist was, for older men, a source of ridicule and jokes at beer parties, and monogamous men were often urged to take a second wife. We suspect that the old ideal of attaining "immortality" by founding a lineage still forms a part of the motivations for polygyny. If he has many sons and grandsons, a man's descendant lineage and the place where he lived may be named after him.

For a man, the ideal preparation for old age is to marry a young wife who will take care of farm work and household chores. Hence, men who have remained monogamous throughout their life plan for their future marriages before their sons reach adulthood and are old enough to protest. When sons become of marriageable age they demand the demarcation of their father's land for their own farms. To provide for a future marriage, monogamous men retain a piece of personal land, *emonga*, on which they can settle with a new wife. This phase was and is filled with conflict, because the father's acquisition of a new wife will divide the estate in half.

Hence, a man takes a considerable risk by marrying a second wife, since he may estrange his first wife and her children. But this is a risk many men have been willing to take, since only a wife can provide the continuous services a man desires for a comfortable old age.

However, there are at least two important sets of factors that counteract polygyny in contemporary Gusii society. First, the relationship between polygyny and political influence is disappearing. Indeed, a few locally prominent men with salaried employment, who serve as county councilors and on cooperative boards, have used their incomes to build large families with two to four wives. But most local potentates, such as party officials, county councilors, and chiefs, are monogamous. Polygyny conflicts with the prevailing Christian ideology, ideas about development, and education. A local leader should be Christian and "modern." Polygyny is regarded as representing underdevelopment and a primitive lifestyle. In addition, today wealthy parents desire to give all their children secondary and post-secondary education. The large number of children that results from polygynous unions is therefore extremely costly. Finally, polygyny is no longer a necessary vehicle for men to build wealth and political influence.

Despite these disincentives, wealthier men may obtain a second wife when they reach fifty or sixty years of age in order to obtain domestic and sexual services. Such polygyny is not a means for personal aggrandizement, as was the large-scale polygyny of the Big Men of earlier times. Indeed, in addition to the risk of alienating their first wives and their children, to take a second young wife may embroil a politically influential man in scandal and gossip as being uncivilized and having broken church rules. A polygynously married man is barred from holy communion; hence, his act is clearly demonstrated each week before the congregation.

Second, economic factors militate against polygyny as an end point in the developmental cycle of families. The decreased land base limits the number of persons who can subsist on a farm and the amount that can be paid for children's education. The rate of polygyny is declining in Gusii Land, and most polygynous families have husbands who are over sixty years old. Although a few younger men have more than one wife, this is becoming increasingly uncommon. The reasons for this decline are many, but an alarming land shortage and changing values and resources among men and women stand out.

It is not surprising that land scarcity is a limitation on plural marriages, since farms today are generally too small to support several families. The high population growth in Kisii District is rapidly making farms smaller for each generation. At the beginning of the 1970s, 42 percent of farms were 1.2 to 2.4 ha, and 40 percent 2.4 to 4.8 ha. By the time that the next generation of male inheritors have divided these farms, the majority of holdings will fall to an average between 1.4 and 3.9 ha (Wielemaker & Boxem, 1982, pp. 95–96). This process had already begun in the early 1980s, when many young men could not establish independent viable rural households because their fathers did not have enough land to divide among their sons.

The drastic decline in polygyny can be illustrated by LeVine's data from his study area "Nyansongo" in the "Morongo" area (R. LeVine & B. LeVine, 1966). In 1956, 44 percent of the married men and 55.8 percent of the married women in Nyansongo were polygynously married; by 1975, these figures had dropped to only 8.9 percent of the married men and 27.9 percent of the married women. This extremely steep decline reflects the scarcities of land and cattle that made polygyny virtually impossible in the 1970s, except for men over fifty years old who had accumulated some wealth. For the "Morongo" area as a whole in 1975, 32.1 percent of the men over fifty, but only 5.4 percent of the men twenty-five to fifty years old, were polygynists. In this later period, Nyansongo was intermediate among Morongo localities in frequency of polygyny. Plural marriages were more frequent in the more prosperous neighborhoods.[5] Wealthy Seventh Day Adventists in particular (paradoxically) could not only afford plural wives but had large enough land holdings for them to cultivate.[6] Thus polygyny remained a possibility for affluent men over fifty years of age; but the majority of children (84.5% of those under five) were now being raised in monogamous homes.

Whether because of land scarcity or other reasons, monogamous men face the risk of being left alone in old age. Illustrative is the case of a man of about seventy whose first wife had died and who had remarried in the beginning of the 1960s. The first wife had given birth to five daughters and one son. The daughters married and therefore lived far away. The married son had left ten years before to settle in the Narok settlements. After quarrels over the man's drinking and his accusations of sexual relationships with other men, his second wife also left him. According to his nephew, "he is suffering because there is no one to cook for him. He cried like a small baby that his wife had run away."

Education and the subsequent employment of children may make the situation even worse, since all the children may have moved to urban areas. The mother of one of the authors' field assistants died and left his father, who was around sixty years old, "alone." The father, a prominent Pentecostal church leader and therefore monogamous, was remarried within a year to a woman in her twenties. Several of his children had moved out from the farm, and he could not expect anyone to stay there and care for him in old age.

To conclude, polygyny is not only a question of wealth and prestige for a man but also a consideration of old-age security and provision of care. The more wives a man has, the more services he can expect and the more grandchildren will surround him. Men have been more prone to use income for further marriages and to value quantity of children rather than "quality" in the form of education. A man's primary day-to day-welfare is dependent on having a wife who takes care of him and the household. Therefore, the children he may get with the new wife are, in a sense, not necessary for his old-age comfort. As one old man expressed it: "Normally you don't expect everybody in the family to be good, so I get help only from some sons, daughters-in-law, and grandchildren, but not all." Until recently, this strategy has been feasible, albeit less and less so, because men have usually left their wives to take the brunt of the costs of raising children.

CONCLUSION

By focusing on the culture-specific constitution of the Gusii family it has been possible to include structural factors in current social and economic processes and thus to go beyond the generalized picture of intergenerational relationships in African societies. While there are built-in structural factors in the relationship between family members that promote an upward flow of benefits, the actual transactions are the result of individuals acting in a contradictory social environment. Not only age but also gender and kinship identities entail different normative expectations between generations in the Gusii family. Rules of avoidance between family members and gender based differentials in authority and resource access generate radically discrepant perspectives on how to achieve a comfortable old age.

Thus, the outcome of investments in children for old-age security and comfort is dependent not only on interactions between parents and children, but also between husbands and wives, between wives and their children, and between the husband and other wives. Whether or not a man marries a second wife affects his first wife's life course and her children's future income earning abilities and his own situation in old age.

The increased importance of investing in children's education has amplified the latent contradictions in the Gusii family as husbands and wives pursue different life course strategies. An aspect of this change is the increased investment in both daughters' and sons' education and the expectation of receiving assistance from all children irrespective of gender. Men to a great extent aim at obtaining a second wife as a provider of daily services. This in turn is a threat to the first wife's ability to invest in her own future. The data presented here indicate that plural marriages indeed have a lower success in educating their children beyond primary school than monogamous families.

Finally, men's desire for polygyny cannot be accounted for only in terms of investment in agricultural production and a desire for descendants, but must also be seen as a form of expansion of a man's access to wifely services in old age. A man's future well-being is not so much dependent on the expensive investment in children's education as on his ability to obtain several wives. Women, who bear the cost of feeding and educating their children, are more concerned about limiting their number of children and nowadays are investing in their future earning capacity instead. However, their ability to control their own fertility has been limited.

During the last thirty years there has been a marked decline in polygyny, and older men can no longer expect to acquire a young wife to provide household services and sexual intercourse. The long-term impact of this trend on women and men is not clear. It will probably decrease the quality of life for men and effect changes in the relationship between children and fathers to accommodate the new family situations with a change in the persons who are going to be caregivers.

NOTES

Maria Cattell and Monica Udvardy have made extensive and insightful comments on earlier versions of this paper. In addition, Monica Udvardy has generously allowed us to draw on material from her unpublished 1985 pilot study of elderly in Gusii Land. We are also indebted to Justus Ogembo for information on certain points.

1. Women's ability to save any surplus income is dependent on a number of factors. If their husbands are working outside the district they can try to hide their savings. In one of my study locations, the priest at the local mission maintained savings accounts for women in order to protect their savings from their husbands. Beer brewing and alcohol distillation are fairly remunerative income sources for women. Traditionally, beer brewing is a female activity, and income therefrom is to some extent controlled by women. However, younger women reported that they could not refuse to give part of their income from brewing to their husbands if they asked for it. In order to protect her savings, a woman can buy a cow, which is considered her house property and the property of her sons and is therefore difficult for her husband to alienate.
2. They came from families that were poor or regular farmers, that is, whose parents had two to four acres of land and little formal education and subsisted on a mixture of agriculture, small scale food marketing, and casual labor.
3. Parkin (1978, pp. 82–85) in his study of urban Luo in Nairobi stressed that polygynous marriages adversely affect the ability of such families to educate their children. Luo wives insist on the ideal of equal division of a husband's resources for the education of all children. This diminishes the chances of providing school fees for any one child's secondary education. In polygynous families it is often the mother who contributes substantially to her children's higher education through trade and the sale of cash crops.
4. The difference in educational success is not related to number of children. There was very little difference in the number of children between the two groups. The lowest number of children was five. One polygynously and one monogamously married woman each had five children. The rest had seven to ten children.
5. Håkansson has observed a similar pattern between his two study communities, Sengera and Suneka. Population density in Suneka is higher than in Sengera, and the former location's closeness to Kisii Town has meant a longer history of wage and salaried work and cash-crop production. The polygyny rate of wives to married men in Sengera is 1.35 to 1 and in Suneka 1.17 to 1. Until recently, land availability has allowed the Sengera population to marry polygynously. There may be other factors involved as well. House type, an economic indicator, shows a much higher number of modern brick and cement houses in Suneka than in Sengera. This implies a different investment pattern in Suneka, where in-

come has been used for business investments, house construction, education, and land purchase to a much greater extent than in Sengera.

6. The Seventh Day Adventist is the strictest denomination with respect to behavioral rules for its members and would be expected to be the least tolerant of polygyny among the different churches in the district. (The other dominant churches are the Pentecostal Assembly of God, the Lutherans, and the Catholic church). Seventh Day Adventists are the foremost representatives of the "Protestant work ethic" and, indeed, a large number of business people are members of this denomination, which prohibits alcohol consumption, coffee drinking, and dancing.

REFERENCES

Caldwell, John. (1982). *Theory of fertility decline*. New York: Academic.

Cattell, Maria. (1990). Models of old age among the Samia of Kenya: Family support of the elderly. *Journal of Cross-Cultural Gerontology, 5*, 375–394.

Fortes, Meyer. (1958). Introduction. In Jack R. Goody (Ed.), *The developmental cycle in domestic groups* (pp. 1–14). Cambridge: Cambridge University Press.

Frank, Odile, & McNicoll, Geoffrey. (1987). An interpretation of fertility and population policy in Kenya. *Population and Development Review, 13*, 209–244

Gray, Robert F., & Gulliver, Philip H. (Eds.). (1964). *The family estate in Africa*. London: Routledge and Kegan Paul.

Goody, Jack R. (1973). Polygyny, economy and the role of women. In Jack R. Goody (Ed.), *The character of kinship* (pp. 175–190). Cambridge: Cambridge University Press.

Government of Kenya. (1979). *Kenya Population Census*, Vols. 1 and 2. Nairobi: Central Bureau of Statistics.

Guyer, Jane. (1994). Lineal identifies and lateral networks: The logic of polyandrous motherhood. In Caroline Bledsoe and Gilles Pison (Eds.), *Nuptuality in Sub-Saharan Africa*. Oxford: Clarendon Press.

Håkansson, N. Thomas. (1980). *Family, labour and trade in Western Kenya*. Uppsala: Scandinavian Institute of African Studies.

Håkansson, N. Thomas. (1985). Why do Gusii women get married? A study of cultural constraints and women's strategies in a rural community in Kenya. *Folk, 27*, 89–114.

Håkansson, N. Thomas. (1988). Bridewealth, women and land: Social change among the Gusii of Kenya. *Uppsala Studies in Cultural Anthropology, 10*. Stockholm: Almqvist & Wiksell International.

Håkansson, N. Thomas. (1989). Family structure, bridewealth, and environment in Eastern Africa: A comparative study of house-property systems. *Ethnology, 28*(2), 117–134.

Håkansson, N. Thomas. (1990). Socioeconomic stratification and marriage payments: Elite marriage and bridewealth among the Gusii of Kenya. In Miriam S. Chaiken & Anne K. Fleuret (Eds.), *Social change and applied anthropology* (pp. 164–181). Boulder: Westview Press.

Kongstad, Paul, & Monsted, Mette. (1980). *Family labour and trade in western Kenya*. Uppsala: Scandinavian Institute of African Studies.

LeVine, Robert A. (1964). The Gusii family. In Robert F. Gray & Philip H. Gulliver (Eds.), *The family estate in Africa* (pp. 63–82). Boston: Boston University Press.

LeVine, Robert A. (1982). Gusii funerals: Meanings of life and death in an African community. *Ethos, 10*, 26–65.

LeVine, Robert A., & LeVine, Barbara B. (1966). *Nyansongo: A Gusii community in Kenya*. New York: Wiley.

Mayer, Iona. (1975). The patriarchal image: Routine dissociation in Gusii families. *African Studies*, *34*, 259–281.

Mayer, Philip. (1949). The lineage principle in Gusii society. *International African Institute Memorandum*, *24*, 1–35.

Mayer, Philip. (1950). Gusii bridewealth, law and custom. *The Rhodes–Livingstone Papers, No. 18*. London: Oxford University Press.

Moore, Sally F. (1978). Old age in life-term social arena: Some Chagga of Kilimanjaro in 1974. In Barbara G. Myerhoff & Andrei Simic (Eds.), *Life's career-aging: Cultural variations on growing old* (pp. 23–76). London: Sage.

Parkin, David. (1978). *The cultural definition of political response*. New York: Academic Press.

Schneider, Harold K. (1979). *Livestock and equality in East Africa*. Bloomington: Indiana University Press.

Udvardy, Monica L., & Cattell, Maria. (1992). Gender, aging and power in Sub-Saharan Africa: Challenges and puzzles. *Journal of Cross-Cultural Gerontology*, *7*(4), 1–14.

White, Douglas R., & Burton, Michael L. (1988). Causes of polygyny: Ecology, economy, kinship, and warfare. *American Anthropologist*, *90*, 871–887.

Wielemaker, W. G., & Boxem, H. W. (1982). *Soils of the Kisii area*. Wageningen: Centre for Agricultural Publishing and Documentation.

13

Polygyny and Resource Allocation in the Lake Victoria Basin

Joseph W. Ssennyonga

INTRODUCTION

The household is not always a single decision-making unit (Hill, 1975; Guyer, 1986; Peters, 1986), so it is not always appropriate to consider it the basic production unit. Recent work has focused on intrahousehold inequality as one reason why households are not a single unit (Haddad & Kanbur, 1990; Thomas, 1989), but little attention has been paid to wives' unequal access to resources in polygynous unions as a reason. Intrahousehold bargaining, for example, is cast almost exclusively in terms of the dyadic relations between husband and wife (Jones, 1986; Guyer, 1986). However, there are also important intra-uxorial factors that bring about unequal ownership and control of resources. These neglected factors are the major focus of this paper.

Many societies use the temporal order in which wives are married to a single spouse as a basis for allocating resources. Another criterion is the number of surviving male children born to a woman. Favoritism, though difficult to establish, is also an important determinant of resource allocation to wives. Theoretically, a wife's education could also be used as a basis for allocating resources such as businesses that require literacy.

This chapter presents empirical data showing how uxorial rank is used as a criterion for allocating resources to wives in polygynous unions and how this resource-allocation system affects the offspring. It goes further to analyze the human ecological advantages of this resource allocation system and how change in the human ecology of the two regions is affecting polygyny itself and the socioeconomic status of wives and their offspring. A case in point is educational attainment, which is increasingly recognized as a powerful catalyst for change because of its dual role as a vehicle for technological change and as a criterion for economic reward. Would one, for example, expect junior wives with far higher educational attainment than senior wives to accept a resource-allocation system based on uxorial seniority? Other trade-offs generated by forces of development are also examined.

The family institutions and resource allocation system discussed are those of the Luo, a Nilotic people inhabiting the Lake Victoria Basin in Kenya, who number about three million. The data were collected from two field sites south of the Nyanza Gulf, Rusinga Island and Lambwe Valley. These sites are inhabited mostly by the Luo-Basuba, originally a Bantu speaking people from Uganda and Tanzania, who, since the introduction of colonialism, have been gradually absorbed both linguistically and culturally (Ayot, 1979).

However, the material presented is not from a single study designed to investigate polygyny and resource allocation. It is distilled from several studies carried out with a view to enhancing the social acceptability, economic viability, and sustainability of integrated tick and tsetse vector-management technologies being developed at the International Centre of Insect Physiology and Ecology. Partly because of this piecing together of several studies, there are gaps in the information presented, especially on the incipient catalytic forces of change and the way it is impacting the resource-allocation system.

The chapter is organized into three major sections. The first section describes three major features of marriage that directly affect the resource allocation system. The second section presents statistical data on the distribution of resources by rank of wife. The third section discusses the implications of the resource allocation system for development in the study area.

PRINCIPAL CHARACTERISTICS AFFECTING THE RESOURCE ALLOCATION SYSTEMS

Prevalence of Polygyny

Polygyny is prevalent in the Lake Victoria Basin. For example, a 1984 survey shows that the percentages of currently married women in polygynous unions are thirty-eight, forty-seven, and forty-one for Kisumu, Siaya, and South Nyanza districts respectively (Republic of Kenya, 1986). A 1987 survey on Rusinga Island provides higher ratios: 34 percent of the married men and 56 percent of the women are living in polygynous unions. The number of polygynous marriages appears to increase with men's age. For example, the percentage of married men in polygynous unions is highest (59%) for the oldest men (homestead heads), intermediate (18%) for their younger brothers, and lowest (10%) for their sons (Ssennyonga, forthcoming).

Widening Age Gap between a Man and Subsequent Wives

A notable feature in the Lake Victoria Basin is the widening gap between the mean ages of a man and each of his subsequent wives. The data presented in Figure 13.1 show that whereas a man's mean age rises at each subsequent marriage, that of his later wives declines, hence the widening gap in the age of a man and his

Figure 13.1
Mean Age at Marriage of Polygynous Men and Their Wives

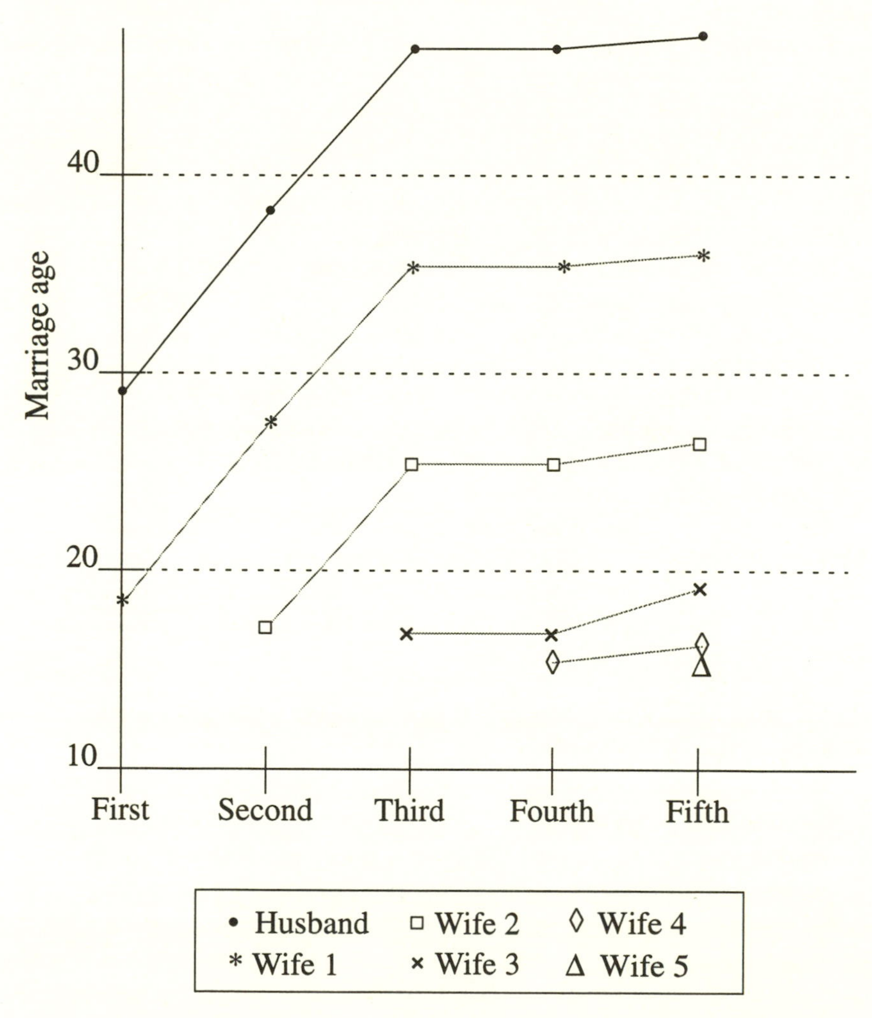

later wives. As can be noted, the mean age of a man marrying his fifth wife is forty-eight years, while that of his bride is about fifteen years. There is also a parallel widening gap between the ages of older and younger cowives. The 1984 survey provides corroborating evidence that girls marry early in the Lake Victoria Basin. For example, the percentages of girls under fifteen marrying for the first time are nineteen, twenty-four, and twenty-six for Kisumu, Siaya, and South Nyanza districts respectively. For those aged fifteen to seventeen years, the percentages are thirty-nine, forty, and forty-five for the same districts. These findings are in conformity with the cultural norm that each subsequent wife should be younger than any of the wives already married to the husband. The data are also consistent with demographers' generalizations associating high rates of polygyny with early marriage of girls (Lesthaeghe, 1984).

The Levirate

The wide gap in the ages of male and female spouses inevitably creates a large number of widows, many of whom are in their prime. The levirate, the marriage of the widow to the brother of the deceased husband, is a traditional arrangement that partly solves this problem. A survey of 170 homesteads on Rusinga Island shows that 32 percent of homesteads have at least one widow, of whom 79.6 percent are remarried, 63 percent of them to the brothers of their dead husbands. It is also legitimate for one of the cousins, *jalibamba*, of the deceased husband to remarry the widow (11.1% in this sample). In rare instances (1.8% in this sample), one of the sons of the dead man may marry any of his father's widows except his own mother. If the man marrying the widow is not yet married, he must marry a woman of his own as well, a custom that reinforces the practice of polygyny. If he is already married, he must first consult his wife, who is entitled to ascertain the widow's character.

If the widow loses a child before her remarriage, none of her husband's relatives may remarry her. Instead, a stranger, *jakowiny*, usually a man of inferior status or one believed to be bewitched, is sought and sometimes induced with a payment to remarry the widow. In the Rusinga sample, 3.7 percent of the women are remarried to strangers.

Of the 20 percent of widows who are not remarried, 14.8 percent declined to do so because of their Christian faith; one claimed she had promised her late husband not to remarry; four said they remained unmarried because of old age; one was still breast-feeding; while another was waiting for the funeral rituals to be performed in full (see Table 13.1).

Table 13.1
Relationship Between Deceased and Current Husbands of Remarried Widows, Rusinga Island

Relationship to deceased husband	Number	%
Brother	34	63.0
Cousin	6	11.1
Son	1	1.8
No relation	2	3.7
Widow is not remarried	11	20.4

Note: N = 54.

RANK ORDER AND THE SPATIAL ECOLOGY OF THE HOMESTEAD

Directly facing the gate to the Luo homestead, *dala*, is the house, *ot*, of the first or only wife. To its right is the house of the second wife, to its left is the third wife's house. Houses of subsequent wives are likewise erected on alternate sides of the first wife's house. In the past, a man used to build for himself a separate house, *abila*, in the middle of the compound, where he received and entertained, in particular male visitors. Each wife served food to him and other children from the homestead, thereby giving all children access to an adequate diet. Occasionally, he also slept in the *abila*, but, with its virtual disappearance, men sleep in rotation among their wives' houses (see Figure 13.2).

Figure 13.2
Spatial Ecology of a Luo Homestead

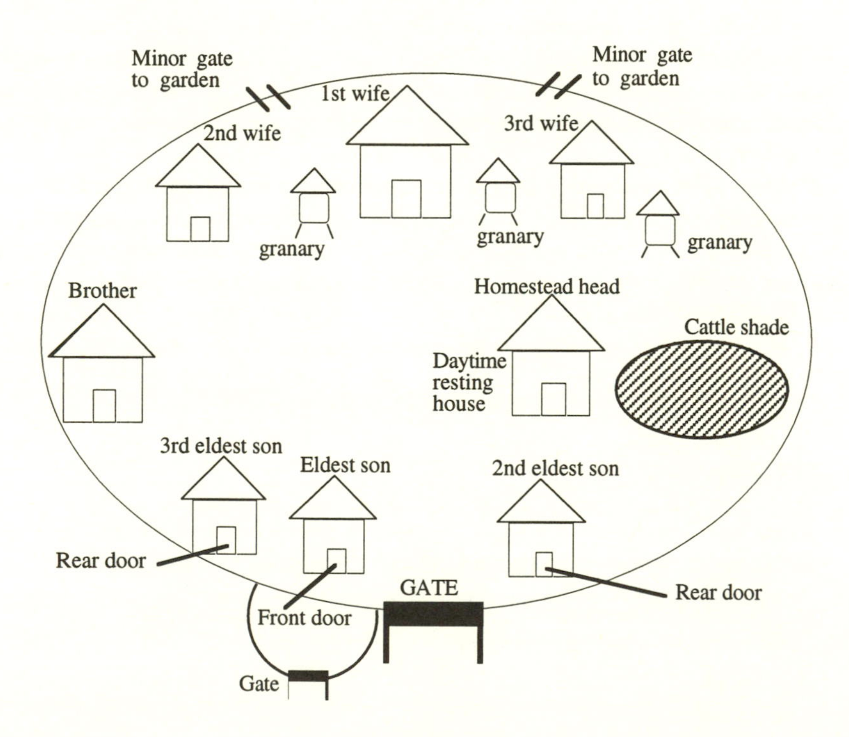

A wife's house is not inherited by her husband at her death, so he cannot allocate it to another wife. Her children and grandchildren can continue living in it up to the time they establish their own separate houses. Subsequently, her married daughters and agnates can stay in it when they come for short visits.

Sons' houses are also erected in order of rank. The eldest son builds his boyhood house, *simba*, by the right side of the gate; the second-eldest son erects his on the left side of the gate. Subsequent sons build their boyhood houses on alternate sides of the gate in line with their natal rank regardless of their mothers' ranks. Sons also establish their own homesteads according to the same seniority rank order. Thus, the eldest son should be the first to move out of his boyhood hut and set up his own homestead elsewhere, on one of the land plots allocated to his mother. But, with rising population pressure, it is increasingly becoming difficult, and sometimes impossible, for a man to allocate land even to the first son. Under these circumstances, sons are now transforming their boyhood houses into adult homes by turning the back of the house into the front and erecting a semicircular fence in front of the new home, with a main gate (see Figure 13.2)

Wife's Rank and Quality of House

Besides being symbolized by positioning, uxorial rank is also reflected in the size and function of a house. For example, the first wife's house is the largest and has unique functions; it is the venue where conflicts are settled and where the corpse of the homestead head lies in state before being buried in the courtyard in front of it. The introduction of new construction technology, in particular new building materials, has added a new mark of status differentiation among cowives. Uxorial rank is also reflected in the quality and value of the house a wife is allocated. Such is the concern for the preservation of this symbolism that if a son of the second or lower-rank wife wishes to build a good house for his mother, he must ensure that the first wife's house is of better quality, upgrading it or building her a new one if necessary, before proceeding to build one for his mother. He may not build a good-quality house for himself before building one for his mother.

Table 13.2
Type of House and Aggregated Money Values by Rank of Wife

Rank	No. of Women	Type of House			Total Value all Types	Mean House Value
		Temporary	Semipermanent	Permanent		
First	97	419,020	35,1728	859,100	1,629,848	16, 803
Second	93	459,200	203,632	343,640	1,006,472	10,822
Third	38	200,900	37,024	171,820	409,744	10,783
Fourth	10	51,660	18,512	0	70,172	7,017
Fifth	2	11,480	0	0	11,480	5,740
Mean		5,740	18,512	171,820		

In order to test whether this norm holds in reality, we collected information on 240 houses in Lambwe Valley in 1992. Houses are classified and defined as follows. A temporary house is built of mud and wattle walls and covered with a grass thatched roof. A semipermanent house has mud and wattle walls and a roof covered with corrugated iron sheets. A permanent house is built of brick walls and a roof covered with iron sheets or tiles. In order to compare the values of these different types of house, we worked with two professional builders to estimate the cash value of eighteen houses: seven temporary, seven semipermanent, and four permanent. The mean values were as follows: K.Sh. 5,740 for a temporary house,

K.Sh.18,512 for a semipermanent house, and K.Sh.171,820 for a permanent one. (US$ 1 = K.Sh. 36.00 in December, 1992.)

Using these estimates, we assigned cash values to all the houses, as shown in Table 13.2. The mean values for the various types of houses by rank of wife, shown in the last column, support the hypothesis that rank of a wife is reflected in the quality of the house allocated to her. For example, the mean value of a house of a first wife, at K.Sh. 16,803, is 1.55 times greater than that of a second wife, K.Sh. 10,822, and 2.39 times greater than that of a fourth wife, K.Sh. 7,017.

Wife's Rank and Allocated Land

Luo traditional land ownership and transactions are regulated by legal conventions embedded in a patrilineal system. Three features of this system are of importance to our argument. The first is the localization of lineages—that is, all members of the lineage reside in one contiguous territory. The second is ownership of lineage territory, in particular land, by the lineage as a corporate entity. The third is exogamy—that is, members of one lineage must marry spouses from another lineage. In this case, it is the men who bring in women from other lineages. In order to stop land being passed on through marriage to men of alien lineages, land is passed on through males only.

Women gain access to land through their husbands' marriages; a man has the obligation to allocate at least one plot of arable land to each wife, which will be inherited by the wives' sons. The rule states a man should give preference to the first wife by allocating to her the largest share of prime land, regardless of whether she has any children. Some informants report that a man allocates land to subsequent wives as he wishes, without taking rank or number of sons into account. Other informants hold the contrary view, that the share and quality of land allocated to junior wives must be in line with their rank and number of sons. Be that as it may, the data presented in Table 13.3 show that the amount of land allocated rises with wife's rank. Information on number of male children would have enabled us to determine differential association between land and rank, on the one

Table 13.3
Allocation of Land by Rank of Wife, Rusinga Island

Rank of Wife	No. of Women[a]	Mean Size of Land (in acres)[b]
First	85	4.3
Second	87	3.6
Third	28	2.6
Fourth	11	2.3
Fifth	3	2.7

[a] Only wives of living polygynous heads of homesteads are recorded.
[b] Mean values are calculated from aggregations of scattered land plots

hand, and land and number of sons, on the other. Unfortunately, such information was not compiled.

Wife's Rank and Access to Livestock

Livestock, like land, is passed on through male members of the lineage. Ownership and management, especially of large stock, are vested in the homestead head. A man must allocate cattle to each of his wives, but they do not acquire disposal rights. A man must give cattle to his son to pay bridewealth. A man also allocates livestock either directly to his son or through his wife after the son is married, but the son does not have full control of the cattle until after setting up his own homestead. If women or sons buy cattle, they have ownership over it but must seek the permission of the homestead head before selling or farming it out. But wives have full control over poultry and dairy products, which they can sell without informing their husband.

The homestead head applies the same criteria in allocating livestock to his wives as he does for land. Field data from Rusinga Island confirm this pattern, with mean number of heads of cattle allocated highest for the first wife and declining as rank drops (see Table 13.4). For example, the mean number of cattle is three for the third wife and one for the fourth.

Table 13.4
Allotment of Cattle by Rank of Wife, Rusinga Island

	Mean Number of Female Cattle Allotted		
Rank of wife	Immature	Calving	Total
First	1	5	6
Second	1	2	3
Third	2	1	3
Fourth	1	0	1

Wife's Rank and Resource Management Roles

In this context, management is defined as an economic resource that comprises technical functions such as planning, directing, supervision, coordination, control and motivation, all of which are associated with the administration of resources (Abercrombie, Hill, & Turner, 1984; Mullins, 1991). In our case, the resources are space for building a house, house, land, and livestock. Married women perform several management tasks.

The first wife of the homestead head assumes the role of the homestead head if her husband dies before any of his sons is judged mature enough to take over. She may sell or allocate livestock without consulting anyone. She can also allocate land, but she would have to consult with the male agnates of her deceased husband before selling it. She is responsible for resolving conflicts and enforcing discipline at the homestead. Other categories of widows do not have such power. However, wives of migrant husbands, including the first wife of the homestead head, can sell or dispose of only small stock, not cattle, and cannot allocate or dispose of land without being authorized by their husbands. Ssennyonga and Mungai (1992) report that 22.2 percent of homesteads in Lambwe Valley (n = 311) are headed by women, 70 percent of them widows of deceased homestead heads and 30 percent of them wives of migrant homestead heads. If the wives of deceased or migrant sons and brothers of homestead heads were to be included, the proportion of female headed households would be much higher. Homestead heads make up only 20 percent of the employed workforce, 93 percent of whom live away from home. Senior wives of migrant husbands therefore play a key role in managing the homestead and resources therein.

Educational Attainment versus Uxorial Rank

Western education emphasizes individualism, competition, and achievement as hallmarks of upward mobility. Grades at examinations provide the basis for recruitment into the highly competitive labor market and access to associated benefits. Education is therefore widely used as a criterion for regulating access to resources. It is also the principal medium for promoting progress through science and technology and a major force for challenging traditional values and social order.

Figure 13.3
Mean Years of Education for Husband and Wives by Rank

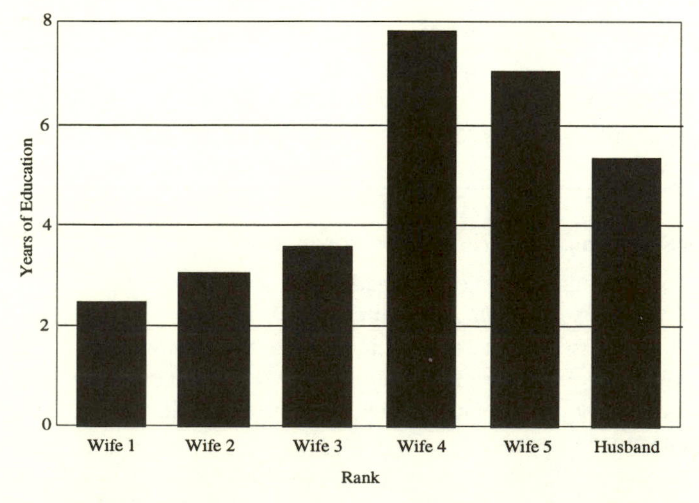

In the three areas studied, there is an inverse relationship between a wife's rank and her educational attainment (see Figure 13.3). For example, the mean years of education attained by first wives is the lowest, 2.2 years, while those for fourth and fifth wives are 7.8 and 6.9 respectively. Although the low number of fourth and fifth wives may have somewhat inflated the means for those two ranks, it is very clear that they have a much higher educational attainment, higher in fact than their husbands.

DISCUSSION

This chapter has thus far used descriptive statistics to portray the resource-allocation system in highly polygynous unions in the Lake Victoria Basin without offering an explanation for its institutional rationality. This section addresses this issue from two perspectives. First, the rationale of polygyny and the associated resource allocation system are analyzed from the viewpoint of human ecology, since the resources discussed are exploited to meet basic survival needs of the family and community in question. This is not to deny these practices their symbolic value, but to emphasize their utilitarian and rational dimensions. This, too, does not imply that all individuals or social groups in the community derive benefits equitably.

Second, some of the major forces of change exerting pressure on polygyny and its associated resource allocation system are also highlighted, albeit with the aid of fragmentary evidence. The purpose of this discussion is to throw into relief a whole new set of research questions for which empirical studies must provide the answers.

The Ecological Basis for Polygyny and Uxorial Rank as a Criterion for Resource Allocation

In the absence of both motor and animal draught power, human labor was the most critical factor of production in the Lake Victoria Basin. In the absence of a labor market, the family, the basic production unit, had to reproduce its own labor. Given a division of labor in which males were principally engaged in livestock rearing and fishing, while women were involved primarily in crop production, and given the absence of a surplus extracting center, agricultural productivity was determined primarily by Chayanov's law (1966): Productivity per worker rises with the dependency ratio up to an optimal level, after which it drops. Given the patrilineal system, under which members of one lineage lay claim to and live in a common territory in which land and livestock are passed on from one generation to another through male members, who also must marry women from outside their lineage, the strategy of marrying several women would not only enhance the prospect of achieving greater acreage and more grain, it would also promote the reproduction of more labor. The viability of this strategy also depended on the maintenance of a favorable man/land ratio, which was the case in the study area. In a noncentralized society without a standing army or institutionalized warrior age grades, families had to ensure their own security. The elaborate residential arrangements and resource transfer to the filial generation were designed to retain male progeny for a prolonged period at the homestead to provide security.

Demographers have demonstrated that while high polygyny is associated with early female marriage and fast remarriage, it lowers age-specific marital fertility in three ways. First, polygyny facilitates prolonged lactation and postpartum abstinence, each of which depresses fertility on its own. Second, the wide gap between younger wives and an older husband reduces the monthly probability of conception. Third, infertile wives are often divorced and remarried as second or third wives. These three mechanisms work in combination to produce a synergy that depresses fertility in traditional societies (Page & Lesthaeghe, 1981; Lesthaeghe, 1984).

In order to achieve high polygyny and prolonged retention of male progeny at the homestead, two additional strategies had to be adopted. It is difficult for a society to maintain high polygyny over time by relying on importing women from neighboring societies. The best solution to this problem is to enforce early marriage for girls and to raise age at first marriage for men. Maintaining late marriage for men was facilitated by the arrangement whereby fathers controlled the essential resources for setting up a marital union—land, livestock, and even space for building a house.

In the past, using uxorial rank as a basis for allocating resources to wives made sense in that, on average, older wives would have a higher mean number of surviving progeny. Giving more management roles and prestige to older women was a mechanism for icing the bitter pill of having to compete with younger wives for the same man. Furthermore, in the past, one would presume that older wives had more knowledge and experience in resource management. But the battery of changes that has been introduced during the past hundred years has eroded most of the advantages outlined. Highlights of these changes follow.

Forces of Change Exerting Pressure on Polygyny and Its Associated Resource-Allocation System

Prevalence of polygyny. There are no reliable quantitative data to show whether and where polygyny is declining, but statements by informants indicate that there may be a decline in this practice. Circumstantial evidence can be adduced from the field studies cited in this chapter, which show that for land-hungry Rusinga Island, the mean number of wives per married man is 1.5 (range = 4), whereas the mean is close to 3 (range = 8) for the land-rich Lambwe Valley. Figures on land and stock holding also show much higher sizes for Lambwe Valley. But, even for Lambwe Valley, the introduction of animal draught power led to a rapidly raising male participation rate in agriculture, thereby undermining the economic basis for marrying several wives. Furthermore, the combined impact of the escalating cost of raising children and the introduction of formal state security agencies such as army and police are making it superfluous to keep many sons at the homestead.

Marriage age. The data presented on age at first marriage for girls suggest that it has not risen, possibly because their enrollment at secondary and tertiary levels is still low. If increased enrollment at higher educational levels raises girls' age at first marriage, a major support for high polygyny will have been removed.

Widow remarriage. Field data show that almost 20 percent of widows are not remarried because of factors associated with change. In addition, informants talk of escalating problems for young widows as brothers of deceased husbands increasingly take them over only as sexual partners and fail to support them and their children because of rising economic problems. The new, dreaded AIDS menace is also likely to reduce the frequency of widow remarriage, if letters in newspaper readers' columns are any indication. Finally, as has been shown, Christianity and western values are also beginning to erode the practice of widow remarriage.

Homestead ecology. Worsening land scarcity is making it difficult for sons to establish new homesteads outside their parents' homesteads. At the same time, the space at the homestead can accommodate a limited number of sons' houses, especially if some opt for polygyny. As has been shown, demographic pressure is already forcing modification in the homestead ecology.

Rank and house. Innovations in house construction technology—notably the use of bricks, corrugated iron sheets, and tiles—and the escalation in house construction costs are incompatible with the traditional practice of abandoning or destroying a wife's house at her death. Younger professional or business wives are beginning to press for good quality houses ahead of senior wives. One of the emerging solutions is to settle such young wives away from the homestead and then build good houses for them, without appearing to violate the rules.

Sons are also showing signs of disaffection for the traditional setup for two reasons. First, with the acquisition of nuclear family values, sons increasingly resent having to put up houses for other wives of their father. Second, sons are beginning to challenge the norm of having to abandon their dead mother's house, especially if it is a high cost one.

Education and polygyny. An inescapable question emerging from the data on education is why young, educated, and or even employed women would accept being married as a second, third, or fourth wife to an older man who may even have an education inferior to theirs? This question implicitly assumes an inverse linear relationship between girls' education and polygyny, which may not necessarily be the case. On the one hand, it might be that female education, especially at tertiary levels, will, by virtue of keeping girls longer at school and instilling in them western values of individualism, competition, and nuclear family, reduce the frequency of polygyny. However, this is likely to be a long-term process; in the short and medium runs, given the fact that age at graduation from secondary school is eighteen years and that less than half of girls complete secondary education, age at first marriage may remain low, supporting one of the conditions of polygyny.

A writer in the Nairobi *Daily Nation* of December 26, 1993, summarized three major arguments advanced in defense of polygyny by well-educated and salaried young women attending a recent international women's conference. They pointed out that a middle aged woman may find it preferable to accept a young cowife rather than risk being divorced by a man who needs a more active sexual life than the older woman is capable of providing. More radically, one young woman took the role of the younger cowife and put it this way: "Why should the first wife feel she is entitled to deny me the man? I could also say the older woman married the man I ought to have married." The third argument is that good men are rare in the world and women should learn to share the few men there are, since they eventually share them anyway.

Regardless of their logical merit, these are the viewpoints of at least some well educated and salaried young women. One wonders if women in this mold would accept the traditional resource allocation system based on uxorial rank. Probably not. They would most likely embrace polygyny, but under renegotiated terms.

Management roles. The criticality of management, though long recognized in industry, is only beginning to receive due attention in agricultural research and development. A case in point is a recent long-term study that shows that the top one-third of farmers in the Philippines have achieved rice yields higher than those of national research institutes and, more surprisingly, than even those of the International Rice Research Institute (IRRI). The authors, attributing this phenomenal performance mainly to better management, wrote, "Farmers who have the ability to learn about the new technologies, discriminate among technologies offered to them by the research system, adapt the technologies to their particular environmental conditions and provide supervision input to ensure the appropriate application of the technology" (Pingali et al., 1990, cited in Kenmore, 1991, p. 5).

Given high male outmigration, the fact that senior wives, who have a mean number of just over two years of education, take up the major managerial roles in the absence of their husbands may be imposing a severe limitation to resources development. It may largely explain the relative stagnation of the agricultural sector and overall development in the Lake Victoria Basin.

There are, however, areas of incipient change, as young wives are beginning to play a more significant role in new technologies. I have observed that young wives play a bigger role in the new horticultural irrigation enterprises in the Lake Victoria Basin. An ongoing study I am conducting in Lambwe Valley will provide information on how education and rank are associated with wives' participation in local organizations and community based tsetse control. More evidence is needed to document this process.

CONCLUDING REMARKS

This chapter has addressed three issues. First, using descriptive statistics, it has examined the resource allocation system based on uxorial rank prevalent in the Lake Victoria Basin. It has shown the institutional rationality of the resource allocation system by relating it to the dynamics of polygyny itself (prevalence, early female marriage, and the levirate). Second, it has argued that the resource allocation system and the form of polygyny in which it is embedded had, in the past, considerable human ecological advantages. Third, it has pinpointed the battery of change that has been put in motion during the past hundred years and that is gradually gaining momentum and, in the process, eroding the institutional rationality of high polygyny, its ancillary institutions, and their inherent human ecological advantages.

However, the quality of evidence presented in support of these propositions is variable. It is strong for the first one, weak for the second one, and even weaker for the third one. Because of the limited data available, one can only speculate about future trends.

In the short and medium terms, high polygyny and its associated resource allocation system will most likely persist despite the erosion of its ecological basis. In the long-term, however, high polygyny and the resource allocation system will inevitably collapse under the weight of causally interrelated factors, some of which deserve mention.

Demographic pressure on land will progressively make it impossible for a man to allocate land outside the homestead for all his sons to build their own homes. Consequently, the rules governing the allocation of residential space will have to change. Furthermore, the high cost of rearing children will make it virtually impossible for a single male breadwinner to feed, clothe, educate, and provide health care to a large number of progeny from several wives.

The levirate, a traditional solution to the problem of the high ratio of widows that results from the wide age gap between male and female spouses, will increasingly become obsolete, mainly because of economic strains, the internalization of western values, and possibly the menace of AIDS.

New house-construction technology has introduced a dimension of permanence and a status symbol that are incompatible with the traditional practice of abandoning or destroying a wife's house at her death. Similarly, the new values associated with the nuclear family promote the ideal of a son inheriting his father's house, especially if it is a high-cost structure.

Increased educational attainment by girls will gradually raise age at first marriage and this will, ipso facto, reduce the frequency of high polygyny. If this is accompanied by the espousal of western values by a significant section of women, there may be negative multiplier effects on polygyny and its associated resource allocation system. But the reported viewpoints of well educated women who staunchly support polygyny serve warning that higher educational attainment may not necessarily have a linear relationship with polygyny.

Finally, there is need to undertake a systematic study whose object is to test formally the validity of the propositions outlined in the last two sections of this chapter. The implications of the findings of a study of this sort are bound to be vital for the family, the socioeconomic status of women and their offspring, and the overall development in the Lake Victoria Basin.

REFERENCES

Abercrombie, N., Hill, S., and Turner, B. (1984). *Dictionary of sociology*. Harmondsworth, England: Penguin Books.

Ayot, H. O. (1979). *History of the Luo-Abasuba of Western Kenya*. Nairobi: Kenya Literature Bureau.

Chayanov, A. V. (1966). *The theory of peasant economy*. Homewood, IL: Irwin.

Guyer, J. I. (1986). Intra-households processes and farming systems research: Perspectives from anthropology. In J. L. Moock (Ed.), *Understanding Africa's rural households and farming systems* (pp. 92–104). Boulder: Westview Press.

Haddad, L., & Kanbur, R. (1990). How serious is the neglect of intra-household inequality? *Economic Journal, 100*, 402, 866–881. Washington, DC: International Food Policy Research Institute.

Handwerker, W. P. (1986). *An anthropological critique of the demographic transition theory*. Boulder: Westview.

Hill, P. (1975). West African farming household. In J. Goody (Ed.), *Changing social structure in Ghana: Essays in the comparative sociology of a new state and old tradition* (pp. 119–136). London: International African Institute.

Jones, C. W. (1986). Intra-household bargaining in response to the introduction of new crops: A case study from north Cameroon. In J. L. Moock (Ed.), *Understanding Africa's rural households and farming systems* (pp.105–123). Boulder: Westview Press.

Kenmore, P. E. (1991). *Indonesia's integrated pest management—A model for Asia*. Manila: FAO Rice IPC Programme.

Lesthaeghe, R. (1984). *Fertility and its proximate determinants in sub-Saharan Africa: The record of the 1960s and 1970s* (Seminar on Integrating Proximate Determinants into the Analysis of Fertility Levels and Trends). Liege, Belgium: International Union for the Scientific Study of Population.

Mullins, L. (1991). *Management and organisational behavior* (2nd ed.). London: Pitman Publishing.

Page, H. J., & Lesthaeghe, R. (Eds.). (1981). *Child-spacing in tropical Africa: Traditions and change*. New York: Academic Press.

Peters, P. E. (1986). Household management in Botswana: Cattle, crops and wage labour. In J. L. Moock (Ed.), *Understanding Africa's rural households and farming systems* (pp. 133–154). Boulder: Westview Press.

Republic of Kenya (1986). *Kenya contraceptive prevalence survey* (Provincial report, Central Bureau of Statistics). Nairobi: Government Printer.

Ssennyonga, J. W. (forthcoming). Socioeconomic aspects of developing methods of controlling ticks: Rusinga case study. In P. Okeyo (Ed.), *Social science interface research at the ICIPE. Case Studies from Western Kenya*. Nairobi: ICIPE Science Press.

Ssennyonga, J. W., & Mungai, P. (1992). *The development of a sampling frame for selecting participating farmers* (Report No. 2). Submitted to the Natural Resources Institute, London.

Thomas, D. (1989). *Intra-household resource allocation: An inferential approach*. Unpublished paper, Yale University.

14

Changing Women's Rights over Property in Western Kenya

Ruth Nasimiyu

Control over labor is crucial to all social formations, although the mechanisms to accomplish control in various communities differs. Among the Luyia of western Kenya, marriage solemnized through the payment of bridewealth gave male elders unquestioned access to the labor of wives and children. Control over women's reproductive capacity strengthened male elders' ability to control other forms of labor. This control was exercised through the rules of precolonial property inheritance and reinforced by new land tenure systems established during the colonial era. Women were far from men's equals during the precolonial era. Nevertheless, the economic policies of colonialism resulted in increased inequalities between men and women.

MODES OF APPROPRIATION AND CONTROL OVER FEMALE AND CHILD LABOR

At the beginning of the twentieth century the Luyia family was an economically self-sufficient unit. The wife and husband, children, and other dependents contributed to the maintenance of the family group by performing tasks allocated within the household through a traditional gender division of labor. Thus, the household fulfilled the dual function of production and reproduction (see Wandibba, this volume).

Among the Luyia, land was never owned in the western sense of the word. In fact, the concept of ownership with reference to land was unknown. Land was communal property. While among communities such as the Luyia with patrilineal African traditions "the power of allocation was not equivalent to ownership" (Okoth-Ogendo, 1978, p. 134), land use and administration were vested in clan elders, who were usually male. The allocation of land to individual members of the clan or lineage was determined by the culture of individual kinship/clan or lineage groups. But in practical terms, the family plot was not owned by the family per se. Ownership of the family plot finally passed into exclusive ownership by the head of the family because the bulk of important land use and disposal capabilities lay in the hands of individual male household heads. Women used land but never controlled it.

Many scholars and policy makers have incorrectly assumed that communal possession of the means of production implies that there is no basis for denying any family member free access. However, as Hindess and Hirst (1975) point out, elders and other adult men played a crucial role in the control of the labor process in patrilineal communal land systems, coordinating and supervising the labor of persons ranked below them in the lineage. Okoth-Ogendo (1978) argues that, in the precolonial context, this economic form provided the basis for the exercise of political authority as well as the transmission of social and technical information from one generation to the next. Thus, intrahousehold exploitation and inequality were a reality, and male control over female and child labor was facilitated by male control over the means of production, land, and cattle.

Women's use of land was nevertheless guaranteed within this patriarchal system. Achola Pala (1976, p. 20) suggests that subsistence production made it "beneficial to the family and village community for women to realize their land and livestock rights." Precolonial communal systems thus recognized women's crucial contributions to food production and provided land for that activity. This contributed significantly to women's economic security and stability in land use rights, at the same time that these rights depended on their roles as wives and mothers and were allocated and controlled by men.

The Luyia of Western Province are a patrilineal community.[1] Traditionally, the power of land use administration was conferred on male elders (*omwami we lichabe* among the Bukusu and *liguru* among the Maragoli and other Luyia communities in what are now Kakamega and Vihiga District). Land was strictly allocated to adult males of the clan or lineage, and rights passed inalienably from father to son (Committee on Native Land Tenure in the North Kavirondo Reserve, 1930, pp. 4–5).[2] Although land continued to be treated as communal property, the administration of parcels allocated to individual households for use was the responsibility of men in their capacity as heads of households. All rights in land were derived from clan membership and inheritance.

Male elders exercised considerable control over both land and cattle, controlling women's access to both (Wagner, 1970). Male elders' control over land included uncultivated land, which was considered the clan's area for possible future expansion. Male elders consequently enjoyed powerful status in Abaluyia society. In addition, C. W. Hobley (1967, p. 279) explained, "each wife in an African family usually has dedicated to her particular use a certain number of cattle, they are not her property, but she has the sole disposal of their milk for use of her children." A woman's cattle rights were usually usufructuary and therefore limited to consumption.

Among the Luyia, each man was allocated a plot from the communal farmland. The man, in turn, divided his plot into strips according to the number of wives he had. In a monogamous home, the piece allocated to a man was automatically cultivated by his wife (see also Ssennyonga, this volume). Again, land was not allocated to women as individuals by clan elders, but through their husbands. Wagner described the allotment of land among wives in precolonial times as follows: "In a polygamous family each wife is apportioned a separate field, the *Omulimi gwa guga* [lands of the grandfather] usually being allotted to the great or senior wife and plots of decreasing size to the junior wives, although adjustments would later be made in accordance with the number of children in each house (Wagner, 1970, vol. 2, p. 86)."[3]

Under this system, a woman's security of tenure was enhanced by the fact that she was entitled, as a wife, to a parcel of land over which she had paramount authority as a cultivator. A woman could also lend out portions of her land to other women who needed to plant potatoes, sorghum, green peas, eleusine, and simsim. Women had absolute control over the disposal of such crops, which enabled them to produce surplus grain which they might not declare to their husbands. This was a clear case of female solidarity, but it required extra labor. As one elderly female informant (seventy-two years old) stated, "Only ambitious, hardworking women managed to cope with additional labor responsibilities."[4] Borrowing land was a survival strategy which enabled Abaluyia women to establish some control over their own labor and thus the disposal of surplus grain. This survival strategy worked well for Bukusu women, for whom land was plentiful; it was less effective in the Maragoli and Bunyore regions because of intense population pressure that began before the twentieth century.

In a polygynous Abaluyia family, each wife eventually established a separate household which was the primary unit of production. The work group within the household consisted of a woman and her children, with occasional support from her husband and extended relations. Children in a polygynous family were grouped with their mothers; they ate and also shared in the house and garden work of their mother's household (see also Ssennyonga, this volume). Among the Bukusu, cowives often cultivated their gardens jointly.[5] Women in polygynous households had several advantages: "the polygamous household may offer women a basis for solidarity and task-sharing. At the household level, cowives cooperate to organize production, consumption and child care. Although friction between co-wives is widely reported, many studies stress the economic and political advantages of polygamy, including the autonomy made possible by shared responsibility (Stamp, 1989, p. 77)."[6]

Additional wives and offspring were valued not only by their husbands, for the extra labor they provided, but by other women. Polygyny was therefore encouraged by both men and women. Additional labor was the basic means of increasing production. Wealth, which was defined in terms of cattle, wives, and numerous children, was a fundamental proof of political leadership and prestige. Among the Luyia, the desire for numerous children was summarized in the saying, "Where there are many children, there will always be plenty of food" (Wagner, 1970, vol. 1, p. 47). Wives, argued Hay (1972), provided the economic surplus necessary for extensive entertaining and for acquiring a reputation for generosity. Thus, female and child labor enhanced the social status of male household heads.

Land-use allocation varied with a wife's work capacity. The size of the strip per wife depended on the industry of the woman who cultivated it. This meant that more industrious women got larger plots than those less so. Among the Luyia, a husband apportioned to his wife one or two fields to grow food crops on behalf of the household. The food crops from these fields were kept in the family store. The woman had limited disposal rights over these crops (Committee on Native Land Tenure in North Kavirondo, 1930; Wagner, 1970, vol. 2).

A man retained a certain number of plots for himself depending on the availability of labor. In rich households, additional labor was obtained from the extended family relations, friends, and communal labor (*ekitayi*). Payment for communal labor was usually in kind (in the form of beer and food parties). Communal labor from friends was based on reciprocal relationships. Only a rich man could afford to provide requisite elaborate entertainment at the end of a day's work when he engaged additional labor (see de Wolf, this volume).

In addition to the one or two fields apportioned to a wife by a husband, Abaluyia women had access to *libubi* (pl. *kamabubi*) and *likunda* (pl. *mwikunda*) fields. *Libubi* was a small field where individual women grew a variety of vegetables and sometimes tobacco. The size of *libubi* fields depended largely on the industry of individual women. One informant observed that "a hardworking woman could expand her *libubi* into a big plot. Her husband could not interfere as long a woman performed her work well. However, a large *libubi* created much work for a woman because she only worked on her *libubi* during her spare-time."[7] *Likunda* was a field that was usually established in the old kraal or homestead site. *Kamabubi* and *Mwikunda* fields belonged to women, and it was here that women exercised their complete authority as cultivators. Hence, the Committee on Land Tenure observed (1930, p. 7): "In the second place, a woman cultivates additional crops entirely by herself in which case she has the right of disposal of that produce although her husband may have helped her with the first clearing."

The location of the *libubi* provided strategic advantages to individual women. *Kamabubi* were close to the house (what are described as kitchen gardens in western societies). All household manure was deposited there. Hence, *kamabubi* fields were always the most fertile plots. Because of the close proximity of *kamabubi* fields to the house, women were able to work on them whenever they had the slightest opportunity. In these fields, women could easily combine and fulfill multiple tasks, especially domestic labor.

Each woman had her own separate grain stores. These included *kitera*, the reserve store of grain, which was drawn upon only in times of shortage; *ekiiagi*, the household foodstore for daily use; and *tsinzoka*, large pots standing five or six feet high where grain was stored over which the woman had the right of disposal (Committee on Native Land Tenure in North Kavirondo, 1930). Produce from *kamabubi* and *mwikunda* fields were stored in *tsinzoka*. Thus, the existence of *kamabubi* fields enabled women, especially industrious women, to establish some control over their labor and the disposal of the surplus grain. For example, bananas were usually grown in *mwikunda* fields. Abaluyia women continue to dominate trading activities involving bananas and vegetables. In addition, as some informants reported, industrious women *barunda* (i.e., exchanged their surplus grain for chicken, goats or sheep) which they later exchanged for cattle.[8]

Women were at a disadvantage relative to men because accumulation of surplus was best held as cattle, a mechanism women could not control. Women who were able to accumulate cattle without their husbands' interference used them for the payment of their sons' bridewealth. Later, when schools were introduced, women sold their cattle to pay school fees for their sons and sometimes their daughters. Payment of bridewealth was the man's responsibility. Thus, women who accumulated cattle reduced men's burdens. In addition, husbands sometimes disposed of their wives' cattle without consulting them. Some men even used their wives' cattle to pay bridewealth for subsequent wives. This was the most oppressive mode of male appropriation of women's property. Women's limited access and control over valuable property such as cattle was a key means of social control and significantly contributed to their low economic status.

APPROPRIATION OF FEMALE AND CHILD LABOR

Mature girls of marriageable age were allocated land by their fathers to cultivate. But they had limited control over the products of their labor. The Committee on Native Land Tenure in North Kavirondo observed (1930, p.6): "When the girl grows up her father may allot to her some of his *mugunda* (land) to cultivate separately, but the produce must be taken to the family grain store. Should the girl wish to sell or barter any of it, she must get her father's permission."

Wagner (1970) writes that Bukusu girls were given their own gardens at the age of fourteen. The crops raised by them were stored in a special granary, which after their marriage were ceremoniously "opened" by their fathers-in-law and served to give them a start in their own household. Bukusu girls used to get married at the ages of eighteen to twenty-one years. The suggestion by Wagner that they used to be given strips of land at the age of fourteen years was probably inaccurate. Furthermore, girls did not dispose of the surplus from their strips of land. The produce from the girl's land was stored separately from the mother's. In case of famine, the father of the girl could exchange the girl's produce for an animal. Such animals were usually given names such as *Nasiaki* (granary). The animal acquired this way belonged to the father and not to the girl.

Although young men were also exploited by elders, they at least received a small share of what they produced. Bridewealth was always paid for them by their fathers, usually in cattle. Cattle were used because they were considered a better method of storing wealth derived from surplus grain. Cattle were the traditional bank, the main form of wealth recognized by Abaluyia society. As a result, ownership of cattle was restricted to the class of patriarchs, which placed male heads of households in a better position to control the labor of male dependents.[9]

The value of cattle, as a status symbol and measure of wealth, also represented, in the form of bridewealth, a measure of labor value provided by women and their reproductive capacity. The distribution of women was regulated through the payment of bridewealth. Large numbers of cattle were usually required for the bridewealth payment. To obtain the necessary cattle for bridewealth, young men had to work for male elders. Thus, control over marriage arrangements gave male elders the means to control the labor and appropriate the surplus value generated by male dependents. At the level of ideology, traditions required that a son show respect to his father, do his bidding, and fear him. However, behind these traditions were concrete relations of production, which had changed by the end of the nineteenth century to means of appropriation and exploitation. Ironically, the father's payment for his sons' bridewealth was produced by the whole family, but its disposal was determined by the father alone.

The payment of bridewealth was a form of labor compensation to the extended family of the girl. Cattle ownership determined the form of surplus appropriation because cattle owners resorted to a mechanism of cattle exchange or transfer to consolidate a relationship between two previously unrelated families (Depelchin, 1977). Consequently, domination of women and their subordination is more severe among cattle owning societies. The woman's labor contribution was central in any marriage arrangements. Every wealthy man in these societies was, and still is, a reflection of the successful appropriation of surplus labor value of women and children. Hay adds, "the nineteenth century descriptions of wealth and wealthy men reflect the labor value of women and not simply the ownership of livestock" (1976, p. 93–94).

The economic importance of women was the basis of polygamous marriages in western Kenya and elsewhere in Africa (see Ssennyonga, this volume).[10] Additional wives were considered a source of extra labor. They, and the children they would bear, were seen as a source of wealth, in the sense that they produced grain which could be exchanged for cattle, and reproduced daughters who, when married off, were also exchanged for cattle. The economic importance of women influenced a man's choice of a wife. Men would look for a wife who was, as one informant put it, "hard working and generally industrious."[11]

For a young man, marriage symbolized the beginning of a transformation period in which he attained the right to appropriate the labor and reproductive potential of others, initially that of his first wife. Men in most African societies were allocated land only at marriage. Among the Luyia, Wagner pointed out, "after a son has established his own household, the father gives him a 'cow for milk' and apportions to him a piece of land which his daughter-in-law may till" (1970, vol. 2, p. 48). There was a clear implication that a woman's participation was essential in proper land management (Rogers, 1979). Henn (1988, p. 10) argues that "before marriage, a man has no means of creating his own sphere of dependents, his labor and its products are controlled by the patriarch upon whom he depends." Through marriage, a man develops his own entourage of dependent wives and children, and he becomes a full-fledged member of the exploiting class (Henn, 1988). Men's appropriation of female and child labor increased their wealth and thus improved their social status in the society. The situation is different for women. According to Wagner, before an Abaluyia woman marries, her father (or his substitute) is her legal guardian. After marriage the guardianship is divided between the father and the husband (Wagner, 1970, vol. II).

The system of redistribution of the products of family labor discriminated against women and daughters. Laws of inheritance and property rights worked to their detriment. Henn (1988) points out that, on a lifetime basis, males appropriated more surplus labor than they provided as dependents of the patriarchal class. Indeed, as Molyneux (1977) argues, although young men were also exploited by elders, they at least received a small share of what they produced because their bridewealth was paid for by their fathers. But women, who were and still are the major producers, did not receive a share of what they produced. Henn underscores the differentiation in terms of young male and female exploitation in society when she states that "female dependence on patriarchs is ideologically defined as permanent and male dependence is temporarily limited to the early years of their life cycle. Thus, the female segment of the subordinate class is more thoroughly dominated and exploited than the male segment" (1988, p. 39).

It has been argued that women's limited access to the productive resources in society, combined with their lack of complete control over their own labor power, weakened their ability to accumulate wealth. In addition, the payment of bridewealth, a form of labor compensation to the extended family of the girl, further incapacitated women's ability to control their own labor. Indeed, the system of bridewealth legitimized male appropriation of female and child labor. Women's ability to accumulate was inhibited by their inability to inherit property and their lack of free access to productive resources. Clearly, in patrilineal and exogamous societies like the Luyia society, men had power over the fruits of women's and children's labor because patriarchal traditions gave them a privileged position over women and children. Male appropriation of female and child surplus labor value was therefore culturally defined and defended and translated into severe limitations on women's ability to accumulate property themselves.

LAWS OF INHERITANCE: WOMEN'S AND CHILDREN'S PROPERTY RIGHTS

Since the Luyia were a patrilineal and exogamous society, laws of inheritance of any form of property were largely defined along male lines of descent. The status of sons and daughters differed with regard to the inheritance of family property. When a man died his land was divided among his sons and not among his daughters.[12] A cow or a parcel of land was passed from father to sons and later to grandsons. This is what Wagner had observed in 1939 when he stated, "men had an upper hand in inheritance" (1970, vol. 1, p.30). Women were also inherited as if they were part and parcel of the property. Wagner states: "Claims to inheritance extend a) to the property of the deceased in livestock (cattle, goats, sheep), b) in land, c) in utensils of personal and domestic use (weapons, tools, implements and ornaments), and d) to the rights which the deceased possessed in respect of his wife or wives (the strength of having paid marriage cattle for them)" (1970, vol. 1, p. 84).

After the father's death, the sons of the senior wife (in polygynous families) may "inherit," that is, marry, the junior wife (Wagner, 1970, vol. 1). The payment of bridewealth provided the right to such inheritance. Furthermore, some women were inherited as if they were part of the deceased man's property, which reduced their ability to inherit property themselves.

The legal position of the wife was also inferior to that of the husband with regard to claims over her children. She had no ownership status whatsoever (Wagner, 1970). Children belonged to their father's clan. Therefore, payment of bridewealth helped to consolidate male authority over the wife and her offspring. It was also the basis of male control and appropriation of female and child labor. As Wagner argued:

> The low status of the wife with regard to property is paralleled by the fact that she has no rights over her children in her capacity as a mother. If the marriage is dissolved, even if entirely owing to the husband's fault, the wife can under no circumstances claim any of her children, in the sense that she would have a right to take them with her to her father's house or to her new husband and there bring them up. (Wagner, 1970, p. 46)

The system of patrilineal inheritance was also related to women's contribution and participation in rural economies. Among Abaluyia, the allocation and distribution of productive resources was influenced by the gender division of labor in society. Hence land arrangements recognized women's usufruct rights in land they were assigned to cultivate. But such allocation of property, like land and cattle, did not give the woman the right to inherit. It appears to have only affected the position of her male children. Land and cattle allocated to individuals were for the production of food for their households. However, property assigned to a particular wife—land, cattle, goats, sheep, and any moveables—was inherited by her sons. Indeed, property allocated to individual houses was protected by customary law which also recognized women's usufruct rights in land and cattle. Therefore, while inheritance was patrilineal, specific rights in the patrimony were transmitted through women, whose status as wives was important in determining the inheritance of their sons. Among Abaluyia, land cultivated by an individual woman was thus distributed to her sons. This system of inheritance encouraged subdivision of land. The colonial officials opposed this system, because it increased fragmentation and created uneconomical land units.

Among Abaluyia, the laws of inheritance and property rights follow the house–property complex (Goody & Buckley, 1973; see also Håkansson & LeVine, this volume).[13] The house–property complex recognized the fact that the sons of one woman, as opposed to sons of a cowife, might have specific rights connected with the distribution of that part of the husband's property that their mother herself has worked. The house–property pattern of inheritance was a characteristic feature of polygynous households.[14] Under the house–property system, all cattle allocated to a house by the head of the family or acquired through exchange or barter of surplus grain became the property of the house and could not be alienated or transferred by the family head to another household. Thus, as some informants stated, a woman had a theoretical possession of all the cattle she milked. If a man had more than one wife, his cows literally belonged to the children of the respective wives.[15] This was also true of land. Håkansson (1989, p. 121) states that, "although a woman has no property rights of her own, she is a trustee and manager of her house's property and exercises a great deal of independent decision making in daily affairs."

The house–property complex constituted a kind of social recognition of women's participation in economic production. The traditional gender division of labor in society made adequate provision for women to participate in their economy. Customary laws recognized and protected women's usufructural rights in land and cattle. However, the same laws made it impossible for women to own and inherit property. Whatever social prestige women gained from the system, as long as women failed to control the means of production in partnership with males, their status would remain subordinate, dangerously exposed, and subject to changing economic circumstances.

CHANGES IN THE LAND TENURE SYSTEM AND ITS IMPACT ON WOMEN

The people of Kenya were dispossessed of much of their land through a series of measures instituted by the British colonial government between 1897 and 1926 (Sorrenson, 1968; Wolff, 1974). Starting in 1897, European settlers could secure ninety-nine-year leases on crown lands (Breen, 1976; Sorrenson 1968). In 1901, crown lands were defined as those not being cultivated by Africans (British and Foreign State Papers, 1901). Recall that, in the traditional system, there were no "unused" lands; land was merely lying fallow. In 1913, the meaning of crown lands was expanded to include even those being cultivated (Sorrenson, 1968). Since all land now belonged to the crown, Africans could not alienate the land they occupied, nor could they purchase land.[16] These measures were designed to permit the colonial government to sell land to white settlers. Through these measures, the agricultural development of "unused" lands in Kenya became an exclusively European prerogative. The consequence of these actions by the colonial government was that one fifth of all usable land and half the land considered "worth cultivating" were, by the mid-1930s, under the control of settlers.[17]

African land use was confined to designated reserves in 1926 and placed under the Native Lands Trust Board. The colonial state encouraged the use of the customary land tenure system in areas demarcated as African reserves.[18] Section 68 of the Native Lands Trust Ordinance, 1938 states: "In respect of the occupation, use, control, inheritance, succession and disposal of any land situated in the native lands, every tribe, group, family and individual shall have the rights which they enjoy or may enjoy by virtue of existing native law and custom."

As we have seen, customary land tenure made adequate provisions for women's land use in rural economies. Thus, on the surface at least, the ordinance sustained women's usufructuary rights in land. However, the misinterpretation of customary land tenure by colonial officials ultimately worked against the interests of women. Although it was true that women enjoyed use rights, men had usufructural rights *as well as* rights of control and disposal. The greater rights of men in the traditional system were magnified under colonialism and resulted in the displacement of women from the land, particularly as individual control over land increased amongst Kenyans.

Changes in the system of land allocation, individualization, and privatization of parcels had taken place since the mid-1920s. Okoth-Ogendo (1976, p. 157) argues that "the establishment of fixed ethnic boundaries badly disturbed the equilibrium between patterns of land use and availability of land, a balance which had been maintained through the system of shifting cultivation or nomadic pastoralism." Africans in the "reserve," under the pressure of land shortage, began to want title deeds to protect their land from alienation. As early as 1925 colonial settler farmers encouraged the state to grant title deeds to individual Africans in Kenya. One motive for the creation of title deeds was to develop a land market among the indigenous people. The rationale was that the sale and purchase of land would result in the emergence of a landless class to work on settler farms. This would then provide a permanent solution to the settlers' labor-shortage problems.

Colonial land alienation policies, which herded Africans onto crowded reserves, significantly altered the system of land allocation among African communities. Since land was no longer as abundant as it was during the precolonial period, newly commodified land increased in cost. Wagner (1956) reported that land values in western Kenya increased tenfold between 1925 and 1937. A further consequence of the growing shortage of land was the progressive subdivision and fragmentation of individual holdings.

Up to 1940, women's usufructural rights in land were recognized by the colonial state. But the situation was completely different in individual African households in Kenya. Changes in the land tenure system and the creation of land certificates worked to the advantage of men. As land became more scarce, patriarchal structures already in place in the precolonial period protected men rather than women. As individual control over land increased and costs rose, many women lost access to land.

With land shortage, land disputes became an endemic problem, resulting in an increased number of court cases throughout Kenya involving land. Kitching notes that such land disputes "were resolved in practice in favor of the strongest or most influential groups, or those who enjoyed the patronage or support of chiefs, headmen and colonial officials" (1980, p. 285). Since women had no disposal rights over land in the traditional land tenure system, land disputes, like the purchase and sale of land, were men's concerns. However, given the struggle in which men were engaged to acquire land, it was hardly surprising that men enjoyed the support of female members of their families when it came to land disputes.

The Swynnerton Plan accentuated what was already happening in African reserves. The Swynnerton Plan, drawn up by the Assistant Director of Agriculture in 1951, argued that the traditional land tenure system was the main obstacle to greater production and soil conservation and recommended its abandonment. Land was to be surveyed and fragmented holdings consolidated, a process already occurring in heavily populated reserves. Titles were to be granted to household heads.

Swynnerton blamed low agricultural productivity in the African reserves on land fragmentation. However, the governor blamed it on the predominant place of women in the agricultural system, as well as on their lack of education (Kenya National Archives, 1950). Women were the backbone of agricultural production in Kenya, the invisible farmers. But agricultural innovations were directed at men rather than women, and no effort was made to enhance women's productivity in African areas. Certificates of ownership were granted to male occupiers of land, which would restrict fragmentation, provide collateral for agricultural credit, and foster cash crop production. As the governor explained:

> It is suggested that individuals, if they are acceptable to the administrative authorities as good farmers of economic units of land, may apply for the issue of a "special title" in respect of their land. This "special title" will in fact confirm the customary rights of the holder and, in addition, will contain provisions designed to prevent fragmentation. . . . The benefits which this form of "special title" would confer on the holder would be protected against subsequent disputes and litigation as his customary rights and the title could be used as security for the granting of agricultural credit. (Kenya National Archives, 1950, p. 11)

In the majority of cases, land reform meant individual male ownership of land. In Western Province, especially in densely populated areas such as Maragoli and Bunyore, conflicts often arose over local requirements for food and cash. Frequently, people chose to forget about food production and concentrate on a quick cash return (Kenya National Archives, 1950). In Bungoma district, commercialization of agriculture was achieved through the use of the plow. Additional land needed for the production of cash crops was acquired either from the family's uncultivated land, which in most cases was grazing lands, or from the fields previously used by wives for food crop production.

The struggle for control and allocation of land within the household intensified with the diversification of cash crop production. As one informant stated, "Land disputes and land related problems were more intensive during land preparation and planting seasons." During this period, women would often return to their parents' homesteads because their husbands had taken away or not allocated adequate land for the production of food crops for their households.[19] Kitching adds: "Particularly in households with small total holdings, this struggle took the form of the attempt of the male household head to assert complete control over the use and disposal of the usufruct of the entire landholding, and to reduce the distinction between wives' gardens and husbands' (or household) gardens to a purely formal level" (1980, p. 128).

As one informant reported, "If you did not fight back, he took away all your plots." In polygynous households, less industrious women lost substantial portions of their plots because those which were not utilized by individual wives were immediately acquired by the husband for the production of cash crops.[20] The decision to grow cash crops such as coffee or to expand maize production for sale rested entirely with men. The resources allocated to women, even in rural female-headed households, were insufficient. Since women were responsible for food production, a change to cash crop production significantly diminished their ability to produce food crops. As Table 14.1 shows, by 1969 the situation during the 1950s had grown worse. Farms had become very small in most households compared to the precolonial period and even the 1950s era, making these choices over food production as over against cash crop requirements quite critical to women's access to sufficient land.

Table 14.1
Distribution of Farms by Size in Bungoma in 1969

Size of Farm	No. of Parcels	% of Total	Total Hectares	% of Total
0–0.99	1,006	3.1	862	0.4
1.00–1.99	3,634	11.2	6,667	3.1
2.00–2.99	5,354	16.5	15,509	7.2
3.00–4.99	7,398	22.3	34,464	16.0
5.00–9.99	11,161	34.4	93,483	43.4
10.00 and over	3,893	12.0	64,405	29.9
Total	32,446	95.5	215,400	100.0

Since land was used as collateral for loans, women without land titles had no access to loans for the development of their own enterprises. The question of agricultural credit was not a new idea to the Luyia communities of Western Province. Abaluyia enjoyed agricultural credit from the African betterment funds, the brainchild of progressive Luyia farmers.

However, the terms under which the agricultural credit was to be advanced to farmers in Kenya proposed by Swynnerton were new. There were also more financial institutions whose doors were opened to African farmers. Only male progressive farmers enjoyed agricultural credit from the African betterment funds. This formalized what was already happening in African rural areas. Rural underdevelopment in Western Province was exacerbated by women's lack of access to loans and agricultural credit facilities, limiting their ability to purchase improved technology such as tractors, plows, fertilizers, and better seeds. However, when men went out in search of wage employment, women and children remained behind to labor on the men's cash crop farms. Because they did not own land and/or hold title deeds, these women were unable to acquire money and technology.

There were a few unique cases where women were able to get land title deeds. Changes in the land tenure system provided an indirect opportunity for women to purchase and own land in their own right. However, during the colonial period in Kenya, very few women managed to purchase land. Women and children continued to provide labor needed for the production of cash crops, such as maize and coffee, which were marketed through cooperative societies. However, they were not enrolled as members in these societies. By 1952, there were 156 cooperative societies in the province, but none had women members. In Bungoma District, the one coffee cooperative society, established in 1952 in Chwele, had not one female member. By 1956, this cooperative society had a total of 554 members, all of whom were men.[21] Even in 1963, when Chwele Cooperative Coffee Society was the largest society in Western Province, it had no female members. As one female informant stated, "We were not allowed to become members of the cooperative society because we [women] did not grow coffee."[22]

Pressure on land and the resulting social differentiation had worse consequences for women and children than for men (see Bradley, this volume; Kilbride & Kilbride, this volume). The socioeconomic position of individual households was determined by the availability of nonfarm income and the size of land holding (de Wolf, this volume). Poor households, which sold land as a survival strategy, threatened the security of tenure for agricultural productivity in African areas. Changes in the system of land tenure affected women's ability to utilize land in the reserves. Few women could afford to purchase land. Thus, women from poor households became landless peasants, forced to join the laboring poor. Zenebeworke (1984) argues that the disappearance of communal land tenure dispossessed women of land and recognizing men as the new owners of land decreased women's control over productive resources.

CONCLUSION

In precolonial times, women were far from the equals of men. Abaluyia were patriarchal and patrilineal with all that implied in gender relations. While bridewealth cemented a social system, it also categorized women as property. The system was mitigated in that land was plentiful and the role of women was honored. With the coming of colonialism, however, gender inequality increased. Relations that had been primarily social became predominantly economic. Land became scarce, women's access to it became more restricted, and it took on new value, which accrued mostly to males. Title deeds were issued to men, cash crops were favored, and men controlled cash crops at the expense of food crops. Unquestionably, men were struggling to survive in the new colonial situation. But they did so by transferring part of their burdens to the women and children. As credit loomed ever more important, ownership of land became crucial, and women slowly lost their rights. As Barbara Rogers (1979) argued, the history of land policies, from those of colonial administration through those of development planners and land reform programs, is the history of women losing their rights and access to land and the concomitant benefits.[23]

NOTES

1. Dora Earthy's (1968) study on women's land rights observed that in a patrilineal society such as the Lenge women did not have formal power. This compares well with the situation of women in Western Province. For further analysis, see Earthy (1968). For additional information and analysis of the Luyia system of land tenure, see Wagner (1956, pp. 75–100).

2. Similarly, Angelique Haugerud (1995) observed that men in Embu acquired land through first cultivation (or *runo* rights); in addition, land in precolonial Embu was inherited by one or more of a man's sons.

3. *Omuliimi gwa guga* is the garden of the grandfather, that is, the piece of land that the household head inherited from his own father when he established his household, as distinct from other lands that he might have acquired later on. See also Wagner (1970).

4. Sara Nabwala, oral interview, Wamono (Bungoma), February 14, 1988.

5. Sara Nabwala, oral interview, Wamono (Bungoma), February 14, 1988. Wagner (1970, vol. 1, p. 51) suggested that "the senior wife exercised a certain amount of authority over her cowives especially during the first year or two after a young wife's marriage, when the latter has not yet established a household of her own. In all joint activities of the co-wives, however, the senior wife continues to take precedence and cowives generally show her the respect due to a senior relative."

6. Polygyny, observed Christine Obbo (1980), afforded some women leverage within a male-dominated descent system. However, jealousy existed between cowives. On the question of jealousy among and between cowives, Wagner (1970, Vol. 2, p. 54) suggests that "the preference given by most husbands to a 'favorite wife' constitutes a frequent occasion for jealousy and strife among cowives."

7. Luka Namulala, oral interview, Musese, September 14, 1987.

8. Johnstone Khisa, Kimilili, oral interview, February 5,1988; and Luka Namulala, Musese, oral interview, September 14, 1987.

9. For instance, Angelique Haugerud observed that among the Embu "the father's right to decide how his wealth is to be distributed among his sons is an important source of influence and control over their behavior" (1989, pp. 69–70).

10. For a more insightful analysis of polygyny among the Luyia of Western Province, see Wagner (1956, vol. 2, pp. 48–52). See particularly footnote No. 1 on page 50, where a table on polygynous homesteads in Western Province is provided.

11. Luka Namulala, oral interview, Chwele, Bungoma, 1988.

12. Timeleo Wepukhulu and Luka Namaulala, oral interviews, November 5, 1987, and September 14, 1987, Bungoma.

13. The extended family, argued Goody and Buckley (1973), is divided into more or less independent units called houses, which consist of a wife and her children, organized for property use and productive activities. Property allocated to a particular house is inherited by the sons of that house, hence the house–property system. For more details, see pages 117–120.

14. Similarly, among the Luo property was transmitted through women to their sons (Hay, 1972). This point was also emphasized by Obbo (1980), when she stated that in polygynous households, a woman was the medium through which individual rights passed to her sons.

15. Luka Namulala and Timeteo Wepukhulu, oral interviews, Bungoma.

16. Such reservation shall not confer on any tribe or member of any tribe any right to alienate the land so reserved or any part thereof. Crown Lands Ordinance, 1915, Part VI: Reservation of Land of "Native" Tribes, Section 46-50.

17. Kenya National Archives, Ordinance No. 21 of 1902, East Africa Protectorate, Gazette, Crown Lands Ordinance, 1902, Section No. 4–6. 64 Kenya National Archives, Crown Lands Ordinance, 1915 sections 34–38. Ainsworth was the sub-commissioner for Ukambani. See his 1895-1905 report relating to the administration of East Africa Protectorate, Parliamentary Papers, Vol. 80, Cd 2740 Africa No. 6 (1805), p. 15. Kenya National Archives, Agr/5/1/203, Development of Agriculture in Native areas, letter from Depart-

ment of Attorney General's office, Nairobi to the Honourable member of Agriculture and Natural Resources, Nairobi 3/10/1946. Lord Hailey, An African Survey (London: Oxford University Press, 1938), p. 751.

18. This was stated in the Crown Lands Ordinance (Amendment) Ordinance of 1938 and the Kenya (Native Areas) Order-in-Council, 1938.

19. Enock Mukhwana, oral interview, February 18, 1988.

20. Marita Munoko, oral interview, Sirisia, April 10, 1988.

21. Peter Kisuya, Chairman, Chwele Cooperative Society, oral interview, Chwele (Bungoma), August 20, 1987.

22. Selina Wanyonyi, oral interview, Lukhome, Bungoma, October 19, 1987.

23. Women's need for land is beginning to receive international attention and support. For details see the World Conference on Agrarian Reform and Rural Development Report (1979).

REFERENCES

Breen, Rita Mary. (1976). *The politics of land: The Kenya Land Commission (1932–33) and its effect on land policy in Kenya.* Unpublished doctoral dissertation, University of Michigan.

British and Foreign State Papers. (1901). XCV 999–1000, The East Africa (Lands) Order in Council.

Committee on Native Land Tenure in the North Kavirondo Reserve.(1930). Report (CO 533/409/17, October. Kakamega, Kenya.

Depelchin, J. (1977). African history and the ideological reproduction of exploitative relations of production. *African Development, 11.*

Earthy, D. Dora. (1968). *Valenge women: The social and economic life of the Valenge women of Portuguese East Africa; an ethnographic study.* London: Cass Library of African Studies.

Goody, J., & Buckley, J. (1973). Inheritance and women's labour in Africa. *Africa, 63,* 108–121.

Hagerud, Angelique. (1995). *The culture of politics in modern Kenya.* Cambridge: Cambridge University Press.

Håkansson, Thomas N. (1989). Family structure, bridewealth and environment in eastern Africa: A comparative study of house–property system. *Ethnology: An International Journal of Cultural and Social Anthropology, 28,* 117–134.

Hay, Margaret Jean. (1972). *Economic change in Luoland: Kowe, 1895–1945.* Unpublished doctoral dissertation, University of Wisconsin.

Hay, Margaret Jean. (1976). Luo women and economic change during the colonial period. In N. J. Hafkin & Edna G. Bay (Eds.), *Women in Africa: Studies in social and economic change* (pp. 87–110). Stanford: Stanford University Press.

Henn, Jeanne Koopman. (1988). The material basis of sexism: A model of production analysis. In S. B. Stichter & J. L. Parpart (Eds.), *Patriarchy and class: African women in the home and the workforce.* Boulder: Westview Press.

Hindess, B., & Hirst, P. Q. (1975). *Pre-capitalist modes of production.* London: Routledge and Kegan Paul.

Hobley, C. W. (1967). *Bantu beliefs and magic.* London: Frank Cass.

Molyneux, M. (1977). Androcentricism in Marxist anthropology. *Critique of Anthropology, 3.*

Kenya National Archives. (1938). Native Lands Trust Ordinance (Agr/5/1/203, Department of Agriculture).

Kenya National Archives. (1950). Letter from the Governor of Kenya to the Secretary of State for the colonies, 2/6/1950. Agr/KSM/829.

Kitching, G. (1980). *Class and economic change in Kenya: The making of an African petite bourgeoisie 1905–1970.* New Haven: Yale University Press.

Obbo, Christine. (1980). *African women: Their struggle for economic independence.* London: Zed Press.

Okoth-Ogendo, H. W. O. (1976). African land tenure reform. In J. Heyer (Ed.), *Agricultural development in Kenya: An economic assessment.* Nairobi: Oxford University Press.

Okoth-Ogendo, H. W. O. (1978). The changing system of land tenure and the rights of women. In Achola Pala et al. (Eds.), *The participation of women in Kenya society.* Nairobi: Kenya Literature Bureau.

Pala, Achola. (1976). *African women in rural development: Research trends and priorities* (Overseas Liaison Committee Paper No. 2). Washington, DC: American Council on Education.

Rogers, Barbara. (1979). *Domestication of women: Discrimination in developing countries.* New York: St. Martin's Press.

Sorrenson, M. P. K. (1968). *Origins of European settlement in Kenya.* Nairobi: Oxford University Press.

Stamp, Patricia. (1989). *Technology, gender and power in Africa* (Technical Study 63e). Ottawa: Internal Development Research Center.

Wagner, Gunter. (1956). *The Bantu of western Kenya. Vol. 2: The economic life.* Oxford: Oxford University Press.

Wagner, Gunter. (1949/1970). *The Bantu of western Kenya: With special reference to the Vugusu and Logoli, vols. 1 and 2 (Economic life).* London: Oxford University Press.

Wagner, Gunter. (1970). *The changing family among the Bantu of Western Province.* London: Oxford University Press.

Wolff, R. D. (1974). *The economics of colonialism in Britain and Kenya, 1870–1930.* New Haven: Yale University Press.

Zenebeworke, Tadesse. (1984). An overview. In *Rural development and women in Africa.* Geneva: International Labor Organization.

15

Logoli Childhood and the Cultural Reproduction of Sex Differentiation

Robert L. Munroe and Ruth H. Munroe

INTRODUCTION: SEX DIFFERENTIATION AS AN AFRICAN CULTURE COMPLEX

Our aim in this chapter is to help illuminate the process by which gender distinctions come to be culturally reproduced in Maragoli, western Kenya. The issue gains some special interest because male and female gender roles are sharply contrasted throughout most of traditional Africa, so much so that strong sex differentiation can be termed an African "culture complex." By the concept of culture complex we mean a related group of traits manifested over some definable culture area (Winick, 1956).[1] Well-known examples are the cattle complex in East Africa (Herskovits, 1926), the honor/shame syndrome in the Mediterranean (Gilmore, 1987; Peristiany, 1966), and the Plains vision quest (Benedict, 1922). Also discernible in the ethnographic record are analogous complexes of somewhat less definite delineation, for instance, parallel cousin marriage in the Middle East and indirect dowry in the Middle East and Central Asia (Schlegel & Eloul, 1987).

Similarly, strong sex differentiation can be claimed as a distinctive African culture complex, though it is neither limited to the continent nor universally present there. As LeVine (1973) has noted in an essay on personality patterns in Africa, gender distinctions are reflected in many areas of life, including the division of labor, childrearing, structural distinctions, and ideology. Documentation of such an emphasis is available from two sets of holocultural ratings based upon the ethnographic literature. One set of ratings, utilizing a world sample of forty-seven societies (including nine in Africa), takes into account seven sociocultural variables on which societies may or may not make distinctions by gender (Munroe, Whiting, & Hally, 1969). The variables include items that are both structural and behavioral, ranging from kin terminology to residence patterns to eating arrangements.[2] When we calculate the average number of sex distinctions per society for these ratings, we find a significantly higher mean for the African than the non-African societies, 4.9 vs. 3.3, $t(45) = 2.13$, $p < .05$. The second set of ratings involves socialization practices, such as achievement training, for a world sample of 110 societies (including twenty-six in Africa). Barry, Bacon, and Child (1957), in discussing these ratings, cite Africa and Native American cultures in North America as the two culture areas of the world that stress differential treatment of the sexes. Thus, insofar as the holocultural samples are representative, African societies clearly meet expectations as to strong emphasis on gender distinctiveness.

The ratings allow us, in addition, to probe a question about process. The first set of ratings above delineates systemic sex distinctions, and the second set, as noted, describes sex distinctions made during child training and socialization. If, as we might assume, the adult system influences child training so that it tends to *reproduce* that system, then those societies with a high level of systemic sex distinctions should emphasize sex distinctions in their socialization practices.[3] Operationally, that is, scores on the first set of ratings ought to be positively correlated with scores on the second set. Although there is relatively little overlap between the two samples, altogether a set of seventeen cases can be compiled to undertake comparison using Spearman's rank correlation coefficient.[4] The figures presented in Table 15.1 indicate that systemic sex distinctions are significantly related to two scores that measure socialization differences for boys and girls: one, a score for responsibility training, and two, an overall mean score combining socialization indices for responsibility, obedience, nurturance, achievement, self-reliance, and independence.[5] The results are consistent with the idea that training of the young may constitute an important means for effecting reproduction of the ongoing system. Also, as we shall see, the responsibility scores are of particular interest concerning the inculcation of gender differentiation in Logoli culture.

LOGOLI CULTURE AND THE ACQUISITION OF SEX-TYPING

Were the Logoli to be assigned a score for the independent variable in Table 15.1, it would be six points—as high on systemic sex distinctions as any society in the sample and equal to the score for the Gikuyu, the sole African society in the table. (Both the Logoli and the Gikuyu belong among Kenyan Bantu-speaking peoples.) The Logoli place a characteristic African emphasis on gender distinctions and evidence a typical bias toward male privilege. (See the chapter by Nasimiyu, this volume, for historical evidence on gender relations among Abaluyia peoples, of whom the Logoli are one, and the chapter by Whyte and Kariuki, this volume, on gender relations in western Kenya in general.) Thus, besides the meaningful structural and behavioral features that are captured in the sex-distinction scale, we find in Maragoli a strong sexual division of labor, the social and spatial separation of men and women, a lengthy ritual of initiation into manhood (abbreviated in recent times to a short circumcision ceremony), and stereotypes about the sexes (Munroe & Munroe, 1984). (See the chapter by Håkansson & LeVine, this volume, for similar features of gender distinction among the Bantu Gusii.)

Table 15.1
Relationships Between Systemic Sex Distinctions and Two Sex Differences in Socialization: A World Sample

Society	Systemic Sex Distinctions[b]	Sex Differences in Socialization[a]	
		Responsibility Training[c]	General
Aranda	6	3	2.3
Gikuyu	6	2	2.0
Omaha	4	4	3.8
Ifaluk	4	3	2.0
Kaska	4	3	0.7
Mandan	4	2	2.3
Araucanians	4	0	0.6
Comanche	3	3	3.2
Alorese	3	2	1.6
Navaho	3	1	1.8
Papago	2	2	2.2
Chukchee	2	1	1.6
Ontong-Java	2	1	1.5
Tupinamba	2	1	1.5
Marquesans	2	0	0.0
Klamath	1	0	0.8
Ifugao	0	0	0.8
		$r_s = .68$ $p < .005$	$r_s = .47$ $p < .05$

[a] Ratings taken from Barry, Bacon, and Child (1967). Responsibility training scores were the difference between boys' and girls' scores for this variable. The direction of difference was disregarded. General socialization scores were calculated by taking the mean difference between scores for boys and girls on the six socialization variables (including responsibility training), with the criterion for a society's inclusion in the sample being that "confident" ratings were available for more than half the variables. Again direction of difference was disregarded. The Spearman rank correlation coefficient for each socialization variable with degree of systemic sex distinction is given beneath the columns of socialization scores.

[b] Ratings taken from R. L. Munroe, Whiting, and Hally (1969). Possible scores range from 0 to 7.

[c] "'Responsible behavior' refers to the performance of tasks, duties, or routines....The emphasis here is on work" (Barry, Bacon, and Child 1967:296).

The Logoli system of sex differentiation is undoubtedly learned progressively as children gain experience, and we might best track the process by analyzing in detail the ways in which, from birth onward, children in Maragoli learn to become competent members of their culture (cf. Jahoda & Lewis, 1989). Although we possess a certain amount of relevant data along these lines, an optimal approach of this sort would require long-term longitudinal study. What we shall present instead are primarily cross-sectional data indicating the degree to which Logoli children at different age levels display both generic and culture-specific gender distinctions in their knowledge, their preferences, and their everyday behavior. Most of the evidence is based on naturalistic observations that measure cultural competence only partially and indirectly, and it is restricted to children no older than nine years of age. Nevertheless, taken in toto, it makes a case for the regular, age-related acquisition of powerful and appropriate sex-typing in Logoli culture.

Note on Method

The authors worked among the Logoli during three field trips carried out between 1966 and 1978. Most of the data reported herein were gathered in the community of "Vihiga" in early 1978 (cf. Munroe & Munroe, 1991). The community, located in the present Vihiga District in South Maragoli, is typical for the area (Bradley, in press) and is characterized by a pattern of dispersed settlement, patrilineally organized homesteads, traditional hoe horticultural methods with a maize based subsistence system, and some cattle keeping. A large proportion of the males spend a significant part of their early and middle adult years working in urban areas and sending cash remittances to support their families in Vihiga. (See de Wolf's chapter, this volume, comparing Maragoli's low sex ratios—indicating male absence—with those elsewhere in Western Province.) Wives and children are based in the community, but many make occasional visits to urban settings for short stays with the fathers (cf. Ross & Weisner, 1977).

In the present study, standardized data were gathered by local personnel trained to undertake naturalistic observations and to administer tests. The primary sample was composed of six boys and six girls at each of the ages of three, five, seven, and nine, yielding a total sample size of forty-eight children.

Three sources of data were used. The main observational technique, the spot observation, was designed to collect systematic information on each child's activities, locations, and associates (R. H. Munroe & R. L. Munroe, 1971, in press; R. L. Munroe & R. H. Munroe, 1991; Rogoff, 1978). Sample children were each observed thirty times, during nonschoolgoing hours, over a six-to-eight-week period.

A second observational technique was concerned with the child's selective attention to others in the social environment, especially the degree of gazing at males or at females. Children were observed for six ten-minute intervals spaced over a four-to-six-week period (for details, see R. L. Munroe & R. H. Munroe, 1992).

Tests were conducted with respect to the sample children's choices among sex roles (e.g., mother vs. father, father vs. daughter) and among sex-differentiated cultural tasks (e.g., caring for coffee trees, a male task, vs. cooking, a female task). Further details about the measures are discussed below where pertinent.

Sex-Typing in Everyday Activities and Social Groupings

Work activities. We saw in Table 15.1 that sex differences in children's responsibility training, or work assignments, were related to systemic sex distinctions.

That is, societies with strong sex differentiation more frequently assigned routine tasks to girls than to boys. Cross-culturally, little of this labor is of the type done by adult males (Bradley, 1993), because "much men's work (either because it is dangerous or requires a lot of strength) probably cannot be done by boys" (Ember, 1981, p. 557). The tasks assigned young children are therefore for the most part "women's work"—infant care, chores, cooking, and housekeeping activities—but in societies with weak sex differentiation, such tasks are assigned with equal frequency to girls and boys.

Application of the cross-cultural finding to the Logoli case is straightforward. At the adult level, sex differentiation is pervasive in Maragoli, so the clear prediction can be made that for children, tasks should be assigned to girls more often than to boys. Table 15.2 shows the results of a comparison, across age levels, of work frequencies during daylight, nonschool hours. (For convenience in exposition, in Table 15.2 and most subsequent tables, children at ages three and five are grouped together as "younger," those at ages seven and nine as "older." Differences between means in these tables are subjected to one-tailed *t*-tests.)

Table 15.2
Percentage of Time Working by Sex and Age

	Sex		
Age Group[a]	Boys	Girls	
3–5	14	25	Girls > Boys*
7–9	35	51	Girls > Boys***
All	25	38	Girls > Boys**

[a] $N = 24$ for each age group, 12 boys, 12 girls.
*$p < .05$. **$p < .01$. ***$p < .005$.

The expectation of a sex difference in labor frequency is upheld, with both younger and older girls devoting more time to work than their male counterparts. As Table 15.2 indicates, younger girls were involved in work contributions one-quarter of the time, and older girls over half the time. That girls are being inducted into the female labor force may seem an anticlimactic and ineluctable conclusion—after all, what else would be likely to happen?—but we must recall that a sex difference in children's labor does not occur universally. The holocultural evidence in Table 15.1 indicates that the difference emerges where, as among the Logoli, there is strong sex differentiation at the adult level.

A sexual division of labor was also not universal with respect to all Logoli childhood activities. Girls devoted approximately one sixth of their total nonschool time to certain domestic chores, namely, food preparation and cleanup, carrying water, and obtaining firewood, these contributions outweighing those of boys by a three-to-one ratio. But other, less time-consuming domestic chores, including house-tidying and errands (at the market), were more nearly balanced between the sexes. Subsistence activities, too, engaged girls and boys approximately equally (somewhat under 10 percent of their time), except that boys were more likely than girls to be involved in animal care. And, surprisingly, the care of infants and young children was evenly divided, both sexes giving about 5 percent of their daily time to this activity. There is some evidence that cultural changes have eroded the traditional childhood division of labor so far as childcare is concerned, and this matter shall be taken up in the latter part of the chapter.

Social Groupings in Free Time: Self-Aggregation by Sex

Logoli boys, with more free (nonwork) time than girls, were more likely to be involved in toy play and in various rule based games. In the process of pursuing these and other free-time activities, they tended to cluster together with other boys. This same-sex aggregation by young males, which has been observed elsewhere, has been given the colorful label of "swarming" (Omark, Omark, & Edelman, 1975). It is not so much that girls are altogether excluded, but that in a given social setting young boys will usually join forces strongly enough to outnumber girls. Girls typically engage in a milder form of clustering. We illustrate the degree of self-aggregation for each sex independently with both male and female associates, as shown in Tables 15.3 and 15.4, respectively. The data refer to those nonhousehold members with whom sample children were actively participating during free-time observations only.[6]

Table 15.3
Mean Free-time Number of Male Affiliates by Sex and Age

	Sex		
Age Group[a]	Boys	Girls	
3–5	57	16	Boys > Girls*
7–9	47	16	Boys > Girls**
All	52	16	Boys > Girls ***

Note: "Male children" = 3 to 16 year old males, nonhousehold members only.
[a] *N*= 24 for each age group, 12 boys, 12 girls.
[b] Cell entries represent a group mean calculated from individual mean scores for number of male affiliates on free-time observations.
* $p < .05$. ** $p < .01$. *** $p < .005$.

The figures in Table 15.3 represent the mean number of male children, per observation, participating in the same voluntary activity as the sample children. It can be seen from the figures that boys in the sample aggregated significantly more with male children than did girls. There were no age differences, thus the self-aggregation was already established among the younger boys. The numbers are highly stable, each cell mean being based on several hundred protocols.

Table 15.4, showing the mean number of female children participating in voluntary activities with sample members, does feature one similarity to Table 15.3: Older girls in the sample aggregated significantly more with other girls than did older sample boys. To this extent, then, both sexes displayed a spontaneous same-

Table 15.4
Mean Free-time Number of Female Affiliates by Sex and Age

	Sex		
Age Group[a]	Boys	Girls	
3–5	25	19	ns
7–9	7	38	Girls > Boys*
All	16	28	ns

Note: "Female children" = 3 to 16 year old females, nonhousehold members only.
[a] N= 24 for each age group, 12 boys, 12 girls.
[b] Cell entries represent a group mean calculated from individual mean scores for number of female affiliates on free-time observations.
* $p < .05$. ** $p < .01$. *** $p < .005$.

sex clustering tendency in their choice of social mates. Otherwise, however, there were some marked differences between the results in the two tables. Table 15.4 shows that among younger children, girls were no more likely than boys to cluster with female children; the sex difference in same-sex aggregation therefore appeared just for older girls. Also, as the figures show, this latter sex difference was due not only to the positive choices of the older girls but to avoidances by older boys, who had a mean of only .07 females per protocol during voluntary activities.

Finally, by comparing data in Tables 15.3 and 15.4, we find that Logoli boys created larger clusters of same-sex groups (mean = .52) than did girls (mean = .28), $t(22) = 2.05$, $p < .05$. And, if the own-sex and opposite-sex figures are subtracted from each other (again by comparing data in Tables 15.3 and 15.4), it is apparent that boys constructed less "contaminated" same-sex aggregates than girls. That is, Logoli boys had a larger difference between the average number of own-sex and opposite-sex playmates (.52 vs. .16) than did Logoli girls (.28 vs. .16), $t(22) = 2.03$, $p < .05$.

Considered together, Tables 15.3 and 15.4 indicate the following: (a) same-sex aggregation is prominent among Logoli children during free-time activities, but (b) boys display the clustering behavior at an earlier age, and more strongly, than girls, and(c) older boys, besides continuing to aggregate with other boys, also seem to avoid the company of girls. Maccoby (1990a, 1990b) has argued that spontaneous segregation by sex is indicative of children's interest in adopting sex-appropriate behavior, and that boys involve themselves in same-sex aggregation even more strongly than girls. The Logoli data are consistent with Maccoby's position.

Free-time distance from home. Previous research has shown that in free time, Logoli boys typically venture farther from home than do Logoli girls (R. L. Munroe & R. H. Munroe, 1971). In the Vihiga community, with its pattern of dispersed settlement, there are numerous places to which children may repair: the fields surrounding the homes, hillsides near streams bordering the community, paths and roads, and a school compound. These areas attract young boys more often than girls during free time, and the data in Table 15.5 show the degree to which boys and girls venture farther from home. (A scale for distance has been employed in order to avoid the distorting effect of very large figures.)

Boys traveled farther from home base, on average, than did girls, and this difference appeared among both younger and older sample members. (Older children of both sexes increased their free-time distance enough that the "younger-older" comparison was also significant.) For older boys, the scale distance of 1.17 indicates that their free-time activities were carried out "on average" more than a hundred feet from their homes.

Table 15.5
Mean Free-time Distance from Home by Sex and Age

	Sex		
Age Group[a]	Boys	Girls	
3–5	0.53	0.26	Boys > Girls *
7–9	1.17	0.68	Boys > Girls **
All	0.85	0.47	Boys > Girls **

Note: Distance scale: 0–99 ft. = 0; 100–199 ft. = 1; 200–299 ft. = 2; 300–399 ft. = 3; 400–499 ft. = 4; 500 ft.+ = 5.
[a] $N = 24$ for each age group, 12 boys, 12 girls.
[b] Cell entries represent a group mean calculated from individual mean scores for distance from home on free-time observations.
*$p < .05$. **$p < .025$.

Sex-Typing in Gazing Behavior

The findings presented to this point have been based on "molar-level" observations gleaned from the daily routines of Logoli children. We turn here to a type of "molecular" data concerned with boys' and girls' selective attention to the males and females in their immediate surrounds. For these protocols, observers noted the personnel present near the sample child and then recorded the direction of the child's eye gaze for a specified period (R. H. Munroe & R. L. Munroe, in press). Children were given scores indexing their relative attentiveness to various categories of age-sex groupings, taking into account the degree to which such groupings were actually represented in the child's environment during the periods of observation.

This technique, employed comparatively in a total of four societies (in American Samoa, Belize, and Nepal besides among the Logoli), yielded an expected overall sex difference in attention to own-sex figures. (There was no age trend, older children being neither more nor less likely than younger children to overattend to own-sex figures [R. H. Munroe & R. L. Munroe, 1992].) Scores were compiled indicating the degree to which boys and girls differentially attended to twelve categories of persons, six of which were male (infants [0–2 years of age], younger children [3–6 yrs.], older children [7–11 yrs.], teens [12–16 yrs.], adults

Table 15.6
Number of Same-sex Role Preferences by Age and Sex

	Age Group		
Sex[a]	3–5	7–9	
Boys	5.2	6.3	ns
Girls	5.8	7.3	ns
All	5.5	6.8	Older > Younger*

Note: Possible total = 9.
[a] $N = 44$, 21 at ages 3–5 (10 boys, 11 girls), 23 at ages 7–9 (11 boys, 12 girls).
*$p < .05$

[17+ yrs.], and father), and six female (infants, younger children, older children, teens, adult women, and mother).

The six categories of males were always gazed at more frequently by boys than by girls in Maragoli. For the six categories of females, however, no such imbalance was shown, with girls looking more at three of the categories of females and boys looking more at three. Interpretation of these trends is perhaps easiest if we bring our cross-cultural data to bear. Comparatively, the Logoli results for the male categories are unique: In no other culture group did the categories attract a single-sex dominance matching the 6–0 one-sidedness of Logoli boys' attentional behavior to males. Thus the attention findings seem to offer a parallel to the same-sex aggregation data, in that Logoli boys, vis-à-vis the girls, were visually attending to the males who occupied their social space. The finding offers an additional piece of evidence that in Maragoli the sex-typing of boys is in some ways more strongly motivated or "powered" than that of girls.

Sex-Typing in Role and Task Preferences: Data from Tests

The two measures involving choice behavior were identical in structure, each giving children an opportunity on a total of nine separate items to make a same-sex or opposite-sex choice. For the sex-role preferences, sample members were presented with the nine possible paired male versus female combinations of the following roles: father, son, baby boy, mother, daughter, and baby girl. For example, the child was asked in Luragoli: "Would you rather be a daughter or a baby boy?" For the task preferences, children were presented with the nine possible paired male versus female combinations of the following culturally sex-differentiated tasks: herd cattle, care for coffee trees, chop firewood (male); cook, care for chickens, and collect firewood (female). For example, the child was asked in Lulogoli: "Would you rather herd cattle or cook?"

It was expected that children would make more same-sex than opposite-sex choices and that they would do so increasingly with age. These expectations were borne out, as the results in Tables 15.6 and 15.7 indicate, with the findings somewhat stronger for task choices than role preferences. (The results are given in terms of the number of same-sex choices out of the nine possible. Random choices would yield scores varying around a mean of 4.5.)

For the role choices, as shown in Table 15.6, the younger children were above the "chance" value of 4.5, while the older children were well beyond the younger children's level. The moderate sex difference favoring females (girls' mean of 6.6 to boys' mean of 5.8), though not significant, illustrates the strong acceptance by girls of their own sex roles.

Table 15.7
Number of Same-sex Task Preferences by Age and Sex

Sex[a]	Age Group 3–5	Age Group 7–9	
Boys	5.4	6.3	ns
Girls	5.5	6.8	Older > Younger*
All	5.5	6.6	Older > Younger**

Note: Possible total = 9.
[a]$N = 45$, 21 at ages 3–5 (10 boys, 11 girls), 24 at ages 7–9 (12 boys, 12 girls).
*$p < .025$. **$p < .01$.

The task choices were similar in outcome to the role-preference results, with an early same-sex bias and then an age progression in this pattern. Once more the choices by girls were slightly though not significantly stronger than those of boys (girls' mean of 6.2 to boys' mean of 5.9).

The earlier results from the behavioral data (reported in Tables 15.3 to 15.5) showed the boys as more powerfully pursuing sex-differentiating activity, and we might have suspected that the psychological evidence (Tables 15.6 and 15.7) would show much the same thing. Yet on the role and task choices the Logoli girls adopted same-sex preferences every bit as strongly as the boys. This proclivity is not altogether surprising if we recall from the data on children's work (Table 15.2) that girls are given frequent adult female assignments from an early age. In any case, looking at the results as a whole, we see indications throughout that the younger sample children are gradually acquiring appropriate sex-typing responses and that these leanings are solidified by the time children reach the older ages.[7]

Cultural Changes in the Sexual Division of Labor: The Case of Childcare

It was pointed out above, in the section on work activities, that there were no sex differences in the care of infants and young children by our Logoli sample members. We have comparable data from the same community, approximately a decade earlier (1967), that show distinctive childcare patterns for girls and boys. What seems to have occurred by 1978 was a strong drop-off in childcare responsibilities for girls and a modest increase for boys. The reason for the decline among girls was probably related to the decade's major change in female children's lives within the community, that change being girls' attainment of almost universal primary schooling: within our samples, in 1967 the proportion of school-aged girls actually attending school was 69 percent, while in 1978 it had risen to 96 percent. (Boys of the same ages were at 92 percent in 1967 and 100 percent in 1978.) This upward shift meant that in 1978 girls were being removed from the household for major portions of the day and that their caretaking accordingly declined to the overall level of boys'.[8] For our purposes, the point is that at the time of our most recent investigation, a rather important part of the activities distinguishing the lives of girls and boys in Maragoli had disappeared, yet our results show that such a change had not much affected the overall inculcation of strong sex-typing.

The same conclusion can be drawn from another comparison of 1967 and 1978 data. We found in 1967 that the care of one-year-olds was entrusted about half the time to older siblings (R. H. Munroe & R. L. Munroe, 1971). Of these child caretakers, sisters cared for both male and female babies, but brothers cared almost exclusively for male babies. By 1978, however, the boys "avoidance" of female infants—whatever its source—was no longer operative. (In 1967, only 3 percent of the total sibling care of infants was that of boys caring for female infants; by 1978, the figure had changed to 23 percent, which figure would be statistically expectable given unbiased allocations of childcare by boys with respect to sex of the infant.) Once more, an earlier pattern of sex differentiation had by 1978 been dissipated, but without much discernible effect on the strong sex-typing of Logoli children.

DISCUSSION

Insofar as childhood constitutes an important site for the reproduction of sex-typing, we may conclude that in Maragoli the ongoing process is stable and robust. We have found developmentally related sex-typing in activities, playmates, distances, attentional behavior, and preferences—in short, in numerous aspects of Logoli childhood. The decline of a few sex-related differences in childcare from an earlier time seems to have had little effect on the general pattern. Further, occasional acculturative experiences undergone by some of the sample children in urban areas, including Nairobi, does not appear to be creating anything like a new direction in childhood sex-typing.

It is not only the children who have been exposed to influences from outside the sociocultural system itself. All adult males and many of the women have spent time in cities and towns and have observed behavioral patterns more nearly egalitarian than those practiced in their traditional culture. But these and other factors potentially conducive to change, such as information imparted via radio broadcasts, printed matter, and films, have had little impact upon the degree of adult sex differentiation (cf. the Gusii in Håkansson and LeVine's chapter, this volume, for a comparable degree of persistence in gender differentiation). And for the adults, as for the children, we would be willing to predict little near-term decline in the potency and depth of sex-typing in Maragoli.

As indicated in the introductory section of this chapter, the strong sex differentiation of the Logoli is a mirror of systems found over much of Africa. To say that the Logoli form one small part of a vast culture complex increases our confidence in predicting that their patterns of sex differentiation are likely to persist, but the prediction seems little more than a truism; by definition, a culture complex is a culture-historical phenomenon with staying power. Yet we believe that the inertial qualities of cultural complexes allow us to infer something about the dynamics underlying their continuity. Zajonc's (1968) classic psychological research on the "mere-exposure effect" indicates that attitudes toward a stimulus are enhanced given only repeated, unreinforced exposure and nothing more. The exposure effect has been demonstrated in more than two hundred published experiments and has been used to investigate anthropologically relevant phenomena such as stereotypes, social perceptions, and environmental preferences (Bornstein & D'Agostino, 1992). If we translate the underlying principle into terms of interest to us, we can say that prolonged exposure to a culture trait, even in the absence of adaptive or utilitarian factors, is likely to promote a positive attitude toward the trait, thus contributing to its continuance. And the existence of a *complex* of related traits, as in the case of African sex differentiation, would entail for culture members a continual exposure to stimuli associated with gender. In turn, this should enhance dispositions toward the elements that make up the complex and thereby help insure the maintenance and perpetuation of these elements.

Investigations following up Zajonc's finding have discovered that the mere-exposure effect is amplified if, rather than being consciously perceived, stimuli are perceived without awareness (Bornstein & D'Agostino, 1992). That is, stimuli perceived only subliminally are subsequently seen as even more preferable, better liked, and more pleasant. The fact that the "exposure/positive-affect" relationship is particularly strong after subliminal exposure is attributed by Bornstein and D'Agostino (1992) to what they call "perceptual fluency" regarding stimuli. (They argue that conscious awareness induces a correction process that partially offsets positive affect toward the stimuli.) It seems to us that early childhood experience, with its informal, often untutored learning, provides precisely the conditions of unconscious or low-awareness perception that would promote perceptual fluency—and thus positive attitudinal dispositions—toward repeatedly presented stimuli.[9]

Applying the above points to the specific case of sex-typing in Maragoli, we would reason as follows. (a) The system of strong sex differentiation, given its status as a culture complex, should tend toward self-replication by means of the mere-exposure effect alone. (b) For children, however, exposed on a near constant basis to the system of sex differentiation, the elements would for the most part be transmitted implicitly rather than formally, and would therefore be assimilated under conditions conducive to establishing optimal "exposure/positive-affect" relationships.[10] (c) Positive affective responses toward the manifestations of strong sex differentiation would be carried into adulthood, thereby creating further resistance to significant alterations in the received system of sex differentiation.[11]

Sociocultural change occurs everywhere, not least in East Africa, as many of the chapters in this volume make abundantly clear (see especially the chapters by Håkansson and LeVine, this volume, and by P. L. Kilbride and J. C. Kilbride, this volume; cf. also Håkansson, 1988; P. L. Kilbride and J. C. Kilbride, 1990; Weisner, 1973). Accordingly no one would assume that the Logoli system of sex differentiation is immune to change. As we have seen, aspects of the gender distinctions surrounding childcare have undergone modification in recent years, and related areas of sex differentiation obviously could be similarly affected. We posit, however, that such changes would most frequently be due to behavioral contingencies not unlike the increased school attendance which was apparently responsible for girls' reduced childcare activities in 1978 vis-à-vis 1967. These changes, in other words, would often be directly reactive responses to circumstantial demands but would not represent any generalized movement in the direction of weaker sex differentiation.[12] Overall, we expect strong sex differentiation to remain very much characteristic of Logoli culture for the foreseeable future.

As a final comment on the central theoretical issue addressed herein, we want to point out that the gender distinctions of Maragoli are intimately related to value concerns and that central values seem to be a critical feature of many or even most cultural complexes (e.g., the honor/shame complex, the vision quest,[13] and the *machismo* syndrome [Garibay-Patron, 1969]). Values, of course, are closely tied up with affective dispositions, and we may ultimately find that the concepts associated with Zajonc's exposure/positive-affect research will prove to be important guideposts in gaining an understanding of the persistence and resiliency exhibited by the world's culture complexes.

NOTES

Fieldwork conducted among the Logoli in 1978 was supported by the National Science Foundation. Fieldwork conducted in 1966–1967 and 1970–1971 was supported by the Carnegie Corporation of New York while the authors were members of the Child Development Research Unit, University of Nairobi (John W. M. Whiting and Beatrice Blyth Whiting, Directors). The authors are indebted to Beatrice Whiting for helpful comments on an earlier version of this paper. All statements are of course the sole responsibility of the authors.

1. These complexes are not necessarily present throughout the entire area of their primary distribution, and they are certainly not constant in their magnitude nor in the details of their manifestation. Nevertheless, they tend to possess a clear identifiability based on a stable congeries of traits, and they offer potential insights into the processes affecting sociocultural reproduction and change.

2. Five of the variables are social-structural and two behavioral. The social-structural variables are: (1) residence (sex distinction = exclusive residential emphasis on one sex, e.g., patrilocality); (2) authority succession (sex distinction = follows either male or female descent line, e.g., matrilineal); (3) kin groups (sex distinction = unilineal kin groups); (4) avuncular kin terminology (sex distinction = different terms for father's brother and mother's brother); and (5) cousin kin terminology (sex distinction = different terms for any first cousins). The behavioral variables are: (1) eating arrangements (sex distinction = husband and wife eat separately) and(2) attendance at birth (sex distinction = males not allowed to be present at childbirth).

3. It is the emphasis on sexual differentiation that might be common to societies, not a similarity between the specific content of the "adult" system and that of the child-training

practices. We enter here the caution that ratings of this type ought to be used with solid knowledge of the operations by which they are constructed and with proper acknowledgment of the sometimes scanty ethnographic information on which they are based. Barry (1981, p. 99) comments on "the unsystematic and anecdotal nature of most ethnographic descriptions" and points out that for much information, "it is uncertain whether [it] is limited to the typical and frequent events or includes descriptions of unusual or abnormal occurrences."

4. In selecting societies from the study of sex distinctions (Munroe, Whiting, & Hally, 1969), we included cases from a supplementary sample (reported in footnote form in the Munroe et al. study) in order to locate as many eligible cases as possible. For the Barry, Bacon, and Child (1967) ratings, we included all cases that were rated confidently on more than half the variables by two of the analysts conducting the Barry et al. study.

5. The sample is highly skewed, with seven of the seventeen societies falling into the Native American/North American culture area. But even for these seven societies within a single area, one of the two relationships—that between systemic sex distinctions and sex differences in responsibility training—continues to hold, $r_S = .71, p = .05$.

6. Fellow child household members (overwhelmingly siblings) have been excluded from the tabulations in order to allow a more unbiased estimate of the sample children's "pure choices" of playmates. Had household members been included in the figures for Tables 15.3 and 15.4, however, the outcomes would have been only slightly less strong than those presented. The use of only active participants rather than inclusion of all those present in the social scene obviously reduces the magnitude of the figures in the tables. The decision to exclude those "present but not participating" was made for much the same reason as above, namely, to try to get at sample children's preferred partners for social interaction.

7. In comparative perspective, the Logoli children's preferences for same-sex roles and same-sex tasks are not as strong as those of children in some other cultures (R. H. Munroe, Shimmin, & R. L. Munroe, 1984).

8. With the overall level of childcare by older children (siblings) showing a decline in 1978, either someone else in the home was taking up the slack (mothers or adolescents, perhaps) or infants and toddlers were receiving less attention than had been the case in 1967. We hope to take up the question in a future paper.

9. Obviously perception must occur at some level, and Bornstein and D'Agostino (1992) point out that their results do not imply that stimuli must be completely outside awareness to elicit an enhanced mere-exposure effect. The key may be that "repeated stimulus exposures [have] stronger effects on liking judgments than on recognition judgments" (Bornstein & D'Agostino, 1992, p. 551; cf. Reingold & Merikle, 1988). Children, then, under the conditions of low-awareness exposure to repeatedly presented stimuli, could be expected to establish stronger affective connections than cognitive connections.

10. The degree to which Logoli girls' induction into the labor force is accompanied by explicit and consciously formulated associations with the female role is relevant here, but we do not have data on the question. Our point, however, is that the elements making up the system of sex differentiation would *in the main* be transmitted implicitly.

11. Paradoxically, despite the underprivileged situation of females in Logoli culture, defense of the status quo in sex differentiation should apply equally to women and men.

12. LeVine, Klein, and Owen (1967) discovered something very much along these same lines in a comparison of modernizing and traditional Yoruba fathers in Ibadan, Nigeria. Although educated fathers were more willing than traditional fathers to undertake infant care and were more affectionate and less strict in assigning household tasks, there were no significant differences between the two groups of fathers with respect to authority and disci-

pline. An emphasis on authority and compliance is a pan-African trait, one that, like sex differentiation, can be accurately termed a culture complex (Doob, 1965; R. L. Munroe, R. H. Munroe, & LeVine, 1972). Thus moderate behavioral changes in childcare had little or no effect on established patterns of deference demands and on severity of discipline.

13. Many urban Native Americans living today in the Los Angeles area continue to take their adolescents into the California wilderness for questlike experiences, and their justification is very much in terms of the inculcation of fundamental values.

REFERENCES

Barry, Herbert, III. (1981). Uses and limitations of ethnographic descriptions. In Ruth H. Munroe, Robert L. Munroe, & Beatrice B. Whiting (Eds.), *Handbook of cross-cultural human development* (pp. 91–111). New York: Garland STPM Press.

Barry, Herbert, III, Bacon, Margaret K., & Child, Irvin L. (1957). A cross-cultural survey of some sex differences in socialization. *Journal of Abnormal and Social. Psychology, 55*, 327–332.

Barry, Herbert, III, Bacon, Margaret K., & Child, Irvin L. (1967). Definitions, ratings, and bibliographic sources for child training practices of 110 cultures. In Clelland S. Ford (Ed.), *Cross-cultural approaches* (pp. 293–331). New Haven, CT: HRAF Press.

Benedict, Ruth. (1922). The vision in plains culture. *American Anthropologist, 24*, 1–25.

Bornstein, Robert F., & D'Agostino, Paul R. (1992). Stimulus recognition and the mere exposure effect. *Journal of Personality and Social Psychology, 63*, 545–552.

Bradley, Candice. (1993). Women's power, children's labor. *Behavior Science Research, 27*, 70–96.

Bradley, Candice. (in press). Luyia. In David Levinson (Ed.), *Encyclopedia of world cultures*. New Haven, CT: HRAF Press.

Doob, Leonard W. (1965). Psychology. In Robert A. Lystad (Ed.), *The African world* (pp. 373–415). London: Pall Mall Press.

Ember, Carol R. (1981). A cross-cultural perspective on sex differences. In R. H. Munroe, R. L. Munroe, & B. B. Whiting (Eds.), *Handbook of cross-cultural human development* (pp. 531–580). New York: Garland.

Garibay-Patron, M. (1969). La psicología del Mexicano. *Revista Mexicana de Psicología, 3*, 350–354.

Gilmore, David D. (Ed.). (1987). *Honor and shame and the unity of the Mediterranean.*(Special Publication No. 22). Washington, DC: American Anthropological Association.

Håkansson, Thomas N. (1988). *Bridewealth, women and land: Social change among the Gusii of Kenya*. Stockholm: Almquist and Wiksell International.

Herskovits, Melville J. (1926). The cattle complex in East Africa. *American Anthropologist, 28*, 230–272, 361–368, 494–528.

Jahoda, Gustav, & Lewis, I. M. (Eds.). (1989). *Acquiring culture: Cross cultural studies in child development*. London: Routledge.

Kilbride, Philip Leroy, & Kilbride, Janet Capriotti. (1990). *Changing family life in East Africa*. University Park: Pennsylvania State University Press.

LeVine, Robert A. (1973). Patterns of personality in Africa. *Ethos, 1*, 123–152.

LeVine, Robert A., Klein, Nancy H., & Owen, Constance R. (1967). Father-child relationships and changing life-styles in Ibadan, Nigeria. In Horace Miner (Ed.), *The city in modern Africa* (pp. 215–255). New York: Frederick A. Praeger.

Maccoby, Eleanor E. (1990a). Children are "ruthless stereotypers." Excerpts from keynote speech, meeting of American Psychological Society. *APS Observer, 3* (4), 5–7.

Maccoby, Eleanor E. (1990b). Gender and relationships. A developmental account. *American Psychologist, 45*, 513–520.

Munroe, Robert L., & Munroe, Ruth H. (1971). Effect of environmental experience on spatial ability in an East African society. *Journal of Social Psychology, 83*, 15–22.

Munroe, Robert L., & Munroe, Ruth H. (1991). *Logoli time allocation* (rev. ed.). Cross-Cultural Studies in Time Allocation (Vol. 5, Series Ed. Allen Johnson). New Haven, CT: HRAF Press.

Munroe, Robert L., & Munroe, Ruth H. (1992). Fathers in children's environments: A four culture study. In Barry S. Hewlett (Ed.), *Father–child relations* (pp. 213–229). New York: Aldine de Gruyter.

Munroe, Robert L., Munroe, Ruth H., & LeVine, Robert A. (1972). Africa. In Francis L. K. Hsu (Ed.), *Psychological anthropology* (2nd ed) (pp. 71–120). Cambridge, MA: Schenkman.

Munroe, Robert L., Whiting, John W. M., & Hally, David J. (1969). Institutionalized male transvestism and sex distinctions. *American Anthropologist, 71*, 87–91.

Munroe, Ruth H., & Munroe, Robert L. (1971). Household density and infant care in an East African society. *Journal of Social Psychology, 83*, 3–13.

Munroe, Ruth H., & Munroe, Robert L. (1984). *Sex-role stereotypes and their correlates in four cultures.* Paper given at the 7th International Conference of the International Association for Cross-Cultural Psychology, Acapulco.

Munroe, Ruth H., & Munroe, Robert L. (in press). Field observations of behavior as a cross-cultural method. In Philip K. Bock (Ed.), *Handbook of psychological anthropology.* Greenwood Press.

Munroe, Ruth H., Shimmin, Harold S., & Munroe, Robert L. (1984). Gender understanding and sex role preference in four cultures. *Developmental psychology, 20*, 673–682.

Omark, Donald R., Omark, Monica, & Edelman, Murray. (1975). Formation of dominance hierarchies in young children. In Thomas R.Williams (Ed.), *Psychological anthropology* (pp. 289–315). The Hague: Mouton.

Peristiany, Jean G. (Ed.). (1966). *Honor and shame: The values of Mediterranean society.* Chicago: University of Chicago Press.

Reingold, E. M., & Merikle, P. M. (1988). Using direct and indirect measures to study perception without awareness. *Perception and Psychophysics, 44*, 563–575.

Rogoff, Barbara. (1978). Spot observation: An introduction and examination. *Quarterly Newsletter of the Institute for Comparative Human Development,* 2, 21–26.

Ross, Marc Howard, & Weisner, Thomas S. (1977). The rural-urban migrant network in Kenya: Some general implications. *American Ethnologist, 4*, pp. 359–375.

Schlegel, Alice, & Eloul, Rohn. (1987). A new coding of marriage transactions. *Behavior Science Research, 21*, 118–140.

Weisner, Thomas S. (1973). The primary sampling unit: A nongeographically based rural–urban example. *Ethos, 1*, 546–559.

Winick, Charles. (1956). *Dictionary of anthropology.* New York: Philosophical Library.

Zajonc, Robert B. (1968). Attitudinal effects of mere exposure. *Journal of Personality and Social Psychology Monographs, 9*(2, Pt. 2).

CULTURE, FAMILY, AND ECONOMY

16

Right Values and Good Fortune: Bukusu Responses to Ecological Opportunity

Jan J. de Wolf

INTRODUCTION

In many parts of East Africa extreme population density makes it impossible to achieve a decent livelihood from farming alone. Families who are short of land and who are not supported by regular off-farm cash incomes find themselves in a distressing situation. Opportunities for improvement depend heavily on the availability of capital: Agricultural efficiency could be increased through replacing low-value food crops with high-value cash crops, through investment in high-yielding milk cows, and generally through use of better implements, fertilizers, and herbicides and pesticides. Off-farm earning capacities could be maximized through the provision of better education. However, as such solutions depend on the capacity to save earnings for investment, they are often open to only a small minority of the population in these areas.

One of the areas that seems to have avoided this fate is northern Bungoma District in Kenya. At least until the 1970s, farm earnings allowed investment in agriculture as well as education. Higher agricultural productivity in turn generated more employment on farms, while the local availability of off-farm occupations, especially in education but also in commercial agriculture, led to more investment in farming.

How can this felicitous situation be explained? Of course, the circumstances had been favorable. Not only are the soils in northern Bungoma District fertile, the population density was also fairly low and, until the 1950s, it was possible to find unoccupied land within the district boundaries. The policies of the colonial administration towards the white farmers in the Kenyan Highlands favored the establishment of commercial maize farming in the African reserves in the 1930s and 1940s. The decision to extend smallholder coffee farming by Africans in the 1950s was also of great benefit, as northern Bungoma District was high enough and had sufficient rainfall for the establishment of Arabica coffee.

The culture of the Bukusu people, whose values emphasize both cooperation and the achievement of individual progress through the exploitation of new opportunities, was also instrumental. In the first part of this chapter I want to show that northern Bungoma District is indeed in a favorable position in comparison with other areas in Western Province by presenting independent evidence from socioeconomic surveys. Then I will demonstrate the importance of social organization and community values in explaining variations in responses to macro socioeconomic developments. I further explore the uniqueness of the Bukusu in this respect by comparing them with the Iteso and Nyole, among whom intensive anthropological field work was conducted at the same time that I worked with the Bukusu. In a final section, I compare the Bukusu with the Gisu, culturally and linguistically their nearest relatives.

In Bugisu, where the Gisu are located, the late 1960s were a time of crisis and the breakdown of law and order. In Bungoma District, they were a time of hope. The Bukusu had finally achieved a district of their own (although it still contained locally important Kalenjin minorities) and believed that this would allow them to spend whatever money they could on education so that they could profit from the employment opportunities created by the departure of Europeans and Asians. This raises the question of whether the situation in Bugisu differed so much from that in Bungoma District because the Bukusu followed a very different historical trajectory or because there were also basic cultural differences that helped to form such historical experiences in a decisive way.

POPULATION PRESSURE AND POVERTY IN WESTERN PROVINCE

In the 1970s the Dutch Organization for International Relations (NOVIB), a nongovernmental organization, was involved in various initiatives to establish multipurpose cooperatives in some villages in the eastern half of Western Province. Jan Lavrijsen conducted socioeconomic studies of communities where such cooperatives were set up. It turned out that the resource base of the villages in Isukha and Idakho locations to the south of Kakamega was insufficient to allow for the development of eventually self-supporting cooperative enterprises: There was no regular production of agricultural surpluses, and off-farm sources of employment and income were scarce. The situation in Kimilili Location to the north of Bungoma was much more promising. As a result, NOVIB decided to concentrate further efforts in support of these cooperatives in the latter area (Lavrijsen, 1984).

At first glance it would appear that the differences between the southern and northern parts of Western Province were essentially due to population pressure. In close cooperation with the Department of Geography of Utrecht University, Lavrijsen selected three villages in which to study this problem more closely. Two of the villages had already been investigated when Lavrijsen conducted his baseline studies, while a third, in North Maragoli Location, with even higher population density, was added to test the hypothesis that living conditions there would also be worse. In the village of Kimalewa, in the north, the population density was 169 per km^2, and farm incomes was relatively high. In the south, farm incomes were much lower than in the north, but surprisingly the standard of living in Isinzi (North Maragoli), with a population density of 1221 per km^2, was higher than in Shikokho (Idakho), with a density of 576 per km^2 (Lavrijsen, 1984).

The unit of investigation was the household. At Shikokho and Isinzi, about fifty households living in a contiguous area were questioned; at Kimalewa, fifty-five households in four different areas were visited. These areas were selected as representative of the whole region covered by the local cooperative society. Mean household size at Kimalewa was 8.7 persons, at Shikokho 5.6, and at Isinzi 5.4. According to Lavrijsen (1984), the larger family size at Kimalewa was caused by more and larger extended families, a higher frequency of polygamy, and a smaller volume of labor migration. However, Lavrijsen did not consider the pattern of dual households. In the southern part of Western Province, where Shikokho and Isinzi are located, it is not unusual for men who have permanent employment in town to establish dual households. This makes it possible for one wife to stay in town and the other on the farm, and the household composition changes frequently (cf. Weisner, 1976; Moock, 1976).

The sex ratios (males per 100 females) at Kimalewa, Shikokho, and Isinzi were 100, 108 and 79; for the age-group fifteen to fifty-nine years, they were 99, 97, and 65. At Kimalewa, there was little labor migration, as local employment opportunities were quite good. Isinzi is typically an area with much labor migration; young men from Shikokho are much less successful in finding employment outside their village. A closer examination shows that many young men remained bachelors because they could not support a family of their own. Young women, on the other hand, tended to move away and marry elsewhere, in areas where conditions were more favorable (Lavrijsen, 1984).

At Kimalewa, the reported average annual per capita income was K.Sh. 1,168; at Shikokho, K.Sh. 604; and at Isinzi, K.Sh. 606. (US$ = K.Sh. 36.00 in December, 1992). Farms at Kimalewa are much larger, averaging 5.09 ha, compared with 0.91 ha at Shikokho and 0.44 ha at Isinzi (1 hectare = 2.5 acres). At Kimalewa, 56 percent of gross income was derived from the sale of farm produce; at Shikokho, this figure was 20 percent, and at Isinzi only 13 percent (Lavrijsen, 1984). Access to salaried jobs was also important in determining the amount and composition of incomes. In rural areas the great majority of such jobs are provided by ministries or parastatal organizations. At Kimalewa, people with permanent employment in the area itself earned K.Sh. 67,000 annually, of which two-thirds came from teaching; in the other villages these earning were much smaller: K.Sh. 5,000 at Isinzi and K.Shs. 6,000 at Shikokho. If we look at the importance of money transfers from elsewhere in Kenya for the household income, we find that Kimalewa again formed an exception. At Kimalewa, money transfers amounted to 27 percent of off-farm income; at Shikokho and Isinzi this figure was 56 percent (Lavrijsen, 1984).

What do these figures mean in terms of living conditions? Lavrijsen established a poverty line based on food requirements expressed in the local costs of maize and an estimated annual average per capita need for cash expenditure of

K.Sh. 200 (1984). By this standard, 12 percent of the households at Kimalewa are poor, while at Isinzi 38 percent of the household were poor and at Shikokho as many as 56 percent. The difference between Kimalewa and the other villages is due to commercialization of agriculture, possible because of the large farm sizes, and to locally earned salaries. It is more difficult to explain the difference between Isinzi and Shikokho. How is it possible that the income situation at Isinzi is better, although the farm size is half of that at Shikokho?

Lavrijsen (1984) tried to provide an answer by looking at historical developments. He argued that around the turn of the century there was hardly any regional socioeconomic differentiation, but that since the 1920s it has become increasingly difficult to accommodate population growth at Isinzi and Shikokho. At a very early date, Isinzi became an area characterized by much labor migration. Maragoli was one of the first areas where Christianity made significant headway. Consequently children received the education necessary to participate in the formal, especially urban, sector of the economy. A network of people from Isinzi was established with a sufficient grip on employment opportunities. Moreover, a system of two annual harvests on the same fields was introduced when the traditional fallow periods could no longer be maintained because of land shortage. The fertility of the soil is maintained with cow dung. A cattle density of 4.32 animals per ha (compared with 1.49 for Shikokho and 1.54 for Kimalewa) makes this possible. Such a high density is achieved through a system of zero grazing and hand feeding.

In the 1930s, gold was discovered in the neighborhood of Shikokho, which led to a great demand for food and labor. It was easy to earn money near home. But when the mines were exhausted, it was difficult to find the same income opportunities through labor migration. Nor was it possible to intensify agriculture, although the climate and soil do not differ significantly from those found at Isinzi. Lavrijsen (1984) attributes the failure to intensify agriculture to lack of cattle after the closing of the mines, the disappearance of cattle sharing customs, and a market oriented production. He implies that the transition to dual cropping was accepted at Isinzi because there it concerned only the production of food for consumption. He reasons that if some farmers at Shikokho planted a second crop, the costs of guarding it would be too high, as the harvest would coincide with the hungry period for the rest of the population; a second crop planted only for sale and not for one's own consumption might be damaged out of jealousy or hostility.

Lavrijsen posits a clear connection between external macro socioeconomic factors and the reactions of the households in the different villages he investigated. At Isinzi, adaptation to increasing population pressure was possible through a tradition of labor migration and the introduction of a system of very intensive mixed farming. At Kimalewa, it was possible to achieve a thoroughgoing agricultural commercialization because sufficient land and well salaried positions were available. But at Shikokho, neither of these developments occurred. As a consequence, Shikokho is characterized by what Lavrijsen calls "community stress": Lack of trust, corruption and deception, drunkenness, quarrels, fighting, theft, rape, arson, poisoning, witchcraft, and even cases of murder and suicide have become a "normal" part of everyday life. Such phenomena are largely absent at Isinzi and Kimalewa, at least according to Lavrijsen (1984).

The data which Lavrijsen used were collected mainly through the administration of questionnaires. The responses were influenced by the difficulty of remembering income and expenditure over an extended period and by respondents' reluctance to give accurate information on wealth and poverty. This was certainly the case with people with very low incomes. Investigators found it too painful to enquire exhaustively how people living near the barest subsistence minimum could nevertheless remain alive with the help of others (Steenwinkel, 1979; cf. Lavrijsen, 1984). People often reported improbably high crop yields. Attempts were made to correct such figures immediately or when a first analysis showed them to be inconsistent with other data (Steenwinkel, 1979; cf. Lavrijsen 1984).

On the other hand, Lavrijsen's survey data are consistent with information gathered in the course of intensive anthropological field work among the Bukusu and the Logoli, who live in the areas where Kimalewa and Isinzi, respectively, are situated. A median annual net total household income of K.Sh. 5,505 at Kimalewa seems to tally quite well with size of income of selected households in the nearby Kibichori Water Scheme, especially when we take into consideration that the farm plots at Kibichori are much smaller than at Kimalewa (Storgaard, Arnfred, & Mululu, 1971). The median annual net total household income of K.Sh. 2,155 (about US$ 300 at the time) at Isinzi corresponds well with the estimated basic annual expenditures for six-person farm units of K.Sh.1,905 reported for a village in South Maragoli (Moock, 1976). The average farm size of 1.75 acres is somewhere in between that of Isinzi and Shikokho.

Lavrijsen does not address patterns of cooperation between households. Yet the social structure of the communities he investigated may well have been a decisive influence in the establishment of conditions favorable to the adaptation of the individual households to changing circumstances—or may explain their failure to adapt. Kimalewa's success was in large measure due to local, off-farm opportunities to earn money. Apart from a functioning cooperative, it is especially the educational system that provided employment. Its importance may be assessed by looking at the number of years of schooling reported by the interviewed household heads. At Kimalewa, the median was 3.6 years, as against 2.0 at Isinzi and only 0.3 at Shikokho (Lavrijsen, 1984, p. 80). In this part of Kenya, local initiative has always been important for the establishment and development of schools. The schools as well as the cooperative at Kimalewa are dependent on a community spirit that values cooperation for a common aim more highly than the acquisition of advantages for one's own clan or subclan. This can be seen as a consequence of the small size of localized clan fragments among the Bukusu, the members of which are always heavily dependent on the other fragments with whom they are connected through frequent marriages (cf. de Wolf, 1977).

The importance of the clan was much greater among the Idakho (Shikokho) and Logoli (Isinzi) than among the Bukusu (Bode, 1978). This could easily lead to factionalism. In the southern part of Western Province such rivalries were most prominent among the Idakho (Bode, 1978). The situation in Idakho Location was aggravated by the corrupt practices of the colonial chiefs, who used their power for their own advantage rather than for the common good in their divided location (Bode, 1978). The demise of the NOVIB sponsored cooperative at Shikokho was due not only to a lack of sufficient economic resources in the area but also to clan rivalries in the management committee (Steenwinkel, 1979). It is not clear whether the clan still plays an important role at Isinzi. If this is no longer the case, one could expect that church affiliation could be important for the organization of communal activities (cf. Moock, 1976).

SOCIAL STRUCTURE AND THE ORGANIZATION OF PRODUCTION

In this section I explore how social structure mediates between macro socioeconomic conditions and the way people relate to their ecological situation by comparing the Bukusu with the Nyole and Iteso. The point of reference is the situation around 1970, when Susan and Michael Whyte did research among the Nyole of eastern Uganda (Whyte, 1974), Ivan Karp among the Iteso in western Kenya (1978), and I among the neighboring Bukusu, also in western Kenya (de Wolf, 1977).

The area where the Nyole live is a gently rolling landscape bounded to the north and west by slowly moving rivers and cut through by other water courses that are either permanent or seasonally flooded. Altitude varies between 3,500 and 3,700 feet. Annual average rainfall is between fifty and sixty inches. Soils are mainly of medium to very low fertility. The country of the Iteso is characterized by a series of hills running north–south, and its altitude varies between 3,500 and 4,000 feet. Annual average rainfall is between sixty and seventy inches. Flooding is a serious problem, as one out of every five years there is too much rain. Soils are moderately fertile. The area of the Bukusu considered here (near Sirisia in South Malakisi Location) is part of the foothills of Mount Elgon and varies in altitude between 4,600 and 5,400 feet. Annual average rainfall is between sixty and seventy inches. Soils are fairly fertile (Whyte, 1974; Karp, 1978; Karp & Karp, 1979; de Wolf, 1977).

The population density based on overall figures is 245 per square mile for the Iteso, 297 for the Nyole, and 375 for the Bukusu. The areas investigated by Karp and de Wolf seem fairly representative, but in the area of Nyole where the Whytes did their research, density reached the 400 per square mile mark because of the quality of the land, high and sufficiently well drained to be immune to flooding in the rainy seasons (Karp, 1978; de Wolf, 1977; Whyte, 1974).

The geographical differences between the areas of the Iteso and Nyole, on the one hand, and that of the Bukusu, on the other hand, are partly reflected in patterns of crop production. Among the Bukusu, Arabica coffee is the most important cash crop next to maize, which is also the staple subsistence food crop. Secondary food crops are bananas and sweet potatoes. In the 1960s, onions became an important cash crop, while cotton is distinctly marginal and limited to the very lowest parts. Among the Iteso, cotton and maize are cash crops, but maize is not normally consumed as food nor used for brewing local beer. Millet is much preferred for beer production as well as for a staple food. It is grown either alone or in stands mixed with cassava, the most important secondary food crop. Cassava grows well on soils with a fertility too low for other crops and can endure very irregular rainfall. Millet mixes well with cassava flour and can be kept for a longer time in the granary than maize, which is said to remain good for only nine months. Because millet can be mixed and stored in this way, people can avoid paying cash for food. Perhaps it is also significant that maize yields are higher at the altitudes where the Bukusu can grow this crop. Among the Nyole, cotton is the only important cash crop, millet the preferred staple food, and bananas and sweet potatoes important secondary food crops. Maize is not important either as a food crop or cash crop, because millet stores well in humid conditions and is therefore better suited than maize to be cultivated at a time that labor requirements for cotton are low. Moreover, in Uganda maize has been officially discouraged because it harbors cotton pests (de Wolf, 1977; Karp, 1978; Heald, 1991; Whyte, 1974; Acland, 1971).

Traditionally Bukusu were as much pastoralists as cultivators, and cattle are still important. Although overall figures amount to one head per capita, in the western areas the figure is 0.7 per capita, which is almost the same as that obtaining among the Iteso (de Wolf, 1977; Karp, 1978). However, since the population density for the Bukusu areas is higher, the Bukusu keep more cattle on the same area of land. This may be due partly to the use of cattle dung as manure, which would reduce fallow and make more land available for grazing, and partly to greater wealth, which results in cattle being kept as a capital investment. Overall figures for Bukedi District, where the Nyole live, indicate that Iteso and Bukusu have twice the number of cattle per capita (United Nations, 1967).

Among the Iteso and Bukusu, the enclosure of land was completed in around 1955. Sons who want to get married and become the head of a household of their own expect to receive a piece of land from their fathers (de Wolf, 1977; Karp, 1978). Land can also be sold, but this seems to be more common among Bukusu than Iteso. Among the former, buyers often belong to the salaried elite. Sons for whom a father has bought an expensive education may be expected to buy their own farms, leaving their share in the family farm to other children. Among the Nyole, a son remains in the compound of his father after marriage and uses part of the land that was allocated to his mother when she married. Only after many years does a son move away to build a separate home, and only then will he get a separate plot of his own. That is also the time that he may take a second wife. Reallocation of land within households is rare, and between independent households nonexistent (Whyte, 1974). But among the Iteso and Bukusu, land given to wives for cultivation can be taken back by their husbands and be reallocated as they see fit (Karp, 1978; de Wolf, 1977).

The three ethnic groups considered here all have concepts that can be translated as 'clan' and 'lineage,' yet none of them organizes its society as a segmentary system of corporate groups with political or economic functions. Nyole clans are thought of as perpetual exogamous units, while Iteso and Bukusu clans may be divided into exogamous subclans between which marriage is possible. Exogamous (sub-)clans are especially important because no one is allowed to marry into any of the four (sub-)clans to which his or her grandparents belong. Membership is acquired patrilineally at birth (Whyte, 1983; Karp, 1978; de Wolf, 1977).

Lineages consist of the patrilineal descendants of an ancestor one or two generations removed from the eldest living men. Among the Nyole, the span of the minimal lineage may vary with the function that it has for its members. The lineage, which is particularly concerned with access to land, is less inclusive than the group of agnates within which widows can be inherited (Whyte, 1983). Lineages are clearly marked off at funeral ceremonies (Whyte, 1983). Among the Iteso, the lineage conducts funeral rituals and is involved in all domestic ceremonies at which the wives of all the men of this group need to be present, even if they have to travel far (Karp, 1978). Among the Bukusu, the paternal descendants of a common grandfather assist each other with bridewealth payments for sons and share those received for daughters. They are known as 'the people who share the meat,' clansmen who would invite each other when killing the 'ox of splitting' as middle-aged men, a ceremony rarely performed nowadays (de Wolf, 1977).

Nyole have an Omaha kinship terminology, which emphasizes the unity of the clan of the wife-givers and also establishes a single category for all the children of a clanswoman belonging to a man's own or an older generation. Wife-givers are superior to wife-takers (Whyte, 1974). Bukusu and Iteso have a terminology that is largely generational. Yet among the Iteso there is also a tendency to regard wife-givers as superior to wife-takers (Karp, 1978). Bukusu prefer brothers to marry into different clans, and sororal polygamy is definitely ruled out (cf. Wagner, 1949).

Neighborhoods are heterogeneous in terms of clan or lineage membership. Among the Nyole, heads of households of the same clan rarely number more than thirty and frequently as few as a half-dozen (Whyte, 1974). The largest lineage in the Iteso area surveyed by Karp, occupied by seventy households, consisted of twenty-seven heads of households (Karp, 1978). Among the Bukusu, an investigation of clanship of over five hundred officially registered plot owners yielded about sixty different clan names. There were only eight clans which had more than the median number of plots, which was twenty-four (de Wolf, 1977). But the rules of exogamy ensure that no matter how heterogeneous a community is in terms of clan membership, the network of affinal and cognatic relationships will become very dense, especially when there is a tendency for neighbors to intermarry, as is well documented for the Bukusu (de Wolf, 1977). The predominance of kinship models for ordering daily interactions is reflected in the use of kinship terms among the Iteso and Bukusu, even when genealogical links are absent (Karp, 1978; de Wolf, 1977). This is perhaps also the case among the Nyole, but specific information is lacking.

Among the Nyole there exists a typical "house property complex." The relative independence of the different subsistence units within the same household, which come into existence when in-marrying women are given plots to support themselves and their children, extends to the cultivation and sale of cotton and occasionally other cash crops. The household head retains some land for himself, and a married man will expect to receive more labor from his wives than he himself contributes to their fields (Whyte, 1983). Discrepancy between the needs for food and cash and shortage of land in individual cases, aggravated by a general population pressure, has led to extensive temporary renting of land, which is paid for in money and food. Buying and selling of land, which could be another solution to this problem, is uncommon. Agnatic relatives do not have any special claims to get loans of land. The system emphasizes a total network of agnates, cognates, and friends (Whyte, 1974). Work parties are not necessary for agricultural production. Farmers may, however, employ each other for cash during short periods, for example, for weeding a cotton plot or plowing a field (Whyte, 1974).

Among the Iteso, sons get a piece of land from their father when they marry. When the father dies, the rest of the land is divided, as is the cattle. The eldest son of each wife is expected to get a larger share than the other sons. Cattle received as bridewealth for full sisters or its offspring go to their brothers (Karp, 1978). Although among the Iteso the allocation of fields and cows to women can be changed at any time, a husband and his wife or wives can be largely independent of each other economically. Women have to earn the cash to pay school fees and to buy household supplies for their own matrisegments. Although they are not required to provide labor for their husbands' cash crops, they often help them with the sowing, weeding, and harvesting of their cotton and maize. Husbands are only required to clear the fields for their wives (Karp, 1978). Heald suggests that women do not object to helping their husbands cultivate cotton, because such fields are very suitable for subsequent cultivation of millet. However, they do object to the cultivation of tobacco, which was introduced as a cash crop in the north of the Iteso area in the 1980s. Tobacco competes directly with the millet crop for female labor, as the husband recognizes no automatic responsibility for buying food crops. This is also one of the reasons that maize did not replace millet (Heald, 1991).

The relative autonomy of husband and wife is counterbalanced by the frequent organization of communal work parties. Iteso define a neighborhood in terms of proper neighborly behavior, which consists mainly of cooperation in agricultural pursuits and a good deal of shared consumption of food and beer. When a household wants a piece of work to be done, it is announced that beer will be ready on a certain day. People who want to come to the party in the late afternoon will work for the host until the midday meal, which he also provides. Although Karp stresses the agronomic necessity of short periods of intensive work effort, he also mentions that some old men and women would otherwise be unable to finish the necessary work in the fields. The discrepancy between land and labor is solved through sharing labor rather than land as among the Nyole (Karp, 1978).

Among the Bukusu, sons who marry also get a piece of land from their father, unless they can get farms elsewhere because they earn enough to buy one or qualify for loans. In the 1960s, many eldest sons were able to acquire farms in this way in the settlement schemes in the former White Highlands. When the father dies, cattle are divided among all sons, keeping in mind their bridewealth requirements. However, cattle received for girls does not remain within their matrisegment. The household head controls the sale of cash crops and cattle, and wives and children are certainly required to help their husband and father with cultivation. On the other hand, men also help their wives with the food crops for which they are responsible. Heald (1991) remarks that Bukusu sell maize at the time of harvest in order to invest in cattle that can be converted back into food during the time of shortage. Women may earn money from the sale of food crops, chickens and eggs, and cooked food at the market, and from brewing beer. Storgaard et al. (1971) report that women are responsible for paying school fees in the lower forms of the primary school, but in my experience they are only asked to help if they have some source of cash income. Storgaard et al. also mention the existence of rotating credit associations among women which enable them to raise such money. Work groups for weeding and harvesting are nonexistent in the area considered here. Where they occur elsewhere among the Bukusu, they are organized on the basis of strict reciprocity and not rewarded with a beer party. Neighborhood beer parties among the Bukusu are commercial affairs, at which people have to pay the woman who provides the beer. When farmers need additional labor they pay in money or sometimes in food. Some Bukusu farmers employ one or more permanent laborers. In those cases they often have a salaried job themselves. On their farms one may also find exotic cattle breeds, which give much more milk than native cows, and tractors for plowing instead of oxen (de Wolf, 1977).

The cash income generated among the Nyole is very small and hardly sufficient for covering consumption needs and social obligations and almost never enough for investment in productive activities (Whyte 1974). The same seems to be true of the Iteso (Karp 1977). The primary cause of this poverty is the low price paid for cotton. Nyole and Iteso economics are characterized by shared poverty. Imbalances of land and labor are corrected through land loans and work parties. Bukusu clearly enjoy a more favorable ecological environment, yet they are also characterized by two factors that helped them to make most of these opportunities, which are absent among the Iteso and Nyole. The control that the household head has over the sale of cash crops and cattle makes productive investments more easily attainable than when matrisegments control such income to a considerable extent. Bukusu also stress the equality and mutual assistance between affines more than Nyole and Iteso. Among the latter, agnatic exclusiveness and inequality between bride-givers and bride-takers are more important.

Among the Nyole, attempts to use clan affiliation for the organization of welfare societies did not succeed (Whyte, 1974). Among the Iteso, leadership is essentially a matter of patronage (in the past) and brokerage (in more recent times), but lacks a corporate ideology that could transcend agnatic identities (Karp, 1978). Cooperation among the Iteso remains limited to patterns of dyadic reciprocity between neighbors, while among the Bukusu, associations for communal welfare constitute themselves as corporate groups. This was certainly the key to their early and self-sustaining interest in schooling, which led to the achievement of well-paid, often urban-based jobs, and also to investments in agricultural development. It also formed the basis of many maize-selling cooperatives through which Bukusu tried to circumvent Asian traders in the late colonial period (de Wolf, 1977). But it also made possible the introduction and marketing of onions in the late 60s.

It could only succeed because farmers organized themselves as a growers' association, which guaranteed paying back credit for buying onion seed and improved local roads to allow trucks to reach the farms for collecting the harvest. The communal aspects were emphasized through devoting the (quite modest) membership fees to local community development projects: building a preschool nursery and a dispensary (de Wolf, 1977).

VALUES AND SOCIAL CHANGE

Linguistically and culturally the Bukusu are closely related to the Gisu, their neighbors on the slopes and foothills of Mount Elgon at the other side of the international border in Uganda. Yet among them the key value of cooperation, which I thought to be characteristic of the Bukusu, is absent. Instead we find an unrestrained individualism and, especially in the postcolonial era, an escalation of acts of interpersonal violence (Heald, 1989). This difference is partly a response to extreme population pressure and a virtual collapse of the rural administrative machine that had been developed in colonial times for the maintenance of law and order. The population density in Bugisu was 329 per square mile in 1959, 441 in 1969, and in the more fertile mountain areas attaining even 1,500. For the Bukusu it was still possible to find unoccupied land within the boundaries of their district in the 1950s, and in the 1960s a considerable area of the White Highlands was opened up for Bukusu settlement.

In both Kenya and Uganda, native courts were abolished after independence, but the consequences were more serious in Uganda. In Kenya, the official judicial role of the chiefs had been abolished in the 1930s, but in Uganda they had had such responsibilities throughout the colonial period. If anything, in Kenya access to the courts became easier as their number increased after independence. Moreover, land registration in Kenya after independence was accompanied by land adjudication. At least in the part of Bungoma District where I worked, the committees that were put in charge of this process were constituted so as to reach a maximal consensus from the people concerned. In Uganda people did not make full use of the new courts, and much pressure was put on the chiefs and their assistants also to stop unofficial arbitration (Heald, 1989; de Wolf, 1977).

In contrast to Kenya, chiefs in Uganda were part of local government and not under direct control of the president. Curtailing their power was part of Obote's policy of strengthening central control. In colonial times Gisu peasants gained concessions from the central government through local elites, as their economic contribution was considered essential for sufficient state revenues. But after independence, gaining, maintaining, and expanding political power took precedence over economic development and administrative efficiency (Bunker, 1987). Such developments were less pronounced in Kenya, at least during the Kenyatta era and the earlier years of the Moi regime.

Demographic and political differences between Gisu and Bukusu are obvious, but their consequences can only be understood in terms of traditional values. Even if the Bukusu had had to face the same circumstances, their response would have been different. As Gisu see it, men (in contrast to women) are characterized by a special kind of willpower that gives them the necessary drive to assert themselves against other men. They get this power through taking part in a circumcision ritual during their late adolescence. It is the source of their courage to endure this ordeal and at the same time the proof that they have acquired this power, called *lirima*. Although this power may impel men to resort to violence when they feel that their individual rights are neglected, many acts of physical aggression are also inspired by fear and suspicion that men may have set aside the ordinary moral restraints in pursuing their interests. A striking instance is the resort to violence of sons whose fathers (or their inheritors) procrastinate or even refuse to give them a piece of land on which to establish an independent household (Heald, 1989). Eventually such behavior is counterproductive, because it gives the young man a reputation for antisocial behavior, which will only make it more difficult for him to escape the predicament of being considered a bachelor wastrel to whom no one owes moral responsibility. But it is not only young men whose *lirima* causes them to go astray; old men can use various kinds of supernatural means such as cursing and witchcraft whenever they feel slighted by the younger generation (Heald, 1989). *Lirima*, as a legitimate mode of self-assertion, can only be exercised by an autonomous man who, in defending his own rights, has no reason to envy others. Those who cannot live up to this requirement are typically the young and the old, but also people who suffer misfortune or fall ill. Generally, the growing shortage of land leads to increased insecurity of tenure for the poorer sections of the community, whose chances of obtaining land or holding on to a small plot diminish over time. This harsh economic reality provides the backcloth for the equally harsh attitudes the Gisu take towards the poor. Fears of theft and witchcraft are associated with the jealousies and resentments of the poor, a product of their *lirima* (Heald, 1989). Once people get a bad reputation, this is believed to be the result of an inherent disposition. A bad character cannot be reformed. Killing such a person is justified because there is no other remedy. Very often the immediate cause may be trivial—theft of a bunch of bananas, verbal insults uttered in drunkenness—but when it is a symptom of degeneration, the culprit gets what he deserves (Heald, 1989).

Bukusu know the word *lirima*, but it does not seem to be a key concept as among the Gisu. It is not a special power inherent in men and acquired at circumcision. The age at which Bukusu boys are circumcised is generally lower. Rather than symbolizing access to adult status, circumcision indicates sexual maturity. It requires single-handedness of purpose on the part of the candidates, but also evokes the support and sympathy of kinsfolk, some of whom play indispensable roles in this ritual, and of neighbors. It establishes enduring bonds between men circumcised in the same year. At the circumcision of a son, a man kills an animal for his agemates. Gisu believe that these agemates may curse the boy if he does not do this. But "the practise came into such disrepute, inciting so many threats of cursing and violence that in 1954 the local government passed a bylaw forbidding it" (La Fontaine, 1959, p. 42; cited by Heald, 1989, p. 122). I never heard of such abuses among the Bukusu.

Although affinal relationships are very important among the Gisu and are seen as the ideal basis upon which the individual can develop lifelong friendships, their traditional role was different from the function they fulfilled among the Bukusu. Among the Bukusu, in-laws were important for political leaders who tried to recruit people to help them build and defend a walled fort; among the Gisu, intermarriage often merely strengthened the already existing association between patrilineal lineages and localities. For Gisu there are no rules of exogamy extending beyond the actual descendants of one's great-grandparents. As a consequence, men who are distantly related patrilineally renew the bonds of consanguinity through marrying related women (Heald, 1989). Warfare between Gisu was endemic in precolonial times. Clans and subclans were identified with specific territories, and interclan fighting is described as frequently bitter and of long duration. Within these territories shallow lineages, linked through parochial marriages, formed tenuous coalitions. "Deep and bitter factionalisation within local areas was evidently marked and receives much comment in missionary reports and letters, as it was seen to hinder the success of the missions because different families refused to work collectively on mission buildings or even attend church services together. It also receives early recognition by the administration" (Heald, 1989, p. 154).

In his study of the role of the coffee cooperative societies in the political development of the Gisu, Bunker says that "suspicion and jealousy between lineages and regions always lay close to the surface of Bagisu ethnic unity" (1987, p. 46). All this is in striking contrast with Bukusu traditions of warfare. Bukusu united against external enemies and did not fight among themselves (de Wolf, 1977). The expression *lirango lienjofu*, 'the thigh of the elephant' symbolizes the common destiny and solidarity of the Bukusu (Makila, 1978).

CONCLUSION

In this article I have compared the Bukusu with other ethnic groups in the same region of East Africa with whom they share many characteristics. In this way one gets a greater understanding of the possible reasons for the differences, which are also important. My aim was not to establish generalizations about relations between variables but rather to explore interpretations of typical patterns that seem to fit together because their different parts imply each other. They are the result of complex interactions between ecological opportunities, traditional values, and large scale economic and political developments such as capitalism and colonialism. This project is also part of a continuous evaluation of my experiences in northern Bungoma District in the late 1960s. I am acutely aware that the images and models with which I tried to order my fieldwork data are a product of my personal biography and of the anthropological tradition within which I try to communicate the results of my investigations. I am therefore grateful for the publications of colleagues who worked in similar circumstances because they are a source of alternative perspectives on Bukusu culture and society. The work of Ivan Karp

(1978) led me to consider the role of patterns of cooperation within the household, which was supported by additional material which I could find in the work of Lavrijsen (1984), Storgaard et al. (1971), and Heald (1991). My ideas about the importance among the Bukusu of cooperation for common political and economic goals were checked in the historical accounts of other societies in western Kenya and eastern Uganda by Bode (1978), Karp (1978), and Bunker (1987). Finally, my speculations about the enduring relevance of certain fundamental traditional values were rendered more likely through the splendid contrast provided by Heald in her study of Gisu violence and concepts of personhood (1989).

I pointed out that certain traditional values concerning the division of labor and the control of property within families, as well as the way in which cooperation between families at the community level and beyond is organized, can help explain why the Bukusu seem to have made so much of their favorable environment and of the political decisions pertaining to African involvement in cash crop production in colonial times.

This does not mean that these values themselves need no explanation or cannot be changed. The differences between Bukusu and Gisu are in accordance with characteristics that are typical of other culturally and linguistically closely related groups, which are divided into agriculturalists and pastoralists. Bukusu values such as independence and self-control, cooperation and industriousness, and a socially cohesive focus are also typical of other pastoralist groups. Gisu, on the other hand, share the central core of the values of other farming groups, namely interpersonal tension, hostility, anxiety, and sensitivity to insults, which lead to litigation and witchcraft. They also sometimes produce impulsive physical attack when open aggression does occur (Edgerton, 1971).

The central role of the husband–father among the Bukusu as manager of labor and capital resources and the relatively high cash incomes from agriculture and animal husbandry set them off from the other groups considered here. The Bukusu developed this pattern not merely because traditionally the autonomy of the matrisegments was limited but also because the advantages of this combination were demonstrated by Christian converts. Their monogamy avoided complications arising from multiple responsibilities of plural marriages, and it also set resources free for investment in commercial agriculture and education. Once it became clear that such investment was very rewarding, people also tried to realize it in polygamous households (de Wolf, 1977). A similar process was identified by Heald among the Iteso. When tobacco was introduced among them in the 1980s, the high monetary rewards of flue cured tobacco made it possible to pay secondary school fees, which were normally quite beyond their peasant incomes. In this situation a new ideal of a unitary household with flexible resource management over time and a need for reciprocity emerged (Heald, 1991).

REFERENCES

Acland, J. D. (1971). *East African crops*. London: Longman.

Bode, Francis C. (1978). *Leadership and politics among the Abaluyia of Kenya, 1894–1963*. Unpublished doctoral dissertation, Yale University.
Bunker, Stephen G. (1987). *Peasants against the state: The politics of market control in Bugisu, Uganda, 1900–1983*. Urbana: University of Illinois Press.
Edgerton, Robert A. (1971). *The individual in cultural adaptation: A study of four East African peoples*. Berkeley: University of California Press.
Heald, Suzette. (1989). *Controlling anger: The sociology of Gisu violence*. Manchester: Manchester University Press for the International African Institute.
Heald, Suzette. (1991). Tobacco, time and the household economy in two Kenya societies: The Teso and the Kuria. *Comparative Studies in Society and History, 33*, 130–157.
Karp, Ivan. (1978). *Fields of change among the Iteso of Kenya*. London: Routledge and Kegan Paul.
Karp, Ivan, & Karp, Patricia. (1979). Living with the spirits of the death. In Z. Ademuwagun, John A. A. Ayoade, Ira E. Harrison, & Dennis M. Warren (Eds.), *African therapeutic systems* (pp. 22–35). Waltham, MA: Crossroads Press.
La Fontaine, J. S. (1959). *The Gisu of Uganda*. London: International African Institute.
Lavrijsen, J. S. G. (1984). *Rural poverty and impoverishment in Western Kenya*. Utrecht: Department of Geography, University of Utrecht.
Makila, F. E. (1978). *An outline history of the Babukusu*. Nairobi: Kenya Literature Bureau.
Moock, Joyce Lewinger. (1976). *The migration process and differential economic behavior in South Maragoli, Western Kenya*. Unpublished doctoral dissertation, Columbia University.
Steenwinkel, John. (1979). *Rurale instituties en regionale differentiatie in West Kenya*. Unpublished master's thesis, Rijksuniversiteit, Utrecht.
Storgaard, Birgit, Arnfred, Niels, & Mululu, Joseph. (1971). *Report on the Kibichori Water Scheme*. Aarhus: University of Aarhus.
United Nations. (1967). *East African livestock survey II*. Rome: Food and Agricultural Organization.
Wagner, Günter. (1949). *The Bantu of North Kavirondo* (Vol. 1). London: Oxford University Press for the International African Institute.
Weisner, Thomas S. (1976). The structure of sociability: Urban migration and urban–rural ties in Kenya. *Urban Anthropology, 5*, 199–223.
de Wolf, Jan J. (1977). *Differentiation and integration in Western Kenya: A study of religious innovation and social change among the Bukusu*. The Hague: Mouton.
Whyte, Michael Anthony. (1974). *The ideology of descent in Bunyole*. Unpublished doctoral dissertation, University of Washington.
Whyte, Michael Anthony. (1983). Clan versus lineage: Notes on the semantics of solidarity and conflict among the Ugandan Nyole. *Folk, 25*, 129–45.

17

Changing Roles in the Bukusu Family

Simiyu Wandibba

INTRODUCTION

This chapter addresses the changing productive roles of the Bukusu nuclear family unit from precolonial times to present. Precolonially, the family division of labor by age and gender was quite marked, and family members performed prescribed roles for which they were trained within the family unit. With the beginning of the colonial era, formal education, the introduction of cash cropping, and wage-labor migration changed the entire household division of labor, affecting not only the roles of men and women but also the training and socialization of children. These changes were solidified with independence, such that the contemporary sexual division of labor within the Bukusu family resembles little of its precolonial predecessor. Nowadays, the family is no longer the locus of most food production in Bungoma, and the Bukusu woman shoulders most of the burden of the productive responsibilities that remain.

Babukusu are the majority ethnic community in the Bungoma District of Western Province. The other original inhabitants of the district include the culturally and linguistically related Abatachoni, Sabaot, and Iteso, in descending order of numerical superiority. Because of the long historical links, the four groups of people have had a lot of cultural intermingling, mainly as a result of intermarriages and assimilation.

Information for this chapter was obtained from randomly selected opinion leaders in the Bukusu community. Selection was based on age and continuous residence in Bungoma District. Informal discussions were held with men and women over fifty years of age, on an individual basis and at various times, in order to tap their knowledge of productive roles of family members from an historical perspective. The communication involved simply a brief description of activities that were related to home food production by gender and age before, during, and after the colonial period. To put the discussion in proper perspective, however, it might be worthwhile to first briefly describe the Bukusu family.

THE BUKUSU FAMILY

Babukusu define their family on the basis of marriage, residence, and the attendant economic cooperation. This means that a family consists of a married couple or married couples and their child(ren), and that in this relationship individuals have certain responsibilities in ensuring the economic survival of the family. On the basis of residence, two types of family are recognized: *enju* and *chinju*. In its ordinary meaning the term *enju* refers to a house, but when applied to the concept of family it stands for what Eurocentric scholars call the nuclear family. Its plural form, *chinju*, is the equivalent of the so-called extended family.

Enju consists of a man, his wife or wives, and all their children. *Chinju*, on the other hand, comprise the parents of the man, his wife or wives, and their children as well as their close relatives. Members of an *enju* tend to cooperate most extensively in all day-to-day activities. Its members also tend to be characterized by occupational differentiation, on the one hand, and a clearly defined sexual division of labor, on the other. In this chapter, the discussion is restricted to this type of family, that is, to the nuclear family.

THE PRECOLONIAL PERIOD

During the precolonial era, family ties in the Bukusu community were much stronger than they are today. During the same period, the roles played by the individual members of each family were much more defined than they are now. Both the family links and the roles of each individual were governed by cultural norms known to and obeyed by all members of the community.

Education played an important role in the specification of the duties of the different members in a family. The content of that education was determined by both the physical and the social environment (Sifuna, 1985). The physical environment determined the nature of economic activities that were carried out. The economic activities included cultivation, animal husbandry, hunting, gathering, and fishing, in order of descending importance. According to Sifuna (1985), elders aimed at adapting children to their physical surroundings and teaching them how to use such surroundings from their earliest years. Within the homestead and its surroundings, siblings, parents, and older relatives were responsible for training in economic responsibilities.

Up to about six years of age, children learned how to exploit their immediate surroundings. They were taught about edible plants, insects, and birds. At this age the children were not expected to contribute to the family food as such. Rather, they were given this knowledge so that they could use it to acquire foodstuffs for use as snacks, and insects such as grasshoppers became a favorite snack for children. Various types of fruits were also gathered by the children and consumed, generally on the spot. The fruits most often consumed were those obtained from trees that grew near homes, for example, various types of *busangura* (Rhus spp.), *chimbunue* (Physalis peruviana), *bufutumbwe* (Vitex fischeri), *chifutu* (Vitex doniana), *kamafwora* (Annona senegalensis), *kamakomosi* (Vangueria madagascariensis), and *kamakhuyu* (Ficus sp.). In general, the acquisition of these fruits did not require much assistance from anybody; children obtained them largely on their own. With the assistance of older siblings, children could also catch some of the smaller birds for their own consumption. Note, however, that although these snacks were supposed to be consumed by the children, more often than not the children shared them with their older siblings as well as their mothers. By and large, these snacks satisfied the basic nutritional needs of the children. This, in turn, meant that the children did not keep on pestering their older siblings and/or mothers for food. Consequently, adults would spend more of their time on other productive roles.

Between the ages of six and ten, children were expected to contribute in simple ways to the family's food production and acquisition. They participated in simple agricultural activities such as weeding sorghum, millet, and bananas and the planting and weeding of various types of vegetables. This was also the period when the sexual division of labor started being emphasized. Through imitation and observation, children learned about their future roles in society. The young girls were introduced to some of the issues pertaining to womanhood and motherhood. Thus young girls would accompany their mothers in search of food, especially vegetables, water, and firewood. They were also expected to have small gardens in which they cultivated their own vegetables. The principal vegetable cultivated by Babukusu was *chisaka* (Gynondropsis gynandra). Other types of domesticated vegetables included *murere* (Corchorus olitorius), *litoto* (Amaranthus hybridus), *emboka*(Amaranthus lividus), *kimiro* (Crotalaria brevidens), *endelema* (Basella alba), and two types of *kimisiebebe* (Cucurbita moschata and C. pepo). Of these vegetables, the easiest to cultivate were *endelema* and *kimisiebebe*. On their part, the boys were taught about some responsibilities associated with manhood and fatherhood. They looked after calves and the small stock within the homesteads. In addition, they assisted in simple agricultural activities such as burning bushes before cultivation and weeding.

In addition to the roles outlined above, children of both sexes continued to learn about the different animals, plants, and insects that they could exploit for food, both for themselves and for the family. Trapping termites and gathering mushrooms became important roles in food acquisition for children in this age range. Termites could be eaten as a snack or as a relish with *ugali*, the staple food. On the other hand, mushroom stew was cherished by everyone and was eaten with any main dish. This was also the time when children of both sexes would be taught skills in cooking. At first this was nothing more than boiling water for vegetables or *ugali*, keeping the fire burning, plucking vegetables, or straining traditional salt from ashes. Children at this age were also expected to know how to clean cooking pots and various utensils used in dishing and serving food, as well as gourds used for the storage of milk. The children also learned to churn milk. Finally, children of both sexes played an important role in sibling caretaking (Weisner, this volume). This allowed older members of the family to concentrate more on economically related activities.

Between ten and fifteen years, children became more closely associated with the family's social life and that of the community at large. The sexual division of roles also became much more marked. Girls were taught about the intricacies of womanhood and motherhood by their grandmothers. They also took on more responsibilities in the production and acquisition of food for the family. They were now expected to fetch water and firewood, gather vegetables, participate in grinding the necessary cereals such as millet, and cook food that would be eaten by one, a few, or all members of the family as their age permitted. As they grew older within this age range, the girls were expected to and did till their own plots, where they planted their own vegetables, potatoes, and millet. The size of the plots to be cultivated was increased as the girls grew older. Ultimately, each girl would have a plot big enough to produce millet that could fill her own granary.

Boys, on the other hand, were taught about manhood and fatherhood. They were expected to tend the calves and the young of the small stock on their own. They also participated, depending on age, in clearing farms before cultivation and in planting, weeding, and harvesting. It was also during this age that the boys became active in trapping birds and small game and in fishing in the rivers near their homes.

Both boys and girls were taught how to milk cows and goats, starting with the latter. The children also continued with their activities of gathering wild fruits and mushrooms. Those fruits found a little bit far from home became important, including *kamachabungwe* (Saba comoronsis), *busolamalwa* (Mussaenda acuarta), *kamasalila* (Afromomum sp.), *busongolamunwa* (Dovyalis macrocalyx), *bukararambi* (Rubus rigidus), *busemwa* (Syzguim cordatum and S. guineense), and *chikhomeli* (Garciania buchananii). At this age, the children were also taught how to trap termites.

At about the age of fifteen, both boys and girls underwent puberty rites, the most notable of which was circumcision. On the average, girls married soon after the initiation ceremonies. On the other hand, boys were expected to go through a further process of maturation before getting married. Strong and healthy boys were trained as fighters, while the others specialized in hunting skills as a common activity for young men.

As adults, men and women had different roles in ensuring that their families were provided for with the necessary food. Farming played a leading role in the Bukusu economy. According to Nasimiyu (1985a, 1985b), the Bukusu precapitalist agriculture was a simple subsistence system, growing enough for consumption for one season. In this system, men's participation in agricultural production involved mainly clearing the land before cultivation. However, they also participated in weeding and harvesting the staple cereals, that is, millet and sorghum. On the other hand, women cultivated the land, planted, weeded, harvested, processed, and stored these cereals. In addition, it was exclusively the woman's responsibility to grow certain food crops such as sweet potatoes, simsim, groundnuts, and various types of vegetables. The actual processing of the different foods eaten by the family was also the work of women. However, in cases of illness and where no assistance could be enlisted from anywhere, the man could step in and process the food.

In animal husbandry, the men looked after the animals. It was also the duty of men to slaughter the animal and to skin and dismember it. Bleeding cattle for blood was also the exclusive responsibility of men. On the other hand, the women cleaned the places where the animals slept. Milking was done by both men and women, but more often than not the women did most of the milking. Churning milk on a large scale was done in a big gourd, which was strapped on one of the pillars in the house. This was the work of women and children. In addition, it was the women who processed the resultant butter to obtain oil and ghee (*libonda*). *Libonda* was eaten as a relish with *ugali*. The oil was used in frying vegetables, among other uses.

THE COLONIAL PERIOD

Kenya was declared a British colony in 1895. During the first three or so decades of colonial rule, the roles played by Bukusu family members in the production and acquisition of food remained largely unchanged. However, starting from the 1920s, people sent their sons to school in large numbers. This was especially true in the northern parts of Bukusuland. Putting the boys in school meant that these children now had to divide their time between the school and the family. They would participate in family chores only in the afternoons, evenings, and weekends and during the school holidays. On the other hand, at first there was less enthusiasm on the part of parents to educate their daughters. The main reason for this was that girls were generally seen in terms of their growing up to get married and produce children and of how much bridewealth they could bring in to their fathers. Western education was therefore initially seen as something that was likely to push up the marriage age of girls and thereby delay their actual roles of producing children and enriching their fathers. In any case, the mothers wanted their daughters to stay at home to assist them in various domestic chores.

Starting from the 1930s, there was a noticeable desire on the part of parents to educate their daughters. One reason for this change of heart lay in the fact that education was seen as something that would make girls better wives and mothers. Second—and this ties in with the first reason—fathers with literate girls started asking for and receiving higher amounts of bridewealth than those with illiterate girls. This trend has continued to this day and could be one reason why the Bukusu community does not discriminate against their children on the basis of sex when it comes to education (Wandibba, n.d.). Nevertheless, in the 1940s, the number of girls attending school was not as high as that of boys, as can be seen in Table 17.1.

From Table 17.1, it is clear that the higher the level of education, the fewer the girls in school. This must have been due to the higher dropout rate of girls as compared to boys. In fact, out of the 333 boys registered at Lugulu Primary School in the first term of 1947, there were still 308 boys in the third term, as compared to

Table 17.1
Kibabi Primary School Enrollment for 1945

Class	Boys ($N = 227$)	Girls ($N = 103$)
Substandard		
A	67	30
B	24	28
Standard		
I	65	18
II	39	13
III	12	10
IV	20	4

Source: Kenya Nation Archives, File No. PC/NZA/3/6/92 (ED/3/5/10, Kibabii MHM, 1935-1945)]

103 and 36 girls for the same terms, respectively, during the same period (1947–1954). All the same, the fact that more children of both sexes were now attending school meant that the parents had to rely less and less on their children for assistance.

Before 1937 there was hardly any plowing in our area of study. However, with the introduction of the single-bladed plow in the 1940s, the use of the plow became common. As the use of the plow became more and more generalized, the men did the plowing and the children became more engaged in planting; this was especially the case with maize, which had to be planted in rows. Because larger pieces of land were now being cultivated, communal weeding and harvesting became more prevalent. In either case, those who came to assist were mainly adults of both sexes and their services were paid for in the form of a beer party.

The 1950s witnessed the introduction of coffee growing in Bukusuland. As a cash crop, coffee was very appealing to people living in the designated areas. Because the crop needed much more attention than the other crops cultivated by these people, more of the family labor became tied to coffee farming. The situation was especially critical during the berry-picking period. Although men, women, and children all participated in picking the coffee, most of this work was done by the children of both sexes. Some boys from the non-coffee growing areas migrated to the coffee areas to provide cheap labor. Such boys no longer contributed to the food eaten by their families.

Changes in attitude towards education meant that parents had to rely less and less on certain roles played by their school-going children. Nevertheless, such children continued to provide assistance in such areas as plowing, planting, weeding, and harvesting after school, on weekends, and during the holidays. Since the mode of cultivation had changed with the introduction of the plow, plowing the fields was now done only by boys. All the same, girls continued to play crucial roles in food processing activities.

THE POSTCOLONIAL PERIOD

The postcolonial period has witnessed major changes in the attitudes of the Bukusu society, especially in regard to education. High levels of educational attainment have resulted in migration elsewhere for cash employment. The need for money has motivated even those who lack technical skills to search for employment. Consequently, many Bukusu families are now to be found in various urban centers throughout the country. In fact, a fair number of these families live in the urban centers on a more or less permanent basis. All these factors combined have affected the traditional roles assigned on the basis of gender and age.

As already stated, Babukusu do not discriminate against their children on the basis of gender when it comes to education. Thus, most of the children of school-going age are in school, many of them in boarding schools. Because of this, many parents have to do without the traditional contributions of their children to the family economy. This has also meant that many of the duties that were prescribed by gender and age in the past are done by anyone around. Women now find themselves looking after cattle and other domestic herds. Men also find themselves engaged in activities traditionally meant for children, such as tethering calves. By and large, therefore, the mother is increasingly becoming the sole breadwinner for the family. If the husband happens to be away in town, her plight is even worse. This is attributed to the fact that some men are unlikely to find financially rewarding employment away from home. Such men do not, generally, remit any money to their wives in the rural areas. Therefore, it is the woman who has to ensure that the farm is plowed and that the planting, weeding, and harvesting have been undertaken. She also has to make sure that the animals are looked after. The net effect of all this is, of course, a marked reduction in her efficiency regarding home productivity. Given these circumstances, the women are hardly able to produce enough food to last the family until the next harvest.

Today children spend most of their time in school and away from their grandparents and other members of the extended family. It is evident that the socialization role of the extended family members according to gender and age has been curtailed not only by this fact, but also by migration of some male parents to urban areas. Unfortunately, the procedure of socialization in schools does not involve the traditional concept of gender role counseling. The children therefore grow up without this necessary aspect of education for the future.

CONCLUSION

The purpose of this chapter was to give an overview of some changes that have occurred in the Bukusu family over the last one hundred years or so. The changes discussed concern the production and acquisition of food within the nuclear family system. It has been shown that during the precolonial period, the division of labor by gender and age within the family was quite marked. Children were taught from a very early age about their physical surroundings and what these offered in terms of food. The children were in this way able to know what vegetable, insect, bird, or animal foods they could exploit. At first this knowledge was merely meant to assist the children in acquiring food for their own consumption, so that they could feed themselves when older siblings or adults were not there to feed them. As the children progressed in age, so was their knowledge of the environment expanded. Ultimately, whatever was obtained by the children would then be expected to be shared by other members of the family. Also, as the children grew older the range of their responsibilities was increased, and the sexual division of labor became much more emphasized.

In agricultural production, men cleared the fields, made granaries for the storage of grain, and assisted in weeding, harvesting, and transporting millet and sorghum. The women planted, weeded, harvested, transported, and also stored these grains. The women were also entirely responsible for the cultivation of groundpeas, simsim, and vegetables. For bananas, the men dug the holes, planted the suckers, and assisted in pruning, while the women weeded and harvested the crop. Children of both sexes generally participated in the planting, weeding, harvesting, and transportation of these various crops. The actual processing of food for consumption was done by women with the assistance of girls.

The colonial period witnessed some changes in the roles played by the various family members in the production and acquisition of food for the family. At first, these were not that marked. However, as a result of the introduction of western education and later on coffee, the traditional roles as defined on the basis of gender and age could no longer be totally adhered to. The fact that children now had to spend much of their time in school meant that parents had to learn to do without the children's contribution to the family economy except at specified times, namely, when the children were not in school. The introduction of coffee meant that people living in the designated areas had to spend more time tending it than they could spend on looking for food. Children, especially, were kept very busy trying to ensure that the harvest was good. Parents, therefore, had to cope with this loss of labor in the procurement of food for the family.

The coming of independence opened up more avenues for Kenyans to education and employment. This has meant an unprecedented expansion in the education of Bukusu children, as well as migration of Bukusu men into various urban centers in search of employment. The net effect of these two developments has been an almost complete breakdown in the traditional system of feeding the family. Most members of the family now contribute very little to what is eaten by the family. It is now the mother who shoulders the greatest burden in this regard.

REFERENCES

Nasimiyu, R. (1985a). The participation of women in Bukusu economy: The situation as of the end of the nineteenth century. In S. Wandibba (Ed.), *History and culture in Western Kenya: The people of Bungoma District through time* (pp. 51–64). Nairobi: Gideon S. Were Press.

Nasimiyu, R. (1985b). Women in the colonial economy of Bungoma District: Role of women in agriculture, 1902–1960. *Journal of Eastern African Research and Development, 15*, 56–3.

Sifuna, D. N. (1985, August). *Indigenous education in Western Kenya.* Paper presented at the Western Province Cultural Festival Symposium, August 8–11, 1985, Kakamega, Kenya.

Wandibba, S. (n.d.). Education and training. In G. S. Were & O. Odak (Eds.), *Bungoma District sociocultural profile—draft report* (Mimeo, pp. 61–76). Nairobi: University of Nairobi, Institute of African Studies, and Ministry of Planning and National Development.

18

Modernization, Family Life, and Child Development in Kokwet

Charles M. Super and Sara Harkness

Modernization is frequently seen as a phenomenon occurring at the national or regional level of nation-states, and in this view the term summarizes a number of discrete but related changes, such as increases in large-scale agriculture, manufacturing, infrastructure, per capita wealth, and education. Each of the components may have its own complexities and special determinants, but there is a coherent dynamism to the system of change. As a group the components are seen to develop over the same general period of time in the same kinds of ways. Water supplies are increased, health improves, the cash economy grows, industrialization expands, more children go to school—all this is modernization.

Another, closer view sees national or regional modernization to be an aggregate of decisions made somewhat independently by a large number of individuals and families. Although these individuals all respond within the same general framework of social and economic conditions, they may be in fact making different kinds of decisions based on their personal disposition and the stage of life at which they encounter the national level changes. In this view, modernization is a phenomenon that takes places at the individual level (Inkeles & Smith, 1974; see also Bradley, this volume); and the shape of modernization at the national or regional level is determined not so much by the internal dynamics of factors operating there, but rather by the proportion of decision-making units (individuals and families) who, for their own reasons, have chosen one path of change or another.

In such an individualized view of modernization, intergenerational effects can be seen to be of special significance (see also Weisner, this volume, and Bradley, this volume). The progressive decision by men and women in one cohort to send their children, especially their daughters, to school, for example, may have dramatically multiplied effects in the next generation. For instance, the level of schooling attained by women is associated in many countries with lower fertility and with lower mortality among their children, even when other socioeconomic factors are controlled (Caldwell & Caldwell, 1987; Lesthaeghe, Vanderhoeft, Gaisie, & Delaine, 1989; LeVine, Le Vine, Richman, Tapia Uribe, Sunderland Correa, & Miller, 1991). Although there may be group-level contextual effects that occur when a certain proportion of women receive a moderate level of education (Lesthaeghe, Vanderhoeft, Becker, & Kibet, 1985), there is also evidence of behavioral outcomes at the individual level in areas as diverse as breast-feeding, health practices, and style of verbal interaction with children (Ahmed, Zeitlin, Beiser, Super, & Gershoff, 1993; LeVine, LeVine, Richman, Tapia Uribe, & Sunderland Correa, 1991). Thus one phenomenon in one cohort—sending girls to school— may have broad and unanticipated effects in the next generation (e.g., infant mortality).

In the present chapter we examine pathways of change chosen by individual families during a specific period of time and the initial consequences of these choices for children. In doing this, we emphasize three features of modernization and family life. First, the kinds of adaptation to and production of social change made by families in the Western Highlands of Kenya is influenced to a significant degree by the particular life histories of the individuals involved: Faced with rapid and dramatic change at the national level, older men and women have responded differently than younger ones; Christian families have chosen a different strategy of advancement than those who had not embraced the church; and so on. Second, the various pathways chosen by different types of families may lead at times to similar intermediate outcomes, such as increased wealth, but the meaning of those outcomes and the use to which they are put may be quite divergent. Finally, it is the construction from these choices of a developmental niche for the next generation (Super & Harkness, 1986) that will determine the transformations of change into the next generation of citizens.

THE COMMUNITY OF KOKWET

The village of Kokwet (a pseudonym) is a rural farming community in the Western Highlands of Kenya. The people of Kokwet are Kipsigis, a Highland Nilotic people (Sutton, 1968) numbering about half a million. Their traditional life at the turn of the century was seminomadic; their economic base was pastoral with some simple agriculture. More permanent residence and land tenure became common in the first few decades of the present century as a result of increasing contact with British settlers, missionaries, and colonial administrators (Manners, 1967). In modern Kenya, Kipsigis participate in all spheres of national life, including politics, business, education, the military, and civil service. The greatest number, however, are in the rural areas west of the Rift Valley. They are self-supporting as small farmers and integrated with the national scene, to varying degrees, through cash crop marketing, political administration, mass media, and the education of children.

Kokwet itself lies about two hundred miles west of Nairobi in the fertile, rolling hills where the Western Highlands slope down toward the Mara savannah lands. At the time of this research (1972–1975), the fifty-four homesteads of Kokwet were spread out over about six square miles. Each family's living quarters, consisting of traditional round, mud-and-wattle, thatched-roofed huts and the newer rectangular, tin-roofed buildings, were clustered at a focal point on the family plot, surrounded by fields for maize and pyrethrum and pastures for the family cows. A dirt road ran the length of the community, providing access for the few tractors borrowed or hired to plow new fields, oxen carrying milk to the creamery pick up station, cows being driven to the community dip for a weekly insecticidal bath, or people on their way to the local markets and the main road. This road, intersecting the community road at one end, led to larger towns where western hospitals and missionary complexes were located and where one could connect with bus transportation to other regions. On each of the two hills adjoining Kokwet were an elementary school and small shops where one could buy soap, consult a local medical practitioner, or drink beer at the bars. At the far end of the community, where the dirt road ended, was the "Reserve" as it was still called—land that had never been claimed by European settlers and that included the Mau Forest, an area forbidden to habitation except by the hunting and gathering Dorobo people.

The typical household in Kokwet consisted of a husband and wife and about five children; in one quarter of the homesteads a second wife and her children formed a second household. As a government-sponsored "settlement scheme," established at Independence to repatriate Kipsigis people on land farmed by the British during the colonial period, Kokwet was deliberately modern in its agriculture and animal husbandry. The land had been divided into equal plots of land of about eighteen acres each, and the farmers signed agreements regulating the use of traditional cows and other practices. Because the community was only a decade old at the time of our fieldwork, most of the plots were still being farmed by their original owners, though a few had already been subdivided for married sons.

Despite these formal pressures toward modern change, many features of traditional life remained. Most women and nearly half of the men had no formal education. Polygyny was the preferred form of marriage for most men who could afford it, and the traditional brideprice was paid in cattle. Although Catholic and Protestant missions have been active in the area for several decades, most adults were, in their own words, "not yet" converted to the church. Traditional forms of preparation for adult life continued in the home and in the community, including adolescent initiation and circumcision rites for both boys and girls, who almost uniformly chose to participate in this central symbolic feature of Kipsigis life.

SOURCES OF DATA

Five kinds of data are used in this analysis. These include a survey of all adults covering household and homestead functioning, participation in traditional and Christian rituals, education, employment, aspirations, and questions indicating knowledge and experience beyond the local area.[1] Second, we gathered information from the cooperatives through which men sold their major cash crops and from the households on acreage, productivity, dairy stock, agricultural investments, and household food requirements, in order to estimate net cash agricultural income. Third, we carried out spot observations (Munroe and Munroe, 1971; Rogoff, 1978) of infants, toddlers, and family members to gather data on individual and household activities.[2] Fourth, all eighty-two mothers of the community were interviewed concerning childrearing practices. Finally, various censuses, updated on a regular basis, yielded data on fertility, educational, and household composition (see Super & Harkness, 1987).

DATA ANALYSIS

The core method of data analysis is correlational, using the measures specified in Table 18.1.[3] The complex results are summarized by multidimensional scaling (MDS), a procedure which uses the "similarity" expressed in the correlations to derive an overall spatial representation (see Kruskal & Wish, 1978; Shepard, Romney, & Nerlove, 1972).[4] In the figures presented here, measures that are highly correlated are drawn close to each other, while other measures, less well or even negatively correlated, are drawn further apart. Physical closeness of items in the figures represents strong positive correlations.

Figure 18.1 presents MDS results for the plot holders, that is, the 51 men who purchased land at the founding of the settlement scheme to which Kokwet belongs.[5] This is the functional economic unit for activities that result in the cooperative marketing of maize, milk, and pyrethrum.[6] Included in Figure 18.1 are the primary measures of economic functioning, agricultural and husbandry practices, men's knowledge and experience, orientation to traditional or Christian values, and demographic measures of men's age, education, and household composition. Table 18.1 provides a key to the abbreviations used.

Two axes have been drawn to provide a common orientation in this and the next figure.[7] One axis connects at its opposite ends the father's age (*Fa-age*, lower left) to the father's education (*Fa-educ*, center right). The second axis is drawn perpendicular to the first with an X intercept of 0. The negative relationship between age and education is reflected in the fact that these two variables lie at opposite extremes: The old men of the community have generally not been to school, while the younger ones have ($r = -.44^{***}$; mean of education = 2.2 years, range = 0–8; mean of age = 43.8, range = 20–74). In contrast, the father's education is closely associated ($r = +.59^{***}$) with his score on the test of knowledge of the outside world (*Fa-know*), found in Figure 18.1 just below *Fa-educ*. Membership in a Christian church, participating in a relatively intimate and egalitarian marital relationship, experience in visiting towns such as the district or provincial capitals, and ownership of modern household amenities (radio, fork, wristwatch, suitcase) are also significantly correlated with the fathers' education. On the other hand, having a large number of older and initiated children and, to a lesser extent, having work experience outside of the immediate area are more characteristic of the older men. The location of various farming practices are as one would expect, with use of the traditional cow exchange (*kimanagen*) being associated with the older men, while exclusive use of hybrid cows and modern crop rotation are more likely to be characteristic of the younger, educated men.[8]

Figure 18.1
Multidimensional Scaling Results of Plot-level Modernization

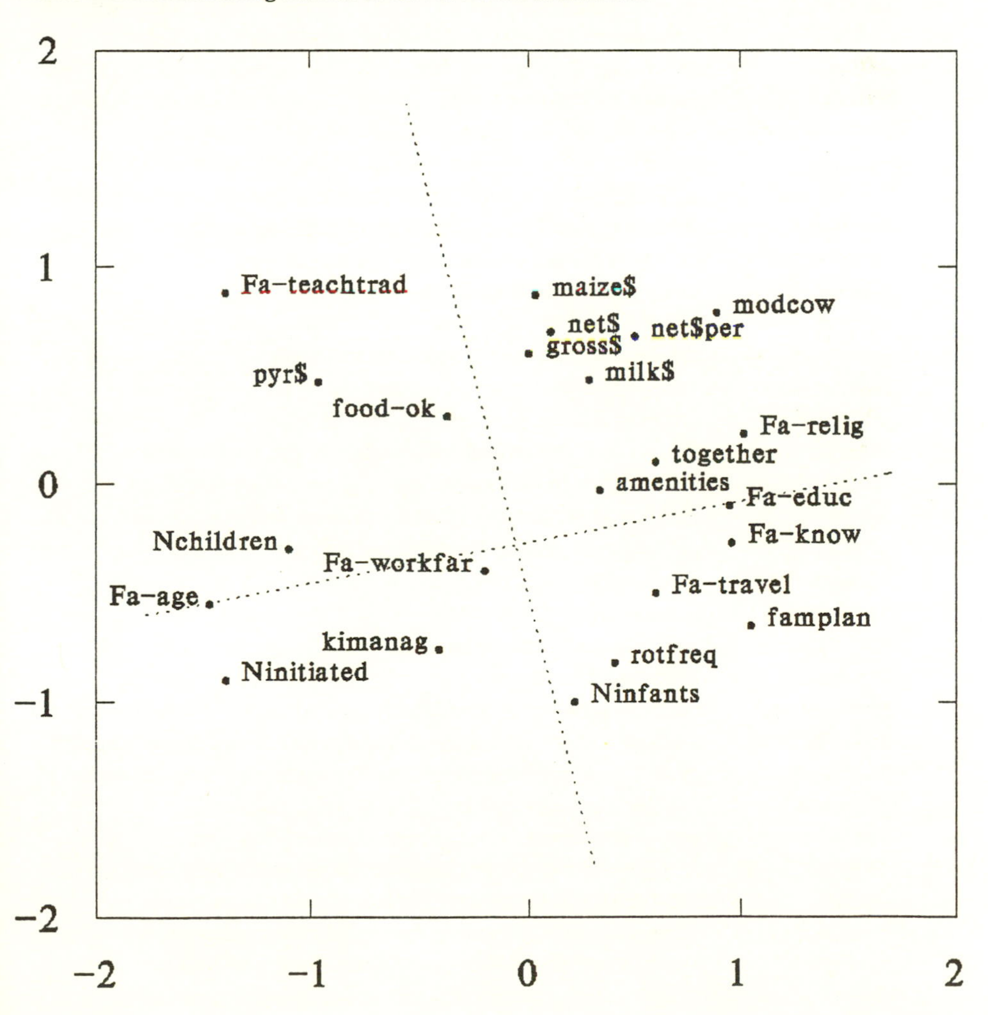

Table 18.1
Abbreviations of Measures in Figures

Abbreviation	Measure
amenities	number of household amenities
Ch-Fa-pres	proportion of time father present: 6- to 10-year-olds
Ch-Mo-pres	proportion of time mother present: 6- to 10-year-olds
Ch-Npeople	observed number of people present: 6- to 10-year-olds
Ch-%work	proportion of time 6- to 10-year-olds observed in economically productive work
Fa-age	father's age
Fa-educ	father's education
Fa-know	father's knowledge of outside world
Fa-relig	father's religion (lo = non-Christian, hi = African Gospel Church)
Fa-teachtrad	father's desire to teach traditional ways to sons
Fa-travel	father's experience in traveling to specified towns
Fa-workfar	father has worked outside of Kipsigis area
famplan	mother and father have discussed family planning
food-ok	family never ran out of food
gross$	family gross income from agricultural sales
infant-hlth	observed health: infants
inf-Npeop	observed number of people present: infants
kimanag	father's use of traditional cow exchange
maize$	family income from maize sales
milk$	family cash income from milk sales to cooperative
modcow	proportion of modern ("grade") vs. tradition (*zebu*) cows
Mo-age	mother's age
Mo-birthage	mother's age at first birth
Mo-IBI	mother's average interbirth interval
Mo-educ	mother's education
Mo-Nkids	number of live births to mother
Mo-relig	mother's religion (lo = non-Christian, hi = African Gospel Church)
Mo-tradrites	mother's use of traditional rites with infants and young children
Nchildren	number of resident children, 2 to 16 years old
net$	family net income from agricultural sales
net$per	family net income from agricultural sales, per capita
Ninfants	number of resident infants (under 2 years)
Ninitiated	number of resident children over 16 years old (initiated)
pyr$	family cash income from pyrethrum sales
rotfreq	father's frequency of rotating crops (hi = recommended)
school-p	probability of school-age child being enrolled in school
school-young	father's expressed desire that children enter school before 7 years old
toddler-hlth	observed health: toddlers
todd-Npeop	observed number of people present: toddlers
together	mother and father eat meals together

The relationship of economic functioning to this primary dimension of contrast is particularly important, for the availability (or perceived availability) of cash funds for school fees and school uniforms was a critical factor in school enrollment in the mid-1970s, when primary education was not yet universally available. Of the three primary cash crops (milk, maize, and pyrethrum), gross income from the first two (upper right quadrant of Figure 18.1) are moderately associated with the younger, more educated farmers (r = .19 and .32*), while the last, pyrethrum, is moderately associated with the older men (upper left quadrant, r = .27*). This pattern reflects differences in both production and consumption. Pyrethrum is a labor intensive crop, requiring frequent weeding and harvesting, and care in sun-drying. The older men, who have more wives, more children, and especially more older, initiated children living at home, manage an agricultural team able to meet this need. For younger, educated men, with younger families, a more available route to cash lies in hybrid cows for milk (Fa-educ and modcow, r =.37**) and modern techniques such as crop rotation (rotfreq, r =.24*) and chemical fertilizers for maize yield. However, the larger families of the older men also consume more maize and milk, reducing the cash income from these crops. This is not true, of course, for pyrethrum. Hence the great differentiation of cash income source. On balance, net cash income remains slightly higher for the younger, more educated plot owner (r = .25*), and this relationship is even greater when net income is calculated per capita, as these men have smaller families (see the upper right quadrant in Figure 18.1, r = .42**).

This analysis omits families in which the father is the grown son of the plot owner. A dozen plot owners, among the eldest, had begun to divide their land this way among their resident sons and their families. Including them in a repeat of this analysis introduces two closely related problems. With regard to the availability of data, information on cash crop incomes was collected from the cooperative records, which exist only at the level of registered plot owners; thus mature sons' cash incomes cannot be separated for analysis. With regard to interpretation, this pooling of resources for recordkeeping does reflect, to varying and unknown degrees, the pooling of resources within the extended family. To some degree the total income for the plot represents a cash resource that could, in theory, be drawn upon for school expenses for a child from any of the households; but the degree to which this happens no doubt varies greatly from family to family, and it remains an unknown factor in the present analysis.

Reflecting both this technical problem and its possible meaning for the larger families, plot-level income measures were used not only for the plot owner but also for his resident sons when repeating the above analysis for all fathers in Kokwet (adequate information was available for sixty-three households). The twelve men thus added to the analysis were among the youngest and most educated fathers, but the plot-level income with which they were associated (and might or might not have been able to call upon) was actually that of their older and less educated fathers. The net effect of this change was to reduce the correlations between age and education on the one side, and income measures on the other. This analysis of all fathers in Kokwet retains the overall structure indicated in Figure

18.1, but almost all the income measures are shifted toward the neutral center of the scaling. There are two exceptions: Pyrethrum income remains correlated with fathers' age *r = .27*), and net income per capita remains associated with the younger, more educated men, but now less so than earlier (r = .30*). In short, when all the households of Kokwet are considered, the relationship of father's age and education to potentially available cash income is minimized, although overall the families of more educated men still retain a small advantage.

To summarize, the primary dimension derived from scaling a number of measures of modernization illustrates vividly the generational aspects of social change in Western Kenya. Men in the younger cohort of plot owners, those in their thirties, are more educated than their seniors and are more likely to have more modern marriages, farms, and households. They are somewhat more effective overall in producing crops for cash income. However, still younger men who are starting families as residents on land still owned by their fathers remain tied in some ways to the economics of their larger extended families. Hence at this one point in time there is a clear association of younger families with higher education, more intimate marriages, and more modern farming techniques. But from the point of view of economics, the very youngest families, sharing and still resident on the grandfather's land, have not acquired at this time the cash income flow of the somewhat more established and independent families of educated men just older. In the mid-1970s, therefore, transitions in agriculture, education, and traditional values were taking place not only in general across the population, but also particularly across generations and in relationship to family stage.

These transitions hold a number of important consequences for the children of Kokwet. Figure 18.2 presents the two-dimension MDS solution to a correlational matrix that includes the primary variables of Figure 18.1, along with measures of child health, daily life, and school experience.[9] In this child-based representation (maximum n = 266) the father's, and now the mother's, education and religion are again found on the right, along with measures of marital intimacy; parental age again contrasts on the left. The cash income measures (not shown) are only weakly associated with the educated families (e.g., the correlation for milk sales is .14*), but per capita cash income (net$per, upper right quadrant) retains a modest association with these smaller households (r = .26***).[10]

Of new interest are the measures of the children's everyday social environment, their health, and their educational progress. The last are particularly strongly associated with the younger, more educated families. These parents want their children to begin school early (*school-young*, *r* = .57***), and in fact their children do have greater probability of attending school (*school-p*, *r* = .31***). In contrast, the older, less educated parents are more likely to invoke traditional learning (*Fa-tradteach*) and ceremonies (*Mo-tradrites*) for their children.

Figure 18.2
Multidimensional Scaling Results of Child-based Variables

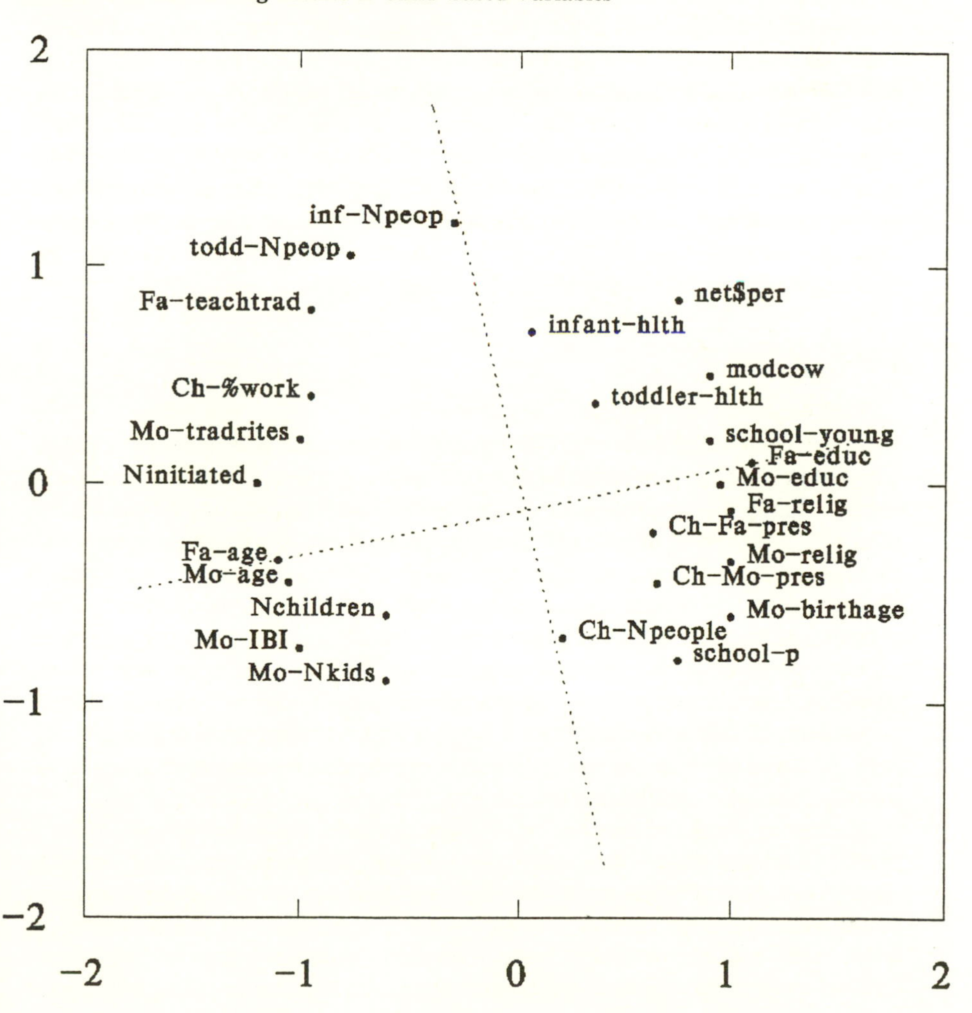

Children's activities and social settings also vary along this same dimension. The six-to-ten-year-old children of younger parents are more frequently found, in spot observations, to be in the presence of their parents (*C-Mo-pres* and *Ch-Fa-pres*, *r* = .26*, .24*), whereas same-age children of older, less educated parents are more often found to be engaged in economically productive activities (*Ch = %work*), such as cow herding, which takes them out of sight of their parents (*r* = .34**). These results suggest that family life in general, not just the marital relationship, is closer in the more "modern" families.

Children's health shows a different, more independent pattern of associations. For both infants (*infant-hlth*) and toddlers (*toddler-hlth*) the relationship of observed health to father's and mother's age and education is weak (*r* with education = .10, .05 for infants, .39, -.08 for toddlers, *n* = 35 and 22). The possible advantages of a modern orientation to health care appear to be offset by negative fertility trends associated with maternal age and education: The more educated mothers are younger at their first birth (*Mo-birthage*, *r* = .33***) and have shorter average interbirth intervals (*Mo-IBI*, *r*= -.21**), both of which increase health risks for themselves and their children (Harkness & Super, 1987).

CONCLUSIONS

Four major conclusions can be drawn about the process of modernization in the families of Kokwet in the mid-1970s. First, father's age and education, themselves closely related, form a major dimension of contrast, carrying with them other measures of family functioning and intimacy. Second, cash productivity is moderately related to this primary dimension, although younger and older men's families exploit different routes to generating cash income. Third, children's school attendance is strongly related to the parental age and education dimension: The younger, more educated, and Christian parents have somewhat greater access to cash per capita for school fees and uniforms, and they are much more effective in enrolling their children in school. Finally, child health during infancy and toddlerhood is not closely related to either the age–education dimension or family economics. It seems rather that several conflicting associations combine to yield no overall advantage to children from any one type of household identified here.

These conclusions necessarily reflect only the state of affairs in the mid-1970s, and two cautions must be mentioned. Because the data are all cross-sectional, the stage of family development is confounded with parental age and education. Thus, young, educated families who now appear to be less invested in labor-intensive crops could become, in theory, more involved in producing such crops as their families grow in size. Second, the present state of affairs does not necessarily reflect the future outcome of the children of these families. The greater investment in education, for example, may lead to divergent health outcomes later, when the children are grown.

It is this long-term process—the intergenerational transmission of change—that best exemplifies the dynamics of social change. Choices made by members of one generation with regard to agricultural methods, education, religion, marital relations, or any other sphere of life can be seen as more or less embracing of social change and contributing to it in their own right. But these choices also shape the developmental niche for their children. The greatest effect of these choices may be seen only when the resulting paths set out for the next generation become more evident: a small angle of difference, played out over a long trajectory, will lead to a very different place.

NOTES

This research was supported in part by grants from the Carnegie Corporation of New York, the W. T. Grant Foundation, the National Institute of Mental Health (USA), and the Spencer Foundation. All statements made and opinions expressed are solely the responsibility of the authors.

1. This survey was carried out as an individual interview with each head of household during the second quarter of 1974 by two male Kipsigis undergraduates at the University of Nairobi, under our direction.

2. Spot observations were collected by trained and supervised local female research assistants who had an average of four years secondary education. As the observer approached the homestead, she mentally noted the location and activity of the target child and others present, before they were altered by the observer's arrival. After exchanging greetings, the observer recorded in a standard format: the child's state of arousal, physical position, and activity; the age, sex, and kinship status of all persons present; and other relevant information such as health status. As daily activities in Kokwet generally took place in the open yard area surrounding the house, the procedure worked smoothly and provided accurate data. The data used here come from 1,363 weekly observations on all sixty-eight infants who were under one year old between January 1973 and April 1975; from 218 spot observations of twenty-one "toddlers," either eighteen or twenty-four months old, and from 2,358 individual observations resulting from ten spot observations on each of the families in Kokwet, carried out in a balanced formula over the course of one full year, with the location and activity of each family member being recorded separately.

3. The correlations come from several different "levels" of analysis, reflecting the social and family structure of Kokwet. At the "lowest" level are child-based measures, such as the health of toddlers and the observed distance of infants to the closest caretaker. Second, some variables refer to mothers, each of whom maintains her own household, with her house and fireplace at its center; these mothers may have more than one child in the sample. Maternal age and education are examples at this level. Third, some measures exist only at the level of fathers. As polygyny is common in Kokwet, any particular father (of one age and religion) may be married to several women (mothers) who differ in such qualities as age and religion. Fourth and finally, the largest unit of economic activity is the legal plot of land, owned by a senior man, but inhabited by him, his wives and young children, and some of his married sons and their wives and children. Thus measures such as income from pyrethrum production may exist at a level that includes several fathers, all of them being sons of the same senior resident male.

4. The version used here is MINISSA, as implemented by the Anthropac computer program (Borgatti, 1990).

5. Overall, this two-dimensional arrangement captures only moderately well the empirical relationships of the full correlation matrix. The Stress Index is .20, a result that is not

unsatisfactory, given the broad range of measures. Adding further dimensions to the scaling improves the stress measure only gradually and without further conceptual clarity.

6. The correlations used in Figure 18.1 are based only on information from the level of plot ownership. This necessarily omits data from women and children, but it yields the "cleanest" picture of the economic relationships, for each plot owner is represented in the analysis only once.

7. Unlike factor plots, in which the rotation of axes is rigidly determined by some function of variance, the axes in MDS can be rotated in various ways to highlight underlying patterns.

8. The measure of association used here is the Pearson *r*. In reporting the correlations, a single asterisk indicates a *p* value less than .05, two signify less than .01, and three, less than .001.

9. Stress Index = .21.

10. The correlations used for Figure 18.2 are based on individual children. Maternal households, paternal families, and legal plots are therefore represented as many times as there are children of a particular age. In addition, the children contributing to one cell in the matrix may be different from those contributing to another (for example, the relationship of maternal education to infant health or the relationship to school attendance). Although one can imagine that very different results would be found depending on the level of the analysis, experimentation with a number of different approaches indicate this not to be the case, and it can be seen that the fundamental relationships in Figure 18.1 replicate in Figure 18.2 with only minor differences in the placement of individual variables.

REFERENCES

Ahmed, N. U., Zeitlin, M. F., Beiser, A. S., Super, C. M., & Gershoff, S. N. (1993). A longitudinal study of the impact of behavioral change intervention on cleanliness, diarrhoeal morbidity, and growth of children in rural Bangladesh. *Social Science and Medicine*, *37*, 159–171.

Borgatti, S. P. (1990). *Anthropac* (Ver. 3.23) (Computer program). Columbia, SC: Author.

Caldwell, J. C., & Caldwell, P. (1987). The cultural context of high fertility in subsaharan Africa. *Population and Development Review*, *11*, 29–51.

Harkness, S., & Super, C. M. (1987). Fertility change, child survival, and child development: Observations on a rural Kenyan community. In N. Scheper-Hughes (Ed.), *Child survival: Anthropological perspectives on the treatment and maltreatment of children* (pp. 59–70). Boston: D. Reidel.

Inkeles, A., & Smith, D. A. (1974). *Becoming modern: Individual change in six developing countries*. Cambridge, MA: Harvard University Press.

Kruskal, J. B., & Wish, M. (1978). *Multidimensional scaling* (University Paper Series on Quantitative Applications in the Social Sciences 07-011). Beverly Hills: Sage.

Lesthaeghe, R., Vanderhoeft, C., Becker, S., & Kibet, M. (1985). Individual and contextual effects of education on proximate fertility determinants and on life-time fertility in Kenya. In J. B. Casterline (Ed.), *The collection and analysis of community data* (pp. 31–63). Voorburg, The Netherlands: International Statistics Institute.

Lesthaeghe, R., Vanderhoeft, C., Gaisie, S., & Delaine, G. (1989). Regional variation in components of child-spacing: The role of women's education. In R. J. Lesthaeghe (Ed.), *Reproduction and social organization in sub-Saharan Africa*, (pp. 122–166). Berkeley, CA: University of California Press.

LeVine, R. A., Levine, S. E., Richman, A., Tapia Uribe, F. M., Sunderland Correa, C., & Miller, P. M. (1994). Schooling and survival: The impact of maternal education on health and reproduction in the Third World. In A. Kleinman, L. C. Chen, & N. Ware (Eds.), *Health and social change*. New York: Oxford Press.

Manners, R. A. (1967). The Kipsigis of Kenya: Culture change in a "model" east African tribe. In J. H. Steward (Ed.), *Three African tribes in transition* (pp. 205–362). Urbana, IL: University of Illinois Press.

Munroe, R. H., & Munroe, R. L. (1971). Household density and infant care in an East African society. *Journal of Social Psychology*, *83*, 3–13.

Rogoff, B. (1978). Spot observations: An introduction and examination. *Quarterly Newsletter of the Institute for Comparative Human Development*, 2, 21–26.

Shepard, R. N., Romney, A. K., & Nerlove, S. B. (1972). *Multidimensional scaling: Theory and applications in the behavioral sciences*. New York: Seminar Press.

Super, C. M., & Harkness, S. (1986). The developmental niche: A conceptualization at the interface of child and culture. *International Journal of Behavioral Development*, *9*, 545–569.

Sutton, J. E. G. (1968). The settlement of east Africa. In B. A. Ogot (Ed.), *Zamani: A survey of east African history* (pp. 70–97). Nairobi: East African Publishing House.

Index

About the Contributors

Susan Abbott is Associate Professor in the Department of Anthropology, University of Kentucky. She received her Ph.D. from the University of North Carolina, Chapel Hill, in 1974. Her research interests lie in the areas of comparative family, gender, and child socialization and in cultural factors in mental health. Her past research in Kenya has been supplemented with recent extended visits to Ghana and Sierra Leone and current research in the southern Appalachian United States focusing on a comparative understanding of the effects of global economic and social change on gender roles and family.

Joshua Akong'a is Professor in the Department of Anthropology, Moi University, Kenya. He received his Ph.D. from the University of California, San Diego in 1979. His main areas of research include social, cultural, and psychological concomitants of development, especially as they affect individuals and families; drought and famine management at the family level; family planning and the effect of urbanization on the individual and family.

Candice Bradley is Associate Professor of Anthropology at Lawrence University in Appleton, Wisconsin. Dr. Bradley received her Ph.D. in social sciences from the University of California, Irvine, in 1987. She is currently working on a monograph about Maragoli, Kenya, where she did research on fertility decline, gender, and intergenerational relationships between 1988 and 1992.

Maria G. Cattell is Research Associate in the Departments of Anthropology at both Bryn Mawr College and the Field Museum. She received her Ph.D. from Bryn Mawr in 1989. She has been doing fieldwork on family life, the elderly, and intergenerational relations among Abaluyia of Kenya in rural and urban locations since 1982. Her focus on social and cultural change and on gender, personhood, and life stories brings together her view of anthropology as history and as humanistic science. She is coauthor (with Steven M. Albert) of *Old Age in Global Perspective: Cross-cultural and Cross-national Views* (1994). Currently she is working on twin accounts of her long-term research among the Samia: an ethnography of aging and an ethnohistorical "from generation to generation" novel.

Carolyn Pope Edwards is Professor of Family Studies at the University of Kentucky. She received her Ed.D. from Harvard University in 1974. She has studied how factors such as maternal and child work roles and household composition affect boys' and girls' development of prosocial behavior (*Children of Different Worlds: The Formation of Social Behavior*, with Beatrice Whiting). She has also written about the cross-cultural validity of cognitive developmental models of moral judgment stages and how educational experiences influence the moral perspectives of Kenyan secondary and university students.

N. Thomas Håkansson was Assistant Professor in the Department of Anthropology at the University of Kentucky. He received his Ph.D. from Uppsala University in 1987. His research focuses on the interface between social structure and the economy, with special emphasis on family organization, marriage, and socioeconomic stratification. He is especially interested in processes of change in contemporary and precolonial societies in eastern Africa.

Sara Harkness is Professor in the School of Family Studies, University of Connecticut. Previously she taught in the Department of Population Sciences at the Harvard School of Public Health and the Department of Human Development and Family Studies at Pennsylvania State University. She received a B.A. in Comparative Literature from Brown University and a Ph.D. in Social Anthropology from Harvard, where she also was a National Institute of Mental Health Postdoctoral Research Fellow and earned a Master of Public Health degree. She has carried out research on culture, health, and human development in Guatemala, Kenya, the Netherlands, and the United States. Currently she is directing a collaborative crosscultural study of parents' cultural belief systems, cultural practices, and children's transition to school in seven countries. She is coeditor (with Charles M. Super) of *Parents' Cultural Belief Systems: Their Origins, Expressions, and Consequences*.

Priscilla Wanjiru Kariuki is Professor of Psychology at the University of Nairobi. She received her Ph.D. from the University of Edmonton, Alberta, Canada, in 1980. Her areas of specialization are psychology, education, and gender analysis. Much of her research revolves around the role of women in attempting to make the delicate balance between culture change and family stability in Kenya.

Janet C. Kilbride is a researcher and writer. She has been affiliated with the University of Delaware, Bryn Mawr College, Pitzer College, and the Philadelphia Geriatric Institute. She received her Ph.D. from Bryn Mawr College in 1976. In field research in Uganda, Zambia, and Kenya she has focused on infant sensorimotor development, the recognition of emotions, and child development in the context of family life, both traditionally and as affected by culture change. She has published numerous journal articles and coauthored with Philip Kilbride, *Changing Family Life in East Africa: Women and Children at Risk* (1990).

Philip L. Kilbride is the Mary Hale Chase Chair in the Social Sciences and Social Work and Social Research, and Professor of Anthropology at Bryn Mawr College. He received his Ph.D. from the University of Missouri in 1970. He has published on family life in East Africa and the United States, including *Changing Family Life in East Africa* with Janet Kilbride and *Plural Marriage for Our Times: A Reinvented Option?* (1994). His other publications are drawn from the fields of American ethnicity, social change in East Africa, the anthropology of deviance, and psychological anthropology, particularly affect and perception.

Robert A. LeVine is Roy E. Larsen Professor of Education and a Professor of Anthropology at Harvard University. He received his Ph.D. from Harvard in 1958. His research interests include parenthood and early childhood development among the Gusii and other peoples of sub-Saharan Africa.

Robert L. Munroe is Research Professor of Anthropology at Pitzer College. He received his Ph.D. from Harvard University in 1964. His primary interest is comparative anthropology, with an emphasis on cross-cultural human development. Under the auspices of the Child Development Research Unit, Nairobi, Kenya, he has conducted research with Ruth Munroe among the Gusii, Kikuyu, Kipsigis, Logoli, and Luo. He has coauthored scores of articles and chapters on culture and human development, including *Cross-Cultural Human Development* (with Ruth Munroe), and has been elected President of the Society for Psychological Anthropology and the Society for Cross-Cultural Research.

Ruth H. Munroe was Professor of Psychology at Pitzer College. She received her Ed.D. from Harvard University in 1964. Her primary interests included children's personality and social development, particularly with respect to the family's influence. With Robert Munroe she conducted research in Central America, Asia, and the Pacific as well as in East Africa. She published extensively in the study of culture, cognition, and childhood, and was coeditor (with Robert Munroe and Beatrice Whiting) of *The Handbook of Cross-Cultural Human Development.*

Ruth Nasimiyu is on the faculty of the Institute of African Studies, University of Nairobi. Dr. Nasimiyu did her research and postgraduate training in Canada. Her research interests are in the study of gender and change in contemporary Kenya and East Africa.

A. B. C. Ocholla-Ayayo is Associate Professor of Anthropology and Population Studies at the Population Studies and Research Institute, University of Nairobi. He received his Ph.D. from Uppsala University, Sweden, in 1976. He is currently doing research on sociocultural mechanisms of demographic processes and change in East Africa. Prof. Ocholla-Ayayo has authored numerous papers and several books on sexuality, fertility, Kenyan culture, and adolescence, most notably *Traditional Ideology and Ethics among the Southern Luo*, *The Luo Culture*, and *The Spirit of a Nation*.

Walter H. Sangree is Professor of Anthropology at the University of Rochester. He received his Ph.D. from the University of Chicago in 1959. His professional publications reflect his continuing interest in various aspects of the life cycle, particularly as manifested in adolescent initiation rites and age groupings in Tiriki Kenya, and ascendancy to positions of political, judicial, and religious authority, both in Tiriki and in Irigwe, Nigeria, where he has conducted extensive fieldwork. Recently he has been exploring social and cultural factors relevant both to fertility and to the status and care of the elderly in these two societies.

Joseph W. Ssennyonga is Senior Research Scientist at the International Centre of Insect Physiology and Ecology, Social Science Interface Research Unit. He received his Ph.D. from the University of Sussex in 1980. For Dr. Ssenyonga, human ecology has provided a conceptual perspective facilitating continued interest in three research areas, namely, demographic anthropology (Western Kenya, 1974–1979), organization and management of small scale irrigation (Kenya, 1979–1986), and since 1986 the socioeconomics of integrated pest management.

Charles M. Super is Professor and Dean in the School of Family Studies at the University of Connecticut. He received his B.A. in Psychology from Yale and a Ph.D. in psychology from Harvard University. He completed his child clinical training at the Judge Baker Children's Center in Boston, Massachusetts and has served as licensed psychologist in Massachusetts and Pennsylvania. He has carried out research on children and families in Kenya, Zambia, Colombia, Guatemala, Bangladesh, the Netherlands, and the United States and served as consultant in Haiti, India, and Bangladesh for the United Nations Development Program, the United States Agency for International Development, WHO, and UNICEF. He is coeditor (with S. Harkness) of *Parents' Cultural Belief Systems: Their Origins, Expressions, and Consequences* and (with Donald E. Super and Branimir Sverko) of *Life Roles, Values, and Careers: International Findings of the Work Importance Study.*

Simiyu Wandibba is the Director of the Institute of African Studies, University of Nairobi. He received his Ph.D. from the University of South Hampton in 1980. His current research interests involve sociocultural changes at the household level. He has been using ethnographic data and pottery to study these processes.

Thomas S. Weisner is Professor of Anthropology in the Departments of Psychiatry (Division of Social Psychiatry) and Anthropology, University of California,

Los Angeles. He received his Ph.D. from Harvard in 1973. His research interests are culture, the family, and human development. He has done field research in Kisa Location and in Nairobi, Kenya, as well as among Native Hawaiians in Hawaii, Native Americans in Los Angeles, and Euro-American families in California.

Beatrice Blyth Whiting is Professor Emerita of Anthropology and Education, Harvard University Graduate School of Education. She received her Ph.D. from Yale University in 1942. Her research has focused on comparative human development. Her many studies have included family life of the Kikuyu, social behavior of Kikuyu children, and profiles of Kenyan women.

John W. M. Whiting is Professor Emeritus of Anthropology, Harvard University. He received his Ph.D. from Yale University in 1938. His research has focused on comparative human development. He has conducted studies in Kenya among the Kikuyu, Kipsigis, Luo, Maasai, Kamba, and Giriama.

Michael A. Whyte is Associate Professor at the Institute of Anthropology, University of Copenhagen. He received his Ph.D. from the University of Washington in 1974. He has been working on issues of family and kinship, language, ethnicity, local level production, and agriculture in eastern Uganda and western Kenya since 1969. More generally, he is interested in the increasingly complex linkages between rural societies, state structures, and the wider world.

Susan Reynolds Whyte is Associate Professor at the Institute of Anthropology, University of Copenhagen. She received her Ph.D. from the University of Washington in 1973. She has done fieldwork in Kenya, Tanzania, and Uganda in the areas of gender relations, cosmology, and health. Her current research interests are changing conceptions of personhood and misfortune, transformations in health care systems, and pharmaceuticals in local settings.

Jan J. de Wolf is Associate Professor in the Department of Cultural Anthropology, Utrecht University. He received his Ph.D. from London University in 1971. He has specialized in nontraditional religion and social change in East Africa. His other interests include oral literature and rural development.

ISBN 0-89789-473-1
90000>
EAN
9 780897 894739
HARDCOVER BAR CODE